WHAT IS A CITY?

WHAT IS A CITY?

RETHINKING THE URBAN
AFTER HURRICANE KATRINA

EDITED BY

PHIL STEINBERG
& ROB SHIELDS

THE UNIVERSITY OF GEORGIA PRESS | ATHENS AND LONDON

A SARAH MILLS HODGE FUND PUBLICATION

This publication is made possible in part through a grant
from the Hodge Foundation in memory of its founder,
Sarah Mills Hodge, who devoted her life to the relief and
education of African Americans in Savannah, Georgia.

© 2008 by the University of Georgia Press
Athens, Georgia 30602
www.ugapress.org
All rights reserved
Set in Electra LH by Graphic Composition, Inc.,
    Bogart, Georgia
Printed and bound by Thomson-Shore
The paper in this book meets the guidelines for
permanence and durability of the Committee on
Production Guidelines for Book Longevity of the
Council on Library Resources.

Printed in the United States of America
12 11 10 09 08 C 5 4 3 2 1
12 11 10 09 08 P 5 4 3 2 1

Library of Congress Cataloging-in-Publication Data

What is a city? : rethinking the urban after Hurricane
    Katrina / edited by Phil Steinberg & Rob Shields.
        p. cm.
    Includes bibliographical references and index.
    ISBN-13: 978-0-8203-2964-2 (hardcover : alk. paper)
    ISBN-10: 0-8203-2964-9 (hardcover : alk. paper)
    ISBN-13: 978-0-8203-3094-5 (pbk. : alk. paper)
    ISBN-10: 0-8203-3094-9 (pbk. : alk. paper)
    1. City planning—United States. 2. Urban geography—
United States. 3. City planning—Louisiana—New
Orleans. 4. Urban geography—Louisiana—New
Orleans. 5. Hurricane Katrina, 2005—Social aspects.
6. Disasters—Social aspects—Louisiana—New Orleans.
7. Hurricanes—Social aspects—Louisiana—New
Orleans. I. Steinberg, Philip E. II. Shields, Rob, 1961–
HT167.W43 2008
307.1′2160973—dc22   2008003983

British Library Cataloging-in-Publication Data available

CONTENTS

ACKNOWLEDGMENTS

Although this book is neither a set of conference proceedings nor an expanded version of a journal issue, it has its origins in both a conference and a journal. When the Katrina disaster occurred, Phil Steinberg had just begun a one-year position as a visiting fellow with the Center for Cultural Studies at the University of California, Santa Cruz. Phil, who had never thought of himself as either a southerner or a hazards geographer, suddenly found that he was being looked to as both by his new colleagues who were seeking to understand the details and implications of the unfolding disaster. In response to their suggestions that he contribute to the national (and international) conversation that was rapidly emerging, Phil organized a conference on the implications of Hurricane Katrina for urban thought. The conference, Reflections on Katrina: Place, Persistence, and the Lives of Cities, was sponsored by the Center for Cultural Studies and was held on January 21, 2006, on the UC Santa Cruz campus.

At around the same time, in the aftermath of Hurricane Katrina, Rob Shields, as an editor of the journal *Space and Culture*, issued a call for one-thousand-word post-Katrina essays on issues such as "What have we learned? How does New Orleans reveal shortcomings in theoretical positions and in accepted social attitudes and practices? What new questions should be asked?" The special issue of *Space and Culture* (vol. 9, no. 1, February 2006) that resulted from these interventions contained twenty-eight essays on a broad range of Katrina-related topics, written within a month of the hurricane. The journal issue, which was published in electronic form at the end of December 2005, was the first peer-refereed response to the disaster.

Rob arrived at the January 2006 Santa Cruz conference (at which he was the keynote speaker) with freshly printed copies of the *Space and Culture* issue in hand, leading to fruitful discussions there between Rob and Phil. Out of these discussions, the concept for this book emerged, and selected authors and presenters from the *Space and Culture* issue and the Santa Cruz conference were asked to expand their essays and lectures for inclusion in this book. The chapters in this book by Flaherty and Spelman derive from papers that they presented at the Santa Cruz conference, while the chapters by Manaugh and Twilley, Bartling, Tiessen, Harvey, Fisher, Wagner, and Anjaria, as well as the provocation by Lara, developed from their (much shorter) essays in *Space and Culture*.

Our first acknowledgments, therefore, go to our respective associates at UC Santa Cruz and *Space and Culture* who made their portions of this collaboration possible. At UC Santa Cruz, the conference (and hence this book) would never have happened were it not for the encouragement and logistical support of Center for Cultural Studies codirectors Chris Connery and Gail Hershatter as well as staff members Shann Ritchie and Stephanie Casher. Funding for the conference (as well as Phil's fellowship in Santa Cruz) was made possible by the Rockefeller Foundation. At the University of Alberta, Rob thanks the referees and assistants who made the issue of *Space and Culture* possible, especially Phillip Boyle.

Once the plan for this book congealed, it would have remained stillborn were it not for the intervention of Derek Krissoff at the University of Georgia Press. In addition to Derek, we are grateful for assistance from countless other people at Georgia, as well as the photographers and cartographers, credited within, who made their images available to us. We also thank the anonymous reviewers for some very helpful suggestions and Ondine Park and Seth Bassett for eleventh-hour assistance preparing the manuscript for final submission.

This book was conceived while Phil was itinerant during the 2005–2006 academic year, but most of the editing occurred during 2006–2007, while Rob was in a state of perpetual motion between Canada, Brazil, Argentina, Italy, and France. We are grateful for partners, loved ones, children, and visiting house guests who learned to deal with us dropping everything when that telltale Skype jingle rang out from our computers, beckoning us to another impromptu conference call/editing session.

Finally, we express solidarity with the people of New Orleans and the other communities affected by the Katrina disaster. It is with some trepidation that we take what was for them a life-changing (or, in some cases, life-extinguishing) event and turn it into a learning object. Our hope, however, is that the questions and insights spurred by this book will go on to inform urban theory and practice, thereby bettering the lives of urban residents in New Orleans and elsewhere. As a further expression of solidarity, we will be donating our royalties from this book to the People's Hurricane Relief Fund.

Phil Steinberg
Tallahassee, Florida

Rob Shields
Edmonton, Alberta

PART ONE

INTRODUCTIONS

CHAPTER ONE

What Is a City? Katrina's Answers

Phil Steinberg

Katrina's Questions

When Hurricane Katrina slammed into the Louisiana-Mississippi coast on August 29, 2005, and in the subsequent days when bureaucratic incompetence, institutionalized racism, class inequality, engineering failures, and a lack of political will combined to leave thousands dead and hundreds of thousands homeless in New Orleans and beyond, few observers likely were considering what the experience meant for the way we think about, plan for, or live in cities. Initial media reports tended to emphasize the city's uniqueness. Stressing the city's racial composition (over two-thirds African American), its history of political corruption, its high crime rate, and its insularity, New Orleans appeared to some to be more like the nearby Caribbean islands — places that, in the popular imagination, fused laid-back partying with grinding poverty — than like the adjacent United States. These "unique" characteristics of New Orleans formed the basis of the dominant explanatory narrative that emerged in the days immediately following the disaster (for critiques, see Dyson 2006, Faux and Kim 2006, and chapter 11 by Jonathan Anjaria in this book), only to be partially supplanted by later works of investigative journalism that sought to understand New Orleans and the impact of Katrina in a broader context (Brinkley 2006, Horne 2006, Rose 2006, *Times-Picayune* 2006).

Even before the floodwaters had subsided, though, scholars and planners were beginning to reflect on Hurricane Katrina and its disastrous aftermath, and they were beginning to ask bigger questions with implications for cities as a whole. These scholars have recognized that New Orleans faces problems typical of most, if not all, cities, but that during the Katrina disaster it experienced these problems in a particularly intense and hence potentially instructive way. By studying the impact of Hurricane Katrina and its aftermath on New Orleans — why the disaster occurred, why it had the impact that it had, and how the city responded — these scholars felt that they could gain insights into specific urban social or policy problems. To this end, hazard research-ers have begun to ask what lessons one can draw from the Katrina disaster for managing (or preventing) future urban disasters (Birch and Wachter 2006; Comfort 2006; Daniels, Kettl, and Kunreuther 2006), while others, noting the extreme divisions and inequalities of race and class that were evident in New Orleans and especially in its citizens' ability to cope with Katrina's challenges, have used the experience to probe deeper into issues of race, class, and, more broadly, social power in the United States and its cities (Childs 2005, Dreier 2006, Dyson 2006, Hartman and Squires 2006, South End Press Collective 2007; see also Davis 2004b for an eerily prescient reflection on race and class dynamics in New Orleans' evacuation to Hurricane Ivan in 2004).

Like this latter round of books, this book also adopts the perspective that the challenges faced by New Orleans before, during, and after the Katrina disaster are in many ways typical of the challenges faced by all cities. However, unlike the books that focus specifically on disaster management or social inequalities, this book uses the Katrina experience to probe the fundamental questions of urban theory: What is the nature of a city, what are its social dynamics, what are its specifically urban processes and tensions, and what are a society's moral responsibilities to maintain (or restore) a city's people, its architecture, its econ-omy, and its culture? To this end, each of this book's sections focuses on one of the main tensions that are present in all cities: the contradiction between a city's natural and built environments, the contradiction between the ways in which a city fosters attachment and the ways in which it facilitates mobility, the contradiction between urban residents' desire to remember and their desire to forget, and the contradiction between a city's tendency to unite communities and its tendency to divide. Although these contradictions can be observed in all cities, they have long been particularly intense in New Orleans (Baumbach and Borah 1981; Campanella 2002; Colten 2000, 2005; Foley and Lauria 2003; Kelman 2003; Spain 1979; Whelan, Young, and Lauria 1994). Amid the experi-ence of Katrina and the questions concerning the city's post-Katrina reconstruc-tion, these contradictions have been confronted with unusual directness.

It is in this context that this volume is being presented, not as a recitation of local knowledge of New Orleans nor of the experience of the Katrina disas-ter (only three of this volume's authors—Jordan Flaherty, Daina Harvey, and Jacob Wagner—have been residents of New Orleans and only one [Flaherty] was there when Hurricane Katrina hit). Instead, this book presents a series of investigations into what questions concerning New Orleans' flooding and, in particular, its reconstruction can tell us about how cities work and, more fun-damentally, what they are and can (or should) be.

This is not to say that New Orleans is not a unique place. In his classic study of New Orleans, Peirce Lewis (1976) stresses how the city defies all the usual city-categories. Arnold Hirsch similarly begins his study with the sentence "New Orleans never fits in" (Hirsch 1983, 100). Indeed, most of the chapters in this book focus on some specific characteristic of New Orleans, elaborating, for instance, on New Orleans' particularities as a delta city (chapter 4 by Rob Shields) or as a creole city (chapter 10 by Jacob Wagner). However, these investigations are used to query larger questions about the nature and future of cities in general.

To this end, the next two sections of this introductory chapter ask: "What is a city?" Although rarely considered explicitly, this question is continually being asked and answered by those individuals seeking to understand what happened during the Katrina disaster and by those offering plans for the city's reconstruction. The following two sections of this chapter briefly introduce New Orleans and the Katrina disaster, presenting an empirical foundation for the chapters that follow. The final section of this chapter introduces the four themes that are explored in the book's remaining chapters.

What Is a City?

To begin our consideration of what a city is, it is useful to review a typology offered by Lewis Mumford (1970) in his 1938 book *The Culture of Cities*. While Mumford's work is not beyond criticism (see, for instance, the point made later in this chapter about his inattention to issues of social power), his broad-brush historical approach leads him to consider the range of perspectives from which one can view the city as an architectural, natural, social, and/or cultural object. His work thus provides a useful entry point to the numerous questions about cities that are raised by the experience of Hurricane Katrina.

ENVIRONMENT

Immediately following the introductory paragraph of *The Culture of Cities*, Mumford offers his first perspective:

> Cities are a product of the earth. They reflect the peasant's cunning in dominating the earth; technically they but carry further his skill in turning the soil to productive uses, in enfolding his cattle for safety, in regulating the waters that moisten his fields, in providing storage bins and barns for his crops. (Mumford 1970, 3)

Here, Mumford argues that urban spaces are not qualitatively different from agricultural spaces. Like agricultural spaces, cities are socially constructed environments in which humans transform and control nature (ultimately through the construction of permanent structures). When seen from this perspective, the city is effectively an *urban village*, an environment in which the landscape has been transformed so as to enable and sustain human habitation. This pragmatic perspective continues to inform many geographical and sociological studies of the politics and everyday lives of urban residents, as well as their adaptations to, and transformations of, the surrounding nature. In the literature on New Orleans, this perspective is particularly evident in the work of Craig Colten (2000, 2005).

DENSITY

In the next paragraph, Mumford goes on to suggest a second perspective on the city. Here, he considers the city as a social space in which the density of social activities and material artifacts gives a new speed and intensity to life:

> Within the city the essence of each type of soil and labor and economic goal is concentrated: thus arise greater possibilities for interchange and for new combinations not given in the isolation of their original inhabitants. (Mumford 1970, 4)

In contrast to his first perspective, Mumford here is suggesting that there is something distinctive about a city, in the way that its density captures (and generates) energy and speed (see also Wirth 1938). Elements of this perspective, which emphasizes *concentration and combination*, can be seen in the works of those who identify the city with a specific, crucial location within circuits of capital, where capital moves with increasing speed between circuits of production, the built environment, and social welfare infrastructure (Harvey 1985) as well as those who identify the city as a site of collective consumption and, therefore, political struggle (Castells 1977).

HEARTH

Mumford then offers a third perspective on the city: the city as *culture hearth*:

> Cities are a product of time. They are the molds in which men's lifetimes have cooled and congealed, giving lasting shape, by way of art, to moments that would otherwise vanish with the living and leave no means of renewal or wider participation behind them. In the city, time becomes visible: buildings and monuments and public ways, more open than the written record, more subject to the gaze of many men than the scattered artifacts of the countryside, leave an imprint upon the minds even of the ignorant or the indifferent. (Mumford 1970, 4)

Here, Mumford argues that the city, by embedding time in its architecture and urban form, is a repository of memories and meanings. In short, the city provides the location for culture, a theme emphasized in the "social ecology" literature of the Chicago School of urban sociology (see Park 1925, Simmel 1950; for a critique, see Gottdiener 1985) and the tendency to associate social forms with particular places, as in the title of one famous 1940s study, "Street Corner Society" (Whyte 1993).

COMPLEXITY

Mumford then offers a fourth perspective that focuses on the city as a site of *social complexity*:

> Through its complex orchestration of time and space no less than through the social division of labor, life in the city takes on the character of a symphony: specialized human aptitudes, specialized instruments, give rise to sonorous results which, neither in volume nor in quality, could be achieved by any single piece. (Mumford 1970, 4)

Here the city is a site of social (and technological) innovation. In a manner that resonates with structural-functionalist (Parsons 1949) and modernization theories (Rostow 1960), Mumford suggests that the city is a space where modernity is born (and reproduced), as specialization begets innovation which begets further specialization, leading to a rise in productivity and the overall "progress" of society. The economics of this perspective have been systematically analyzed in the Marxist tradition (Harvey 1982) and in studies of urban competitiveness (Florida 2004) and innovation (Lundvall 1992).

HUB

Mumford's final perspective hails the city as a *cosmopolitan hub* or what Lefebvre (2003) dubs "social centrality" (see also the Introduction to part 5 of this book, "Divisions and Connections"):

> In the city remote forces and influences intermingle with the local: their conflicts are no less significant than their harmonies. And here, through the concentration of the means of intercourse in the market and the meeting place, alternative modes of living present themselves: the deeply rutted ways of the village cease to be coercive and the ancestral goals cease to be all-sufficient: strange men and women, strange interests, and stranger gods loosen the traditional ties of blood and neighborhood. A sailing ship, a caravan, stopping at the city, may bring a new dye for wool, a new glaze for the potter's dish, a new system of signs for long-

distance communication, or a new thought about human destiny. (Mumford 1970, 4–5)

With this final definition, Mumford stresses the role of the city as a meeting place, a node at which commodities, ideas, and people intersect to form new identities and cultures. This perspective has been elaborated on by recent scholars who stress that world cities have greater connections with each other, across networks of flows, than they do with their contiguous hinterlands (Castells 1996, King 1990, Sassen 2006).

The Value of Cities

All of Mumford's perspectives are, in a certain sense, functionalist. Each one focuses on something that the city *produces* for society — permanency, concentrations and combinations, culture, social/economic/technical development, or interconnections across space, respectively — and these functions, for Mumford, spur social change. However, Mumford also reminds the reader that the city does more than *shape* society; it also *reflects* the ideals of a society:

> [The city is] a conscious work of art, and it holds within its communal framework many simpler and more personal forms of art. Mind takes form in the city; and in turn, urban forms condition mind. . . . The dome and the spire, the open avenue and the closed court, tell the story, not merely of different physical accommodations, but of essentially different concepts of man's destiny. The city is both a physical utility for collective living and a symbol of those collective purposes and unanimities that arise under such favoring circumstance. With language itself, it remains man's greatest work of art. (Mumford 1970, 5)

Mumford's attribution of "consciousness" to the builders of a city is problematic; a more nuanced analysis might see the city reflecting the intersection of economic and cultural relations rather than an ineffable "mind" (Dear 2002a). Then, when one considers the city as a construction (like a work of art), two crucial questions emerge. The first concerns issues of power: Who has the resources to leave their imprint on the city's landscape, its significations, its cultural institutions, and its social structures? Second, we need to ask what vision of a city — that is, which of Mumford's perspectives — is being proffered by those engaged in these activities that build and reproduce cities.

The intersection of these issues — power and perspective — is particularly clear in the debates surrounding the reconstruction of New Orleans. Consider, for instance, an article by Edward Glaeser (2005), published shortly after Hurricane Katrina in *The Economist's Voice*. Glaeser notes that New Orleans' functional contribution to the U.S. economy, as the port that moves traffic between the Mississippi River and the Gulf of Mexico, requires the services of only a tiny portion of the city's 485,000 pre-Katrina residents. Glaeser thus asks why the U.S. government should spend money to maintain this population in what he identifies as an environmentally unsustainable location. Noting that reconstruction estimates at the time his article was published (December 2005) were around $200 billion, Glaeser wonders if the total happiness of New Orleans residents might not be maximized by simply giving each individual a check for his or her portion of that amount. Even if half of the $200 billion were spent on rehabilitating the port and restoring conditions so that a few thousand workers directly employed in port-related activities could remain in New Orleans, this would leave $100 billion for everyone else. Distributed over five hundred thousand people, each New Orleans resident would receive a check for two hundred thousand dollars, a substantial windfall for a population whose per capita income was less than twenty thousand dollars.

One can counter Glaeser by noting that New Orleans' "function" goes far beyond the city's port activities. It is also a site of community, a home for its residents, and a cultural resource for New Orleanians and non–New Orleanians alike. Furthermore, if a city is indeed like a work of art, an "oeuvre" (Lefebvre 1991) that defies utilitarian assessment, it may have value beyond any recognizable "function." Like all cities, New Orleans is, as Glaeser would have it, a node in the circulation of goods. But, as Mumford's multiple perspectives suggest, it also was, and remains, much more.

Locating New Orleans

New Orleans, like all cities, has multiple characteristics and functions. Its complexity can be seen in the power of four images that prevail in media depictions: New Orleans as a center of global interchange, New Orleans as an insular backwater, New Orleans as a center of African-American (and African-Caribbean) culture, and New Orleans as a site of environmental danger.

HUB CITY

As a port, New Orleans has been cosmopolitan from its very beginnings. Its origins lay in global economic ventures, as the mercantile empires of Spain,

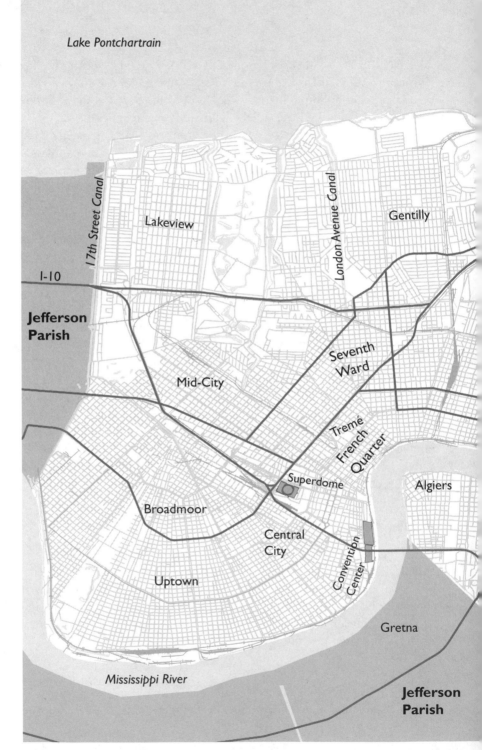

MAP OF NEW ORLEANS.

Map by Jacob A. Wagner, based on data from City of New Orleans (2006),
Louisiana Geographic Information Center (2002), and U.S. Census Bureau
(1990, 2000); image courtesy of the cartographer.

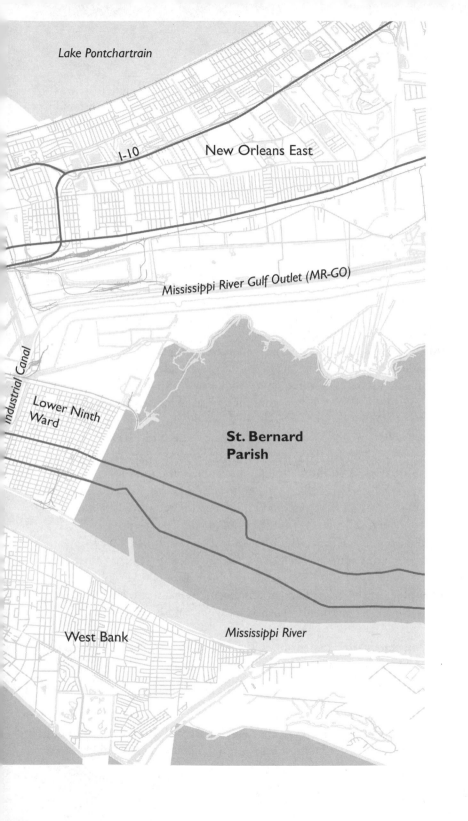

Lake Pontchartrain

I-10

New Orleans East

Mississippi River Gulf Outlet (MR-GO)

Industrial Canal

Lower Ninth Ward

St. Bernard Parish

West Bank

Mississippi River

France, England, and the United States constructed and coveted the city as a base for expanding their reach into resource-rich hinterlands. The city rapidly became a trans-shipment hub for the sugar economy of the Caribbean, the cotton economy of the southern United States, the grain economy of the midwestern United States, and the petroleum economy of the Gulf of Mexico. At the same time, New Orleans failed to emerge as the commercial center of any of these industries or regions. Thus, while the city, like most large port cities, attracted a diverse population from around the world, it had only limited growth as a site of large-scale productive investment and industrial development (Hirsch 1983). It remained an "island," unusually disconnected from its adjacent hinterland (Lewis 1976). From this perspective, New Orleans was a hub amid long-distance routes — a node in the Gulf of Mexico economic-cultural region (Gruesz 2006) — much more than it was a place (or urban village) with local roots (see chapter 4 by Rob Shields for more on how New Orleans' location combines centrality with marginality).

Over time, another economic sector based on connections became key in New Orleans' economy: tourism. Already in the late nineteenth century, New Orleans was marketing its culture to tourists. The famed brothels of Storyville, in particular, provided a means for tourists to transgress racial barriers while the Cotton Centennial Exposition, a world's fair held in New Orleans in 1884, is often credited with helping to spawn the birth of jazz (Gotham 2002, Souther 2006). By 1970, New Orleans' economy could be categorized as "tripartite," based on the shipping, petrochemicals, and tourism sectors. However, about that time, the petrochemical industry began consolidating around Houston, and the shipping industry sharply reduced its labor needs due to containerization and concentration (Gotham 2002, Hirsch 1983). As a result, the city became increasingly dependent on tourism, and New Orleans joined the growing number of cities around the world that were basing their economic development trajectories on the marketing of their culture (Judd and Fainstein 1999). Soon tourism was driving not just the city's economy but also its political and housing dynamics (Foley and Lauria 2003, Gotham 2005).

The tourism industry touted New Orleans' distinctive culture and architecture that blended elements of African American, Anglo-American, French, Spanish, and Caribbean society in a multiethnic "gumbo." New Orleans was marketed as unique but accessible, the birthplace of iconic U.S. art forms including jazz and, by some accounts, the blues. Historic markers, storefronts, and nightclubs in the French Quarter celebrated the *diversity* of this port city while attempting to steer tourists clear of the *difference* that would become evident if one were to set foot outside the Quarter (Souther 2006).[1] Marketing brochures promoted sanitized versions of voodoo rituals and Mardi Gras parades that made them accessible to outsiders who had little time for (or, perhaps, little interest in) understanding the social complexities of these practices (Gotham 2002, Jacobs 2001).

Pre-Katrina New Orleans was extremely successful as a tourism destination. According to the New Orleans Convention and Visitors Bureau, in 2004 the tourism industry attracted 10.1 million visitors and generated $4.9 billion, propelling the city to its position as the nation's fifth-largest convention destination (even though it ranked twenty-first in population among U.S. cities). The Convention and Visitors Bureau's promotional materials fuse the city's role as a tourist destination with its ongoing role as a cosmopolitan hub of commerce. Its Web site (using pre-Katrina data) intersperses statistics celebrating the city's vital tourist economy with the fact that "New Orleans is the largest port in the U.S. and second only to Rotterdam in the worldwide value of foreign commerce and total waterborne commerce" and that "over 6,000 ships from 60 countries dock here every year, and the port handles an average of 11.2 million tons of cargo volume each year." According to this image, New Orleans, disconnected from its hinterland but connected with the world, is a cosmopolitan hub amid global flows of people, commodities, capital, and culture.

BACKWATER CITY

Complementing (and contradicting) this image of New Orleans is an equally pervasive image of New Orleans as an insular backwater. Hirsch (1983), for instance, depicts New Orleans as plagued by a dual economy. At one end, a large percentage of the population persists in an informal economy characterized by poverty and crime. At the other end, the city's elite is exceptionally conservative and inbred:

> The Crescent City's elite is preoccupied with social rituals, such as Mardi Gras, which reinforce and emphasize its status. . . . It is a town where, in contrast to its more businesslike competitors, it is perfectly proper to "keep a luncheon club member at the rummy table while a client waits at the office.". . .
>
> In no other American city does birth, as opposed to achievement, count for so much. Such values and the social intimacy of the group mean that newcomers, no matter how successful, have great difficulty circulating in the city's highest circles. This, of course, has had serious economic consequences for the city. It has stifled the rise of new leadership . . . [and] discouraged new business and industry from locating there. In the generation after World War II, it meant that New Orleans,

bound by complacency, stagnated while other Sunbelt cities developed rapidly. (Hirsch 1983, 118–119)

These themes were frequently picked up by post-hurricane commentators. Three months after the hurricane, for instance, *The New York Times* published a story that centered on how post-Katrina returnees, many of whom had traveled away from home for the first time in their lives, were now questioning the city's inadequacies and inequalities. Explaining this phenomenon, the article noted:

> Cities are often naturally transient. New Orleans before the hurricane was not.
> Of 70 localities in the nation with populations of at least 250,000, New Orleans ranked second in the percentage of its American-born population born in the state — 83 percent, according to the census. . . .
> Consider the Lower Ninth Ward, a mostly poor, black neighborhood wiped out in the flooding. The census found that 54 percent of its residents had been in their homes for 10 years or more, according to the Greater New Orleans Community Data Center. Nationally, the figure was 35 percent. (Levy 2005)

In some cases, the image of New Orleans as an insular backwater with a semifeudal social structure has been employed to explain why the hurricane had such a devastating and long-lasting impact on the city. For instance, early in 2007 another article in *The New York Times*, analyzing the city's failure to repopulate after Katrina, lay part of the blame on the city's stagnant economy. However, the article goes on to note other factors:

> Haunting the city's effort to repopulate, too, is the incalculable toll inflicted by ghosts from the past — a political legacy of corruption and patronage, and a deep racial division with a far more distressing passage toward integration than was experienced, say, in Atlanta. (Nossiter 2007)

This article further observes that these factors have combined to construct a city in which an unusually large percentage of the (pre-Katrina) population was apparently consigned to a nonproductive existence:

> The poorest 30 percent of households had a lower share of the city's total income than the comparable slice in any other similar Southern city, [Tulane University economist William] Oakland found.
> "The job mobility was very low among the poor, so they just stay where they are, and the social welfare system shored them up" [said Oakland]. (Nossiter 2007)

The two sides of the "insular backwater" image work together. According to this narrative, the city's inbred, feudal elite are unwilling to progress while its stagnant, marginalized poor are unable to progress. From this perspective, it is hardly surprising that post-Katrina recovery has been agonizingly slow.

BLACK CITY

While both of these images — cosmopolitan hub and insular backwater — commonly appear in representations of New Orleans, either image, on its own, leads to an incomplete understanding of the city's history, its social structures, or the hurdles that it continues to face. When one views New Orleans as a cosmopolitan hub, the city is reduced to its function as a node for long-distance commerce and its image is reduced to the one that is projected to tourists. When one adopts this perspective, there is little to stop one from calling for a population purge in the name of efficiency (as has been advocated by Glaeser [2005]) or gentrification in the interest of tourism marketing (as has occurred in the French Quarter [Gotham 2005]). The everyday lives of New Orleanians fade from view. In fact, New Orleans residents' experiences, and indeed their very existence, become expendable.

On the other hand, when one sees New Orleans as an insular backwater, one loses sight of the world beyond the city's borders which in so many ways has been responsible for the city's being "left behind." Neoliberal economic policies have led to disinvestment in countless urban neighborhoods throughout the nation even as others are propped up through gentrification (Smith 1996). Economic and political forces that originate far beyond the borders of New Orleans are responsible for the situation where crucial infrastructure (including levees) had been allowed to decay amid the construction of new superhighways (Reed 2006). New Orleans' crime and unemployment statistics and its reputation for corrupt and inept government paint a picture of urban dysfunction, but this picture fails to identify complicit forces behind the nation's abandonment of New Orleans.

Despite the failings of both of these representations of New Orleans, they persist, and at times they even fuse with each other. This is particularly the case in a third popular image: New Orleans as an African American city.

From the "backwater" perspective, observers such as Adam Nossiter, the *New York Times* reporter quoted above, stress New Orleans' large African American population and associate this with historical and ongoing racial segregation, class stratification, crime, and poverty. In 2000, 33.8 percent of the city's African American population lived below the poverty line (at that time, $8,501 for an individual or $17,029 for a four-person household). By comparison, 11.0 percent of the city's white population lived in poverty (U.S. Census Bureau 2000). Prior to Katrina, four out of ten men in the working-age population were unemployed or not looking for a job (compared with fewer than three in ten nationally). More than half of young black men aged sixteen to twenty-four were not in the labor force, and the unemployment rate for young black men was over 25 percent (Nossiter 2007). In 2004, the last full year before Katrina, New Orleans' murder rate was 60 per 100,000 residents, compared to a national average of 5.5 murders per 100,000 residents and an average of 12.5 for cities with populations over 250,000 (U.S. Federal Bureau of Investigation 2005).

For many outsiders, this impression of New Orleans as a disproportionately black (and poor and crime-ridden) city likely was confirmed during the Katrina disaster by television footage of impoverished New Orleans residents (almost all African American) pleading for help and reinforced by stories (many of which were later found to be untrue) of senseless black-on-black violence and looting. In short, images of New Orleans in the wake of Katrina confirmed a long-held impression of New Orleans as a prime example of the black, decadent, crime- and poverty-stricken city that is the antithesis of an American national mythology that, in its essence, remains white, wholesome, safe, wealthy, and rural or suburban (Dyson 2006).

On the other hand, New Orleans is also heralded as the "Black Vatican" (Woods 2005). From this perspective, far from being an insular backwater forgotten by the progress of the global economy, New Orleans is a central hub of African American culture (and, by some accounts, the global African diaspora). Proponents of this view note that the city has long had a vibrant, if small, black middle class, which dates back to the days of slavery when New Orleans had the largest population of "free persons of color" in North America (Hirsch and Logsdon 1992) and to its location on the border of the Jim Crow South (where a simple black-white racial binary prevailed) and the Caribbean (where a more complex, if not necessarily more flexible, system of race, class, and gender division was the norm). Thus, for instance, tourists learning about the diversity (if not the difference) of New Orleans are invariably taught about the category of Creoles (most typically defined as the "mixed-race" descendants of free people of African descent and eighteenth-century French and Spanish settlers), and, less commonly, the city's historic Afro-Caribbean and Latin American (especially Honduran) populations, as well as its population of black and white Anglos (Souther 2006).

Prior to Katrina, New Orleans managed the delicate balance between these images, but just barely. Tourists were directed to the city's famous St. Louis Cemetery #1, just across Rampart Street from the French Quarter, but they were advised to proceed there with care. The French Quarter's Mardi Gras celebration became increasingly disconnected from the celebrations that prevailed in New Orleans' neighborhoods. In retrospect, perhaps it is not surprising that, when Katrina hit, this delicate balance collapsed. For some time at least, the image of New Orleans as a cosmopolitan multicultural "gumbo" or as a hearth of African American culture was overtaken by the image of the city as a "Third World" hell of poverty and violence.

SINKING CITY

This fragile balance of contradictory images of New Orleans is symbolized — and exacerbated — by the instability of its very location. The Mississippi River has been the dominant force controlling the evolution of the delta plain along the north central coast of the Gulf of Mexico, where New Orleans is located. But the Mississippi itself is anything but a stable object. Frequent shifts of the Mississippi have left abandoned channels and inlets or "bayous" in which water moves slowly. Each shift involves a cycle of coastal progradation (sinking) and sedimentation to form sandy barrier islands. These provide buffers for marshes, but also overextend and thus reduce the slope of the river channel. Eventually this leads to a diversion of the river somewhere upstream. Wetlands deprived of continual flows of water and sediment subside as underlying clays dry and compact, with the result that the marshes in the abandoned, prograding channels become brackish as they are inundated by saltwater. This effect leads to a decline in wildlife habitat but a temporary surge in saltwater fish fertility, which in turn is responsible for Louisiana's position as the U.S. leader in fisheries production (Perret and Chatry 1991).

Since the 1930s, the construction of dams and levees has further reduced flooding and the volume of sediment transported by the river to the wetlands, leaving them vulnerable to progradation and erosion. The Mississippi Delta has the highest erosion rate in the nation, losing one hundred square kilometers a year, or the equivalent of a tennis court every thirteen seconds (Williams, Penland, and Sallenger 1991). The attendant loss of buffers between New Orleans and the sea has further increased the city's exposure to Gulf storms, as there are fewer wetlands that might serve as "speedbumps" for storms blowing inland (Dunne 2005).

Thus, if New Orleans' pre-Katrina image rested on a delicate balance of insular backwater and cosmopolitan hub and its physical geography rested on a parallel balance of fixed architecture and mobile land (see chapter 3 by Geoff Manaugh and Nicola Twilley), Katrina and its aftermath have led all parties involved to search for a new balance. Amid a series of new flows — the *inflow* of storm waters and relief funds and plans, the *outflow* of residents and images of poverty and neglect — one is forced to reconsider the responsibility of local and national institutions to preserve the city's architecture, rebuild its communities, honor its memories, rectify its structural inequalities, care for its displaced citizens, and redevelop its economic sectors.

To find a balance between these imperatives, one must revisit the question of just what a city is: Is a city a place of memory embedded in architecture, a locus of investment, a center of social differentiation and technological innovation, a location in regional and global networks, a site where nature is transformed, or an arena wherein communities form and reproduce themselves? It seems likely that most urban scholars (and, indeed, most urban residents) would identify cities as encompassing all of these elements. However, as Glaeser's article demonstrates, the emphasis that one places on one element or another will significantly alter decisions made by the displaced resident who is deciding whether or not to return, the urban planning official who is deciding what (and where) to rebuild, or the disaster manager who is attempting to lessen the social impact of a future storm. In other words, using the experience of Katrina to rethink the qualities of cities spurs us to revisit how we think about, plan for, and live in them. Each of the authors in this book addresses this challenge.

The Katrina Disaster

Hurricane Katrina formed as a tropical depression over the southeastern Bahamas on August 23, 2005, and was upgraded to a hurricane two days later, just hours before making landfall on the southeastern coast of Florida.[2] Although it lost hurricane strength while traveling across the Florida peninsula, it rapidly regained strength in the Gulf of Mexico, eventually becoming what was at the time the fourth-strongest Atlantic hurricane ever recorded, a Category Five storm with sustained winds of 175 miles per hour (280 kilometers per hour). By the time the hurricane made landfall, first on peninsular Louisiana about sixty miles southeast of New Orleans and then on the mainland near the Louisiana-Mississippi border about thirty-five miles northeast of New Orleans, the hurricane's strength was reduced to a Category Three storm with sustained winds of around 120 miles per hour (195 kilometers per hour) (Knabb, Rhome, and Brown 2006).

Although Katrina was exceptional as a hurricane, it was not unexpected. Within one hundred miles of New Orleans, hurricanes had made landfall approximately every ten to fifteen years. Prior to Katrina, the area suffered major hurricane damage in 1893, 1906, 1915, 1916, 1947, 1965 (Hurricane Betsy, with $400 million in damages), and 1969. That year, Hurricane Camille

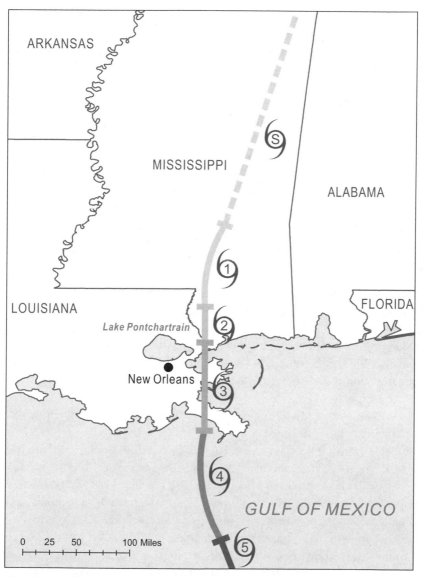

HURRICANE KATRINA TRACK

Numbers reflect the storm's rating according to the
Saffir-Simpson scale (S = tropical storm).
Map by Tao Zhang, derived from Kent (2005), with data from
Knabb, Rhome, and Brown (2006); image courtesy of the cartographer.

(a Category Five hurricane) left 144 dead, $500 million in damages locally, and billions of dollars in damages nationally (Godschalk, Brower, and Beatley 1989). By the time Katrina hit, the region's vulnerability had been exacerbated not only by attempts to "fix" the region's hydrology, which had reduced wetlands buffer zones and the Mississippi's coping capacity, but also by a coastal building boom that had occurred during the 1970s. This boom had been spurred by a cyclical low in hurricane activities, by local zoning ordinances that promoted high-density commercial development in an effort to stimulate the post-Camille rehabilitation of devastated areas, and by "images of coastal enjoyment [that are] deeply ingrained in our collective psyche, coupled with steeply rising coastal real estate values" (Godschalk, Brower, and Beatley 1989, 2–3). Into this environment came a dramatic increase in hurricane activity in the early years of the twenty-first century, particularly in the Gulf of Mexico.

Amid this increase, 2005 stands out as the most active year in recorded history, with a record number of storms and with two subsequent hurricanes (Rita and Wilma) that actually surpassed Katrina in maximum sustained wind speed. While some of the increase in hurricane activity during the early twenty-first century may have been due to cyclical climatic events, many climatologists associate this increased activity with an ongoing rise in ocean temperatures (Intergovernmental Panel on Climate Change 2007, Union of Concerned Scientists 2005). Since this rise in ocean temperatures is associated with global climate change which, in turn, is associated with the worldwide increase in the combustion of fossil fuels, the rise of hurricane activity in the Gulf of Mexico represents a particularly cruel example of the Gulf's petrochemical wealth coming home to wreak havoc.

Once Katrina hit the Gulf Coast, its impacts were devastating, and not just in New Orleans. While most of the 1,833 Katrina-related deaths were in Louisiana, deaths also occurred in Mississippi (238), Florida (14), Georgia (2), and Alabama (2) (Knabb, Rhome, and Brown 2006). The impacts were quickly felt globally too, due to the hurricane's impacts on offshore petroleum production and onshore refining and distribution facilities.

Ironically, the one place where Katrina's impact might not have been expected to be severe was New Orleans. New Orleans was located on the weaker, western side of the hurricane and it experienced only Category One–level winds (approximately ninety miles per hour). Such winds pose flying-object hazards to individuals walking on the street, but large cities are typically capable of enduring winds of this force with little structural damage (U.S. National Hurricane Center, Pielke 2007). Indeed, reports from just after the hurricane had passed through New Orleans abound with statements of relief over the city having, once again, just avoided "the big one." However, although Katrina's eye passed to the east of New Orleans, it was an exceptionally large (and hence wet) hurricane. This, together with the aforementioned coastal engineering (especially the construction of the Mississippi River Gulf Outlet shipping channel in the 1960s and its subsequent widening), led to an unusually large storm surge and water-level rise in Lake Pontchartrain, which lies directly north of New Orleans. Holding back the lake's waters was a levee system that in many instances had been poorly designed and, in any event, was poorly maintained. Levees in many places were overtopped, and at several points they crumbled, leaving storm water to pour into the city from the lake, adjacent canals, and the Mississippi River Gulf Outlet.

Eighty percent of New Orleans flooded, and 71 percent of the city's housing stock suffered at least some damage. Almost eighty thousand housing units — 42 percent of the city's dwellings — suffered "severe damage" or were destroyed (U.S. Department of Housing and Urban Development 2006). As might be expected, such a devastating blow is having a long-term impact on the city's future. Repopulation estimates vary, but one study conducted one year after Katrina found that that there were only 929,554 people resident in greater New Orleans (a 30.5 percent drop from the 2000 population of 1,337,726) and 200,665 in the city proper (a 58.6 percent drop from the 2000 population of 484,674). Poorer residents have had particular difficulty reestablishing themselves. The number of black households in the city proper suffered a 72.2 percent drop, from 322,792 in 2000 to just 89,891 in 2006 (Louisiana Recovery Authority 2007, U.S. Census Bureau 2000).[3]

On August 28, the day before the hurricane hit, the mayor issued a mandatory evacuation order, but few provisions were made for the evacuation of those who lacked private vehicles. Shelters were established within the city — most famously in the Superdome sports arena — but government and private aid agencies failed to equip these shelters with resources adequate for the large number of city residents (overwhelmingly poor and black) who converged there. The roof of the Superdome itself was damaged by hurricane winds and the power failed, and images from there and the Convention Center, the other main staging area for those who were unable to evacuate prior to the storm, were transmitted widely, spreading the message to the world that New Orleans was a city in chaos.

The failure of city and state authorities to adequately provide basic support to residents in city-approved shelters and to gather buses that could be mobilized to evacuate homeless survivors after the storm had passed was compounded by the failure of the Federal Emergency Management Agency (FEMA) to promptly coordinate rescue and relief efforts. Eventually, almost a week after the hurricane hit, survivors were removed from the Superdome and the Convention Center, and over the next days the levees received temporary repairs, although it took weeks for the floodwaters to be drained from the city.

As several authors note in the chapters that follow, the flooding of New Orleans was not a natural disaster. It was a disaster that, while sparked by Hurricane Katrina, can be attributed to poor environmental planning, political incompetence, and faulty engineering. But it also can be attributed to more structural and larger-scale factors. Urban imaginaries frequently involve processes of forgetting (see chapter 7 by Daina Harvey), and it appears as though, in this case, government officials forgot about a large number of their citizens, leaving them behind as the city was evacuated. Or, even worse, perhaps these citizens and neighborhoods were remembered but were deemed expendable.

To some extent, the tragedy of Hurricane Katrina can be attributed to governmental neglect that had skewed infrastructural investments at all levels of government and that had led to FEMA being assigned a director with no emergency management experience. However, this neglect was exacerbated by a longstanding trend toward cutting back government services and abandoning responsibilities in line with prevailing neoliberal, neoconservative, antiurban ideologies. The U.S. government's focus on the war in Iraq and on an infinitely expansive "global war on terror" further distracted government planners. Materially, the deployment of National Guard units in Iraq made them unavailable for local disaster duty, which normally is one of their primary functions, while the country's war-fighting machine had diverted military resources from the Army Corps of Engineers, which is responsible for the upkeep of the city's levees. Additionally, in the wake of the attacks of September 11, 2001, disaster relief had been placed within the framework of military security (exemplified most clearly by the inclusion of FEMA within the newly created Department of Homeland Security). As a result, when the federal government eventually responded to the tragedy it adopted an exceptionally militaristic posture, in which the hurricane's victims were often treated as the enemy (Dyson 2006, Graham 2006).

After Katrina

The story of Katrina leaves us not simply with data about how a hurricane impacts a city but also with questions about what cities are and how they function. Katrina can teach us about the ways in which cities as urban forms mediate between nature, community, and commerce. Katrina can teach us about the paired impulses toward nostalgia and progress. Katrina can teach us about the relationship between fixity and movement. Katrina can teach us about the cycles by which cities are born, die, and are reborn. And Katrina can teach us about how the politics and governance of a place can serve both to unite and to divide its residents. These issues among others are addressed in the chapters that follow.

Before we can abstract insights from a study of the Katrina disaster and apply them to a general understanding of cities, however, we first must gain a better understanding of the community that was in place in New Orleans prior to the hurricane, how it was affected, and how it has responded. Underlying all of Mumford's definitions of the city is the city as a collectivity of individuals, and each of these individuals experiences his or her city as moments of joy and pain, solidarities and disappointments. To this end, the next chapter, by New Orleans–based journalist and community activist Jordan Flaherty, paints a picture of life in New Orleans before, during, and after Katrina. For Flaherty, the essence of New Orleans (and, for that matter, any city) is *community*. This is the aspect of the city most profoundly experienced by its residents as they go about their everyday lives and struggles, and Flaherty reminds us that this aspect of the city needs to be recalled continually as one proceeds through the chapters that follow.

Following Flaherty's chapter, the remainder of this book is divided into four parts, each of which uses the example of Hurricane Katrina and its impact on New Orleans to consider a different aspect of the city: materialities, mobilities, memories, and divisions and connections. While these four topics fail to cover the entirety of issues that are raised by the Katrina disaster or considered by urban theorists, taken together they raise a cross section of the issues that emerge when one considers a city that, to paraphrase Henri Lefebvre's (1991) typology, is simultaneously an environment that is perceived by individuals as they navigate through its nature, architecture, and infrastructure (an arena of spatial practices); a planned space that gives order to society as it is conceived from above (a space of representations); and a space that is lived through as one projects one's ideals through the spatial practices that add meaning and materiality to one's urban environment (a representational space).

We begin our survey of urban issues brought to light by Hurricane Katrina with an investigation of the materiality of the city, which is defined by the relationship between a city's architecture, its infrastructure, and its nature. Most cities arise where they do because of an area's nature, and yet every city is perpetually trying to abstract itself from that nature, by bridging its rivers, diversifying its economy, paving its roads, and raising its levees. This is a central point made by Peirce Lewis (1976), when he distinguishes between New Orleans' fortuitous (and what he sees as "inevitable") situation — its contextual position at the mouth of the enormous Mississippi-Missouri-Ohio River drainage basin — and its unfortunate site — below sea level and nearly surrounded by water. This conceptual distinction between situation and site, or between context and nature, begins to unravel, however, as one looks at the social life that transpires within and transforms a city. The city itself becomes a second nature for the activities that occur there: a social nature, or a built environment (Smith 1990). Thus, as we search for lessons that can be learned from Katrina and its aftermath, we begin, in part 2 of this book, with the relationship between the city and the nature that it both encounters and creates.

In the first chapter of part 2, Geoff Manaugh and Nicola Twilley use the example of New Orleans' levee system to query the relationship between a city's architecture and its nature. Identifying a contradiction between the militaristic rigidity of the solutions developed by the Army Corps of Engineers and the fluid character of the river that these solutions seek to contain, they call for a more flexible urbanism that works with, instead of against, nature. The nature of New Orleans and, more generally, delta cities is further explored by Rob Shields in the next chapter. Shields sets New Orleans within the context of the world's great delta cities, liminal sites that serve as meeting points between land and sea, the national and the foreign, and the native and the migrant. The rise and fall (and rise again?) of New Orleans suggest the significance of these cities, with their blend of precariousness and vibrancy, for cultural innovation. Thus a link is made between several of Mumford's perspectives: the city as an urban village (or engineered landscape), the city as a cosmopolitan hub, and the city as a culture hearth. Additionally, both of these chapters direct attention away from the control and segmentation of a city's spaces, its people, and its nature that is usually associated with urban governance. Instead, they stress processes of mobility — of people and of nature — both within and beyond a city's borders.

The theme of mobility is approached directly in part 3 of this book. Most successful cities have thrived by serving as nodes on paths of movement, and individual urbanites' survival skills likewise are based on mastery of intra- and interurban mobility. But this is not to say that movement is necessarily a positive thing. As anthropologists who have studied mobility within the context of (post)modernity have shown, the processes of movement are complex and uneven (Appadurai 1996), and they may be experienced in highly particularized, and not always positive, ways (Ong 1999). The tourist is very different from the economic migrant, the exile, or the transported slave (Chambers 1994,

Gilroy 1993). The ambiguous relationship between mobility and city life is demonstrated by the *New York Times* article quoted above that stressed the historic immobility of New Orleanians and the shock that they experienced when forced to leave their homes (Levy 2005). As the article makes clear, this forced temporary relocation led some to question (and attempt to improve) their lives. For others, however, the experience likely was traumatic. For many, it was probably both. For some, it was a short-term displacement. Others had few means to return.

Just as the experience of mobility is ambiguous, it is also difficult to rank degrees of mobility. At first glance, the jet-setting tourist coming to New Orleans to enjoy Mardi Gras in the French Quarter is much more mobile than the homebound New Orleans resident portrayed in the *New York Times* article. At second glance, though, this tourist may feel confined to a few blocks of the Quarter for safety's sake, while the resident may be able to use local knowledge to travel the city at will.

The lesson here is that to understand mobility in the (post)modern world (or the [post]modern city) one must not simply look at aggregate flows of commodities, images, ideas, money, or people, as might be done by a scholar informed solely by Mumford's "cosmopolitan hub" perspective. One must also look at how individuals claim or are denied the right to move within and beyond the boundaries of urban space. The 1960s' call for a "right to the city" (Lefebvre 1968, 1996) has become a desire for a "right to space" which is more utopian still. In the first chapter of part 3, Hugh Bartling turns to the mobility of individual urbanites as he examines how the facilitation of mobility has become privatized in North American urban governance, leading to a "mobility deficit," which was evidenced in the inability of many New Orleanians to evacuate from the city. This deficit, for Bartling, is one of the most pressing obstacles to urban social justice.

The link between mobility and social justice, and the parallel link between uneven access to mobility and uneven social power, is explored in the second chapter of part 3 by Matthew Tiessen. Making links with Mumford's second perspective (the city as a space of speed and combination) as well as his fifth perspective (the city as a cosmopolitan hub), Tiessen considers the equation of urbanity with mobility that is an increasingly common theme in the urban literature. Through an interrogation of the works of John Urry and Paul Virilio, Tiessen, like Bartling, suggests that any understanding of urban mobility must begin and end with a consideration of power.

If urbanites are necessarily mobile, they also, paradoxically, are necessarily rooted. Every city is an accumulation of memories, embedded in its architecture, a point stressed by Mumford in his perspective on the city as a culture hearth. A city's places are locations in time as well as in space, and the post-Katrina testimony of New Orleans residents in countless newspaper articles, blogs, and Web sites exemplifies the mutual dependence of a city on both its architecture and its memories.

The relationship between place, architecture, and memory is complex, however. Gaston Bachelard (1958), for instance, uses architecture as a metaphor with which to explore place. For Bachelard, as we move through architecture, we experience place, and through this process we endow places with meaning. Others suggest that the identities of places depend on their changing relations to other places in a wider network of sites and spaces. From this point of view, New Orleans' marginal location is particularly relevant to its identity (Shields 1991). Still others suggest that place is a process, inseparable from time, and thus places are without essences; they have only multiple pasts and multiple futures (Massey 2005). From this perspective, a building (or an object) in place is as much a vector through time as it is a point in space. To repeat a quotation from Mumford, "In the city, time becomes visible" (Mumford 1970, 4). While this statement seems particularly appropriate for a city like New Orleans, which is so conscious of its past and, especially now, so wary about its future, it requires further clarification about *what* time is present in the city and *how* it is made visible.

These questions regarding the relationship between architecture/object on the one hand and memory/time on the other, how they are used to ascribe meaning to urban places, and how the subsequent location within these meaning-laden urban places fosters a sense of identity and community are taken up in part 4. In the first chapter, Daina Harvey explores the process of urban signification. While Harvey acknowledges that urban memories are always contested, he concentrates on the ways that these struggles are played out in different kinds of spaces of memory: spaces of amnesia (where memories are lost or willfully destroyed), spaces of anamnesis (where absence fosters memory), and asemiotic spaces (where a multitude of emotive associations leaves memory continually open to a variety of narratives that may coexist in one place). Reflecting on recent research in New Orleans, Harvey explores how the trauma of Hurricane Katrina has allowed multiple urban tropes to rise to the surface, a multiplicity that may bode well for the prospect of the city's recovery.

In the chapter that follows, Elizabeth Spelman focuses specifically on individuals' connections to objects and the role that material culture plays in connecting individuals with place and the past. Objects, for Spelman, play a mediating role between the individual and the place, and the restoration and recovery of objects can play a crucial role in the process by which one restores and recovers one's place (and one's identity). Thus, by conceiving of places as arenas in which objects are used, and by considering objects as "scaffolds" for memories, Spelman suggests that one can establish a framework whereby places, objects, and individuals' livelihoods may be recovered. At the same time, because objects are (often) portable, they can provide a tool for connecting people with memories that have been dis-placed.

While Harvey and Spelman focus on the connections made between people and places, the contributors to part 5 focus on connections (and divisions) among people. In the context of New Orleans, any discussion of social divisions inevitably turns to the categories of race and class; as has been noted, these divisions have been particularly stark in New Orleans, and they have been reproduced and magnified in the images of Hurricane Katrina and its aftermath. Here we must take leave of Mumford's five perspectives on the city, for the divisions of race and class are most certainly about power, and power is strangely absent from all of Mumford's perspectives. Of course, power may be grafted onto any of his perspectives (for instance, one can look at the conflicts that emerge and the power that is exercised as different groups of individuals transform nature to construct dwellings), but Mumford does not locate the city as necessarily lying within the dynamics of power and conflict, which are central themes in later urban research (Betsky 1997, Castells 1996, Harvey 1973, Lefebvre 1991, Sassen 2002; for a historical overview, see Savage and Warde 1993). Power is certainly not absent in the prior parts of this book — parts 2 through 4 deal, respectively, with struggles over who has the power to construct the city, who has the power to move, and who has the power to remember — but power becomes even more central in part 5 as we turn to the divisions and connections that are employed and reproduced in the images and experiences of pre- and post-Katrina New Orleans.

In the first chapter of part 5, C. Tabor Fisher examines the divisions between the observer who looks into the city from the outside and the urban resident who is living not only *in* but also *through* the city. Fisher warns that any attempt to understand the fabric of power and inequities that characterize the modern city must avoid mimicking the systems of abstractions and "representations of space" through which these inequities are reproduced. The distance between the disembodied observer and the city-as-object reproduces the notion of the city as abstract space, and this epistemological perspective inadvertently reproduces divisions between urban residents. Drawing on the work of María Lugones, Fisher proposes as an alternative that one adopt the position of a "streetwalker theorist" who picks up bits of knowledge from the stories of on-the-ground individuals and who concatenates these stories into provisional explanations. Employing Henri Lefebvre's (1991) terminology, she advocates this method as a means for allowing spaces of representation to be understood against the dominant background of official representations of what the city is.

In the next chapter, Jacob Wagner takes on the role of a "streetwalker theorist," viewing New Orleans not as a patchwork of defined and static neighborhoods nor as a gumbo of diverse but assimilated ethnicities, but as an environment of hybridity and continual interaction and transformation. Wagner develops the concept of creole urbanism to describe the city's resilient urban culture and built environment, a concept that resonates with the deltaic urbanism that Shields celebrates in chapter 4. From its culture that fuses a multitude of margins together to its vibrant public spaces, Wagner emphasizes connections amid difference, a far cry from the images of urban dysfunction and division that dominated media images of New Orleans before, during, and after the Katrina disaster.

In the final chapter, Jonathan Shapiro Anjaria examines some different sets of divisions and connections. In addition to identifying the division drawn in the U.S. media between white, non-inner-city America and cities like New Orleans, Anjaria also notes the connections that the media makes between all places that appear chaotic and are populated by nonwhite people. These are the imagined places of the "Third World." Anjaria also, like Wagner, notes another set of connections: the cooperative connections that frequently exist among individuals in these "Third World" places, media representations of looting and violence notwithstanding.

To develop this point, Anjaria expands his focus from New Orleans to Mumbai, India, which, one month prior to Katrina, also experienced devastating floods. Anjaria suggests that the cooperative spirit that prevailed in Mumbai was due to a general rejection of bourgeois ideals (in personal attitudes and in city planning), and thus he concludes that the lesson of Katrina is that, as we rethink the design of our cities in anticipation of the next disaster, we must simultaneously rethink our values and aspirations. In other words, we cannot answer the question "what is a city?" without concurrently answering the questions of who we are and who we want to be.

Notes

In addition to editorial input from Rob Shields, I am indebted to Jacob Wagner for some excellent comments on an earlier draft of this chapter.

1. Here I utilize Homi Bhabha's (1994) distinction between "diversity" and "difference," a distinction that is also implied (although not using these terms) by Jacob Wagner in chapter 10 of this book.

2. For a more in-depth and personal account of how Hurricane Katrina and its aftermath were experienced by New Orleans residents, see the next chapter in this book by Jordan Flaherty.

3. As another indicator of displacement, in January 2007 FEMA reported that there were still 1,289,353 individuals receiving emergency aid, concentrated in Louisiana, Mississippi, and Alabama, as well as in Houston and San Antonio, Texas, and Atlanta, Georgia (U.S. Federal Emergency Management Agency 2007). For updated figures, see Greater New Orleans Community Data Center (2007), with links also to the Brookings Institution's monthly *Katrina Index*.

CHAPTER TWO

New Orleans' Culture of Resistance

Jordan Flaherty

The devastation of New Orleans began long before Katrina, and didn't stop when hurricane season ended. The damage to New Orleans came from decades of brutal negligence and a criminally slow response on the part of local, state, and federal governments that didn't care about the people of New Orleans, and still don't.

The U.S. government's abdication of responsibility, the images broadcast around the world of a people abandoned, and the escalating chaos all served as the opening act of what has turned out to be a long struggle over the characteristics of relief and reconstruction. One side has an agenda that encompasses the corporatization, criminalization, militarization, and privatization of relief. On the other side are the people of New Orleans, historically overexploited and underserved by our government and politicians, fighting for community control of both the decisions and the finances behind the reconstruction of our city.

Relief and reconstruction thus are among the many arenas wherein a struggle is being waged between, on the one hand, the notion of the city as a space to be governed, managed, and policed, and, on the other hand, the notion of the city as a space of community. In this chapter, I explore the ongoing tension between these two perspectives on New Orleans. At every step along the way, attempts to control the city have been met by a vibrant culture of resistance in the city's pre-Katrina history, in the ways in which the residents of the city coped with the disaster, and in the ongoing struggles to rebuild its schools, its neighborhoods, and its physical and social infrastructure. Drawing in large part on my own experience living in New Orleans, I recount this ongoing struggle between community and control, concluding with an extended discussion of the role of nonprofit organizations that, depending on the specific organization, work in cooperation with, in the service of, or, all too often, in opposition to the underlying grassroots culture of resistance.

Privilege and Profit

As a white male organizer who moved to New Orleans several years before Katrina, I have profited from the inequality that has been intrinsic to the contours
of this disaster. In everything from employment opportunities to housing to the
amplification my writing has received in the national media, I have benefited
from intersecting levels of privilege — especially privilege based on race, but
also gender, class, and geography.

In writing this piece, I need to acknowledge that in important ways it is not
my own. My analysis of what has happened in New Orleans, the filter through
which I have interpreted what I have seen here, has been developed through
education I have received from countless hours of conversation and work with
people from New Orleans, especially African American grassroots community organizers from organizations such as Safe Streets/Strong Communities,
INCITE! Women of Color Against Violence, the People's Institute for Survival
and Beyond, Community Labor United, and many more. The grassroots resistance that these groups have led has inspired and educated me.

The fact that my voice has been more prominent than some of these other
much more informed voices is a part of this disaster that must be acknowledged: black people of New Orleans have not only been killed and displaced
and robbed, but also silenced.

The same people of New Orleans whom the national media portrayed as
murderers and looters remain silenced today. Even in the noncorporate media,
white voices like mine have been overrepresented instead of black voices, and
black female voices are doubly missing.

Beyond race, there are also other issues of privilege. As one community organizer expressed to me in the days following the storm, "There's a difference between New Orleans residents and New Orleans natives. The voices I've heard
speaking for us have been people who moved to New Orleans. Many of them
are currently staying with family or friends from somewhere else. They're in a
different situation. I'm from New Orleans; my family is from New Orleans. I
don't have anywhere else." The access I've had to networks outside New Orleans gave me an advantage in the days following the evacuation in everything
from housing and work to media exposure.

The City

For those who have not lived in New Orleans, you have missed an incredible,
glorious, vital city — a place with a culture and energy unlike anywhere else

in the world; a 70 percent African American city where resistance to white
supremacy supported a generous, subversive, and unique culture of vivid
beauty.

From jazz, blues, and hip-hop to second lines, Mardi Gras Indians, jazz funerals, and the citywide tradition of red beans and rice on Monday nights, New
Orleans is a place of art and music and traditions and sexuality and liberation
unlike anywhere else in the world.

New Orleans was, as more than one former resident has said, North America's African city. It is a city steeped in a culture that is specifically African
American. Many attribute this at least partly to the legacy of the different form
that French colonialism took. For example, the existence in New Orleans of a
neighborhood (Tremé) of free black people as early as 1770 meant that African
cultural traditions were maintained in a way that they were not elsewhere in
the United States.

New Orleans was the number-one African American tourist destination in
the United States. The Bayou Classic and Essence Festival, two major black
community events, brought tens of thousands of tourists to the city every
year.

It is a city with its own holidays, like Indian Sunday, in which black men —
and some women — dress in elaborate costumes that they have sewed and constructed all year. The costuming began at least in part as a tribute to the Native American community, for the support that community gave black people
during the times of slavery, such as reservations serving as stops on the Underground Railroad. These Mardi Gras Indians — as they are called — are just part
of the cultural tradition of New Orleans that outsiders rarely see. These are
neighborhood traditions — put on by members of a community, for the benefit
of others in the community.

Culture and Resistance

Shortly after the city was flooded, Cornel West stated:

> New Orleans has always been a city that lived on the edge . . . with Elysian Fields
> and cemeteries and the quest for paradise. When you live so close to death, be-
> hind the levees, you live more intensely, sexually, gastronomically, psychologically.
> Louis Armstrong came out of that unbelievable cultural breakthrough unprece-
> dented in the history of American civilization. The rural blues, the urban jazz. It is
> the tragicomic lyricism that gives you the courage to get through the darkest storm.
> Charlie Parker would have killed somebody if he had not blown his horn. The

Mardi Gras Indians.

Photograph by Jordan Flaherty; image courtesy of the photographer.

history of black people in America is one of unbelievable resilience in the face of crushing white supremacist powers. (quoted in Walters 2005)

More than anywhere else in the United States, New Orleans is a city where people live in one neighborhood their whole lives, and where generations live in the same community. All of this is to say that New Orleans is not just a tourist stop. New Orleans is a unique culture, one that is resilient, and with a history of community and resistance.

The community traditions of New Orleans have generally existed outside the police and white power structure of the city. Mardi Gras Indians, for example, have never had the support of city government, and have in fact faced police repression.

In spring of 2005, as the Indians were parading on another of their official holidays (St. Joseph's Night), scores of officers descended on the scene and disrupted the event, scaring the children present and arresting several of the performers.

Several weeks later, at a city council hearing on the incident, Tootie Montana, the chief of chiefs of the Mardi Gras Indians, spoke. At eighty-two years old, Tootie had been a Mardi Gras Indian chief for five decades. He captivated the assembled crowd with details of a long history of police repression, tied into racial discrimination, beginning with a police crackdown at his very first Mardi Gras many decades ago. Tootie ended his speech with the words, "This has to stop." Those would be his last words. Tootie Montana stepped back from the microphone and collapsed to the floor. He was pronounced dead of a heart attack shortly afterward.

His funeral was a moving combination of cultural celebration and political demonstration. Thousands of people came out, dressed in all manner of costume, to commemorate the life of this brave fighter for freedom. Longtime community activist Jerome Smith inflamed the crowd: "This is about a life that has passed, but it is also about the struggle against institutionalized racism in our city." The link between New Orleans culture, especially the culture of black Mardi Gras, and liberation was clear to everyone in attendance.

Community

I didn't really understand community until I moved to New Orleans. It is a city of kindness and hospitality, where walking down the block can take two hours because you stop and talk to someone on every porch, and where everyone pulls together when someone is in need. It is a city of extended families and social networks filling the gaps left by city, state, and federal governments that have abdicated their responsibility for the public welfare. It is a city where people you walk past on the street not only ask how you are; they wait for an answer. New Orleans is a place where someone always wants to feed you.

It is a city and people who have resisted white supremacy for centuries, a city of slave revolts and uprisings. This is the city where in 1892 Homer Plessy and the Citizens Committee planned the direct action that brought the first (unsuccessful) legal challenge to the doctrine of "separate but equal" — the challenge that became the Supreme Court case of *Plessy v. Ferguson*.

Social aid and pleasure clubs, local black cultural institutions that began during the reconstruction era both for mutual aid and to maintain the community's culture, still thrive today, and in fact have been an important force in bringing back residents of the city.

New Orleans activists were on the front lines of civil rights organizing. "Wherever you went across the South," Congress of Racial Equality (CORE) veteran Mattheo "Flukie" Suarez told New Orleans journalist Katy Reckdahl (2005), "there were always New Orleans people working in the civil-rights movement."

New Orleans was also part of the more militant post–civil rights era. In 1970 the New Orleans Black Panthers held off the police from the Desire housing projects and also formed one of the nation's first Black Panther chapters in prison. Nationwide, Panthers and other radical groups were inspired by the Deacons for Defense, an armed self-defense group formed in rural central Louisiana in 1964.

Despite these rich traditions, New Orleans has long been a city in crisis.

It was a violent city. New Orleans had a pre-Katrina population of fewer than five hundred thousand and was expecting three hundred murders in 2005, most of them centered on just a few, overwhelmingly black, neighborhoods. Murder suspects are rarely convicted. Often, a few days after a shooting, the attacker is shot in revenge. Distrust of police is so high that even when murders happen in front of large crowds, officers can find no witnesses. The district attorney's office had three convictions for the 162 murders in 2006.

New Orleans had a 47 percent functional illiteracy rate by some measures (Center for Arts and Culture 2003), and over 50 percent of black ninth-graders did not graduate in four years. Louisiana spends on average $4,724 per child's education each year and ranked forty-eighth in the country for lowest teacher salaries (Juvenile Justice Project of Louisiana Web site).

New Orleans is a city where industry has left, and most remaining jobs are low-paying, transient, insecure jobs in the service economy. It has always been a city you fall in love with, and a city you have to fight to improve.

The Evacuation

When I evacuated from New Orleans, five days after the city flooded, I traveled from a Mid-City apartment by boat to a helicopter to an evacuee camp, on the I-10 freeway just outside of New Orleans. In the camp, thousands of people — by my estimate 90 percent black and poor — were forced to stand or sit in mud and trash behind metal barricades, under an unforgiving sun, with heavily armed soldiers standing guard over them.

When a bus would come through, it would stop at a different spot every time, state police would open a gap in one of the barricades, and people would rush for the bus, with no information given about where the bus was going. Once inside, evacuees would find out where the bus was taking them; Baton Rouge, Houston, Arkansas, Dallas, or some other location.

I was told that if you boarded a bus bound for Little Rock, for example, even people with family and a place to stay in Baton Rouge would not be allowed to get out of the bus as it passed through that much closer city. You had no choice but to go to the shelter in Arkansas. If you had people willing to come to New Orleans to pick you up, they could not come within seventeen miles of the camp.

In this atmosphere of chaos, family members were separated, and fear and misinformation dominated. Given the choice of being shipped off to somewhere unknown or staying behind, many people were on the side, not even trying to get on a bus. Children, people in wheelchairs, and everyone else waited in the sun by the side of the highway.

I traveled throughout the camp and spoke to Red Cross supervisors, Salvation Army workers, National Guard soldiers, and state police. No one could give me any details on when buses would arrive, how many, where they would go to, or any other information. I spoke to the several teams of journalists nearby, and asked if any of them had been able to get any information from any federal or state officials on any of these questions, and all of them, from German photographers to producers with a local Fox affiliate, complained of an unorganized, noncommunicative mess.

There was also no visible attempt by any of those running the camp to set up any sort of transparent and consistent system — for instance, a line to get on buses, a way to register contact information or find family members, special-needs services for children and the infirm, phone services, treatment for possible disease exposure, or even a single trash can.

The individual soldiers and police were friendly and polite—at least to me—but nobody seemed to know what was going on. As wave after wave of evacuees arrived, they were ushered behind the barricades onto mud and garbage, while heavily armed soldiers looked on.

My memories of that place still haunt me. Everyone I spoke to had a horrible story to tell, of a home destroyed, of swimming across town, of bodies and fights, gunshots, vigilantes, and fear.

While most people there had no choice but to wait for whatever was dealt to them, my intersecting layers of privilege as a journalist and as a white male allowed me to escape via a ride from an Australian TV crew. From there, the resources I have as a nonnative of New Orleans meant that a stay in a shelter was never a fear. Weeks later, I was back in the city. The majority of those who were in the camp with me no doubt remain exiled to this day, perhaps in Houston, or a trailer camp in Baton Rouge, or somewhere further removed.

Later, watching media coverage of the disaster, seeing how black New Orleanians were portrayed, I felt anger and dismay. The city I loved was demonized, the people criminalized, their homes stolen, and a culture was in the process of being erased.

Shelter and Safety

Days after evacuating, I went to the River Road shelter in Baton Rouge as part of a project initiated by a grassroots organization called Families and Friends of Louisiana's Incarcerated Children to help displaced New Orleans residents reconnect with loved ones who were lost in the labyrinth of Louisiana's corrections system.

Everyone I met was desperately trying to find a sister or brother or child or other family member lost in the system. Many people who were picked up for minor infractions in the days before the hurricane ended up being shipped to prisons upstate, including the infamous Angola Prison, a former slave plantation where the warden has estimated that over 90 percent of inmates sent there will die within its walls (Gordon 2005).

Most of the family members I spoke with in the shelter just wanted to get a message to their loved ones. "Tell him that we've been looking for him, that we made it out of New Orleans, and that we love him," said an evacuated New Orleans East resident named Angela.

While Barbara Bush famously declared how fortunate the shelter residents were, in the real world New Orleans evacuees were feeling anything but sheltered. One woman I spoke with in the River Street shelter said that she had barely slept since she arrived in the shelter system. "I sleep with one eye open," she told me. "It's not safe in there."

Christina Kucera, a Planned Parenthood organizer from New Orleans, explained it this way: "Issues of safety and shelter are intricately tied to gender. This has hit women particularly hard. It's the collapse of community. We've lost neighbors and systems within our communities that helped keep us safe."

For many who experienced the shelter system, abuse and revictimization were rampant. There were widespread reports of racism and discrimination in Red Cross shelters, especially in Lafayette, Lake Charles, and Baton Rouge. According to Jodie Escobedo (2005), a doctor from California who was volunteering in the Baton Rouge shelters, "Local officials, including politicians, select Red Cross personnel and an especially well placed but small segment of the Louisiana medical community, have managed to get themselves into positions of power where their prejudices result in the hoarding of supplies, vilification of the needy and substandard treatment of volunteers and refugees alike."

As a medical volunteer with a firsthand view, Escobedo painted a devastating portrait.

> I witnessed Red Cross staff treated abusively by shelter administration who also expressed contempt for the sheltered population. Dental abscesses abounded and when several cases of small individual cases of Scope were donated, Red Cross staff was told not to distribute it because "they will drink it and get drunk." At the River Center the Red Cross hoarded hygiene supplies and basic necessities on a giant loading dock while kids could not go to school because they had no pants or shoes, babies drank from dirty baby bottles, people slept on the floor and donated clothes sat inaccessible. I tried for 4 days to get access to the Red Cross storehouse of hand sanitizer which was unfortunately off site.

Shortly after the storm, an aid worker with the relief organization Save the Children expressed to me shame at her profiting from the disaster. "We're getting a big per-diem, on top of our salaries," she confessed. Frustrated with her experience with the organization, she continued, "Things take forever to be approved—sometimes so long that by the time we have the support we need, the effort has passed. There's so much money behind us—we can do pretty much whatever we want and don't have to worry about funding, but it feeds lifestyles that are much more demanding than I'd hope relief workers would be."

New Orleans was a blueprint for a new, militarized form of relief. The Chicago police camped out in a bar on Bourbon Street, while an Israeli security company named Instinctive Shooting International was hired to guard uptown mansions. National Guard and Blackwater mercenaries were seemingly everywhere. Meanwhile, white vigilante gangs patrolled the West Bank, with the tacit permission of local authorities. As one central city resident complained to me, "Why don't they send some of these troops with tools to rebuild instead of just weapons? I guess they don't want it rebuilt."

Criminalizing the Survivors

If the "rescue" were not bad enough, for the thousands of New Orleanians caught up in the criminal justice system, things keep getting worse. The continuing debacle of this broken system inspires in me a sense of indignation I thought was lost to cynicism long ago.

Ursula Price, an investigator for indigent defense cases, spent months after the storm speaking with several thousand hurricane survivors who were imprisoned at the time of the hurricane, and her stories chill me. "I grew up in small-town Mississippi," she tells me. "We had the Klan marching down our main street, but I've never seen anything like this."

Safe Streets/Strong Communities, a New Orleans–based criminal justice reform coalition, released a devastating report in March 2006 based on more than one hundred interviews with prisoners incarcerated since pre-Katrina and spread across thirteen prisons and hundreds of miles. They found the average number of days people had been held without a trial was 385 days. One person had been locked up for 1,289 days. None of them had been convicted of any crime.

"I've been working in the system for the while. I do capital cases, and I've seen the worst that the criminal justice system has to offer," Price explained. "But even I am shocked that there has been so much disregard for the value of these people's lives, especially people who have not been proved to have done anything wrong." According to a pre-Katrina report from the Metropolitan Crime Commission, 65 percent of those arrested in New Orleans are eventually released without ever having been charged with any crime (Metropolitan Crime Commission 2005).

Samuel Nicholas (his friends call him Nick) was imprisoned in Orleans Parish Prison (OPP) on a misdemeanor charge, and was due to be released August 31. Instead, after a harrowing journey of several months, he was released February 1. Nick told me he still shudders when he thinks of those days in OPP.

House on St. Claude Avenue, Bywater.
Photograph by Jordan Flaherty; image courtesy of the photographer.

"We heard boats leaving, and one of the guys said, 'Hey man, all the deputies gone,'" Nick relates. "We took it upon ourselves to try to survive. They left us in the gym for two days with nothing. Some of those guys stayed in a cell four or five days. People were hollering, 'Get me out, I don't want to drown, I don't want to die.' We were locked in with no ventilation, no water, nothing to eat. It's just the grace of God that a lot of us survived."

Systemic Problems

Pre-Katrina, the New Orleans public defender system was already dangerously overloaded, with forty-two attorneys and six investigators. For almost a year after the storm, New Orleans was down to six public defenders and one investigator. And these defenders were not necessarily full-time, nor committed to their clients. One attorney was known to spend his days in court working on crossword puzzles instead of talking to his clients. "We have a system that was broken before Katrina," Price tells me, "that was then torn apart, and is waiting to be rebuilt."

"This ain't just started, it's been going on," Nick tells me. "I want to talk about it, but at the same time it hurts to talk about it. It's not the judge, it's not the lawyers, it's the criminal justice system. Everybody who goes to jail isn't guilty. You got guys who were drunk in public, treated like they committed murder."

I talked to Nick in a neighborhood bar in Central City, just before he was going to Mardi Gras Indian practice. As with many people from his community, Nick is active in creating and sustaining New Orleans' unique culture. "I'm making this interview so that things get better," he explains. "The prison system, the judicial system, the police. We got to make a change, and we all got to come together as a community to make this change. I want to stop all this harassment and brutality."

For many New Orleanians, it is community that has brought security. And that's why the police and National Guard and security companies on our streets didn't bring the security that people wanted. That's why locking up our neighbors in prisons and throwing away the key is no solution.

"Despite all of the horror we are seeing daily, my hope is this is an opportunity for change," Price said. "OPP corruption is being laid bare. People being held past their time is nothing new in this system. It's just more extreme now. This is something to organize around and fight against."

Since its founding, Safe Streets/Strong Communities has done just that, combining a grassroots organizing strategy — working directly with the incarcerated, formerly incarcerated, and their family members — with political pressure and legal support. In its first months, Safe Streets/Strong Communities succeeded in radically transforming the city's indigent defense board from a corrupt and negligent home of cronyism to a body staffed with criminal justice reform advocates, while simultaneously becoming a force in city and state government and mobilizing a large grassroots base (Flaherty 2006).

The Schools

Post-Katrina New Orleans has become a battleground in the national fight over competing visions for the future of urban education. Weeks after Katrina, with the city evacuated and all the schools closed, no parents or students or teachers around, suddenly anything became possible. Instead of making gradual changes to an existing system, there was no system, and virtually no rules or limits on what could be changed. Just days after New Orleans was flooded, the Heritage Foundation, a right-wing think tank based in Washington, DC, was already advocating for vouchers and "market solutions" to the city's education problems. "The framework has been exploded since the storm," confirms New Orleans–based education reform advocate Aesha Rasheed. "It's almost a blank slate for whatever agenda people want to bring."

Before the storm and displacement, New Orleans had 128 public schools, four thousand teachers, and sixty thousand students. The system was widely regarded as in crisis. Three quarters of eighth-graders failed to score at the basic level on state English assessments. In some schools, JROTC, the high school military recruiting program, was a mandatory class, mostly because funding was not available for other programs. Ten school superintendents in ten years had been fired or quit. Many parents, especially white parents, had pulled their kids out of the system; almost half of the city's students were enrolled in private schools and parochial schools. Advocates accused the school system of functioning as little more than a warehousing program for black youth.

While the city's private schools saw almost 90 percent of their students return, spring 2006 saw only 20 percent of public school students return. Those who returned are attending a system completely different from the one they left, what some have referred to as a grand experiment in school reform, with thirty-five out of the fifty-six schools open in fall of 2006 transformed to publicly sanctioned but privately operated charter schools. In other words, New Orleans now has a school system in which the majority of publicly funded schools have been freed from many of the rules and oversight that previously had applied to public schools in the system.

Nationwide, the fight over charter schools has crossed traditional boundaries of left and right, with many progressives supporting charter schools as a potential tool for community control, and an opportunity to try education strategies that would not be possible through the common bureaucracy of public schools. Opponents, however, see charter schools as a backdoor strategy used by conservatives to undermine public schools and to create a two-tiered "separate but equal" hierarchy within the public education system. They worry that the new administrations running the schools are inexperienced and unprepared to take over the New Orleans system. "They say this is an experiment," Tracie Washington, an NAACP lawyer and education advocate, explains, speaking about the plans of charter school advocates. Referring to the forty-year-long "scientific study" under which African American men were allowed to die of syphilis, she continued, "Tuskegee was an experiment. We have reason to be suspicious of experiments."

The question of the role of the teachers' union — previously the largest and perhaps strongest in the city — is another contentious issue tied up in the dispute over charters. The School Board voted in the fall to lay off all but sixty-one of the seven thousand employees, and in June let the teachers' union contract expire with little comment and no fanfare. Those rehired at charter schools return without their union.

For many New Orleanians, the union represents an important black-led political base advocating for justice within the education system. "Elites of the city may prefer the teachers don't come back because they represent an educated class of black New Orleans, with steady income, seniority, job protection," explained Jacques Morial, community advocate and brother of former mayor Marc Morial.

According to education activists, students whose parents are able to actively advocate for them have been able to get into improved public schools, but for those who have difficulty managing the system of applications and red tape, their options are reduced. "Suffice it to say that the old system worked for people with higher education, with more resources," Mtangulizi Sanyinka, project manager of New Orleans' African American Leadership Project, tells me. "It wasn't that the system didn't work at all. It didn't work for poor people."

"There is an access barrier," Rasheed confirms. "In the old New Orleans, charters were an island in a sea of city schools. That's no longer the case. There's currently a big group of kids that don't have a school. Some think it was one or two thousand in the spring 2006 semester. That's a lot, considering you had only twelve thousand total enrolled."

Pre-Katrina, thousands of kids every year did not preregister for any school—they simply showed up at their neighborhood school on the first day, and the school found them a place. Now, most of those neighborhood schools do not exist, and those that do are no longer obligated to place students who just show up.

The struggle over what form the education system will take is also fundamental to the larger issue of who will return and when. At forums, at neighborhood meetings, and throughout the city and its diaspora, parents are anxious. In Houston and Atlanta, displaced parents question if their kids will have a school if they return.

At John McDonogh, a city school under state supervision, students formed an activist group—called the Fyre Youth Squad—to fight against what they saw as unfair treatment and an unequal system. "Our school has thirty-four security guards and twenty-one teachers," one student told me. "How do we learn in that environment? Do they even want us to learn?" Fyre Youth Squad organized demonstrations and press conferences and brought national attention to the plight of students in the most underfunded schools—another example of an inspiring, locally led effort.

Advocates are attempting to fight for the students who will be left behind, but it's an uphill struggle with more questions than answers. Despite all of the promises from charter school advocates, Tracie Washington, civil rights attorney and adult ally of the Youth Squad, is suspicious of their motives. "If you kick me out of my kitchen because you say you can cook better than me," she says, "then your gumbo better taste better than mine."

Disaster and Politics

Disaster response has political repercussions. Corruption and stealing of post-earthquake disaster aid in 1972 contributed to the fall of the Somoza dictatorship in Nicaragua. The faulty federal response to the 1985 earthquake that hit Mexico City ignited a grassroots movement in Mexico that helped to end the PRI government's decades of one-party rule. And, of course, the 1927 flooding of the Mississippi River helped to elect Huey P. Long governor of Louisiana.

Within two weeks after Katrina, Michael Brown of the Federal Emergency Management Agency (FEMA) resigned. New Orleans police superintendent Eddie Compass followed soon after. In January 2006, Marsha Evans, president of the Red Cross, was forced out. The Bush administration poll numbers began their fall after the failures of Katrina. This disaster was made by politics, the "recovery" has been guided by politics, and the consequences continue to be felt in politics.

When I saw the floodwaters rising in New Orleans, I expected that poor people would be cut out of the reconstruction money. What has surprised me is the extent to which the entire city has been left out. While some local elites have profited, on a deeper level — from levees to housing aid to business loans — the money necessary to rebuild New Orleans simply never came. The largest program for bringing federal money to New Orleans — the Louisiana Road Home program — has been acknowledged by all to be a catastrophe (e.g., see Associated Press 2006).

Part of the justification for the federal abandonment of the city is New Orleans' famously corrupt politics. "The money will just be embezzled or squandered" is the widely repeated refrain. This is also used against the people of New Orleans, who are accused of "wasting" their aid from FEMA or the Red Cross on liquor stores and strip clubs.

However, the truth is that all of this is an excuse to cover up the federal government's corporate agenda, which has never been to support poor people or cities, and especially not a majority African American city. The city has been demonized just as Reagan had demonized "welfare queens" twenty years earlier, as part of an overall strategy to attack poor people. The right-wing think tanks saw this as an opportunity to push their privatization agenda.

Bush needed to come long enough for a few photo opportunities and to pretend that he cared. But in reality, national elites care very little about what happens to New Orleans. The complaints about corruption are just a way to muddy the waters.

We have more than our share of corrupt politicians in New Orleans, but our problem is not politicians wasting recovery aid. Nor do our problems come from misspent FEMA checks. Our problem is oil companies — and the federal government — profiting off of Louisiana off-coast drilling while Louisiana gets coastal erosion and environmental devastation. Our problem is multinational corporations making millions while refusing to pay their employees above minimum wage. Our problem is contractors and subcontractors and sub-subcontractors victimizing immigrant workers with low pay and hazardous working conditions. Our problem is that the federal government refused to allocate the money for levees and coastal restoration to protect our city. Our problem is the whole United States being enriched by the culture created in this city, while the people who created that culture have been either demonized or rendered invisible.

Resistance Everywhere

Resistance to displacement has been present wherever New Orleanians have found themselves, including hotels, shelters, and trailer parks. In spring 2006 I visited Renaissance Village, an evacuee community of over five hundred trailers located north of Baton Rouge on land owned by a youth prison. Residents I spoke to were aching to come home. "Last year I was a middle-income American, a homeowner. I never imagined I'd come to this," said Hillary Moore Jr., a former city employee and New Orleans property owner exiled in a small trailer in the middle of the complex. Living alone, Moore barely fits in his trailer. When he talks about the family of five living next door, I can't imagine how they could possibly squeeze in.

As with all of the residents I spoke with, Moore was unhappy in his trailer home. "Why would they buy this for as much money as they paid? This thing is designed for a weekend. Can you imagine someone trying to live in here for six or seven months?"

I asked him why he agreed to move in. "When you've been living in a gymnasium with one-hundred-plus people, a travel trailer sounds like a mansion to you, and when they tell you sign here so you can end standing in line to get a shower, you don't question anything. You sign and you jump at the opportunity." An over-capacity housing market from Baton Rouge to New Orleans made other options scarce.

On the day I visited, residents voiced some of their recent complaints, most involving the logistics of living in an isolated, underserved community. Many of the occupants had no means of transportation in and out. The only bus service was to Wal-Mart and back.

Not long after moving in, Moore and others organized a residents' council. "We got tired of a lot of things Keta [the contractor company managing the park] was doing, and we decided to organize because we realized there is strength in numbers," he tells me. The residents' council formed an elected board and held open meetings every week.

The Neighborhoods

The most dramatic example of grassroots community responses may be in the rise in prominence and influence of another element of New Orleans' communities: neighborhood associations.

These organizations — most of which existed pre-Katrina, but have seen their membership numbers and involvement multiply along with their influence — have become important as a place for everyone from politicians to architects and designers and planners to foundations and other funders to go to for input and to lend support.

This development is encouraging, in that these neighborhood associations represent a possibility of direct democracy and community involvement. They have had real successes, in designing their own plans for rebuilding, in resisting the destruction of their neighborhoods, in fighting a landfill near residences in New Orleans East, getting trash pickup started, and much more. However, with so much of the city still displaced, the membership of these organizations is biased toward residents who have returned, which reflects the racist and classist nature of this disaster. For example, even neighborhoods that are majority African American, such as Gentilly and Broadmoor, were represented in this process by neighborhood associations that are majority white (Sontag 2005).

The planning process has been intensely confusing, with legions of planners coming down to work with neighborhood groups, while the mayor and city council hired separate planners. For more than a year after Katrina, there seemed to be many simultaneous processes, with perhaps none having any real hope of being funded.

Eventually, Mayor Ray Nagin and the city council agreed on the hire of Ed Blakely, an internationally recognized expert on rebuilding, as city recovery czar. Blakely moved forward on a much less ambitious — but in some ways more inclusive — rebuilding plan, which contained strong support for the

Lower Ninth Ward and New Orleans East. It remains to be seen, perhaps after years or even decades, what all the planning will add up to.

The Corporate Left

Despite the attention New Orleans has received from the left, progressive resources have been comparatively scarce. Liberal foundations and nonprofits earmarked millions of dollars toward the Gulf, but most of that money did not go to New Orleans–initiated projects, and in fact much of it went to the same East Coast and West Coast nonprofits that have traditionally received the majority of grants.

New Orleans — and poor communities in general — have a long history of outsiders spending large sums of money for organizing without community leadership or involvement. Efforts like these almost always fail. Meanwhile, vital local projects go unfunded and unrecognized.

Poststorm, local organizations with no paid staff or grants immediately started doing crucial work with virtually no funding or attention from outside New Orleans. New Orleans residents struggled to rebuild their lives and city. During this same time, they saw many outside organizations visit, conduct interviews, write reports, and receive grants.

National Allies

In an open letter to funders and national nonprofits released in December 2006, a wide alliance of New Orleans' grassroots organizations declared, "From the perspective of the poorest and least powerful, it appears that the work of national allies on our behalf has either not happened, or if it has happened it has been a failure."

In conversations with scores of New Orleans residents, including organizers, advocates, health-care providers, educators, artists, and media makers, I heard countless stories of diverted funding and unmet needs. While many stressed that they have had important positive experiences with national allies, few reported receiving anything close to the funding, resources, or staff they need for their work, and in fact most were still working unsustainable hours while living in a devastated city.

Research backs up the anecdotal reports. A January 2006 article by Pablo Eisenberg in the *Chronicle of Philanthropy* argued that the amount given to post-Katrina New Orleans was "small-potato giving for America's foundations, which collectively have $500 billion in assets." The article also asserted, "Just as deplorable as the small sums poured into the region are the choices foundations have made about where the money should go" (Eisenberg 2006). In other words, very little of the money had gone to organizations directed by or accountable to New Orleanians. One prominent New Orleans–born advocate and lobbyist called this phenomenon the "Halliburtization of the nonprofit sector."

A February 2006 report from the Foundation Center points out that the Red Cross, which raised perhaps $2 billion for Katrina relief despite widespread accusations of racism and mismanagement, "ranked as by far the largest named recipient of contributions from foundation and corporate donors in response to hurricanes Katrina and Rita," receiving almost 35 percent of all aid. At the time of the report, another 35 percent of the money the foundations designated had not been spent. The Bush-Clinton Katrina Fund, Salvation Army, and United Way together made up another 13 percent. The rest was mostly spread between other national relief organizations.

Accountability

Foundations, according to the *Chronicle* article, "seem to have been preoccupied with the issue of accountability. Many foundations wondered how they could be certain that grants to local groups would be well spent and, therefore, publicly accountable" (Eisenberg 2006).

While those are reasonable concerns, many in New Orleans see a double standard in this view. Eisenberg goes on to state, "The question of accountability didn't seem to bother the large foundations that gave so generously to the Red Cross, which had a questionable record of competence to begin with and attracted even more criticism in the aftermath of Katrina over its unwise use of funds, high administrative costs, and lack of outreach to minorities."

Many feel that the message from major funders has been that New Orleanians cannot handle the money appropriately. "Twenty-seven years running a business, and they don't trust us with money," comments Jennifer Turner of the Community Book Center, a vital Seventh Ward neighborhood gathering space, when asked about her feeling toward national funders. "They think we're all stupid or corrupt."

Many feel that media depictions of New Orleans, and the bias and racism that were in many cases reflected, are in part to blame for the reluctance of major funders to give money directly to the people most affected. In other words, the popular view of the people of New Orleans is as looters and criminals, or at the least too helplessly poor and ignorant to be trustworthy partners in the rebuilding of their city. Even today, many news stories about New Orleans post-Katrina focus on FEMA payments that were misused or obtained through fraud, rather than the bigger story of corporate fraud.

"They figure if they give poor people money they'll buy crack and cigarettes," People's Organizing Committee and People's Hurricane Relief Fund cofounder Curtis Muhammad summarized.

Historically Exploited

For a region of the country that has been historically underfunded, these issues are nothing new. "I'm very much afraid of this 'foundation complex,'" civil rights organizer Ella Baker said in 1963, referring to the changes happening then in the structure of grassroots movements (quoted in Uhlenbeck 2005, 25).

In a 2007 book chapter about New Orleans post-Katrina, members of INCITE! Women of Color Against Violence write, "Though hundreds of nonprofits, NGOs, university urban planning departments, and foundations have come through the city, they have paid little attention to the organizing led by people of color that existed before Katrina and that is struggling now more than ever" (Bierria, Liebenthal, and INCITE! 2007, 39).

Echoing this analysis, the *Chronicle of Philanthropy* article complains of a "long-term lack of concern and neglect that foundations that operate nationally and in the Gulf Coast region have shown for poor and minority Gulf Coast residents, even as some grant makers proudly strutted their awards to national antipoverty and antiracism programs" (Eisenberg 2006).

The INCITE! authors posit that successful organizing is rooted in the community and takes a long time to bear fruit. Mainstream funders don't appreciate this, and "a look at who and what gets funding in New Orleans, from foundations to support work, reveals the priorities of these foundations and the entire nonprofit system. Organizations that represent their work through quick and quantifiable accomplishments are rewarded by the system. Foundations are not only drawn to them but are pressured by their own donors to fund them."

For many in the nonprofit field nationally, post-Katrina New Orleans has been an opportunity for career advancement. While local residents were too overwhelmed by tragedy to apply for grants, a few well-placed national individuals and organizations have not hesitated to take their place in line. Although some have no relation to New Orleans, they often have previous relationships with the foundations, as well as resources that translate into easier access to funding, such as development staff, Web site designers, and professional promotional materials. One director of a Gulf Coast organization reported that when she went on a trip to Washington, DC, she met someone whose job title was "Katrina expert." This expert had never visited the Gulf Coast.[1]

The Nonprofit Industrial Complex

Foundations are not to blame for the continuing crisis in New Orleans, nor do they possess a special responsibility to help the city. However, many foundations have expressed a desire to support New Orleans' recovery, and funding is desperately needed on the ground. Because of this, their actions have taken on added scrutiny from people in New Orleans.

Foundations are an integral part of the current structure of U.S. nonprofits, a system that INCITE! has called the Nonprofit Industrial Complex, to emphasize the intersecting, dependent, and corporatized ways in which the system is constructed. It is a system in which organizations are frequently pitted against each other for funding, where organizers are discouraged from being active in their own community, where accountability to and leadership from those most affected has become increasingly rare, and where, in many cases, the priorities of the "movement" are guided by those with money rather than being led by those most affected.

Perhaps the biggest lesson of Katrina for people concerned about social justice is that the structures of U.S. movements are in serious crisis. As the director of one base-building organization asked, making reference to the section of the U.S. tax code that grants tax-exempt status to nonprofit organizations, "What's wrong with the 501(c)3 structure that everyone could come down for a five-day tour but no one could come to actually do the work for a month? What's wrong with a 501(c)3 structure where everyone is already so underresourced and then tied to projects and promised outcomes that the biggest disaster this nation has seen in decades occurs and no one can stop what they are working on to come down and help? What's wrong with the foundation world that they have to produce 207 fancy glossy interview reports to their board in order to shuffle a few thousand dollars our way?"

One thing that is clear is that the current paradigm simply doesn't work. Without community accountability, projects aimed to bring justice to that community are weaker and sometimes counterproductive.

INCITE! members argue that the structures of this nonaccountable movement stopped organizations from responding more capably to the disaster when it happened, and that a movement more responsive to the local community would have been more effective. "Community organizing and community-based accountability are the things we have left when the systems have collapsed," they argue.

Many organizers told me that, in dealing with foundations, they were expected to be responsive to the foundations instead of to any concrete needs on the ground. "It's not just that you have to jump when they tell you to jump," the manager of one organization told me. "You also have to act like you wanted to jump anyway."

These issues have been developing for a long time. More than forty years ago, Fannie Lou Hamer, civil rights leader and cofounder of the Mississippi Freedom Democratic Party, complained, "I can't see a leader leading me nowhere if he's in New York and I'm down here catching hell" (quoted in Lal 2007).

"What's wrong with our movement and our organizations," the director of another grassroots organization asked me, "that they couldn't collaborate and coordinate and offer us some organized plan of assistance instead of asking us to do more and more to help them help us? What's wrong with funders that they couldn't coordinate, the way they ask us to, so that they could come down once, together, and not on fifteen separate trips?"

Solutions

When asked for solutions, many in New Orleans have called for allies to bring a deeper respect for the experiences of the people on the ground. Others have expressed an overall need for movements to move away from reliance on foundations and large donors.

Several organizers have highlighted the examples of positive experiences. "National Immigration Law Center (NILC) came here in a principled way, looking to hire someone local, and to support already existing local projects," Rosana Cruz, who worked with NILC and the New Orleans Worker Justice Coalition, explained. "Advancement Project does litigation led by and in support of grassroots organizing campaigns. OXFAM is a major international organization, but they came in and worked responsibly with small organizations on the ground they had previous relationships with. And they made multiyear commitments. They didn't just come and dump money — or worse, come and promise money then disappear, as some did."

"Ironically, many of the folks who have come through for us are southern groups, who are themselves underresourced," the managing director of one organization told me. "Organizations like Project South and Southerners On

New Ground (SONG) have been stronger allies than many larger national groups."

The *Chronicle of Philanthropy* article asks foundations to play a role in "strengthening nonprofit organizations that serve low-income people and African-Americans, as well as other minorities . . . America's foundations need to move from a policy of neglect of the nation's most vulnerable organizations to one of affirmative action, an approach that will mean changing the way many foundations do business" (Eisenberg 2006).

"I would ask national organizing groups to send a staff person down for six to twelve months," begins the executive director of another organization. "I would also recommend all progressive and liberal foundations with Katrina money to do an analysis of funding and jointly release the results along with the plan for funding in 2007 and 2008."

Others listed specific needs they felt were unmet. "We need seed money, technical training, and leadership development," explained Mayaba Lieben-thal, an organizer active with the New Orleans chapters of Critical Resistance and INCITE!

The stakes are far beyond New Orleans. This is a struggle with national and international implications. Questions of race, class, gender, education, health care, food access, policing, housing, privatization, mental health, and much more are on vivid display. "Everyone is here right now, or has come through," comments community organizer Curtis Muhammad, referring to the vast array of organizations and individuals who have visited the city. "If the movement continues to grow, New Orleans will be seen as a turning point." But, despite all of the resilience on display here, the people of New Orleans can't do it alone.

The Volunteers

From the first days after the disaster, people from around the world wanted to come and help in some way. For radicals and progressives, there were two main organizations that welcomed mass numbers of volunteers from all over: the People's Hurricane Relief Fund, and Common Ground.

While the city was still flooded, progressives around the world responded to the declaration put out by an eight-year-old coalition of grassroots social justice organizations called Community Labor United: "The people of New Orleans will not go quietly into the night, scattering across this country to become homeless in countless other cities while federal relief funds are funneled into rebuilding casinos, hotels, chemical plants and the wealthy white districts of

New Orleans, like the French Quarter and the Garden District" (Common Dreams News Center 2005; see also http://www.peopleshurricane.org).

The document announced the founding of a new organization, the People's Hurricane Relief Fund and Organizing Committee (PHRF). Their high profile and deliberative pace brought criticism, and some of the founders eventually formed a new organization — People's Organizing Committee — in a highly publicized split. However, both PHRF and People's Organizing Committee have united individuals from New Orleans and around the United States in black-led coalition with other organizations with the potential and desire to lead a principled, radical struggle for reconstruction with justice.

While the People's Hurricane Relief Fund received much of its support from the black left, Common Ground Relief Collective attracted a whiter support base. This was an unfortunate continuation of the segregated history of New Orleans, but also was the result of alternate strategies of outreach and organizing.

While many people fled the city, former New Orleans Black Panther Malik Rahim refused to leave, and invited concerned individuals from around the United States to join him. In this racially charged situation, while white vigilantes were patrolling the streets of New Orleans, Malik's call was especially aimed toward white allies who could come to stand between black community members and white vigilantes. His call went out widely, and soon Malik's house was a campsite of mostly white, mostly young and anarchist, volunteers. As word continued to spread, more volunteers arrived, with supplies, a lot of energy, and a wide array of skills. Soon Malik had arranged for his neighborhood mosque to be transformed into a free community health clinic. Other volunteers set up a wireless Internet zone, a solar-powered shower, and more projects every day.

Within a month the newly-formed Common Ground Collective had a distribution network reaching sixteen thousand people in the New Orleans area and a free health clinic serving hundreds of patients, many who had not seen a doctor in years or even decades. By November, they had issued a mass call for volunteers, with at least three hundred mostly young and white activists coming through on the week of Thanksgiving, hundreds more arriving in the weeks that followed, and thousands more by the following spring. By summer of 2006 they had gutted hundreds of houses, started a newspaper and radio station, reopened at least one school, and much more. By 2007, the health clinic had paid staff and a board of directors, and had in most ways severed its relationship — amicably — with the rest of Common Ground.

Common Ground and PHRF became the radical organizations with the widest reputation across the United States, at least in part because they were the organizations most welcoming to mass numbers of outside volunteers. But they are just part of a much wider picture that included more mainstream organizations such as Habitat for Humanity and ACORN, as well as countless church groups and other smaller projects.

Also missing from this view are the smaller networks of volunteers who came and worked with grassroots, pre-Katrina organizations such as INCITE! Women of Color Against Violence, Critical Resistance, and the Ashe Cultural Arts Center. There is much inspiration to be found in the successes of these local, grassroots, mostly volunteer efforts. Tens of thousands of volunteers came through New Orleans with organizations such as these. Some gave a day, some ended up moving here. But almost all learned crucial lessons. First, they learned about the nature of this disaster; they saw firsthand what disaster capitalism is, and the brutal face of racism and profiteering exposed. Second, they were able to see, and be inspired by, local, grassroots resistance.

Whatever happens in New Orleans, it is clear that the next generation of student leaders, of activists and organizers, will have had their views shaped by their experience in New Orleans. The legacy of this city will live on in the struggles they will lead.

The Next Fight

This has been a sad time for anyone from New Orleans, or anyone who cares about the people of the city. It has been a time of increased drinking and depression. The suicide rate has more than tripled (Freemantle 2006). New Orleanians are still dispersed around the United States. No one knows how many will come home, or when, but they are missed. In the weeks after the hurricane a friend told me through tears, "I just want to go back as if this never happened. I want to go back to my friends and my neighbors and my community."

It has also been a beautiful and inspiring time, and this is not the end of our struggle. As the recovery drags on, New Orleanians will keep fighting. Whatever the results, there is much for progressives around the world to learn from and be moved by in the spirit of New Orleanians. For the next city or region devastated by disaster, there will certainly be lessons from both our victories and our failures.

Every time I see a family moving back to New Orleans, I am inspired by this small act of resistance and courage, this dedication to community and to the further life of the city. Every day, I see other little acts of resistance, in the second-line street dancing that accompanies funeral processions and other parades, and in other cultural expressions. I see people going to what seems like the thousandth neighborhood planning meeting and still remaining fresh. I see people demonstrating in the streets. I see people being generous in the face of the cruelty of the city's elite who tried to keep them out. I see people giving their neighbors places to stay, a gift of food, a friendly greeting.

What's really going to bring people back to our city are the people themselves, fighting on the front lines to come home. In hundreds of small struggles, in grassroots organizing and demonstrations around the city, the fight continues. As Beverly Wright, director of Dillard University's Deep South Center for Environmental Justice, declared during a 2006 forum sponsored by the African American Leadership Project, "They've underestimated the determination of people like me to fight to our last breath."

The people of New Orleans are standing up and fighting back, joined by progressive allies from around the world, and reinforced by a tradition and culture of resistance. This culture of resistance, of community and caring, continues to inspire those of us who love New Orleans. It has sustained and inspired me when it seems hopeless. In the end, it may be the best hope this city—or any city—has.

Notes

Some of the reporting on which this chapter was based originally appeared in *Colorlines Magazine* and *Left Turn Magazine*.

1. Because many of those interviewed for this chapter work with organizations that are in some way dependent on these foundations, they were reluctant in many cases to be identified by name.

PART TWO

MATERIALITIES

Explicit Ruins: Architecture Is More Visible When It Fails

By Fernando Lara

It is pouring outside. It is dark in the middle of the afternoon. Heavy dark clouds are moving fast, rotating around a new center of gravity that competes with the earth, pushing everything up. Gutters and storm pipes cannot cope with the amount of water. Lights are off. Phone lines are off. Cell phones get no signal. You are left alone with architecture. Suddenly you cannot hide behind a wireless phone nor dive yourself into the Internet. In the absence of gadgets, space (or what is left of it) is all you have.

We like to think of architecture as this other materiality that tells us who we are by opposing our own materiality. It constrains us. We can go neither through here nor into there. Only our eyes can go beyond the small concession offered by a window. Otherwise, we have to maneuver around the obstacles that architecture disposes against our freedom of movement, looking for even rarer concessions like a door or a flight of stairs that would allow our body to move from one space to another. But by opposing our immediate desires with elements that are often many times heavier and harder than us, architecture helps to define who we are.

However, as much as we like to believe that architecture is an important component of our culture or a mirror of our own condition as a society, it is only when it falters that we become fully aware of its presence. Even if it is not a natural disaster, all it takes is a disruption in the energy flow. As soon as electricity ceases to work we are confronted with architecture. And what that means is that time is decompressed again and we have to deal with the full weight and hardness of the materiality of the built environment. In a natural disaster we are forced to face the real dimensions of time and space with the limits of our own body. We can only walk so far and so (not) fast.

Our voices can only be heard for a limited distance. Our own material existence is not really ready to survive without a refrigerator nearby. Our own psychological balance is not ready to endure many days or weeks without phone calls or e-mail messages.

Remember when, yesterday, you had no real idea of distance because you could reach anybody in another continent with your fingers only? Remember when you used time to measure distance: the street was three minutes away by elevator, the bookshop was twenty minutes away by subway, home was fifty minutes away by commuter train, London was six hours away. No more. Now the street is twenty-five floors or four hundred steps away. The bookshop is five miles away and home is twenty-five miles or at least seven hours away if you insist on measuring it with time.

When a natural disaster strikes and our digital network is disrupted we are forced to face the unbearable rashness of our built environment. Forget Virilio and Baudrillard and the virtual realities; there is no compression of time and space anymore. You are left alone with the dis-virtual reality of space.

You have to deal with space, you must deal with the real dimensions of space. There is nothing to mediate your relationship with the materiality of the built space that surrounds you. Without neons and electronics space becomes what it has always been and you have never perceived.

Now, with the lights off and without any operable transportation system, not only do you have to deal with space and its mighty three dimensions, but now you realize that there are also others in the same space. They're on the stairway, down the street, on rooftops, or gathering under a bridge. It's dark and as a result you start to see that you're living amid a world of people. Isn't that amazing? Where were they before? Hiding behind their own instruments or turned invisible by your gadgets. The diversity forces you to confront who you are and who you are not: white, black, rich, poor.

Architecture becomes your single protection, the only device left to mediate your relationships with the others. You need a wall to protect yourself from that obnoxious colleague walking toward you when all you needed before was a phone call or a computer screen. You need a door to walk through and reach whomever you want to reach. You are suddenly aware of the weight and the materiality of the wall. You are suddenly aware of the air circulation (or absence of it) in your home. You are suddenly aware of the weight and the materiality of water between you and the dry areas or the roof that used to separate you from the falling sky.

In case you are far from home you need even more architecture to protect you. You need a bridge to cross over the highway or the river and you need it right here. The next bridge might be too far for you. Maybe the only bridge is out of reach of your legs. You might have to rest somewhere on your way to a safer place and you need steps to use as a sofa. If you cannot walk there, you might need to sleep on those

Morning, Lower Garden District.
Photograph by Jacob A. Wagner; image courtesy of the photographer.

steps and you become aware that they are made of stone. And stone is cold and hard, very hard. Your back hurts. Your leg hurts. Your feet hurt. You became aware of distance and aware of the inevitable materiality of the built world in which you live. Architecture pulses in front of you with all its force.

Yes, architecture (like so many other important things) is most visible when it is most needed. We experience it in the state of distracted perception articulated so well by Walter Benjamin almost seventy years ago, and although it affects all our senses, we are barely aware of it. Unless it fails, floods, or goes up in flames, 99 percent of our built environment fades into the background, and we perceive it as just an envelope for our activities. Nevertheless, when architecture does become visible because an entire neighborhood was flooded by a failing levee or filled with debris from a suicide terrorist attack, what does it say? What is the image articulated by architecture once it is made visible in the aftermath of those tragic events? Once it exposes itself, architecture also exposes all the nasty injustices of our society — why some build on higher ground while others can only afford to do so below the water levels.

At this point the reflection becomes rather grim. After spending so much of our time complaining that globalization, consumerism, and suburbanization have made architecture invisible if not irrelevant, what do we have to show when all eyes, for a moment, turn to our architecture? Let's face it: when our built environment is made visible, the image is ugly.

It seems likely that the New Orleanians portrayed in the previous chapter by Jordan Flaherty would not recognize the traumatized and disoriented city dweller of the above essay by Fernando Lara. Whereas Flaherty emphasizes the resilience that arises from community, Lara's provocation portrays a lone individual who attempts to use infrastructure to control nature: storm pipes and electricity will keep water and darkness at bay. When the infrastructure fails, Lara's ironic hero turns to architecture, seeking safety in the idealized (feminine) cocoon of the nurturing home, free from any nature (human or liquid) that might threaten this lone individual's self-created space. When the architecture fails as well, the narrator is left with nothing except fear. Lara's city dweller's survival is based on control (or, at least, psychological survival is based on maintaining the *illusion* of control), and when one senses that one can no longer control the situation, the lone, modernist subject feels lost and vulnerable. Although this vulnerability fosters a new level of awareness about one's place in a stratified society, the overall narrative is of an individual exist-ing in opposition to the surrounding city that stifles as it closes in. One can imagine the narrator spiraling into a cycle of self-pity, anger, awareness, and fear, until the lights come on, the waters recede, architecture resumes its in-visible function, and the narrator's detached, commanding, and self-centered persona is restored.

Yet, as Flaherty's chapter makes clear, we do not live alone in cities; we live in communities. And, especially when normal life patterns are disrupted, we do not live in opposition to nature; we live with nature. This alternate per-spective raises interesting questions for urban design. Instead of attempting to abstract the built environment from nature, what if cities were designed to enable us to navigate *through* nature? Likewise, instead of designing archi-tecture that is conceived amid the assumption that nature exists in a constant (i.e., controlled) state, what if architecture were designed to adapt to shifts in the surrounding nature?

Place

These questions are asked (and provisionally answered) in part 2 of this vol-ume, and they are not solely questions of architecture or engineering. Indeed, they refer us back to the question posed in the introductory chapter — what is a city? — or, perhaps more profoundly, what is a *place*?

For the phenomenologist, place is the essence around which consciousness, and hence life, is formed: "To live is to live locally, and to know is first of all to know the place that one is in" (Casey 1996, 18). For Lara's city dweller, urban life is based on knowledge and the sense of control that knowledge makes possible. Deprived of knowledge amid darkness and floodwaters, he feels out of control. The city, like the floodwaters themselves, emerges as a threat, and architecture remains his only defense, and a fairly ineffective one at that.

An alternate perspective sees a place as a site of *experience*. Since all experience is individual, all knowledge is partial. Control, therefore, is impossible. Instead, survival is dependent on forging links across a community of people with divergent experiences, knowledges, and senses of place. This is the perspective adopted by Doreen Massey (1994) in her account of her home in Kilburn, a London neighborhood that has long served as a destination for immigrants from Ireland and that now hosts immigrants from around the world:

> Kilburn is a place for which I have a great affection; I have lived there many years. It certainly "has a character of its own" . . . [but] it is absolutely not a seamless, coherent identity, a single sense of place which everyone shares. It could hardly be less so. People's routes through the place, their favourite haunts within it, the connections they make (physically, or by phone or post, or in memory and imagination) between here and the rest of the world vary enormously. If it is now recognized that people have multiple identities then the same point can be made in relation to places. (153)

For Massey, sense of place is based on a *lack* of total understanding. She acknowledges that her experiences in Kilburn (as a professional who relocated there) are quite different from that of the third-generation working-class Irish Kilburn resident or the recent immigrant from Pakistan, and that she can never really know Kilburn as they know Kilburn (or vice versa). But out of this confluence of different experiences and partial knowledges, the energy of a place like Kilburn emerges. Massey has "a great affection" for Kilburn, but her knowledge is restricted to the situated knowledge of a "streetwalker theorist," an epistemological position elaborated on by C. Tabor Fisher in chapter 9.

This perspective on a city, as a place that escapes total knowledge and hence is immune to control, has implications for how one thinks about a city's materiality: its nature, its architecture, its infrastructure, its form, and the interactions between these elements and the bodies that inhabit the city. As engineering projects that are designed to control nature are abandoned for those that adapt to nature (a focus of chapter 3, by Geoff Manaugh and Nicola Twilley), accompanying discourses of militarism, planning, and social stratification are called into question. And as cities are reconceived as marginal spaces amid flows, rather than as central places characterized by rootedness (a focus of chapter 4 by Rob Shields), the city reemerges as a space of betweenness or liminality, less a place to be controlled than one to be appreciated for its mysteries and its affects. To use a term elaborated on by Daina Harvey in chapter 7, the city becomes an arena of asemiotic spaces, spaces with multiple evocations based on multiple experiences.

Every city is much more than its materialities, but every city begins with an encounter among material bodies, human and nonhuman, built and "natural." And yet materiality need not necessarily imply solidity. "Cities are a product of the earth," writes Mumford (1970, 3), but, as the case of New Orleans makes particularly clear, that underlying earth is not necessarily solid. Architects and planners have historically assumed a solid earth and a unitary sense of place, and they have planned their material contributions based on ideals of knowledge and control of this fixed environment. Chapters 3 and 4 offer alternative conceptualizations wherein the city's materialities — its nature, its infrastructure, its buildings, and its bodies — are all in interdependent states of flux.

CHAPTER THREE

On Flexible Urbanism

Geoff Manaugh and Nicola Twilley

A Landscape under Martial Law

It is all too easy to blame Hurricane Katrina's catastrophic impact and after-math on the Army Corps of Engineers, but it is also worth remembering that New Orleans — in fact, most of the lower Mississippi delta — is a manufactured landscape.[1] Through its interaction with the Corps, the lower Mississippi has become, over the last century at least, something of a military artifact. To say, therefore, that New Orleans, in the aftermath of Katrina, was a city placed under martial law is rather redundant: the city's landscape has never been under anything *but* martial law.

The lower Mississippi is literally nothing other than landscape design by military hydrologists.

Like all rivers, the Mississippi is not a rigid system. It does not have one floodplain or even one riverbed; its long path to the Gulf of Mexico has moved back and forth across hundreds of miles over thousands of years. As John McPhee explains, in *The Control of Nature* (1990), "The Mississippi River, with its sand and silt, has created most of Louisiana, and it could not have done so by remaining in one channel" (5). Yet keeping the river "in one channel" is exactly what the Army Corps has sought to do.

The Mississippi's cargo of sediment, combined with a riverine imperative to reach the sea by the shortest and steepest route, means that roughly once each millennium the river radically changes course. Over time, "the mouth advances southward and the river lengthens." This means that "the gradient declines, the current slows, and sediment builds up the bed. Eventually, it builds up so much that the river spills to one side" (McPhee 1990, 5) — breaking its banks to flow off in a whole new direction. The former main channel is then reduced to a backwater bayou.

Land building and channel changing are hence equally inevitable impulses of the Mississippi's natural flow.

The Mississippi River, geological records indicate, settled into its present course in approximately A.D. 1000. However, McPhee tells us, "By the nineteen-fifties, the Mississippi River had advanced so far past New Orleans and out into the Gulf that it was about to shift again." Water had already started escaping the Mississippi, sometimes in sufficient volume to "quintuple the falls at Niagara" (McPhee 1990, 6, 7). One of the Mississippi's former meander bends, called the Old River, acted as a conduit to the nearby Atchafalaya River, whose own route across the deltaic plain was less than half the length of the master stream. The more Mississippi water flowed down the Atchafalaya, the more the Atchafalaya widened and deepened, "preparing for nothing less than an absolute capture" (McPhee 1990, 4). For more than fifty years, in other words, the Mississippi has been on the cusp of switching direction — leaving New Orleans, in a geological instant, both land-locked and dry.

The consequences of such capture would be, on the one hand, gradual land accretion in the Atchafalaya basin, and, on the other, "the virtual destruction of New Orleans . . . its fresh water gone, its harbor a silt bar, its economy disconnected from inland commerce" (McPhee 1990, 6). After all, the shores of the Mississippi between New Orleans and Baton Rouge have become something of an "American Ruhr," home to big industrial names such as Union Carbide, Dow Chemical, Monsanto, and Shell. As McPhee points out, "These industries were there because of the river . . . its navigational convenience and its fresh water. They would not, and could not, linger beside a tidal creek" (McPhee 1990, 6).

The obvious economic impact of letting nature take its course was unthinkable, unaffordable — indeed, "Nature, in this place, had become an enemy of the state" (McPhee 1990, 7). The Old River, then, as the Mississippi's preferred route of escape between the Mississippi and the Atchafalaya, became the site of a "civil-works project of the highest national priority" (McPhee 1990, 48). There, the Corps deployed not one but two so-called control structures. These were assembled from concrete revetments, buttresses, jetties, towers, and piers all designed to freeze the course of the Mississippi in both space and time. The Corps hoped — indeed, still hopes — for nothing less than the preservation of the Mississippi River as it was in 1950, indefinitely.

Thus, for the past fifty years at least, we have been living through the afterlife of New Orleans, a city that sinks deeper into the Mississippi's alluvial fan every day, even as that very river, now trapped in a course it has long since outgrown, steadily rises in elevation above it.

New Orleans, of course, has been fighting something of a losing battle with the river ever since the city's inception. As Elizabeth Kolbert (2006) describes it, in 1718, as the French laid out their new city — its location ideal for both military and commercial purposes — the foundations flooded. The man considered responsible for founding New Orleans, Jean-Baptiste Le Moyne de Bienville, had declared only ten years earlier, "I do not see how settlers can be placed on this river" (Kolbert 2006). Indeed, southern Louisiana consists almost entirely of a deltaic "palimpsest of bayous and distributary streams in forested paludal basins," with the result that "there is no terra firma" (McPhee 1990, 31). The consistency of the region's soil, according to Kolbert, can reasonably be likened to "warm Jell-O" (2006) — and this warm Jell-O has an interesting geographical pedigree:

> In some form or another, the Mississippi has been flowing for tens of millions of years, and all the while it has been carrying great loads of sediment — in the eighteen-hundreds, some four hundred million tons per year — which tended to settle out where the river, slowing, emptied into the sea. In this way, what is now the Louisiana Gulf Coast was formed out of bits and pieces of Missouri and Arkansas and Kentucky and Iowa and Illinois and Minnesota. (Kolbert 2006)

Kolbert adds that "there are no rocks in southern Louisiana, except for those that have been imported to, for example, shore up the sinking roads." This makes the very idea of modern human settlement in southern Louisiana (including, of course, the city of New Orleans) something of a geo-anthropological project — an exercise in optimism and denial that reveals itself, upon closer inspection, as a literally monumental federal landscape installation.

So how could urbanism in any form, let alone its American incarnation of gridded rigidity and settled address, find a home amid such ancient, wandering hydrology? The region's native inhabitants could "fish and forage and . . . move their teepees," but, as the Corps of Engineers' own public relations director tells McPhee (1990), "You can't move Vicksburg" (32).

Thus, the decision is already made: in southern Louisiana you cannot "create a city, or even a cluster of modest steadings — without declaring war on nature" (McPhee 1990, 32).

Accordingly, six years after New Orleans was founded, the French colonial governor ordered all homeowners to build levees to a height of three feet; he then declared the city flood-proof. Nonetheless, the Mississippi managed to engulf New Orleans in 1735 — and countless times then onward. Each time, residents have demanded new, larger levees. They were supported in this by the Corps, which was granted total control of the Mississippi River in 1879 with a congressional mandate to "prevent destructive floods," and which remained committed to a disastrous "hold by levees" policy for forty-eight years (McPhee

1990, 37). Based on the theories of seventeenth-century Italian engineer Giovanni Domenico Guglielmini, the Corps believed that levees would force the river to scour its own bed, producing a deeper channel that would more effectively hold floodwaters, as well as make the Mississippi more navigable, thus strengthening the economic foundation for the city of New Orleans.

This did not turn out to be the case. Confined by levees, the river actually rises; meanwhile, deprived of fresh sedimentary reinforcement, Kolbert's warm Jell-O of unconsolidated silt deposits — on which New Orleans is built — compresses, compacts, and sinks in a geological process known as down-warping. Even as levees are raised, they start sinking, pressing down on the mud beneath them and squeezing it out to the sides. The Corps ends up adding five feet of material to the levees, McPhee writes, gaining only two feet of defense. This effect was making itself known as recently as the end of May 2006, when a "setback was announced" by the Corps in their attempt to rebuild the hurricane-damaged levees. Specifically, a "400-foot section of levee in Plaquemines Parish, south of New Orleans, shifted as it neared completion. The marshy soil of the area could not support the weight of the earthen levee structure, which slumped and bulged." With almost comic understatement, *The New York Times* adds: "It is being repaired" (Schwartz 2006).

Unsurprisingly, then, as the land around it subsides, the Mississippi River, walled in on either side, has begun "to stand up like a large vein on the back of a hand" (McPhee 1990, 37). The river now flows through New Orleans "like an elevated highway" (McPhee 1990, 61).

In the Corps' hydrological version of the Maginot Line, a "ring of levees [was built] around New Orleans," McPhee (1990) writes, "thus creating New Avignon, a walled medieval city accessed by an interstate that jumps over the walls" (63). Yet, following historical precedent, these rigid and immobile fortifications ironically contributed to the city's subsequent catastrophe. "We've been living in this bowl," explained geologist Shea Penland, in an interview with *The New York Times*. "And then Katrina broke channels into the bowl and the bowl filled. And now the bowl is connected to the Gulf of Mexico" (Dean and Revkin 2005). The Corps, of course, built that bowl — and New Orleans has now experienced the consequences.

Hurricane Katrina, in this context, becomes a problem of landscape design.

More Protection Than Levees Can Offer

If at first you don't succeed, try ever more elaborate feats of hydrological engineering. In the wake of Hurricane Katrina, the Corps — supported, for a while, by American popular opinion — has again taken the "bigger, better, more" approach to urban reconstruction. This time around, ever larger and more elaborate levees have been proposed, and they will be supported by nothing less than artificially created marshlands, strengthened canals, and an entirely new delta for the Mississippi River. More of the disease is the cure for the disease.

As Michael Behar writes, in the February 2006 issue of *Popular Science*, "New Orleans needs more protection than levees alone can offer." While neglecting to mention that securing the city's protection might actually require moving it out of the deltaic plain altogether, Behar is quick to add that "Katrina changed everything," both for urban planners and for the Corps. "All ideas — no matter how costly or far-fetched — are back on the table" (Behar 2006).

Behar's article outlines five such "far-fetched" proposals, all of which take New Orleans' present geographical location for granted. Two of the more interesting projects include "a row of giant sea gates" that "would together span about 3,000 feet," and a "$14 billion, 30-year wetland restoration plan called *Coast 2050*" (Behar 2006).

This latter plan is particularly fascinating, as it involves transforming the Mississippi delta into something substantially more artificial and technologically controlled than it already is today. The Coast 2050 plan requires "pumping sediment from the Mississippi River through huge pipelines into surrounding marshes and swamps. Over decades, this will fill in open areas and stimulate the spread of native vegetation" (Behar 2006). This process hopes to reproduce, in fast forward, the river's "natural" land-building impulse, laying down vital inches of silty *terra nova*, whose solidity — or lack thereof — will either save or doom future generations.

This postnatural condition — an almost literal unearthliness — is made all the more explicit by the plan's second phase, which would require developing new genetic lines for local plantlife. Herry Utomo, of Louisiana State University's AgCenter, hopes to "genetically enhance wetland grasses to grow in almost any environment, deep or shallow, salt or fresh. The experimental grasses will produce hearty seeds that sprout readily after being airdropped by crop dusters — no more hand planting" (Behar 2006). This vision of manmade plantlife — dropped by airplane — growing on manmade land only furthers the engineered deterrestrialization of the lower Mississippi. This, of course, while technologically exhilarating, is yet more of the shortsighted mania for landscape engineering that got New Orleans into so much trouble in the first place.

Another idea outlined by Behar would all but turn New Orleans into an inhabitable flood control mechanism, an urban valvescape or hydrological machine: "Submarines and aircraft carriers," he notes, "are divided into many compartments. Should one begin to leak, crew members can seal hatches and isolate the flooded compartment before the entire vessel sinks." This model of compartmentalized flood control could be "easily incorporated into a new levee system for New Orleans." In other words, engineers would use "an interlocking network of reinforced floodwalls that would divide New Orleans" into districts called "community havens" (Behar 2006). As flooding begins, or levees are breached, each "community haven" would seal itself off from the rest, containing the floodwaters and protecting — or perhaps "enfiefing" is the more accurate word — its inhabitants.

But surely this planned re-division of the city would only set the stage for more numerous, more openly hostile, interdistrict conflicts? If Katrina brought socioeconomic and racial divisions to the surface with unexpected rapidity and aggression, then these fortified "community havens" risk complete hydrological apartheid.[2]

In any case, these projects serve as evidence that Hurricane Katrina and its immediate urban aftermath struck an imaginative chord unlike any other natural disaster in modern history — the flooded city, the failed barriers, the regional anarchy, floating corpses broadcast live on TV. The post-Katrina proposals described by Michael Behar share the same estranged, cinematic, and vaguely science-fictional aura that cloaked New Orleans' unfolding catastrophe.

Transfixed by harrowing coverage of rising floodwaters and stranded families, it was not therefore surprising to hear the frequency with which another hydrologically engineered civilization was mentioned. Atlantis, Platonic island-city of dikes and levees, and a common reference point for nightly news coverage during Hurricane Katrina, was itself a fortified metropolis, lording over canals and inland seas. A self-contained world of concentric and symmetrical hydrological planning, it, too, was swallowed by the oceans and destroyed.

New Orleans' underwater fate was thus long ago rehearsed in myth.

Perhaps one could say it was even expected.

The Flood Market

Invoked by the city's collapse, science fiction can also serve unironically as a rough guide to a future New Orleans.

In his novel *The Scar*, for instance, China Miéville (2003) proposes a kind of counter-Atlantis called Armada, "the ship-city." Armada is a city of maritime flux and flexibility, made from the hulls of captured ships that have been lashed together into one floating metropolitan unit. It is a "flotilla of dwellings. A city built on old boat bones" (100).

Early on, a woman looks out "across the vista of reconfigured masts and bowsprits, a cityscape of beak-heads and forecastles." She sees "many hundreds of ships lashed together, spread over almost a square mile of sea, and the city built on them . . . Tangled in ropes and moving wooden walkways, hundreds of vessels facing all directions rode the swells" (100–101).

Miéville's ship-city is not locked into its topography. It is dynamic, responsive, buoyant, and supple: "Armada moved constantly, its bridges swinging side to side, its towers heeling. The city shifted on the water" (101).

> What had once been berths and bulkheads had become houses; there were workshops in old gundecks. But the city had not been bounded by the ships' existing skins. It reshaped them. They were built up, topped with structure, styles and materials shoved together from a hundred histories and aesthetics into a compound architecture. Centuries-old pagodas tottered on the decks of ancient oarships, and cement monoliths rose like extra smokestacks on paddlers stolen from southern seas. The streets between the buildings were tight. They passed over the converted vessels on bridges, between mazes and plazas, and what might have been mansions. Parklands crawled across clippers, above armouries in deeply hidden decks. Decktop houses were cracked and strained from the boats' constant motion. (101)

This architectural bricolage — made of artifacts from the traditional built environment — is "bobbing randomly, moving very slowly with whatever currents took it" (110–111).

Here, we encounter an issue of genre. Though Miéville's city is considered science fiction, it resembles a project already built — and under expansion — in the Netherlands.

In spring 2005, *The New Yorker* ran a series of articles by Elizabeth Kolbert, entitled "The Climate of Man." These explored the subject of human-induced climate change. The third article ends with a description of how "one of the Netherlands' largest construction firms, Dura Vermeer, received permission to turn a former R.V. park into a development of 'amphibious homes.'" It would be a floating city, in other words; an Armada.

As Dura Vermeer's environmental director tells Elizabeth Kolbert: "There is a flood market emerging."

"The amphibious homes all look alike," Kolbert writes. Floating on the River Meuse in Maasbommel, Holland, "They resemble a row of toasters.

Each one is moored to a metal pole and sits on a set of hollow concrete pontoons. Assuming that all goes according to plan, when the Meuse floods the homes will bob up and then, when the water recedes, they will gently be deposited back on land."

Dura Vermeer is also looking into the design of "buoyant roads."[3]

It has now become clear that, if there is a post-Katrina world, or, rather, if Katrina's impact now shapes the practice of urban design in the twenty-first century, then this world will have to include "a complete rethinking of water: not as a threat, but as a real estate opportunity" (Kessler 2006). This "opportunity" primarily means the design and construction of "waterborne housing," Kristina Kessler of the Urban Land Institute writes, or "mixed-use development on water" (2006). Also in the Netherlands, we find Frits Schoute, a former professor at Delft University, who is "developing a stabilizing platform that allows communities to live in the middle of the oceans, unaffected by waves. He expects people to start living and working on these platforms by 2020, and envisions floating cities by 2050" (Kessler 2006). *The Guardian* describes this optimistically as "colonising the sea" (Burkeman 2005).

Kessler concludes that a future consisting of "entire communities of seaworthy structures on subdivided water lots that embrace flooding rather than walling it off no longer seems so far-fetched." Indeed, the *Christian Science Monitor* reassures us that practicality is at the heart of Schoute's ultimate plan: "One of Schoute's designs," they write, "features dampers that would not only protect floating houses from waves, but would also act as generators to exploit the tides for electrical energy. Based on his preliminary calculations, wave dampers could also provide more than enough electricity to live indefinitely on one of Schoute's 'ecoboats'."

This radical take on the concept of maritime urbanism would scrap solid ground altogether. In a further, philosophically vertiginous step away from everyday terrestrial reference, we learn that Dura Vermeer has actually built what sounds "like a bizarre folly: an experimental floating greenhouse" (Burkeman 2005):

> Made out of polystyrene slabs clicked together like Lego pieces, then overlain with concrete, it was built on the water, rather than being constructed on dry land. As a result, there is no obvious limit to the size of the platforms that could be built this way — and Dura Vermeer, certainly, envisages cities of floating homes, floating offices and floating restaurants. (Burkeman 2005)

Almost incredibly, "a further development could allow the greenhouse to move with the sun, so that the plants will grow faster" (Burkeman 2005) — implying

Amphibious community in Maasbommel, the Netherlands.
Artistic rendition by Hans Kuiper; image courtesy of Dura Vermeer.

that this groundless state of dynamic heliotropism carries advantages and opportunities that land-based inflexibility could never offer.

Of course, in many respects, China Miéville's science-fictional city and the design proposals of Frits Schoute can be seen as operating on the same rhetorical plain: *speculative urban design*, here, serves as the default narrative, or discursive condition, for their respective texts and visions. Miéville's words may have been published as a science-fiction novel, and Schoute's proposals may now be considered viable architectural plans, but their shared imaginative vitality makes them all but one and the same thing.

At the risk of overstating the case, then, science fiction would seem to be an even more worthwhile planning resource than, say, community meetings, regional archives, or the Corps' own hydrological models. These latter examples all seem to insist that a New Orleans "subsiding by more than one inch (2.54cm) a year" (*BBC News* 2006) is somehow architecturally feasible.[4] It isn't feasible.

As Elizabeth Kolbert reminds us:

> Five thousand years ago, much of southern Louisiana did not exist. A hundred years from now, it is unclear how much of it will remain. The region, it is often observed, is losing land at the rate of a football field every thirty-eight seconds. Alternatively, it is said, the area is shrinking by a large desktop's worth of ground every second, or a tennis court's worth every thirteen seconds, or twenty-five square miles a year. Between 1930 and 2000, some 1.2 million acres, an area roughly the size of Delaware, disappeared. (Kolbert 2006)

If New Orleans wants to stay where it is, it will have to learn to swim.

Sinking Deeper Each Day

The choices facing New Orleans as it confronts this undersea destiny have an interesting counterpart in London, England.

In London, for example, we find a neighborhood called Little Venice, just east of Notting Hill. It is a small, even quaint, waterlocked urban village, built overlooking man-made canals designed in the early 1800s by Isambard Kingdom Brunel — the same man behind the machines that excavated the tunnels for London's first underground railway.

But Little Venice now offers something of an unintended glimpse, or even a prediction, of the London yet to come: that neighborhood's romantic canals and artificial lakes are a working model for London's own Venetian — if not Atlantean — future.[5]

"Tide levels are steadily increasing owing to a combination of factors," the UK's Environment Agency warns. "These include higher mean sea levels, greater storminess, increasing tide amplitude, the tilting of the British Isles (with the south eastern corner tipping downwards) and the settlement of London on its bed of clay" (Environment Agency 2007). Whether it is this century or in one hundred thousand years, then, London's fate is hydrological encroachment — before it is lost to the sea entirely. It is a new Atlantis, sinking deeper each day into the ocean's embrace.[6]

"Postglacial rebound" is the technical term for this "tilting of the British Isles." The tilt — measured at as much as eight inches per century — comes as northern Scotland's deglaciated mountain valleys rise upward, decompressing from the weight of lost ice caps. This Scottish rebound pushes London downward — and toward doom. The rising waters of climate change only add to the city's worries.

Short of capping the Highlands in new glaciers of lead, or attaching gigantic hot air balloons to the spires of churches to pull the city skyward, London will eventually flood: like New Orleans, like Atlantis—like Mumbai and Shanghai—its undersea fate is geologically inevitable.

Yet, as in New Orleans, rather than responding to the geological conveyor belt of postglacial rebound with urban flexibility—even architectural buoyancy—the politicians, engineers, and urban planners responsible for London's continued survival seem determined to take another route. This is the route of defensive rigidity: buttressed levees, revetments, dikes; a Great Wall—or several—of mechanized barriers.

For example, we read, in an article published nine months before Hurricane Katrina, "Britain might have to block off the whole River Thames with a barrier stretching from Essex to Kent if London is to be protected from rising sea levels." This wall "would stretch up to 10 miles across the Thames estuary from Sheerness, in north Kent, to Southend in Essex, making it one of the biggest engineering projects Britain has undertaken" (Leake 2005).

On the other hand, the London *Times* quickly reminds us, this future seawall may be "the largest in Britain," but it would still be "smaller than some of those constructed by the Dutch, who use such techniques to reclaim land from the sea" (Leake 2005). This wall—still speculative, to be sure—would also include "numerous gates to allow water to flow in and out of the Thames estuary according to the tides, but engineers would also be able to shut the gates if a flood seemed likely. The barrier might also include a road and hydroelectric power generators" (Leake 2005).

It is interesting, of course, that the *Times* compares London's proposed new flood barrier to hydrological strategies used by the Dutch—strategies the Dutch are actually *abandoning* as both unrealistic and too expensive.[7] So, while London's shortsighted attempts to head off the inevitable and wall itself in against the sea will no doubt proceed, future generations may well witness a tiresome, obvious, and entirely all too predictable turn away from these and other militant, bulwarked tactics, toward something more flexible, waterborne, and, we might add, more Miévillian.

Or more Dutch.

But as these plans currently stand, it is easy to imagine the entire southeastern British coastline soon buttressed behind forty-meter-high locks and levees. Thames Water PLC, already struggling to keep the Tube dry and safely defended against the pervasive river and its underground tributaries, might even need its own nuclear power plants, droning into the next century, simply to fuel this complex network of pumps and aquatic regulators. New channels, distributing estuarial surges up toward marshland desalination plants, could store that water in inland seas, huge reservoirs processed for drinking. A new Lake District of artificial holding ponds, militarized and closely surveilled, could then be visited by future Wordsworths; Coleridge and his ancient mariner setting sail up the Thames, now freshly dredged as far as Edinburgh . . .

In this recent burst of enthusiasm for long-term hydrological warfare, even New York City has been reimagined as a site for gargantuan floodwalls.

> If a major hurricane struck close to New York City, the storm surge could raise the local sea level by 8 metres, swamping the financial district in lower Manhattan and parts of Brooklyn, as well as areas of Jersey City. The subway, some road and rail tunnels, and La Guardia and John F. Kennedy airports would be flooded. In total, more than 250 square kilometres could be affected, forcing 2.2 million people to evacuate in New York City alone. (Barry 2006)

To combat this catastrophic — though perhaps lucratively cinematic — scenario, "rotating flood barriers as much as 1.6 kilometres long and rising at least 8 metres above the normal high-water level" have been suggested. There would not be one wall, however, but "four such barriers at key locations around Upper New York Bay" (Barry 2006).

Back in England, meanwhile, Alok Jha of *The Guardian* introduces us to Jacqueline McGlade, a mathematician at University College London, whose specialty is terrain and flood dynamics. McGlade has designed something called *Flood Ranger*,

> a computer game in which the player gets to test out different ways of saving stretches of land. The land is modelled on the east coast of England. Set the game running, and players see what happens to the land as climate change — with varying rainfall and temperatures — takes its course. "As the flood ranger, you have the option, against the backdrop of the changing landscape, to really intervene," she says. "So you can build flood defences, you can allow land to be flooded, habitats created, wetlands, for example." At each step, the player has to manage how the landscape changes in response to climate change, as well as meeting urban needs like more housing, industry, railways and airports. (Jha 2003)

In the process, you become your own private Army Corps of Engineers.

Flexible Urbanism

These examples are simply meant to illustrate how the post-Katrina urban imagination, if such a thing can be identified, seems freshly alert to impera-

FEMA trailers (never hooked up), January 2006.
Photograph by Jacob A. Wagner; image courtesy of the photographer.

tives of hydrological control and adaptation. However, despite the exemplary pontoon urbanism of the Dutch, and despite three centuries of failed engineering in the Mississippi floodplain, this renewed concern still seems fixated on the concept of *protective muscularity*: rigid attempts at resisting the fluid dynamics of an encroaching sea. But as Hurricane Katrina, the catastrophic unreadiness of New Orleans' flood defenses, and the inept response of government planners, such as FEMA, all collaborated to demonstrate, when a system locked into place gives way even slightly total chaos can ensue.

Reflooded terrains—a strategy known as "managed retreat"—and floating architecture should not only be considered as viable options for the future of New Orleans, but as possible next steps for London, New York, Miami, Hamburg, Mumbai, and so on—indeed, for any coastal city threatened by rising sea levels or wandering riverways. The maritime urbanism of the future must, by necessity, be both flexible and dynamic.

The very idea that there is a "future" for New Orleans, then, is hydrologically questionable. It must be accepted, with a sense of moral sobriety, that the future of New Orleans may not include New Orleans, as we currently know it, at all. The landscape dynamism of the lower Mississippi — as that river com-petes with the Atchafalaya for dominance over the waters, and as they both collide in fractal, deltaic splendor with the Gulf of Mexico — simply cannot bear a city of barriers, walls, and floodgates.

Indeed, the most important question inside all of this is not which districts to repair first, or which neighborhoods to prioritize, *but whether the city should be there in the first place*. As it is, any suggestion that New Orleans should not be rebuilt at all is either dismissed outright, without real consideration, or it's seen as a kind of veiled insult to national identity.

Rather than acknowledge the inherent fragility of the defensive urban in-frastructure through which New Orleans exists, the *new* New Orleans — one house at a time — seems destined to become a bastion city once again.

The new New Orleans, that is, will be flooded once again.

And yet this fate can be avoided. If we have the will to see it — if we in-sist on rebuilding the city — then we may find that surprisingly realistic, and uniquely inspired, examples of maritime urban architectural viability come from speculative genres outside of official planning charettes and government dossiers.

In other words, we might respond to John McPhee's "austere realities of deltaic geomorphology" (1990, 18) not with more of the same, but with *more imagination*: pursuing both buoyant and elastic architectural adaptations. To adapt to, and adopt, flexible urbanism — whether this means China Miéville's nomadic ship-city or the moored pontoon houses of the Dutch — would mean that New Orleans, perhaps, could ride out the swells of any future hurricane, any flood, any all-too-inevitable failure of dike, wall, or levee.

Until then, corpses will once again float in the oil-stained lake that was New Orleans, and federal authorities will continue to write checks that guarantee the city's future demise.

Notes

1. In fact, the Army Corps of Engineers is now willing to accept much of the blame, admitting that "the levees it built in the city were an incomplete patchwork of protection, containing flaws in design and construction and not built to handle a storm anywhere near the strength of Hur-ricane Katrina." The Corps' chief engineer, Lieutenant General Carl A. Strock, is then quoted as saying, "Call it a mea culpa, or admission, or whatever — but we're not ducking our accountability and responsibility in this" (Schwartz 2006).

2. As *The New York Times* reported in January 2007, these social dividing lines "existed long before Hurricane Katrina . . . In this view, the storm was merely a grim exclamation point to con-ditions decades in the making" (Nossiter 2007). It would seem that further compartmentalizing

the city — with all the attendant questions of socioeconomic priority that will raise — can't help but exacerbate already existing urban tension and class resentment.

3. *Gulf News* has announced that there will soon be a partially floating highway built within the city of Dubai: "A floating bridge, first of its kind in the region, will be built over Dubai Creek as part of the government's 'quick solution' plans to ease traffic congestion in the city," we read. "The 300-metre-long bridge, which will have three lanes on each direction . . . will be built with 20-metre wide hollow concrete blocks that will float on the water" (Ahmed 2006). In that case, perhaps the Dutch are actually behind the times . . .

4. That article actually refers to some of the city's districts as "death traps."

5. Indeed, novelist Richard Doyle has recently imagined this flooded London in a 2002 book entitled *Flood*. Its tagline: "London has stood for 2000 years. Until today." Doyle presents us with a bewildering combination of failed seawalls, badly timed and overlapping low pressure systems, a rammed Thames barrier, and several raging infernos at an oil refinery, all of which threaten — and appear to achieve, in the novel's abrupt ending — the total destruction of the city. Doyle now operates a Web site about London's hydrological fragility; the Web site's title even reads like a sinister suggestion: *Flood London*.

6. Another, more properly science-fictional novel imagining this undersea future for the British capital is J. G. Ballard's *The Drowned World*. There, we read how London has become "a nightmare world of competing organic forms returning rapidly to their Paleozoic past" (19). Ballard continues: "Giant groves of gymnosperms stretched in dense clumps along the rooftops of the submerged buildings, smothering the white rectangular outlines. . . . Narrow creeks, the canopies overhead turning them into green-lit tunnels, wound away from the larger lagoons, eventually joining the six hundred-yard-wide channels which broadened outwards toward the former suburbs of the city. Everywhere the silt encroached, shoring itself in huge banks against a railway viaduct or crescent of offices, oozing through a submerged arcade. . . . Many of the smaller lakes were now filled in by the silt, yellow discs of fungus-covered sludge from which a profuse tangle of competing plant forms emerged, walled gardens in an insane Eden" (52–53).

7. Indeed, the Netherlands provides the most famous example of how urban land has been geotechnically reclaimed from the seafloor. After disastrous flooding in 1953, the Dutch embarked upon Project Delta: an enormous, all-consuming system of dikes, levees, and floodgates, rigorously maintained so as to safeguard former regions of the Atlantic seabed — or "polders," as such reclaimed zones are called (Netherlands Architecture Institute).

CHAPTER FOUR

Delta City

Rob Shields

This chapter expands discussions of New Orleans to consider the *delta city* as a spatial, cultural, and political-economic type. Delta cities are distinct from cities on bays like San Francisco or adjacent to deltas, such as Buenos Aires. This chapter thus begins by considering New Orleans' ties to its natural environment and the Mississippi River. However, the focus here is not so much the topography and hydrology of New Orleans. Instead, cultural, technological, and economic perspectives give a context to the liminal and libidinal image that New Orleans, like many other delta cities around the world, has acquired. These are geographical and cultural margins, or thresholds (*limen*). They acquire and incorporate into their development powerful images not only of marginality and difference but of exteriority and escape from dominant social norms.

Navigating New Orleans

One significance of delta locations is that the various channels tend to make a city relatively inaccessible to those traveling across the delta, even as its location favors access to more distant upstream hinterlands and foreign ports. Indeed, the problem of cross-delta navigation played a strong role in the siting of New Orleans. If New Orleans had been located any closer to the mouth of the Mississippi, east-west intracoastal navigation would have been much more difficult.

In the 1970s, Peirce Lewis proposed a dialectic of site-situation to capture the way in which New Orleans' favorable commercial location is intertwined with a tortuous geography and man-made landscape of levees and hydrological engineering that now even includes re-created marshlands. The city is in a suboptimal site but an optimal situation in terms of commercial opportunity as the port for the Mississippi-Missouri-Ohio basin. "The situation guaranteed New Orleans' prosperity, but the site guaranteed that the city would be plagued by incessant trouble — yellow fever, floods . . ." (Lewis 1976, 17). Thus New Orleans is an "impossible but inevitable city" (Fra Paleo 2006, 20).

But Lewis's language of "guarantees" is too strong. Literary commentators do not use site or situation to "explain" culture. The specific qualities of early New Orleans at the turn of the millennium are the result of an almost three-hundred-year history of interwoven decisions, global and local social change, environmental disasters, and ongoing hydrological processes. For example, from the beginning, the site of the city was hardly scientifically chosen, excepting that it seemed to be relatively high terrain to Jean-Baptiste Le Moyne de Bienville, the founding governor, and his party, who had searched for days in 1718 for a location for their colony that would be accessible by sea. Better sites such as at Baton Rouge were available farther upstream; however, sailing directly up the fast-flowing Mississippi was difficult for fully laden ships of the time. Navigating the shifting sandbars at the mouth of the delta, one hundred miles downstream, was also risky. It was thought that the main access to New Orleans might be via Lake Pontchartrain, which flanked the town site to the north and was partly open to the sea. Goods could then be portaged to river craft.

Settlers persevered despite desertions and hurricanes in 1721 and 1722 that destroyed many of the buildings and most of the ships in port. Flooding in 1732, 1734, and 1740 alternated with years of drought. From the beginning, the solution was to build earthen levees to protect the town. Meanwhile, geopolitical Anglo-French rivalries played a strong part in encouraging the establishment of the colony of Louisiana, along with unproven conjectures that the soil would be richer and the natives more docile than in Acadia and Québec (Clark 1970, 4–5). Thomas Jefferson saw New Orleans as a strategic gateway to the center of the continent: "There is on the globe one spot, the possessor of which is our natural and habitual enemy. It is New Orleans" (cited in Lewis 1976, 10).

By 1803, when the city was purchased by the United States, it was a robust center of a distinctive Franco-Spanish culture: Creole New Orleans was the first non-native, frontier society which the Americans encountered that was better established than its own culture (Gilmore 1944), the fifth-largest city in the United States by the 1810 census and one of its most active ports. However, it was the only major subtropical city in the United States, a Caribbean rather than Atlantic city, and culturally alienated from the Anglo-American mainstream.

Delta Cities

Deltas are typically discussed as natural areas, as in the Okavango in Botswana, or in the context of their vulnerability to sea-level changes (e.g., Bondesan et al. 1995, Chen and Zong 1999). The theme of urbanization and delta locations seems antique: either a relic of the discourse of schoolbooks listing great moments of civilization, or a topic for archaeology (Goodfriend and Stanley 1999, Stanley and Jorstad 2006). New Orleans is the only major delta city in the United States. Although other port cities, such as New York or San Francisco (or, outside the United States, London or Hong Kong), are located at or near the mouths of rivers, they are "embayed." Although these cities are gateways to deltas, they are qualitatively different than delta cities. Although delta cities and other ports share many characteristics, delta cities are unique in at least three ways: their locations are exceptionally unstable (due to both shifts in the river and encroachment from the sea — as outlined in the previous chapter by Geoff Manaugh and Nicola Twilley), they are exceptionally isolated from their proximate hinterland (because the width of the delta typically hinders cross-delta communication and transportation), and they are exceptionally vulnerable to flooding (due to the proximity of wetlands, whose absorption capacities have often been limited as a result of the delta city's growth).

While there are few delta cities in the United States, many contemporary metropolises outside of the United States fit this classification of delta city. They all have developed based on local geographical location and access to both rivers and the sea, they all face challenges of sedimentation and exposure to the landfall of ocean storms and tidal surges, and they all face risks of changes in sea levels. Where they differ is in local traditions and cultural reactions to these commonalities. Reactions to foreign contact and social diversity vary, as do their experiences of invasion and vulnerability to war, and their political responses.

Delta cities are conditioned by their location and the challenging condition of changeable river courses, silt soils, high water tables, and the meeting of fresh and salt water. Many of these cities have developed across low-lying islands or have displaced marshland ecologies. If they are drained, mud and silt soils tend to compact and sink relative to sea level. Problems of tidal flooding are compounded both by the risk of seasonal floods on their rivers and by ill-conceived drainage schemes (Williams, Penland, and Sallenger 1991, 219). Exchanges of experience have been hampered not only by nation-centered disciplines but by language barriers and the different levels of technological sophistication between flood plans and dikes built in different eras. The environmental specificity of delta cities is being rediscovered by urban specialists. As environmental and civil engineers have specialized in relation to river and wetlands management, flood control, the building of levees, and the construction of tidal barriers, comparative and global knowledge has become detached from its urban context. The delta city as a holistic category is thus presumed

Delta Cities

City	River
Marseilles, France	Rhone River
Amsterdam, the Netherlands	Amstel River
Rotterdam, the Netherlands	Rhine River
Kolkata (Calcutta), India	Ganges River
Shanghai, China	Pearl River
Port Harcourt, Nigeria	Niger River
Bangkok, Thailand	Chao Phraya River
Phnom Penh, Cambodia	Mekong River
Basra, Iraq	Tiber River
Alexandria, Egypt	Nile River
Sacramento, California	Sacramento–San Joaquin Rivers
Yangon (Rangoon), Myanmar (Burma)	Ayeyarwady River
St. Petersburg, Russia	Neva River

and not acknowledged as professionals have become more and more specialized.

Delta cities are generally understood to be individually unique. Each is celebrated or critiqued as an incomparable city, notably in cultural and economic terms. This order of exceptionality derives in part from national and territorial frames of reference in the study of cities and planning. Few countries have more than one major delta — more often than not, deltas are borderlands, such as between early twenty-first-century Romania and Ukraine, or between Iraq and Iran. A global, comparative approach seems awkward: who puts Amsterdam, Kolkata, and New Orleans side by side? Yet to resist doing so is to deny the consistency of their geographical locations and geomorphology. We need to reject Lewis's assertion that

> there is scarcely any point for a scholar to study New Orleans, particularly if the scholar is predisposed to study cities in search of general urban theories. . . . Whatever he discovers about New Orleans remains particular to New Orleans. . . . It is enough to turn any scholar into other, more productive undertakings, and apparently it did. (1976, 11)

Engineering the Landscape

Delta cities are characterized by not only a river delta and wetland location. They have three other qualities. First is a location which is an "edge condition" to a territory, classically the interface of land and sea. Historically this has also been a political edge condition as the sea has marked the limits of temporal power and sovereignty.

Second, these cities are associated with systems to divert, manage, or exploit water flows. Their topography and hydrology are artificial and obviously so. Taking their cue from the raised banks or levees formed by river deposits, the first settlers began to construct artificial levees for flood control. New Orleans embodies faith in engineering and technology; it has relied on the invention of the modern pump, levee systems, and pilings for building foundations. Delta cities are thus the locus of intense efforts and expenditures. The resources of the city's hinterland and wider territories are drawn upon in the development and maintenance of these engineering schemes. Karl Wittfogel (1957) famously locates the origins of the state with the rise of such "hydraulic despots." Irrigation canals or flood dikes "harden" sedentary agricultural societies. They require the development of expertise, massive amounts of manual labor, continual adjustment to seasonal water levels, and protection against marauders. These needs militate for the formation of centralized control: corps of experts and military power to procure slaves to construct earthworks and then to protect this infrastructure, as well as to dominate peripheries that can supply resources and tax revenues. As Manaugh and Twilley argue in the previous chapter in this volume, delta cities favor military projects, and this in turn would seem to favor trust in engineering.

Third, not only is engineering necessary but obviously water is central. Delta settlements have water access and shallow or marshlike terrain as a key factor in their development. As a result they are physically, socially, and economically vulnerable to changes in water flows and levels (as opposed to cities adjacent to deltas, such as Buenos Aires). There have to be overriding interests and needs to require the development of these sites. Delta cities are generally driven by strong political and economic forces, and their survival over time is a product of their integration into economic regions as well as successful national states. Cities such as Amsterdam or Bangkok are artifacts of historical forces stabilized around a particular political conjuncture or logistical node.

LEVEES

The Dutch have a long history of reengineering the topography of the Netherlands to escape flooding. From around 500 B.C., *terps* or *wierde*, small rises and hills, were built to accommodate villages and dwellings. Dikes were built from around A.D. 1200 as earth walls whose mass resisted being displaced by tides and whose height protected land on one side from flooding by waters on the other. Amsterdam's position on the Amstel, a branch of the Rhine estuary, was at the river's mouth in the seventeenth century. The Dutch solution was to limit flooding at this vulnerable location by constructing rings of canals, transmuting a defensive military form, the moat, into a way of maximizing the amount of quayside space in the city. A famous example of more extensive hydrological engineering is the Netherlands' system of dikes and floodgates. After extensive floods in 1953, Project Delta was launched as a national effort to protect low-lying areas and "polders" reclaimed from the seafloor with levees. The construction and maintenance of these floodworks became a defining activity for the Dutch state and national industries, but its utility and long-term sustainability have been questioned (see the previous chapter by Manaugh and Twilley). Delta cities are shifting from places that defy nature to cities that embrace the flows that they are astride.

Besides levees, two other technologies are essential in this massive landscaping effort to stabilize the watercourse and keep New Orleans dry. New Orleans has been an important site for the development of pumps and pilings.

PUMPS

To drain rainwater, 22 pumping stations existed in New Orleans and 130 in Jefferson Parish, operated by a Sewerage and Water Board — which had become almost a parallel city administration by 2005. New Orleans figures as a key site in the innovation of water pumps. Initially, a type of paddlewheel was used to push water along drainage canals. More modern axial pumps were invented in New Orleans and installed in 1915. Despite their age, they are still among the most powerful in the world at around 16 million gallons of water per minute (Hayes 2005). More efficient, low-head, high-volume screw pumps twelve feet in bore which use air pressure and siphoning effects to control the ingress and egress of water were pioneered and proven in New Orleans, and were later used around the world, including in the Netherlands (U.S. Army Corps of Engineers 1992, 76; Haydel 1995–1996).

PILINGS

A second significant engineering development was the use of pilings as foundations — vertically driven timbers or steel poles — to allow buildings to be built up to five or six stories, increasing the useable density of the city and allowing multistory warehouses and shop-houses to be built. Wood pile foundations have their origins about six thousand years ago (Timber Piling Council 2004), but they are particularly necessary in New Orleans. Stable soil is seventy feet down beneath New Orleans, meaning that any heavy structure — including levees — faces problems of stability and subsidence. Structures sink into the muddy surface soil, which itself sinks as its water content decreases through drainage. In effect, buildings in New Orleans stand on stilts which go down through watery silt to compacted soil. This approach to foundations is now widespread and used for all major buildings.

Beyond these technologies, the long-term efforts of the Corps have focused on "intelligent conservation," altering the natural topography and environment with flood control works (Viosca 1928). The Army Corps of Engineers publicly describes its efforts as a war against the Mississippi:

> This nation has a large and powerful adversary. Our opponent could cause the United States to lose nearly all her seaborne commerce, to lose her standing as first among trading nations. . . . We are fighting Mother Nature. . . . It's a battle we have to fight day by day, year by year; the health of our economy depends on it. (cited in McPhee 1990, 7)

However, physical mitigation efforts tend to produce other effects: for example, increased settlement and population increases the overall risk (Leyden 1985). Reclamation of coastal marshes also reduces the coastal buffers against storms on the delta (Dunne 2005).

Failures in the Corps of Engineers' engineering of the Mississippi River are often blamed for floods. However, the settlement of the city initially at or barely above sea level and its development in a "bowl" below sea level protected by a ring of levees have required the reengineering of the landscape. This has been placed under even greater stress by more intense hurricanes and predicted increases in sea level resulting from climate change (see Leavitt and Kiefer 2006). It is this broader project of Delta cities and settlements rather than the specific failures of one or another levee that the 2005 flooding of New Orleans brings into question, to the extent that some were prompted to propose abandoning the site. In a national poll commissioned by the *Washington Post* and ABC News shortly after the storm, 43 percent of respondents thought the low-lying neighborhoods should not be rebuilt (Acomb 2005).

Cultural Metropole

Delta cities also have a reputation as innovative cultural margins, especially if they are not the center of authority and national political power. Twentieth-century New Orleans is prima facie evidence against H. L. Mencken's famous comment that the South was without culture, even as the established creole families, black musicians, and white writers in New Orleans themselves dismiss the surrounding rural, Cajun way of life. Numerous authors, musicians, publishers, and critics lived there and wrote or reported about New Orleans—William Faulkner, Tennessee Williams, Truman Capote, Ernest Hemingway, John Kennedy Toole, and Walker Percy. Andrei Codrescu captures this creative spirit:

> The dead pass casually by: Buddy Bolden, the creator of Jazz; young Louis Armstrong; Marie Laveau, voodoo queen . . . Jean Lafitte the pirate . . . beautiful and sad Creole mistresses of French and Spanish aristocrats; old carnival krewes and mobs of others, slaves, sailors, adventurers, writers. . . . there is the Lafayette Cemetery on Prytania Street. Anne Rice's Vampire Lestat lives in one of the tombs. F. Scott Fitzgerald wrote *This Side of Paradise*, his first novel, in an apartment overlooking the cemetery. . . . A few decades later, a young poet, Everette Maddox, moved to New Orleans and rented Fitzgerald's apartment. It's still available, cheap, like everything else in New Orleans. There is no memorial plaque. If New Orleans went into the memorial plaque business for all the writers who ever lived here they would have to brass-plate the whole town. There is a plaque on Pirate's Alley on the house Faulkner lived in but there isn't any on Audubon's house. (Codrescu 1992, v–vi)

Bolden was one of the first great improv players, an innovator who created dance tunes out of the materials of marching bands and other popular music of the late 1800s. He came out of the aggregations of black and creole musicians forced together when creoles were pushed out of the downtown area into Storyville and other neighborhoods by the 1894 "white supremacy" Law 111, enacted by the growing white population. The streets and squares of New Orleans became a virtual academy of music for artists who also worked as laborers. Bands such as the Olympia Brass Band led by coronetist Freddie Keppard from 1900 to 1915, the Original Tuxedo Orchestra formed in 1910, and the Original Creole and Brownskin Bands were among many seminal groups focused on collective improvisation, which formed the ethos of early jazz. Creoles such as clarinetist Alphone Picou learned to improvise from blacks to survive: "Us downtown people, we didn't think so much of this uptown jazz until we couldn't make a living otherwise," complained Paul Dominguez in an interview Alan Lomax collected for the Library of Congress (Lomax 1939). In the first decades of the twentieth century, local blues prodigy Jelly Roll Morton became the first published composer of jazz. Performances and sheet music brought jazz and blues to national audiences.

Sherwood Anderson, around whom a New Orleans literary circle linked to the *Picayune* newspaper and the literary magazine *The Double Dealer* had developed, wrote in 1922 that he had come to New Orleans "because I love something basically cultural in the life here." He extolled

Flooded organ, Gentilly.
Photograph by Jacob A. Wagner; image courtesy of the photographer.

the long quiet walks to be taken on the levee in back-of-town, where old ships, retired from service, thrust their masts up into the evening sky. On the streets here the crowds have a more leisurely stride. . . . I stick to my pronouncement that culture means first of all the enjoyment of life, leisure and a sense of leisure. . . . In a civilization where the fact becomes dominant, submerging the imaginative life, you will have what is dominant in the cities of Pittsburg and Chicago today.

When the fact is made secondary to the desire to live, to love, and to understand life, it may be that we will have in more American cities a charm of place such as one finds in the older part of New Orleans now. (cited in Collins 1958, 17)

These are successful social spaces, sites of "social centrality," or coming together (Lefebvre 2003, see the Introduction to part 5 of this book) even at the margins of the continent. Codrescu describes this constructed time-space:

New Orleans is a small city but it seems spacious because it's always full of people . . . like a crowded barroom at night. At dawn the deserted barroom seems small beyond belief: how did all those people fit? The answer is that space and time are subjective no matter what the merciless clock of late twentieth century America tells us. . . . The city puts up a fight, a funny sad fight composed sometimes of sly stupidities and Third World inefficiency. The city can drive a sober-minded person insane, but it feeds the dreamer . . . stories, music and food. (Codrescu 1992, vi–vii)

One hundred fifty years earlier, in the midst of the young Audubon's observations of natural history, he exclaims about this:

Busling City where no one cares a fig for a Man in my situation. . . .

The Levee early was Crowded by people of all Sorts as well as Colors, the Market very aboundant, the Church Bell ringing (and) the Billiard Balls Knocking, the Guns heard all around. What a Display this is for a Steady Quaker of Philada [sic] or Cincinnati. . . . (Audubon 1992, 83)

This central yet marginal quality appears in literature and other cultural documents. In his *New Orleans Sketches*, Faulkner detects a certain hunger among the inhabitants — for recognition, love, status, and dignity (Collins 1958, 27). The tension between margin and center is explicit in the delta city. Ignatius J. Reilly, the protagonist of John Kennedy Toole's 1960s *A Confederacy of Dunces*, expresses and even embodies the New Orleans which is an outpost against adversity, a place to leave but which is surrounded by risk:

Of course, the worst thing is riding on top in one of those Greyhound Scenicruisers. So high up. Do you remember the time that I went to Baton Rouge in one of those? I vomited several times. . . . Leaving New Orleans also frightened me considerably. Outside of the city limits the heart of darkness, the true wasteland begins. . . .

. . .

Speeding along in that bus was like hurling into the abyss. By the time we had left the swamps and reached those rolling hills near Baton Rouge, I was getting afraid that some rural rednecks might toss bombs at the bus. They love to attack vehicles, which are a symbol of progress, I guess. (Toole 1996, 12–13)

Louis Armstrong's recollections of his youth include a number of mentions of "going away," particularly to Chicago and New York. Armstrong writes about his fellow coronet player, Bix Beiderbecke: "Beiderbecke got popular, the boys grab him, keep him on Broadway — and go, cat. Couldn't touch him then. They had him booked for three, four jobs a night. Very important man, see. So we lost him" (Armstrong 1992, 36). The promise of fame and money meant the loss of local talent and also the risk of having to return in shame:

I used to see so many kids leave New Orleans, and they'd be gone a long time, and then you look around and they have to hobo their way back home. Wasn't nobody going to get *me* to leave New Orleans but King Oliver. . . .

One night playing there in the Lincoln Gardens I suddenly see my mother coming across the dance floor right toward the bandstand, a couple of big paper bundles under the arms. She looked right at me and said, "I come to get you." Seems some cat told her I was stranded in Chicago, and that when he asked me why I didn't go home, I just held my head down and cried. . . . I told her, "Aw, don't believe that." (Armstrong 1992, 36–37)

Liminality and Relations to Otherness

One attraction of delta cities is they are in essence links to elsewhere, sites of cross-cultural contact and entrepots which are nothing without their termini. Notwithstanding, or perhaps because of, their marginality, they are cosmopolitan hubs in the sense identified by Lewis Mumford (see chapter 1 of this book). They are marked by relations of "going away" and returning. In her story "Hoodoo," Zora Neale Hurston noted New Orleans' cultural links to Africa, which did not cease with the end of the slave trade: "New Orleans is now and has ever been the hoodoo capital of America. Great names in rites that vie with those of Hayti [sic] in deeds that keep alive the powers of Africa" (Hurston 1935, 57). Being "on the edge" involves being an interface or site in which the local and foreign intermingle. Being "betwixt and between" cultural and political authorities offers the possibility of not only encounter but the development of unorthodox, hybrid social or cultural forms and innovative, syncretic forms. To an extent, this is true of all port cities, but this condition of "betweenness" may be particularly intense in delta cities because of their tenuous connections to their immediate hinterlands. In the 1969 film *Easy Rider*, Captain America never really feels at home during his psychedelic sojourn in the Crescent City.

New Orleans was portrayed as an eccentric and foreign creole Paris by local writers such as Lafcadio Hearn (Hearn 2001) and visitors such as Mrs. Trollope (Trollope 2006, Woodward 1951). This place-myth has been uncritically accepted in scholarly works. For example, Lewis echoes the exceptionalist position effusively:

After all, New Orleans *is* a different sort of place, and what is more natural than to pay attention to eccentricities — especially when they are colorful and entertaining? After all, what other American city possesses a genuine indigenous cuisine . . . ? What other city, especially a Southern city, exhibited such tolerance to sin, or such an easy-going attitude toward race relations? What other American city is so strongly flavored with Mediterranean Catholicism, with carnivals that bridge the chasm between sacred and profane with such élan? Whose society was so brilliant, so exclusive, and so elusively foreign? What other city had such an illogical and dangerous site, but insouciantly went about its mixed business of commerce and fun in defiance. . . ? (Lewis 1976, 10)

One could take issue with Lewis's depiction on a number of counts. In addition to displaying a Eurocentric bias (where Lewis sees Mediterranean Catholicism, a more Caribbean spirituality is overlooked), Lewis also reproduces a general notion of New Orleans as an exception to the norms and intolerant mores of American society, which went on to frame the initial media coverage of Hurricane Katrina, in which reporters went looking for images that would illustrate a preconceived storyline of Latin Quarter revelers drinking while the hurricane devastated the city (Brinkley 2006).

But New Orleans is arguably more important as a threshold or "limen" to other places. As an entrepôt, it embodies and is a site of links to the foreign, an interface with Otherness more than it is itself an Other. In Jack Kerouac's *On the Road*, New Orleans as a *place* is described as bland, and any riches that it contains are inaccessible to the outsider: "New Orleans is a very dull town. It's against the law to go to the colored section. The bars are insufferably dreary" (Kerouac 1976, 146). What New Orleans (and other port cities like New York and San Francisco) has is the unique placelessness and liminality of connection: "I looked down Market Street [in San Francisco]. I didn't know whether it was that or Canal Street in New Orleans: it led to water, ambiguous, universal water, just as 42nd Street in New York leads to water, and you never know where you are." (Kerouac 1976, 172)

Delta cities thus are simultaneously connected and inaccessible, as both physical and cultural constructs, and this inaccessibility can breed provincialism. Traditions of not only complex social relations and a profane popular culture but also parochial social relations of domination, racism, and corruption are rooted in the interfacial conditions of the delta. This gives rise to hybrid local cultures and economies. A different order from that which it separates necessarily exists within an interface which is "betwixt and between," allowing the coexistence of contradictory social forms (Shields 1991). This is done by suspending the norms that operate elsewhere in everyday life. Rituals and repeated routines create liminal zones, such as the French Quarter, where social identity can be played and experimented with, where one can say one thing and do another, with the possibility (if not the rule) of being reborn back into everyday life with a changed status or self-understanding. Hence the libidinal economy of the culture of the touristic French Quarter, which persists despite

Store window,
French Quarter.
Photograph by Jacob A.
Wagner; image courtesy
of the photographer.

the displacement of illicit and truly libidinal activities to make way for scripted family tourism from the 1980s onward.

The Smell of "Culture"

My thesis concerning New Orleans is that the natural geography and environmental disposition of the city is not incidental to its status and "spatialization" (Shields 1990) as a particular sort of cultural capital and cultural margin. That is to say, that the delta climate, wildlife, topography, and hydrology have been founding ingredients in widely disseminated stories which cast or "spatialize" New Orleans as a unique place. This blending of nature and culture with libidinal resonances is particularly apparent when one turns attention to a city's smells. Smells bind the concepts of "nature" and "culture," or, to be more precise, they bind "nature" *into* "culture." The smell of a place is, by definition, a smell of nature (or matter), but a place's smell invariably becomes an element of (and a metaphor for) its culture. "Nature" and "culture" are both figures of speech, more abstractions and virtuality than material and actual things. And the lie to this distinction is revealed in the smell of a place:

> When writers come here they walk about smelling everything because New Orleans is, above all, a town where the heady scent of jasmine or sweet olive mingles with the cloying stink of sugar refineries and the musky mud smell of the Mississippi. It's an intoxicating brew of rotting and generating, a feeling of death and life simultaneously occurring and inextricably linked. (Codrescu 1992, vi)

The sense of smell is often linked to involuntary memory. Codrescu links it further to death and remembrance, to storytelling and the unconscious (see part 4 of this book). For example, Faulkner describes New Orleans as an aged, outdated courtesan: "There is the scent of incense about her, and her draperies are arranged in formal folds. She lives in an atmosphere of a bygone and more gracious age" (Faulkner 1958, 49; see also Thackeray 1992, 116; Audubon 1992, 83–84). But smell is also a signal, a talisman, of the importance of nature, the river and the silt land on which the city sits.

Smell also appears with frequency in narratives of recovery. Residents returning to New Orleans after Hurricane Katrina frequently noted the city's fierce stench: the smell of mold, decaying bodies, industrial waste, raw sewage, and portside fires. The smell of mold and rotting food in flooded homes and refrigerators, so powerful it gave headaches, after three weeks became

> sour, pungent, with some petroleum, brackish with a tang of dead fish from the lake water, and even a hint of sweetness. That comes from the head-high piles of dead oak and pine and sycamore branches lining the sides of the streets, all turning burnt orange in the sun. (Kamenetz 2005)

After a month, it was not just that the smell of magnolias and gumbo was missing, or that "The air didn't smell bad . . . but it didn't smell like New Orleans, either" (Piazza 2005, 122): "In some neighborhoods, the rancid piles permeate the air with a smell that seems a mix of sour milk, foul river water and rotting meat" (Medina 2005). It is also described again and again as the smell of death or a "smell of fear" (Apostropher 2005).

Each of these smells emanates from a liminal space between liquid and solid, water and land, "nature" and "culture." These divisions — always tenuous in a delta city — had been broken, leading to a new liminality: post-Katrina New Orleans has emerged as a place that is not quite reduced to its "nature" but that is struggling to demonstrate continuity with its "culture." This liminality has been particularly apparent in the wake of the trauma of

Katrina, but, in a sense, it is the perpetual position of delta cities like New Orleans.

Neither the "culture" nor the "nature" of New Orleans can be understood independent of each other or independent of New Orleans' status as a delta city. Observations about smell, flora, and fauna amount to a minor discourse within the major notes of cultural narratives. Smell is a motif that inserts the natural context as a significant reference for New Orleans as a delta city.

Conclusion

The natural geography and environmental disposition of New Orleans is not incidental to its status and spatialization as a liminal and libidinal cultural capital. Its material location as a threshold and position within flows of goods undergirds its cultural qualities. Delta cities tend to be isolated from their immediate region in favor of more distant hinterlands. This gives them an immediate exceptionality and distinction from their surrounding area. The cultural construction of New Orleans as a liminal and libidinal site rests in part on this and on the romanticized narratives of New Orleans' "difference."

When New Orleans is compared with other cities in the United States, as in the prior quotation from *On the Road*, it is frequently with reference to distance, movement, and connection, rather than to any shared internal essence. More often, though, comparisons are made with distant and foreign cities, reinforcing the sense of difference and liminal exoticism. For example, introducing a volume of stories about New Orleans, Andrei Codrescu writes: "There are certain cities and certain areas of certain cities where the official language is dreams. Venice is one. And Paris. North Beach in San Francisco. Wenceslaus Square in Prague. And New Orleans, the city that dreams stories" (Codrescu 1992, v). Anne Rice's *The Vampire Lestat* (Rice 1992), Hurston's *Mules and Men* (Hurston 1935), and even the image of a "second line" of bystanders joining in to jazz funeral marches extend this liminal spatialization to being an interface with the dead and monstrous.

Facing the erosion of coastal wetlands and the increased frequency and strength of the last decade of hurricanes, New Orleans' exceptionalism has limited the ability to focus on the common risks and changes in delta cities. Historically, the expenditures required to resist the hydrological processes at work in a delta suggest that New Orleans is more important — culturally and economically — than the myths of its marginality would suggest. This contradiction is part and parcel of its spatialization. The requirement for strict control over levees and the investment and faith in technological innovations, such as more efficient pumps and new piling materials and techniques, and the history of racial oppression are also in contrast to the freedom from mores suggested by images of Mardi Gras revelers and the hybridity of its black-creole culture. The suspension of norms is itself a mask, part and parcel of the interfacial, liminal role played by the delta city as a shipping entrepôt to the Caribbean and the world. A delta city is in a perpetual state of betweenness, between land and water, between the domestic and the foreign, between stability and vulnerability, between the provincial and the worldly, between "nature" and "culture," between the living and the dead. The challenge for post-Katrina New Orleans is unique, but it mirrors that of all delta cities: to construct *place* from this condition of betweenness.

PART THREE

MOBILITIES

Commonsense approaches often treat cities as objects or environments of objects, a hard infrastructure through which people, money, and goods circulate. Whereas part 2 considered the challenges to stability and fixity necessary in creating New Orleans as a place and a city in the Mississippi Delta, part 3 considers the mobility and flows of objects, persons, and information that reproduce New Orleans. In chapter 5, Hugh Bartling discusses lessons that can be learned from Hurricane Katrina for planning regional relationships and transportation flows across the New Orleans area. In chapter 6, Matthew Tiessen considers the social and political relevance of theories of the speed and fluidity of objects and the importance of efforts to manage the mobilities inherent in social activities.

Mobility Matters

Mobility is more than a question of moving things around. As Bartling notes, access to mobility is uneven across locations and unequal across social class and status, gender, race, and ethnicity. A further complication is the continuing development of informational mobilities, such as access to the information crucial to decision making, whether in everyday life or public management. Modern societies have prized mobility as a right, but tend to neglect the right to stay in one place (Blomley 1994). Many areas are impacted by tourism-related mobilities wherein local, historic, or grassroots cultures are unable to resist the domination of cosmopolitan and commercial influences, or the sheer number of tourists. It was in this context that, following Katrina, New Orleans' leaders banned tours of the Lower Ninth Ward, worried that the neighborhood not only

would become synonymous with disaster but would be locked into that position (see Eggler 2006).

These leaders were concerned about the image of the Lower Ninth Ward
because images, produced through mobility, are themselves exceedingly mobile. Prior to the hurricane, images of New Orleans promoted by the city
and its Convention and Visitors Bureau circulated as advertisements. These
abstracted visions of the city competed with other representations such as
those in Hollywood movies. To these could be added historical and popular place-images and myths of the city conveyed in music and literature (see
chapter 4). In a study of films made between 1985 and 2000 that depict New
Orleans, Bridget Bordelon categorized images of "crime and violence," as well
as unique images such as "Mardi Gras, parades and street festivities, and cemeteries." These prominent images competed with but also complemented official, sanitized tourism-promotion images (Bordelon 2003). Digital technology
permits images to circulate with increased intensity, but the accessibility of
digital production technology also facilitates contestation. Not only do images
of a city literally circulate through print and electronic media, but they refer
to a place-myth (Shields 1991) that circulates not just in media but in the
popular imagination. Even those with firsthand knowledge of New Orleans or
those who live there refer to such "ideas in currency" concerning the city, if
only to deny them. This place-myth is "virtual" in the sense that it is real but
intangible, or "known through its effects"—for example, as an anticipation
that foretells the character of an actual experience of the city.[1] This is both
shared and contested as a central stake in the struggle over the meanings of
New Orleans—for example, as a well-produced jazz entertainment destination versus a capital of black culture, a working container port, or a site of
creole identity.

Struggle over Images

As Paul Virilio argues, a key aspect of power is the control over the speed of the
flow of images (see chapter 6). Images of the disaster circulated with a speed
that caught politicians and government officials by surprise. The Internet allowed bloggers, eyewitnesses with cameras, and the independent media to con-
test stereotyping mass-media coverage with local versions of the disaster that
reflected the pain of residents and the displaced, as well as insider knowledge
of those working in the disaster management and recovery apparatus. Journalists were criticized by bloggers who held reporters responsible for not checking
false stories of black violence and looting that were told to them by police and

politicians (see Peirce 2005, Bunch and commenters 2005, American Progress Action Fund and commenters 2006). CNN reporter Brian Thevenot, for example, was held to account for promoting racist stereotypes of violence (Street 2005; for his defense, see Thevenot 2006). A study for the University of Colorado Natural Hazards Center later suggested that looting was much less significant than reported. Pro-social, volunteer behavior may even have been confused with looting (Barsky, Trainor, and Torres 2006).

The virtual place-myth of New Orleans as a tourism destination for Mardi Gras partying has long overshadowed the actual character of life in the city and its suburbs. Indeed, as the Katrina disaster shattered the previously dominant place-myth of New Orleans as a party capital where *all* that black people did was make music, outside observers found it convenient to turn to the antithetical place-myth that had always lurked beneath the surface: the myth of New Orleans as a den of crime where *all* that black people did was loot and murder. The controversy over the reporting of the events in the weeks immediately following the hurricane and over uneven rebuilding efforts has made New Orleans a prominent symbol for urban race issues (see Brookings Institution 2006). The tragedy of New Orleans is that it took a hurricane to remind policymakers and the public of the reality of urban poverty and disadvantage in parts of New Orleans and its highly racialized character (Shipler 2005). Other elements still remain relatively overlooked, such as the fate of the Latino population and the role of undocumented migrant laborers in rebuilding New Orleans (Dyson 2006).

Although managers of major projects — as New Orleans' rebuilding certainly is — are keenly aware of how a project's image can "stop a project as surely as can bad ground or a shortage of labour and materials" (Lemley 1996), it is questionable whether the full import of imagery is appreciated by planners who are trained to use community "town hall meetings" (which may themselves reproduce place-myths) as ways of proposing and gaining legitimacy for development plans. In the context of postdisaster reconstruction, community input through public meetings is seen simply as part of "an expansive view of public works and infrastructure" as both hard and soft (Watson and Kiel 2006, 281; see also chapter 5).

Mobilities and the City

As the chapters in part 3 show, the answer that one provides to the question posed in chapter 1 — "What is a city?" — includes different elements from the perspective of mobilities. Managing mobility is not just the "regulation of waters" as in Mumford's "urban village" perspective. It also involves managing flows of information in which virtual elements of the city, such as its reputation and how it is imagined by different publics, circulate. It is not just a matter of density and concentration as in Mumford's second perspective ("concentration and combination"), but a qualitative shift that results in speeding up the tempo of everyday life, the fluidity of representations, and, most significantly, the speed at which images and the latent character of cities can be actualized with tangible effects. The virtual qualities of cities become all the more important to urban planners who must attend to the actualization of these virtualities in the built environment. However, this process involves other actors, including the media, literature, and the fine arts, as well. In addition to adding complexity, these actors demand that planners, city managers, and urban designers account for the plurality of understandings of the city, rather than simple majority opinion. This process becomes particularly intricate when one considers Mumford's fourth perspective on the city, as a site of social complexity.

From the perspective of mobilities, cities and environments are not static, simple objects with singular identities, but are understood equivocally and lived and actualized by competing actors with unreconciled interests. Forged amid, and distributed by, mobilities, the image of New Orleans is a bundle of contradictory qualities, held in a tension that is an ongoing scandal of nonconformity, impropriety, and particularity, as well as a productive cultural milieu that has played an important role in the imagination of the American urban character.

Note

1. "Virtual" designates the intangible aspects of New Orleans such as its character and culture rather than abstract representations of the city, whether in the form of images, data, or narratives (see Shields 2003; Peirce 1958, volume 6, subsection 372).

CHAPTER FIVE

Mobility and the Regional Context of Urban Disaster

Hugh Bartling

Hurricane Katrina was unique in that it was a regional catastrophe covering a large metropolitan area and its environs. Typical of most North American metropolises, the New Orleans area has experienced very little in the way of regional planning. Fragmented governance, explicitly and implicitly exclusionary social practices, and public policies that spatially segregated people on the basis of race and class exacerbated the social and ecological dimensions of the regional destruction wrought by Katrina.

What lessons can be learned for urban development? This is an especially pertinent question as the Gulf Coast region engages in the processes of rebuilding — processes increasingly marked by an uneasy tension between a desire to "respect" the region's history and to redress systematic inequalities.

An *ideology of mobility* permeates public policy at every level of the U.S. federalist system. This ideology influenced the contours of official evacuation plans in New Orleans, served as the guiding vision for decades of infrastructural projects that shaped the region's landscape, and exacerbated the challenges faced by many victims of Katrina as they endured the posthurricane flooding. Furthermore, as New Orleans and Mississippi's Gulf Coast engaged in planning for the rebuilding of devastated areas, the patterns assumed by this ideology resurfaced. By "ideology" I mean a structured set of discourses, explanations, beliefs, and underlying behaviors that frame the dominant terrain for social action. These tendencies need not be explicitly promulgated, but rather serve as reference points for what is politically and socially "possible." This understanding of ideology derives from Antonio Gramsci, who argues that this set of ideas or beliefs operates in a hegemonic fashion, framing and shaping the breadth of policy discussion.

New Orleans morning.
Photograph by Jacob A.
Wagner; image courtesy
of the photographer.

Mobility and the City

Commentators on the development of urbanism who come from various disciplinary backgrounds generally acknowledge — either explicitly or implicitly — the central role of mobility in influencing urban form. Lewis Mumford (1961), for instance, in his ambitious work, *The City in History*, places great emphasis on the siting of ancient cities with respect to their advantage for moving goods and people, highlighting the emergence of a built environment that facilitated various commercial flows. From the standpoint of modernist planning, we see a similar sentiment in the work of twentieth-century planners like Daniel Burnham in the United States and Le Corbusier in Europe, who sought to "rationalize" the city through geometrically designed roads and boulevards, improving the city's circulatory flows.

Given the importance of mobility as an organizing feature of the urban landscape and a facilitator of economic production, it remains one of the most underdiscussed subjects in the domains of both policymaking and mainstream culture. A "mobility privilege" operates both culturally and materially through changes to the built environment. Operating in much the same way as does "white privilege," "masculine privilege," or "heterosexist privilege," the privilege of particular forms of mobility contributes to a wide variety of class and policy practices that continue particular forms of dominance.

One could look at metropolitan development in the United States from the immediate post–World War II era to the present as a codification and realization of mobilities of privilege. With the emergence of capitalist industrialization in the nineteenth century, issues of mobility came to be dominant urban problems. Urban expansion in cities like New Orleans, Chicago, St. Louis, and Pittsburgh was facilitated by their advantageous siting. River — and later train — access served as a mechanism of economic expansion, allowing such cities to serve as nodes for distribution of goods and points of attraction for migrants and workers. As economic production diversified, cities increasingly became sites for manufacturing, creating a new set of mobility problems. Exponential rates of population growth required an urban landscape that both accommodated housing for wage workers and enabled them to reach places of employment. Negotiating these demands was seldom seamless, and often contributed to larger disputes between socioeconomic classes.

Simultaneously, new technologies of mobility were developed that restructured the urban landscape. Omnibuses, streetcars, subways, and, finally, automobiles required particular configurations of the built form relating to rights-of-way while also influencing urban architecture. Mobility also made the development of suburbia possible — a process that served to segregate metropolitan inhabitants based on economic status as the upper classes sought to take refuge from the insalubrious environment of the cities which, somewhat ironically, was also the source of their wealth. Thus, the early streetcars and commuter railways that opened up areas far-flung from center cities were largely taken advantage of by a wealthier class who could afford lower-density development and higher transportation costs (Warner 1962). Intrametropolitan mobility, in this sense, set the stage for the processes of mass suburbanization that ensued in the post–World War II era, which, when coupled with the country's legacy of institutionalized racial discrimination, fueled spatial concentration of communities along race, class, and ethnic lines.

In more recent years, understandings of "mobility" have been expanded to reflect the increasing importance of informational technologies in shaping cities and how, in particular, these technologies form the basis of a hyperglobalized economy whereby capital's mobility and flexibility have influenced the urban landscape (see the following chapter in this book by Matthew Tiessen). As the U.S. manufacturing sector has quickly dissipated since 1970 with the increased shifting of manufacturing investment to the Global South, cities have relied on informational and service-centered industries for capital investment. For larger cities like New York or Chicago, the agglomeration of services that facilitate capital flows and mobility has created a class of "global cities" (Sassen 1991). Smaller cities without a critical mass of lucrative telecommunications and financial services industries — like New Orleans — often experience their contemporary postindustrial mobility as being tied up with tourism (Judd and Fainstein 1999). Successful tourist cities require a particular type of "mobility landscape," replete with designated tourist districts, hotels, spaces for consumption, and adequate circulatory linkages to other cities. They rely on the global circulation of the particular city's "image" or "brand" to create incentives for outsiders to visit. Thus, urban mobility operates both virtually (through advertising and promotion) and physically (by providing a space for the visitor that speaks to the image "promised" in the city's promotional material).

Thus, we can think of the city as a circulatory site facilitating flows of capital, people, and information. Mobility, from this perspective, should figure in discussions of other, more prominent aspects of urbanism. Issues of "growth machine" politics that concern urbanists, such as Harvey Molotch (1976), or the persistence of an urban underclass, explored in-depth by William Julius Wilson (1987), have elements relating to the politics of mobility that can enhance traditional economic or cultural accounts of urban social and political relations. As such, the way in which mobility is configured in the urban landscape is not neutral. Rather, it reflects constellations of particular economic, social, and cultural interests and values.

What, then, are the architectonics of the contemporary "mobility privilege," and how is it articulated in urban regions on the Gulf Coast? The waves of suburbanization that characterized post–World War II metropolitan expansion throughout the country were predicated by an infrastructure of mobility, backed by restrictive public policies and a cultural logic of racism. Initially whites fled inner-city residential areas but still maintained access to urban centers of capital circulation through a built environment that facilitated automobile travel.

In the New Orleans region, the unique geography played an important role in the development of suburbanization as the particular hydrological features of the region made more common patterns of contiguous expansion untenable. Craig Colten (2005) has described how, as early as the 1920s, suburban expansion westward into Jefferson Parish required significant state and federal investment in flood control projects, which contributed to a rise in suburban property values. A devastating 1947 hurricane that showed the futility of these projects, however, struck Lake Pontchartrain, inundating it with water that breached the levees constructed two decades prior, resulting in massive flooding in these new suburban areas.

The fundamental embrace of the automobile as a form of regional mobility allowed the development of land far-flung from the flood-prone environs of central New Orleans. In the 1950s large public works projects like the Lake Pontchartrain Causeway and the expansion of the interstate highway system opened up large swaths of land in proximity to New Orleans. People could live distanced from the environmental and social problems of the city, yet its economic and cultural opportunities could be accessed via automobile. As more people of greater economic means moved to suburbia, more capital investment occurred in these areas, further separating inner-city residents from suburban centers of employment and exacerbating social and economic inequalities. While central New Orleans — in particular the downtown and French Quarter districts — has been the beneficiary of investment over the past several decades as the city promoted itself as a cultural and tourist destination, there have been few economic benefits for the city's lower-income communities. A mobility infrastructure linking lower-income residents in need of jobs to places of employment growth has, likewise, not been forthcoming. In the decades prior to Katrina, public investment in regional transportation infrastructure has focused primarily on enhancing opportunities for private automobile travel while investment in forms of public transportation has been stagnant or dedicated primarily to streetcars that reinforce the tourist identity of the city.

Thus, the logic of mobility that informed the urban social and political landscape operating at the time of Hurricane Katrina can be summarized according to the following characteristics:

1. A privileging of the automobile as the primary form of urban and regional mobility.
2. A land-use regime — particularly in the suburban areas — that privileged low-density development. Low-density development reinforces the transportation monoculture of the automobile because it makes the circulation of people in their daily pursuits of labor, housing, and consumption by other means relatively untenable. Low-density development simultaneously exacerbates class segregation as it homogenizes forms of residential development in favor

of single-family homes at the expense of multifamily housing options, having the effect of pricing out of the market people who cannot afford a single-family home.

3. A lack of commitment of resources to developing regional public transportation systems.

It is these characteristics that formed the contours of the mobility deficit and privilege that had a significant impact surrounding the response to the extreme socio-ecological events of Hurricane Katrina.

New Orleans and Suburban Development

While mass suburbanization in the United States is often associated with the postwar era, this wave of expansion was made possible by the rise of electric power earlier in the century. As Daphne Spain (1979) argues, the expansion of the electric streetcar system, coupled with the employment of massive electrified pumps used for drainage (Maygarden et al. 1999), set the stage for the first wave of suburbanization in New Orleans during the 1920s. Legalized segregation exacerbated racial inequalities, as the new areas opened up for development were seized upon by higher-income, primarily white households. Additionally, the streetcars themselves were spaces of segregation. The commonplace experience throughout the South of African Americans having to ride in the rear of public transportation vehicles was given unusual flexibility in New Orleans where mobile "race screens" could be moved forward and backward in streetcars by white passengers to expand or constrict the space allocated to African Americans (Post 2006).

The court-mandated desegregation of streetcars in 1958 coincided with the completion and/or planning of a series of major freeways, including the Lake Pontchartrain Causeway, the Crescent City Bridge, and the Pontchartrain Expressway. In some respects, the blatant processes of Jim Crow segregation morphed into a much more subtle form of discrimination based upon changing practices of mobility. Freeway expansion made the areas in St. Tammany and other outlying parishes more amenable to suburban development. Practices of redlining (Jackson 1985), the use of restrictive covenants, and the focus on building single-family homes in these outlying parishes fostered racial homogeneity. In the case of the New Orleans region, the emphasis on automobiles as the major form of transportation intersected with quasi-legalized racial discrimination, class and race biases in residential mortgage schemes, and autonomy in suburban zoning to result in a regional landscape characterized by clusters of homogeneity — both economically and racially. Simultaneously, the streetcar system was slowly downgraded (Mosher, Keim, and Franques 1995), with numerous lines being shut during the 1960s and 1970s. Although the system was now desegregated, service was inferior, inhibiting mobility for those New Orleans residents unable to afford an automobile.

The logic of private automobility that was solidified by the 1960s has persisted in the intervening decades — except for a successful attempt by historic preservationists to block a Robert Moses–inspired freeway just north of the French Quarter (Moe and Wilkie 1997). Within the city, the move toward automobility fundamentally transformed some largely African American and low-income neighborhoods. While the residents of the French Quarter were battling the city's effort to build Moses's Vieux Carré [French Quarter] Freeway, Claiborne Avenue — a bustling African American business district — was chosen for the site of Interstate Highway 10. The highway is elevated by several dozen feet and runs in excess of two miles, effectively destroying this important economic and cultural institution. By offering connections to the city for suburban settlements while inserting a large, noisy, and pollution-inducing piece of urban infrastructure atop a formerly vibrant neighborhood, Interstate 10 stands as an apposite symbol of the automotive mobility paradigm.

In practice, suburbanization in the New Orleans region had the same demographic effects that were experienced in metropolitan areas across the United States during the late twentieth century. Census data broken down by parish shows stark contrasts. In the 2000 U.S. Census for Orleans Parish, which is contiguous with the City of New Orleans, 28.1 percent of the population identified themselves as white while 67.3 percent identified themselves as African American. By contrast, for suburban St. Tammany Parish, the numbers were 87 percent white and 9.9 percent African American; for Jefferson Parish, 69.8 percent white and 22.9 percent African American; for St. Bernard Parish, 88.3 percent white and 7.6 percent African American. Poverty rates show similar discrepancies. In Orleans Parish, the percentage of the population below the poverty line was 27.94 percent; in St. Tammany Parish, 9.72 percent; in Jefferson Parish, 13.65 percent; and in St. Bernard Parish, 13.11 percent. As one would expect given the higher density in Orleans Parish, only 60.3 percent of workers 16 years and over reported commuting in a private vehicle while 16.1 percent carpooled, 13.7 percent relied on public transportation, and 5.2 percent walked. In St. Tammany, the figures were 80.2 percent private automobile, 13.7 percent carpool, 0.3 percent public transportation, and 0.8 percent walking. While these figures are compiled for commuting to work, thus excluding significant segments of the population (e.g., children, retired people, and the unemployed), they provide a glimpse into the mobility options available to people in different urban and suburban landscapes within the New Orleans metropolitan region.

Thus, the urbanized landscape of New Orleans — as opposed to the suburbanized landscape of neighboring parishes — reflects a different geography of possibility. A significant number of urban residents are able to operate outside the dominant mode of mobility. However, the tragedy of the events surrounding Hurricane Katrina made apparent the rigidity of the dominant logic of mobility and mobility privilege. Alternatives to the private automobile were shown to be inadequate.

This rigidity is most clearly present in the assumptions inherent in the city's evacuation plan. Given the federalist nature of governance in the United States and the regional nature of extreme weather events, such as hurricanes, most planning for evacuation in the case of disasters involves cooperative (or coercive) efforts between state, local, and regional governments. While some states arguably play a stronger role in influencing local land use and transportation decisions relating to disaster reaction (May et al. 1996), there is generally a significant degree of autonomy for local municipalities to develop their own plans.

Plans for responding to natural disasters in the metropolitan context operate in the same way as other arenas of local policymaking in that they adhere to an inherently fragmented governance paradigm. The growth of metropolitan areas over the past fifty years within the context of fragmentation has resulted in uneven development in a variety of policies. Peter Dreier and his colleagues (Dreier, Mollenkopf, and Swanstrom 2004) have mapped the substantive aspect of these patterns in *Place Matters: Metropolitics for the Twenty-first Century*. In their estimation, municipal fragmentation in the areas of zoning, housing, education, economic development, and transportation have created municipal "winners" and "losers" in most metropolitan areas of the United States. In the absence of regional planning, differences in wealth and opportunity within regions are on a path of increasing polarization.

This is clearly apparent in the case of evacuation plans in the hurricane-prone region of southeastern Louisiana. In Louisiana, the Office of Homeland Security and Emergency Preparedness serves as the main state coordinating body for evacuation and disaster response with the authority to determine if/when emergency procedures should be followed and to define the severity of a particular extreme event for the purposes of response. Localities are required to adopt accounting procedures in accordance with state dictates, but the substance of local plans is entirely at the discretion of municipalities (State of

Louisiana 2005), leaving issues such as regional transportation responses effectively uncoordinated (Sundeen, Reed, and Savage 2005).

In the case of New Orleans, the city's geography and the logic of mobility helped to determine the possibilities for evacuation in the immediate hours following the hurricane. The city's evacuation plan relied on private transportation and voluntary compliance for citizen evacuation (DeParle 2005). As the transportation element of the city's 2004 master plan acknowledges, "Hurricane evacuation planning is made more difficult for the city, due to the large percentage of residents without access to a private automobile. . . . Evacuation is also closely related to income. . . . In addition to those unable to afford vehicles or transportation there are the disabled, hospitalized, elderly, and incarcerated who would not be able to drive from the area. Development of alternative means for citizens to leave the area is crucial" (City Planning Commission 2004, 145). This description, written more than two years before Hurricane Katrina, is revealing. It anticipates the challenges faced by many residents as water inundated the city following the passage of the storm.

Perhaps most striking, however, is the plan's uncritical acceptance of the status quo. Comprehensive planning is generally designed to provide both an assessment of the issues facing a city at a particular point in time and, perhaps more importantly, a strategy for policy action focused on alleviating identified problems. Although public transportation is discussed in the document, it is primarily wedded to enhancing mobility for the tourist industry by encouraging the expansion of the streetcar system in conjunction with plans to increase both the size of the city's convention center and its cruise ship capacity, creating seamless mobility between various tourist-centered spaces. This is compounded by a desire to concentrate new capital projects around a new light-rail line linking the central business district with the airport. Regional public transportation linkages to suburban parishes are not discussed in the document. Perhaps most telling is the letter transmitting the plan, wherein the chair of the commission stresses that the plan, as a whole, is a "pragmatic one. It is focused on five priorities: preservation and strategic enhancement of the existing transportation system, creation of a balanced system with a broad range of transportation choices, integration with land use and economic development planning, public safety enhancement, and improved funding, system management and operations" (City Planning Commission 2004, ii). That "pragmatism" is required could be explained by the particular logic of mobility embracing an automobile monoculture that had been in development for upward of half a century. Like any ideology that asserts a seemingly unassailable inner logic, these dominant understandings of mobility limit policy possibilities. When the commission has to argue for transportation's "integration with land use . . . planning" as a "priority," it suggests that this has not been done adequately in the past.

Of course, the separation of land use planning from transportation planning has been a major critique leveled against the overtly "rationalistic" planning practices that were largely responsible for decades of suburban sprawl (Duany, Plater-Zyberk, and Speck 2000). These practices viewed mobility as an afterthought and failed to adequately appreciate the unsustainability of a decentralized system for circulating people and goods. Like all ideologies, the automotive logic apparent in dominant thinking about mobility presents an ostensibly cohesive narrative, which, at its core, is unable to accommodate social phenomena that fail to fit within its logic. This is not to suggest that the simple insertion of a more "transit-oriented" ideology would *necessarily* be more accommodative; rather, the prevailing logic of mobility operates within — and helps to constitute — a variety of other social practices that also contribute to structural discontinuities. What is most problematic about the ideological production analyzed herein is the lack of avenues for critical reflection. The absence of these spaces for calling into question dominant practices inhibits policy choices during the critical juncture of rebuilding.

Reconstruction: An Opportunity for Rethinking Mobility?

Given the national circulation of media images showing individuals' inability to leave the city, it is curious that attempts to revise the mobility paradigm have not been forthcoming. This was not the case in all of the areas affected by Hurricane Katrina. One much-publicized reconstruction effort in Mississippi employed an armada of "New Urbanist" designers who conducted "charettes" in various coastal communities and developed a regional plan that emphasized the major tenets of New Urbanism: higher-density land use, mixed development, accommodation for pedestrians, and multiple modes of transportation. This effort — sponsored by Governor Haley Barbour and overseen by the Chicago-based Congress for New Urbanism — was not received without criticism. The group of architects and town planners was headed by Andres Duany, and the charettes, which were participatory design exercises that were ostensibly intended to bring the public into the planning process, took place just six weeks after the hurricane when many evacuees had not returned to the region. The resulting framework, published under the moniker of the Mississippi Renewal Forum (2005), looked similar to the multiple New Urbanist developments constructed over the past twenty years by Duany's firm, leading to critiques questioning the democratic nature of the planning and the penchant for New Urbanist developments to act as engines of gentrification at the expense of low-income communities (Davis 2005).

With particular reference to transportation and mobility, however, the final report of the Mississippi Renewal Forum envisions a regional rail system linking the major coastal communities in the state as well as connecting them with neighboring cities in Louisiana and Alabama. Additionally, the report advocates for light rail systems for shorter-distance travel and as a magnet for development on the coastal highway. The highway, in turn, would be reconfigured for pedestrian access and tourist redevelopment. Unlike conventional planning, as seen in the New Orleans Master Plan, discussion of transportation is linked specifically to land use and economic redevelopment, and issues of regionalism are placed at the forefront of all of the plan's elements.

The Duany plan, however, suffers from the same plight as many of the conceptual ideas relating to regionalism in other parts of the United States: it relies predominantly on voluntary compliance for implementation of its suggestions. As such, its rather radical conceptions regarding new possibilities for mobility do little to materially challenge dominant paradigms. The plan itself was commissioned by the governor who, in the fragmented system of U.S. governance structures, has generally deferred to municipalities to authorize most land-use decisions. While some municipalities have responded favorably to the Duany plan, the largest — Biloxi — has rejected the Duany suggestions in favor of a conventional approach that was favored by the city's casino industry (Ward 2006).

In the case of New Orleans, the mobility issue was not significantly broached. Mayor Nagin's Bring New Orleans Back Commission had a subcommittee that was charged with assessing the city's public transit opportunities, and its findings figure somewhat significantly in the final report (Bring New Orleans Back Commission 2006). However, it focused almost solely on the state of the city's Regional Transit Authority (RTA), which emerged from the aftermath of the hurricane with much of its fleet destroyed and ridership at anemic numbers. Given the state of emergency experienced by the RTA, this focus is not unwarranted, but it offered no openings for looking at the regional mechanisms of mobility which could call into question the uneven distribution of mobility privilege in the region. Regional public transportation planning has been discussed by the RTA board of commissioners in the aftermath of the Bring New Orleans Back Commission report of early 2006. However, these discussions have been eclipsed by the RTA's reliance on subsidies from the Federal Emergency Management Agency (Donze 2006).

The larger issue in addressing reconstruction from the standpoint of metropolitan mobility is the intransigence of the fragmented structures of governance in the region. As Dreier and colleagues (2004) explain, patterns of intraregional inequality have been on the rise over the past two decades throughout the United States. Thus, in some neighborhoods in a metropolitan area the size of greater New Orleans, certain places have experienced qualitative advantages due to their spatial isolation and their ability to "transcend" isolating structures when needed. Mobility privilege could be considered a flexible mechanism serving to underpin these unequal patterns of social interaction and isolation. The whole suburban project operates by providing a publicly funded modification of the metropolitan landscape that supports access and mobility for some while excluding others.

Therefore, it is not surprising that several suburban municipalities in the New Orleans region appear to be quite content with rebuilding by following the patterns of logic that served them prior to the devastation brought by Hurricane Katrina. St. Tammany Parish, while not suffering nearly the same human death toll as New Orleans, suffered a significant amount of property damage, and public officials there — like their counterparts in New Orleans — developed reconstruction plans in the months following the hurricane. A curious effect of the storm was a significant population increase in St. Tammany, which is situated on the northern shore of Lake Pontchartrain. The parishes north of the lake increased population from 310,000 prior to the storm to 370,000, as of March 2006, while parishes on the south shore of the lake dropped from 1 million to 600,000 (Taimerica Management Company 2006). This population increase has created both challenges and opportunities for the parish. In a March 2006 reconstruction charette, participants highlighted the mitigation of traffic congestion and increasing traffic flow as primary goals for reconstruction. Lacking was any mention of St. Tammany's role in a larger socioeconomic region. For the purposes of the reconstruction document, relief from the hurricane was primarily a traffic problem. This was reinforced three months later when St. Tammany Parish President Kevin Davis gave his annual State of the Parish speech. In the speech he lauded the reconstruction effort and focused on the main accomplishments of the parish since the storm: various road widening projects and road improvements (Davis 2006).

Conclusion

Hurricane Katrina was a *regional* disaster. Like most environmental problems, the hurricane did not pay much attention to political boundaries. However, these human boundaries — social, economic, and political — shaped the ways in which the "natural" disaster was experienced. Decades of suburbanization, building upon centuries of social stratification, created a set of conditions that literally and immediately determined life and death in the region. However, even dramatic tragedies on the scale of Hurricane Katrina may be insufficient to provoke a different vision of urban and metropolitan spaces and mobilities.

In the hurricane's deadly wake, the consequences of decades of spatial incongruities became vividly clear. It did not take long after the levees broke in the city to see spatial incongruities manifest themselves in various ways. An evacuation plan in the city that was predicated on access to private transportation predictably failed those (mostly low-income) people who did not have access to automobiles. As the situation grew more perilous throughout the week in the "shelters of last resort," refugees seeking to flee the city (who were largely people of color) were forcibly turned back by police in neighboring suburbs as they approached the city's limits. This graphically demonstrated the impermeability and intransigence of the "color line" over a hundred years after W. E. B. DuBois's prophetic proclamation of our previous century's greatest "problem."

In New Orleans, the logic of a decades-long pattern of metropolitan development that ignored the city for the sake of suburbia magnified social tensions. Little more than two weeks later, as meteorologists were predicting Hurricane Rita's path across southeast Texas, mobility deficit and privilege became even more apparent. In Houston, fresh memories of people trying to flee New Orleans contributed to overwhelming compliance with local officials' pleas to evacuate.

Whereas mobility privilege allowed people with access to private automobiles to leave New Orleans in advance of Hurricane Katrina, in Houston, thousands clogged the highways heading north, causing traffic to come to a standstill. In this case, the U.S. cultural predilection that asserts a transportation monoculture based upon the private automobile proceeded to its logical conclusion – massive gridlock.

The cultural belief that "freedom" is attained through the inefficient utilization of a highly polluting technology for mobility has dire consequences. In the cases of Hurricanes Katrina and Rita, the response from the federal government was not to rethink the social practices of mobility that contributed to failures of evacuation in both New Orleans and Houston, but rather to use these failures as a way to enhance the spatial networks and systems that support the mobility privileged.

CHAPTER SIX

Uneven Mobilities and Urban Theory
The Power of Fast and Slow

Matthew Tiessen

Introduction: Mobility in a State of Flux

Mobility has become a most suitable trope for our time, an era accelerating at what seems to be ever faster rates of speed, an era penetrated by pervasive and proliferating technologies and riven with the effects of neoliberal economics. "Mobility" is a term whose explanatory and descriptive potency has received particular attention by social and technology theorists. Taking into consideration the urban theories of John Urry, Paul Virilio, and others, this paper addresses the question of how/whether theories of mobility provide an illuminating lens through which to view the urban disaster that saw New Orleans destroyed by Hurricane Katrina. My suggestion will be that although mobility has been receiving increasing theoretical attention, this attention does not describe a new phenomenon; rather, the contemporary penchant to theorize mobility objectifies the degree to which mobilities have been disavowed or gone unrecognized in the past.

Can mobility—the term/the concept—accurately (or adequately) capture or represent contemporary city life? What exactly does this term "mobility" describe? Are there entities, situations, or experiences that theories of mobility cannot address? Alternatively: What *new* work does this recently popular term—"mobility"—do? Hasn't everything *always been* mobile and in flux? Cities, suggests geographer Jennifer Robinson, have been sources of "vital excitement" for urban sociologists and theorists for a century or more (2004, 569). Robinson observes that cities have always had an ability to amaze people who experience them. It is perhaps due to such amazement that those who choose to write academic prose about cities tend to set out on what sometimes seems like "a headlong rush to capture . . . the newness, originality and astonishment of city life" (569). Citing Simmel's 1903 essay "The Metropolis and Mental Life," Robinson argues that the "excitement" of life in the city has "invested" theories of the urban with "a certain frisson and pace" (2004, 570); in turn, this has given rise to a quite particular definition of "the urban" that privileges those cities that are most likely to evoke a palpable sense of astonishment. By contrast, Robinson points out that cities that are "slowing down," that have "intermittent electricity" or "decaying physical environments," are "difficult to fit into these excitable accounts of city life." Hence they are ignored and become invisible in the discourse that favors what she refers to as a particular "phantasmagoria of city-ness" (570). Many less fortunate or less exciting cities, she argues, have become "barely relevant" to that mode of urban theorizing that today is de rigueur. One of the results of this dominant urban paradigm, suggests Robinson, is that when commentators today speak of the "urban" they speak more or less exclusively about cities that can be described as exhibiting a host of multivalent "mobilities."

Mobility is a rather ambiguous term applicable, it might seem, to any number of more or less mobile examples. Mobilities come in all shapes and sizes. Mobile entities can, for instance, be material (cars, airplanes, packages, food) as well as immaterial or virtual (ideas, emails, spoken languages, shared memories). Different mobilities can be interrelated. The mobile trajectories within a network or meshwork intersect and are interdependent; they move and change across space and time. Often the biggest impediment to a mobile virtuality[1] is a less mobile material reality (for instance, an idea that couldn't be actualized, given a particular set of material constraints); similarly, often a material reality will be rendered immobile by an immaterial virtuality (for instance, a particular cultural or social paradigm — pacifism and all its attendant consequences, for instance — may inhibit physical violence or war).

Mobilities are often described as sets of flows (see Shields 1997). Although such a liquid metaphor might seem inadequate to describe a long line at a post office, or the start-and-stop sequence at a traffic light, flows do become apparent when a city is viewed, for instance, using time-lapse photography. Mobilities, then, are all around us and are certainly a feature of contemporary cities. But is the equation "cities = mobilities" (as identified by Robinson above) useful as a generalized observation? And does such a concept provide us with insight into New Orleans' encounter with Hurricane Katrina?

Whether or not contemporary cities are or are not more or less mobile than they used to be (or, indeed, whether contemporary cities are not so much *newly* mobile as they are *differently* mobile) are questions that deserve careful attention. Does today's mobile city change more dramatically than cities used to? Is today's mobile city a more volatile place than cities used to be? The contemporary emphasis on mobility reflects the sense that today's cities exhibit *more* of just about everything. They move at greater speed, their inhabitants travel further, they absorb and expel more varieties of analog and digital information, they (in many instances) welcome more immigrants, they are crossed by ever more goods and services: quantity rather than quality. Of course, cities have always been more or less on the move. Indeed, to make a rather banal but not insignificant point, isn't everything, at the most basic physical level, in a constant, but uneven, state of motion?

Everyday Mobilities

Observing that everything is in a constant state of movement or flow (at the very least at the micro-level) is, of course, not new. In the 1700s Gottfried Wilhelm Leibniz (1646–1716) observed that all things "are, like rivers, in a perpetual flux; small parts enter and leave them continually" (1965a, 160). Leibniz suggested that "the very substance of things" consists in "their force to act and be acted upon" (1965b, 102) and that all that exists is "subject to change" (1965a, 149). More recently, Manuel De Landa (1997 and 2002) has demonstrated how material and immaterial entities — from rocks, to gases, to memories, to concepts — are fluid, but that the complex, divergent, and non-human rates of flow that these entities exhibit have for too long gone unnoticed in everyday life, in turn being regarded as insignificant.

Mobility, then, is not something new: it is the state of things. Rather, it seems that it is the *rate*, and *speed*, and *amount* of change by which mobilities are made manifest that is worthy of note. The contemporary city is not newly mobile; rather, the speed and the amount of mobility are, in effect, literally more of the same. It's not change, but change's rate that signals an alteration. It follows then that the recent focus within social theory on mobility is less "a novel agenda," as John Urry suggests (2000, 186), than it is a reference to the sociology that Urry and others are taking pains to mobilize.

Urry's writings on mobility are seminal. They are motivated by what he describes as the existence of "new temporal-spatial patterns" that crisscross national borders — those borders that so much "twentieth-century sociology" regarded as being representative of relatively closed societies waiting to be surveyed by the sociologist's gaze. What was missed (or ignored), suggests Urry, were the intersections and interactions just below these last-century-sociologists' noses: intersections and interactions between "region, city and place" and/or "class, gender and ethnicity" (2000, 186). Social theorist Zygmunt Bauman (2000) has termed this interconnected and accelerating flux "liquid modernity."

Urry, invoking Leibniz's observations cited above, notes that mobility does not occur only at the level of the metropolis and need not be represented simply by an endless stream of jet-setters. Rather, mobility prevails in urban settings down to the smallest of communities. Often when theorists of mobility are pointing to their objects of study they are motioning toward, for instance, the still incredible phenomenon of transcontinental modes of communication that allow our "virtual" selves to be anywhere on earth (for more on the virtual, see, for instance, Shields 2003); or, perhaps, they are describing how globalization has produced an economic system wherein not only money, but jobs in manufacturing or knowledge economies flow across borders and oceans with impunity (see Harvey 2001 and 2005). Despite these exceptional spatio-temporal developments, more localized instances of mobility have not lost their importance. Urry suggests, for example, that face-to-face interaction— "co-presence"—remains an attractive necessity for human beings insofar as it affords them the opportunity for "rich, multi-layered and dense conversations" that involve "not just words," but "indexical expressions, facial gestures, body language, status, voice intonation, pregnant silences, past histories, antici-pated conversations and actions, turn-taking practices and so on" (2002, 259). Whether Urry's observation is true or not—witness, for instance, the rise of the social-networking Web site www.myspace.com ("a place for friends") and its subsequent purchase in 2005 by media magnate Rupert Murdoch for $580 million (Reiss 2006)—he does identify the fact that even face-to-face interac-tions have particular mobilities that are related to them and not achievable through other means.

Urry goes on to point out that comparatively less mobile communities that exhibit a great degree of "co-present propinquity" depend not only on the mo-bilities within the community's boundaries—its "well-worn paths" and "famil-iar roads"—but also on vast numbers of other places whose goods and services they receive, whose media they consume, and whose social paradigms, beliefs, and fashions they adopt (2002, 266). Of course, the relative "need" for face-to-face co-presence functions not only to facilitate exchanges within small, local-ized communities, it also contributes to the need for face-to-face encounters that necessitate transcontinental air travel. In turn, those consumed by a life in flight in pursuit of co-present encounters as the lubricant that cements busi-ness deals (for example) know well that such a life is very much facilitated by their leaving digital "traces of their selves" in that mobile space that is always just a click away: the Internet (266). The Internet's capacity to distribute a little bit of ourselves to us when and where we need it — we check our email or read the news here, we upload a file or check our bank balance there — enables (some of) us to engage in relatively convenient face-to-face meetings across vast distances. It is appropriate, then, that discussions of mobility in contemporary theories of cities focus not exclusively on the *newness* of mobility, but on how mobility has become and is becoming *different*: how amounts and rates of change in many areas seem to be growing and/or accelerating. Indeed, one of the most compelling facets of contemporary life is its propensity to seem to accelerate perpetually.

Nevertheless, the capacity to be mobile, and for this mobility to be controlled by the person with an interest in being mobilized, is a capacity that is distributed unevenly across the socioeconomic and technological landscape. This capacity — to be able to control mobility — is a function of power or, more specifically, of a person's being able to wield power in order to achieve particular ends. When mobility is at its most powerful it is often a mobility that is traveling at very high rates of speed. Whoever or whatever can get "there" first usually wins. This applies in regard to economics, warfare, scientific discovery, geographical exploration, and so on.

(Im)mobility in New Orleans

The degree to which rates of and capacities for mobility are unevenly distributed was made particularly clear on August 29, 2005, when Hurricane Katrina touched down ferociously on the unfortunately immobile city of New Orleans. Large numbers of city residents were immobilized in their homes as the winds roared and the water levels began to rise. Others had escaped in time. These others were, evidently, more mobile — in their automobiles — and were able to get out of town along the mobility-facilitating highways that slice through the landscape of any contemporary urban metropolis.

New Orleans offers many examples of mobilities. With a network of railroads, airports, ports, highways, buses, and streetcars (as well as a proposed light rail system), New Orleans is relatively flush with transportation options. And yet, despite their city's public transportation options, the car-less residents of New Orleans were not afforded the use of these options in the face of Hurricane Katrina (Murdock 2005). New Orleans, then, during and after Katrina's onslaught was a city whose most significant events — the deaths, for instance — were a result not of mobility but of immobility. During the hurricane thousands of people huddled in their homes (and eventually in the Superdome — see the chapter by Flaherty, above), trapped in their city, and thousands more — posthurricane — could not return to the homes they had managed to vacate at some point before, during, or after the storm.

A 2000 U.S. census reported that the population of New Orleans was 484,674; as of June 2006 population estimates ranged from 192,000 (Whoris-key 2006) to 220,000 (Henderson 2006). This drop in population has left New Orleans a smaller and, not incidentally, a whiter place (pre-Katrina New Orleans was 67 percent black; see Edney 2007). This has, in turn, placed stress upon those cities with the largest number of post-Katrina New Orleans citizens, such as Atlanta, Baton Rouge, and Houston. Members of the post-Katrina diaspora — among them those who escaped and those who could not get out prior to the flooding — can be found in all fifty American states. If aid applications to the Federal Emergency Management Agency (FEMA) are any indication, their numbers exceed 1 million displaced people from in or around Louisiana: 1,356,704 as of September 23, 2005 (Ericson, Tse, and Wilgoren 2005).

When Katrina struck it was, of course, equally devastating to the homes of those who left town as to the homes of those who stayed. Thus, whether or not the less mobile (i.e., less financially secure) could get out of town initially, they were eventually forced to leave — forced to experience unchosen mobility — or were trapped when their homes were flooded and ruined. Similarly, those who left in hopes of coming back were forced to relocate when, upon inspection, their homes, too, were condemned. Since the post-Katrina evacuation many more mobile inhabitants have returned; but the large numbers who haven't (250,000-plus) have, due to financial hardship and other debilitating factors, been left immobile in their new diasporic communities. Ironically, then, for the most part it has been New Orleans' least (upwardly) mobile inhabitants who now reside farthest from their pre-Katrina homes. The immobile were made mobile after the storm but in exile seem to have become, again, im-mobilized. Those with the least means have been, literally, blown here and there, powerless in the face of natural, financial, and legislative forces that have decided on their behalf where and how they will move.

The significance of this forced physical dislocation is made especially clear when collective activities requiring local participation occur, such as the first post-Katrina municipal election. Efforts to inform the diaspora about where and when to vote have been harshly criticized as deficient. Indeed, the con-fusion surrounding how to cast votes has been described as a racist effort to squelch the black vote. Representative Barney Frank (D-Mass.) has described the ineffective efforts to include New Orleans' less fortunate residents in cur-rent and future planning efforts "a policy of ethnic cleansing by inaction"

(Dvorak 2006). Of course, one of the more useful tools being used to access individuals displaced by Katrina is the Internet (see Tisserand 2006). However, Internet access (or the lack thereof) by Katrina's diasporic community too often further objectifies the divide that separates mobile from immobile citizens.

Mobility's Speed

Mobility's relationship to power — an issue that inevitably confronts us in the context of this discussion — is explicitly explored in the writings of urban theorist Paul Virilio. For Virilio, mobility and change in the contemporary environment are not novel concepts. Rather, what is significant in our technophilic world is speed. Virilio observes that an everyday experience of speeding up is that things (i.e., the world) become smaller. In this regard Virilio is especially intent on demonstrating and describing the intimate relationship between speed (i.e., hypermobility) and power. Indeed, for Virilio the two are synonymous: "The nature of absolute speed is also to be absolute power" (1999, 17).

Virilio, through his analysis of twentieth-century urbanism, warfare, media, and medical technologies, presents an alarming portrait of our world. In Virilio's eyes, the world is being compelled forward in time by a sort of "technological fundamentalism" that functions as the "religion of those who believe in the absolute power of technology, a ubiquitous, instantaneous, and immediate technology" (Virilio and Armitage 1999, 44). This techno-fundamentalism is bent on eradicating "the gap" between space and time "that used to separate man so unacceptably from his objective" (Virilio 1997, 119). With this goal of abolishing "the gap" increasingly being achieved, hypermobility will have realized its *telos*: to render us fleshy humans disembodied. Finally, then, that apparently disembodied substance known as "information" will be able to flow freely (see Hayles 1999).

While he acknowledges that transportation has been "constantly speeded up too," Virilio observes that the real trajectory of the twentieth century is the increase of the speed of information transmission such that its speed becomes that of "real time" (1997, 36). Once information can be dispatched in "real time," at the "absolute velocity of electromagnetic waves" (1997, 36), all material barriers to mobility disappear, resulting in a world in which overcoming distance becomes unnecessary and falls into obsolescence. For Virilio, "telepresence" (as opposed to Urry's "co-presence") and other virtual technologies have created a world where our sense of earth and sky, material and immaterial has been utterly disoriented: "telecommunication tools, not content to limit extension, . . . are also eradicating all duration, any extension of time in the transmission of messages, images" (1997, 9). He argues that the people (most significantly urban dwellers) who occupy our accelerated, and increasingly physically and digitally mobile societies and cities, by pursuing lives defined by "telepresence" and virtuality, are, in fact, *breeding* physical inaction and willed disability (i.e., immobility).

The hypermobility described by Virilio comes, he warns, with a great cost. He argues that once distances (countries, oceans, continents) can be crossed — virtually if not yet physically — in the blink of an eye, they become insignificant, valueless, giving rise to a world that is "pitiful for all time" (1997, 119). He elaborates:

> From that moment onwards, it is no longer necessary to make any journey: one has already arrived. The consequence of staying in the same place is a sort of Foucauldian imprisonment, but this new type of imprisonment is the ultimate form because it means that the world has been reduced to nothing. The world is reduced, both in terms of surface and extension, to nothing, and this results in a kind of incarceration, in a stasis, which means that it is no longer necessary to go towards the world, to journey, to stand up, to depart, to go to things. Everything is already there. (Virilio and Armitage 1999, 39–40)

Virilio, then, while acknowledging that today's world "no longer has any kind of stability"—that it is "shifting, straddling, gliding away all the time" (1999, 48) — looks not to mobility as its defining characteristic, but to speed, particularly speed's ability to annihilate physical distance and all that with which it comes into contact. But like mobility, this speed he describes as "power itself" is not available to all of us. Instead, speed's uneven distribution creates a pyramidal social structure wherein the higher speeds "belong to the upper reaches of society," while the slower speeds belong to "the bottom" social strata. The wealth pyramid, he goes on to suggest — rich at the top, poor at the bottom — is a "replica" of the velocity (speed) pyramid. Velocity, acceleration, and speed are major political phenomena without which "no understanding of history, and especially history-that-is-in-the-making since the 18th century, is possible" (1999, 35); in sum, "[s]peed and wealth go hand in hand" (1999, 13–14).

Virilio's argument vis à vis mobility is that those persons and entities with a greater capacity for reinvention, transformation, locomotion, transmission, and imagination *within the least amount of time* are those with the greatest amount of power at their disposal. In short, those whose objectives are achieved first win. The role of speed — the capacity to effect change — is, of course, of great consequence in urban environments, particularly those in the midst of an emergency. It is worth considering, then, how speed was and was not applied before, during, and after Hurricane Katrina.

Speed and Desire

The flooding that washed away much of New Orleans was recognized as a potential event for many years. But in the face of this threat the powers that be failed to fortify the levee system and failed to develop a transportation plan that would be able to render mobile New Orleans' most immobile residents. It seems as though the potential urban disaster threatening New Orleans was not sufficient to compel the authorities to prepare adequately for what became a disavowed possibility. Keith Ansell-Pearson (following philosophers Henri Bergson [1998], and Gilles Deleuze and Felix Guattari [1987]) has observed that we err when we observe that the "possible" gives rise to the "actually real"; rather, he observes that our comprehension of the full extent of what might be possible is enabled by our encounter with the actually real. Only when faced with actually real events do we project backward, only then "realizing" that the potential was *actually* (rather than virtually) possible (2002, 72). In everyday language we refer to these "actually possible" events as "risk" and calculate them probabilistically. What happened in New Orleans, then, is an acute example. Whether or not those with the means to act to secure the levies believed (or wanted to believe) in the risks confronting New Orleans, their choice — not to act — was a decision from those in power that, once again, didn't exhibit much speed or mobility at all.[2]

Few would dispute that Hurricane Katrina existed within an American sub-conscious as a sort of disavowed virtual reality. Prior hurricanes had threatened New Orleans; witness the following excerpt from the October 2001 issue of *Scientific American*:

> A major hurricane could swamp New Orleans under 20 feet of water, killing thou-sands. Human activities along the Mississippi River have dramatically increased the risk, and now only massive re-engineering of southeastern Louisiana can save the city. (Fischetti 2001)

And yet it was only when Hurricane Katrina actually appeared physically, only after the bodies became bloated in the rivers that were once streets, that the American populace and administration were compelled, belatedly, to act and to reflect upon the significance of mobility not only for cities at the best of times, but also for cities facing disaster. From an economic point of view, we might remark that the fact that the potential for Hurricane Katrina was ignored is not surprising, given that the risk it represented was not one that could be, literally, capitalized upon by those at the upper echelons of Virilio's pyramid. The risk posed by Katrina threatened (and in turn destroyed) those who were perceived as the expendable of American society, and so there was little urgency to mobilize with speed the powers necessary to prevent the destruction of the city.

The slow response to the foreseeable disaster that was Hurricane Katrina, the apparent disposability of its victims (illustrated by the suggestions by Barbara Bush, the president's mother, that the mostly poor and African American refugees were better off in their displacement — that their disastrous situation was "working very well for them")[3] reveal the difficulty the American administration and its formal and informal representatives had when confronted with the challenge of trying to comprehend and address circumstances that did not suit their interests. In the context of the official response to the Katrina victims, we can see also that the speed, mobility, and spatial compression of our globalized, technologized world, as described by Paul Virilio at least, typically exists only within a space in which that speed is *desired* by those in power to perform or enable it and *applied to accommodate particular interests and agendas*. Speed or hypermobility, when exercised by humans, is speed that is motivated in particular directions and a product of a particular desire. And, as Virilio described above, speed is most pervasively and efficiently (or productively and destructively) deployed by those in positions of power for the sake of the maintenance of this power.

In Virilio's view, the interconnected relationship between speed and power is one of the greatest threats to contemporary humanity. This power-speed assemblage, he suggests, "liquidates you" (2002, 161). If television images of the event are to be believed, Hurricane Katrina's victims were counting on their state and federal aid agencies to provide timely — that is, speedy — help in the wake of the storm. The immobilized folks, pinned down by the storm, swimming in the streets, and suffering inside and outside the Superdome, were expecting to be taken to safety by the mechanisms of mobility they knew were available to their federal government (having, no doubt, watched with awe on television the *uber*-machines deployed by their own military in Gulf Wars I and II). It was precisely on the basis of speed's ability to make the world small that the refugees of New Orleans were expecting a speedy delivery of aid; it was precisely the technologically fortified state, itself a state of speed, on which they were pinning their hopes.

Following Hurricane Katrina television news reports showed hundreds of mostly African Americans chanting, "We need help! We need help!" outside the

Superdome. What was, perhaps, most poignant about these cries was the implied message — the naïve expectation — that there would be, as President Bush suggested, "a lot of help coming" (*BBC News* 2005). These Americans were initially hopeful that they would be well taken care of by their government — the government of the most powerful nation on earth. But this hope soon turned to dismay and anger when "a lot of food, . . . water , . . . boats and choppers" (*BBC News* 2005) did not arrive — were not mobilized — in a timely fashion.

Unfortunately, in this instance those able to exercise speed — those at the top of Virilio's pyramid — were happy to apply it in different directions. The powerful did not desire New Orleans' or Katrina's victims; the mobile was not interested in the immobile. And so speed waited and mobility was left immobile as hundreds of Katrina's most fragile victims suffered a slow death and others underwent unnecessary trauma.

The inaction — the immobility — exhibited during and after Hurricane Katrina was its own sort of action, played out in the face of what Donald Rumsfeld has described as "known knowns."[4] That action — the decision not to fortify the levee system, to invest instead (in the face of real risks) in tax cuts and allegedly illegal wars (*BBC News* 2004) — was not a result of a lack of willpower or desire; rather, this decision — remade repetitively for years — resulted from a very real desire to redirect resources, speed, and technology to sites that would provide more immediate returns on investment. Philosopher Gilles Deleuze tells us that any form of desire "produces" (2004, 232–233). Tragically, the desire that was enacted before and at the moment Katrina hit New Orleans produced death and desolation; the subsequent desire to respond to the disaster with too little urgency produced more death.

As speed continues to be operationalized in some areas but not in others, the "generalized accident" predicted by Virilio — any major catastrophe brought about by a combination of speed and technology, and the tendency of each to connect what were once separate units into interconnected networks — appears to be a result not so much of speed itself, but of its strategic application in some areas and not in others. The horrors exhibited in a contemporary generalized accident like the liquification of New Orleans become a result of both the fast *and* the slow: it seems it is not only speed that kills. But the desire to not apply speed in given situations functions like the proverbial stick in the spokes, to quickly bring to a halt speed and mobility that had been taken for granted.

Conclusion: Mobility's Relationship to Power

In conclusion, the enthusiasm by social and urban theorists for mobility as an apt descriptor for contemporary cities should not go unchallenged. To suggest that mobility is something new, or to observe that the accelerating flux of contemporary globalization has prompted us to attend to theories of mobility is to objectify the degree to which mobilities have been undertheorized in the past. While the speed of contemporary life is indubitably increasing (as described by Virilio), this increase does not make mobility a new phenomenon nor a definitive marker of "the urban." Rather, it is mobility's characteristics, its qualities that demand further investigation; it is mobility's uneven distribution that is increasingly defining life in contemporary cities (such as New Orleans).

Mobility is a concept that is inherently ambiguous, applicable in some instances, but not others. Indeed, its overuse might force us to ask: "What isn't mobility? Isn't everything more or less mobile? And if so, what explanatory power does it have?" Further, as the example of New Orleans before, during, and after Hurricane Katrina demonstrates, it is also slowness and immobility that contribute to what contemporary cities "are." Mobilities and immobilities, speed and slowness are in play in our cities, producing an uneven fabric of opportunities and impediments. To focus the attention on a city's mobilities is to focus exclusively on those at the top of Virilio's pyramid.

Mobility, then, will remain contested terrain both within and beyond academe and the urban. What is certain, however, is that mobility's abilities are in play within macro and micro structures of both power and impotence. Mobilities are means, not ends. Research that focuses on the nature and dynamics of these power structures will be most illuminating in our efforts to come to terms with mobility and immobility in contemporary cities.

Notes

1. For more on the relationship between the virtual and the actual see, for instance, Ansell-Pearson (2002), De Landa (2002), or Massumi (2002).

2. It's worth noting, of course, that often in a capitalist economic system, destruction generates just as much for someone's bottom line as preservation. Witness, for instance, wars as generators of economic activity, or oil spills as opportunities for the companies that clean them up and the work crews that benefit from oil-cleaning employment.

3. "And so many of the people in the arena here, you know, were underprivileged anyway," she said, "so this is working very well for them" (*New York Times* 2005).

4. In the February 12, 2002, Department of Defense news briefing, Donald Rumsfeld said: "As we know, there are known knowns; there are things we know we know. We also know there are known unknowns; that is to say, we know there are some things we do not know. But there are also unknown unknowns, the ones we don't know we don't know. And if one looks throughout the history of our country and other free countries, it is the latter category that tends to be the difficult one."

PART FOUR

MEMORIES

Part 4 introduces an interdisciplinary vein of cultural thought to our discussions of urban development, geography, disaster recovery, and city governance. This part deals primarily with the third of Mumford's perspectives on "what is a city?" presented in the opening chapter: the city as a site of history and culture. These chapters stress that the city is a human site of remembering, without which history is but dusty trivia, and without which repair and "re"-construction would be impossible. As Daina Harvey argues in the next chapter, New Orleans, post-Katrina, highlights the uniquely human process of recalling and retelling as well as forgetting as an *urban* activity, as an integral part of urban culture as well as of the materiality of cities.

We subject memories to tests of truth and routinely demand that those who reminisce provide verification. This is an indicator of not only the fragility of memory but the importance we attach to its accuracy. For, like the past (what was once actually real), a memory is virtual, even if it is no longer actual or tangible (see Shields 2003). Memory is not just cerebral nor simply an abstract representation. Rather, it is an ideal aspect of the real that must be worked up, enacted, or performed each time it is recalled.

Urban Trauma and Racialized Trauma

In New Orleans, memory is forevermore overlit with trauma. Psychological trauma occurs when an experience overwhelms the individual's ability to integrate ideas and emotions into his or her familiar ideas about the world or about what persons or institutions can be depended upon. The resulting confusion or insecurity can produce a feeling of helplessness that persists even when the physical threat

Collapsed church, Lower Ninth Ward.
Photograph by Jacob A. Wagner; image courtesy of the photographer.

has passed, often leading to a loss of self-esteem and confidence. The ensuing sense of alienation and depression, often inexplicable to the sufferer, can further lead to self-destructive and antisocial behaviors.

At one level, trauma is experienced individually, as by the protagonist in Fernando Lara's essay that appears in the introduction to part 2. However, trauma is also a social and symbolic condition. New Orleans is a "traumatic landscape" that has become a symbol for a range of injuries and losses (Kirmayer 1996, Crang and Travlou 2001). Hurricane Katrina and its aftermath have been a source of "urban trauma."

In the eighteen months following the hurricane, New Orleans became an exemplar for a debate on "racialized trauma" among psychologists and social work professionals (Carter 2007, Bryant-Davis 2007). As previous chapters have made clear, the trauma of Katrina and of subsequent decisions regarding where (and where not) to rebuild has fallen disproportionately on the city's African American residents. Some lost belongings, others lost loved ones, others their homes, and still others lost entire communities. The impact on an already disadvantaged community raises sociological questions that go beyond the different psychologies of trauma experienced by individuals. Charges of racism have been common in the months since Katrina.

Clinically, "racialized trauma" refers to measurable posttraumatic stress among those who experience discrimination or lack of cultural recognition (Loo et al. 2001). Located at the intersection of ethnicity, race, and psychology, racialized trauma alerts us to longer-term psychosocial issues that are expressed in the behavior and performance of affected populations. The reconstruction of postdisaster cities thus entails addressing not only direct losses of material objects and economic opportunities, but inequalities and perceptions of comparative injustices in those losses. Inasmuch as these perceptions are based in racial communities or neighborhoods, the response also needs to be at the level of collectives — not so much individual therapy as public rituals of healing; not so much individual repair as the rebuilding of neighborhoods. Some examples might be found in New Orleans' own traditions, such as jazz funeral marches and second lines that orchestrate a collective mourning, or in sod-turning or ribbon-cutting rituals for new buildings and projects that materially demonstrate the return of "normality," the reestablishment of community, or the resolution of conflict or social failures that had contributed to the disaster.

Exile and Memory

The following chapters present approaches to memory, forgetting, and loss that are relevant to all of these different forms of trauma and how individuals and communities deal with them. In addition to the racialized trauma of loss, a related trauma of displacement is likely being experienced by the diaspora of New Orleans residents who, having been evacuated to random, distant cities and having no homes or even neighborhoods to return to, are left with only memories. Trauma is generally inarticulable except as obsessive storytelling in an attempt to "gain access to a traumatic history" (Caruth 1995, 156; see also Jackson 2002). Although this history is not forgotten, neither is it directly accessible. It is a haunting more than an immediate presence. Will Katrina's diaspora demand that a reconstructed New Orleans acknowledge in its (re-) built environment the suffering of displaced and former residents (Burgin 1996)? For children of exiled survivors, "although they have not themselves lived through the trauma of banishment and the destruction of home, [they can] remain always marginal or exiled, always in the Diaspora. 'Home' is always elsewhere" (Hirsch 1996, 662). What of New Orleans' scattered children? The stock of memories of New Orleans has been dislocated from the Delta not only into the media but into the diaspora. While disaster destroys family, neighbor-hood, and community — the thresholds between self and other — storytelling, which may be in the form of public monuments, reintegrates and rebalances the relationship between self and society, private and public. It "retraces one's steps" (Jackson 2002, 245) and allows performative enactments that actualize a given memory or trauma.

Debates over the reconstruction of some inner-city neighborhoods as themed tourist areas reflect the desire to rebuild not just a way of life but an everyday "emotional universe" that was uniquely urban, New Orleans–style (Baum 2000, 93). The risk is that residents' lives, communities, and memo-ries will be forgotten and replaced with a synthesized history made for tour-ist entertainment (see chapter 7). Other urban expressions of remembrance may involve preserved ruins or symbolic objects and landscapes from before or during a disaster. These "object survivors" are indexes of trauma that dem-onstrate that the loss was of something real and tangible, even though virtual and intangible memories may be all that is left for many survivors (Liss 2000; see also chapter 8).

In chapter 1, Steinberg referred to Mumford's perspective on the city as a culture hearth wherein "time becomes visible" (Mumford 1938, 4). In the process, however, time also is selectively remembered, forgotten, frozen, and reenacted in a frenzy of symbols, meanings, and political struggles. In the two chapters that follow, we investigate how these struggles for meaning are being waged within individual New Orleanians' minds as well as in competing re-construction proposals.

CHAPTER SEVEN

Remembering the Forgetting of New Orleans

Daina Cheyenne Harvey

The urban trauma inflicted upon New Orleans has unambiguously reminded us that certain spaces in the city are more vulnerable than others, not only physically but also discursively. Climatic events like Katrina push marginalized spaces into the view of the larger society. These events force us to try and understand spaces and places that we have been socialized to ignore or have long ago forgotten. Every urban area has these types of spaces, but New Orleans, perhaps because of its unique topography (Colten 2000, 2005) or its history, seems to have more of these types of spaces than other American cities. The devastation of these spaces reveals a facet of urbanism that has long been ignored: the crisis of urban memory (Crinson 2005).

Unlike the symbolic violence that urban trauma inflicts on the culture of cities (Lash and Urry 1994), the assault on the memory of the city largely goes unnoticed. In part the crisis of memory is represented not only by the surfeit of memory, but also its abeyance. That is, spaces in the city tend to reflect the dominant mnemonic community (Zerubavel 1997) while allowing us to forget or marginalize others. We thus end up not only with urban amnesia, which we witnessed in New Orleans in the days after Katrina, where entire urban populations were forgotten, we also lose spaces of memory that are important for the culture of our cities. Consequently a discussion of who has rights over the memory of the city must be had along with the discussion of who has the right to the city (Lefebvre 1996).

The crisis of urban memory is not entirely new. Eric Avila (1998), for example, has documented attempts to obliterate and resuscitate Hispanic memory in Los Angeles, while Kirp, Dwyer, and Rosenthal (1995) have done the same with black memory in Camden, New Jersey. As both demonstrate, certain groups control spaces of memory to the detriment of "others," and when urban spaces are destroyed the memory of those spaces is often obliterated as well. Rarely, however, do we witness discussions over the reproduction of place from mnemonic tropes (Harvey 2006a) or urban imagery (Holt 2000) on the scale that we are seeing in New Orleans.

New Orleans provides us with a unique opportunity to reevaluate the urban and the analytical tools that we use to understand the space of the city. First, New Orleans does not fit well in most urban models, and for that reason has often been left out of urban analysis (Hirsch and Logsdon 1992). Although New Orleans is a port city (see chapter 4 in this book by Rob Shields), it is not a postmetropolis (Soja 1997, 2000), an edge city (Garreau 1991), or a creative city (Florida 2002, 2003), nor does it fit into the LA School's focus on sprawl and postmodern urbanism (Byrne 2001, Clarke 1997, Ellin 1996, Davis 1990, Dear 2002b, Soja 1989). And while an analysis rooted in the political economy approach would be useful, it would ultimately miss the crucial symbolic and mnemonic dimensions of the city.[1] Second, its spaces are marked by what Jacob Wagner in chapter 10 of this book terms "creole urbanism." Wagner notes the city's unique street culture, where public and private space continually collapse onto one another, a phenomenon largely missing from other U.S. cities. Wagner also observes that New Orleans is punctuated by diverse cultural spaces that reference its unique creole heritage; the city's urban history is unlike any other in the United States. Third, New Orleans, for the most part, bypassed the first two phases of urban renewal that swept the Northeast and Midwest (Gotham 2001a). Although urban renewal has been used to supplant black space with land uses favored by the city's white-led business establishment — for example, the destruction of antisegregationist Homer Plessy's residence for the building of an interstate highway — many of the buildings and spaces that symbolize historically marginalized communities remain in New Orleans' cityscape (Medley 2000).

Urban traumas like Hurricane Katrina have the potential to form and deform space and spatial relations in a manner similar to that of urban renewal. State authorities in New Orleans were using space as a means of social control long before the destruction wrought by Katrina (Gotham 2001b). Just as many have feared in the aftermath of Katrina, the authorities have imposed "abstract space," the potential of space as seen by developers, to supplant "social space," the existential dimension of space as lived by community members (see chapter 9 of this book by C. Tabor Fisher). Not only has this trauma been seized as an opportunity to change the imagery and materiality of these spaces, but the memory of these spaces as well. Urban traumas provide the opportunity to remove memories from space. An integral component to the story of urban renewal, which unfortunately has been seriously neglected, is the ability to destroy or replace memory. The processes of forgetting and remembering in the city, of investing in certain memories and de-investing in the memories of others, has been overlooked in urban analysis.

The rest of this chapter is an initial step toward rectifying that omission. The following section focuses on spaces of memory that become problematic after urban traumas. The next section, entitled "New Orleans' Mnemonic Battles," looks at how various mnemonic communities (Zerubavel 1997) are already competing for the memory of New Orleans. In that section I discuss the city as a site of collective memory and look at how two New Orleans neighborhoods, Gentilly and Broadmoor, are balancing remembering and forgetting.[2] I end with a brief discussion of what I call "mnemonic triage."

Of course, urban memory is not the only question being asked in the context of New Orleans' reconstruction. However, other questions, many of which center on poverty, race, the shortcomings of various administrators, or the possibility that many of the New Orleans diaspora will not, or perhaps should not return, intersect with the question of urban memory, as residents, planners, and politicians offer their visions of what New Orleans was and what it can (or should) be. Thus, in this chapter, I consider urban memory as a critical point in the dialogue that seeks answers to all the questions that hover over competing visions for New Orleans in particular and cities more generally.

The City and Memory: Remembering and Forgetting

SPACES OF AMNESIA

Urban traumas provide an opportunity to parse the space of the city, and in particular spaces of collective memory within the city, because of the vulnerability of such spaces and memories at that time. The most troubling spaces of memory are spaces of amnesia — spaces that have fallen out of the collective memory. Some examples of spaces of amnesia include Kracauer's "streets without memory" or the spaces of the poor (alleys, abandoned buildings, etc.) that we are socialized to ignore (Gotham 2003, Gotham and Brumley 2002). Other examples include spaces of slavery in the North which have been "disowned" (Melish 1998) by both the black and white mnemonic communities in an attempt to accept the mnemonic trope of southern enslavement and northern abolitionism (Harvey 2006b). Hesse (1997, 87) writes of a "white amnesia" in urban places where whites forget about the spaces of the "other." This is part of the "racing of space" (Mills 1997, Omi and Winant 1994, Wacquant and Wilson 1989) where space becomes reflexively understood as representing the individuals who inhabit it. As Mills writes, "Space must be normed and raced at the macrolevel (entire countries and continents), [and at] the local level (city neighborhoods)" (1997, 43–44). The norming and racing of space allows us to invest in remembering certain spaces and forgetting others.

Perhaps the space of New York City's World Trade Center provides the best example of where urban trauma removes memory from space. After September 11, 2001, the memory of the space as "Little Syria" or "Radio Row" is no longer engaged; neither the imagery of the space nor the collective memory of this space as anything other than a referent to 9/11 exists.[3]

As witnessed in the days immediately before and after Katrina, New Orleans has a number of spaces of amnesia. Despite having the highest concentration of historical structures in the country (Connolly 2005), mnemonic myopia — the tendency to forget the distant past and remember the recent past (Zerubavel 2003) — marks New Orleans. President Bush standing in front of Jackson Square "waiting for life and hope to return" (White House 2005) surely constrains the memory of the space as a site where slaves were hanged for civil disobedience.[4] Spaces such as these are spaces of forgetting. Either by intentionally removing objects in the space or the space itself from the collective memory, as when slave cabins are removed from plantations so tourists will not attend to the memory of slaves (Eichstedt and Small 2002), or simply forgotten over a period of time, such as the Native space replaced by New Orleans, these spaces become increasingly problematic after urban trauma as mnemonic layering further pushes the memory of these spaces down and ultimately out of our collective memory.

SPACES OF ANAMNESIS

The removal of objects from the space, an attempt to change the memory of that space, paradoxically might restore the memory of the space to the collective. This type of mnemonic space is a space of anamnesis (Curtis 2004, Lyotard 2004), where forgetting reminds us to remember. As Gilloch and Kilby note, "[t]he void is also a mnemonic" (2005, 6). The winning design for the World Trade Center site, aptly named "Reflecting Absence," is designed, in the words of the architects Michael Arad and Peter Walker, to evoke the memory of the Towers by creating a void, an absence in the city. Thus just as the removal of slave cabins on plantations might actually provide the opportunity for some tourists to "remember" the existence of slaves on the plantation, the removal of objects or space from the city might provide a reason to remember the space. If the Ninth Ward and other everyday, unmarked black spaces are not rebuilt, whatever replaces them will certainly be located in a space of anamnesis. The void or whatever replaces the original will serve as a "mnemonic prompt." Places such as Madame John's Legacy, which survived the citywide fire of 1794, making it the second-oldest building in the Mississippi Valley, lead us to reflect on their surroundings and prompt us to both remember and wonder what has been removed in the city through previous disasters. Hence spaces of anamnesis need not reference marked spaces; they can reference the everyday, taken for granted, apperceived space.[5] Likewise, the unmarking of space might actually serve to mark the space. The removal of objects from space during urban trauma allows some people to "see" spaces in the city that had previously not been "seen."

ASEMIOTIC SPACES

Most spaces in the city are treated as semiotic. The city as such exists as a "communication machine," conveying representational content and affecting representational contexts (Borer 2006). Treating space as semiotic, however, reduces urban analysis to the understanding of signs. In the city as a sign there is a "process of absorption of signs and absorption by signs . . . There is no longer any contradiction within being, or any problematic of being and appearance. . . . What characterizes this society is the absence of reflection" (Baudrillard 1998, 191–192). We cease to reflect on the memory of space because the space is what it is. By contrast, asemiotic spaces do not explicitly reference the objects in their space. Asemiotic spaces break down the cartography of memory. Urban theory that utilizes semiotic spaces treats these spaces as hard spaces. The mnemonic referent point, the meaning of the space, is dictated. An ideal type of a semiotic space would be the iconical statue or monument accompanied by a placard that fixes the memory of the space. While counter-memory is possible (where the space is seized by multiple mnemonic communities), it is not likely. On the other hand, we can view polysemic spaces as soft spaces of memory. The space is supersaturated with memory and hence references multiple memories. Asemiotic spaces, however, are neither hard nor soft and yet both. They are discursively nondiscursive, difficult to explain and yet understood intuitively. Asemiotic spaces are the spaces of sounds, smells, nonhaptic sensations. It is the confluence of these spaces, the aggregate of these spaces, that mnemonically distinguish urban spaces from other spaces in the city or the city itself from other cities. The sticky smell of pralines, the sounds of Mardi Gras, the omnipresent jazz, the sights of crawfish, the warm breeze coming off of the Mississippi, and the bricolage style of its architecture all reference New Orleans and yet do not signify any particular space. These asemiotic spaces denote the memory of New Orleans because "the city is not only a language but also a practice" (Lefebvre 1996, 143).

New Orleans' Mnemonic Battles

The "trauma of the present" (Bhabha 1994) allows us to remember, and re-membering allows us to comprehend the present trauma. That we remember the city and spaces in the city in different ways, perhaps even more so after a major urban trauma, should not surprise anyone. Ultimately the city is not only a city, but "the city is *many* cities and . . . place-positionality" matters (Westwood and Williams 1997, 6). Multiple groups inhabit the space of the city and each group has its own memory. These groups are what Eviatar Zerubavel (1997) terms mnemonic communities — communities of memory. As he points out, because of the vast "web of sociomental affiliations" (1997, 17), we are members of multiple collectivities, each with its own history, its own way of thinking, and its own memory. Urban traumas have a way of re-vealing not only membership in specific mnemonic communities, but also the battles for memory that occur between different mnemonic communities. These mnemonic battles (Zerubavel 1997) can be subtle, as in the case of the memory of Abraham Lincoln (Schwartz 2000) which evolved over time, or quite direct, as revealed by Jeffrey Olick (2005) in his work on how during the fall of Germany various groups debated how Nazi Germany would be remembered. The mnemonic battles for spaces in New Orleans will undoubt-edly be both subtle and direct, and only time will tell exactly which spaces in New Orleans will be remembered and which ones forgotten, but the contours of these mnemonic battles are already being revealed. In this section, I briefly examine mnemonic battles involving two neighborhoods in New Orleans, Gentilly and Broadmoor, and show how these battles are constructed from understanding space through the cognitive processes of remembering and forgetting.[6]

GENTILLY

Jerold S. Kayden, co-chairman of the urban planning and design depart-ment at Harvard University's Graduate School of Design, says of New Orleans, "In a true sense, physically, in certain parts of the city, there is a tabula rasa, which raises the question of whether there's anything left of a real memory" (Dunlap 2005). The relationship between presence and absence is central to many mnemonic battles in New Orleans' neighborhoods, and we often hear sentiments about memory similar to those made by Professor Kayden. Senator Landrieu likewise says of New Orleans, "There are places that are no longer there" (Dunlap 2005). Kayden and Landrieu seem to be saying that presence marks memory and absence signifies a mnemonic void, yet those familiar with certain spaces in New Orleans' neighborhoods know that memory rests on more than simply presence and absence.

Jen, a tour operator and resident of the Lakeview neighborhood, explains that the relationship between spaces of remembering and spaces of forgetting is in flux in Gentilly. She remarks, "It is sometimes difficult to tell what is being remembered and what is being forgotten. In Gentilly, paradoxically what is present is what has been forgotten and what is absent is what is being remembered." As we ride through Gentilly Jen points out empty green lots and explains that in most instances they signify a space where someone has torn down their home in order to rebuild. Those homes that are untouched have for the most part been abandoned or forgotten. Ben Wilson, a member of Dartmouth College's MOSAIC Project, which is using GIS imaging technology with the residents of Gentilly to map the recovery of the neighborhood, echoes Jen's remarks. He notes that the project color-codes areas that have been remembered — spaces that have been gutted — and areas that have been forgotten — spaces that remain untouched, to give the neighborhood "spatial meaning" (*Dartmouth News* 2006). As Jen and Ben Wilson both realize, spatial meaning revolves around both amnesia and anamnesis — presence and absence. Spaces of memory in the neighborhoods throughout Gentilly drift back and forth, from remembering to forgetting. Unlike other mnemonic battles, the battles in Gentilly do not so much center on *how* to remember as on *what* to remember and on *whether* to remember at all.

The desire to rebuild Gentilly from memory is strong. Reflecting on why residents of Orleans Parish might rebuild according to what they remember, University of Pennsylvania professor of urbanism Witold Rybcznyski notes, "We generally rebuild more or less what was there. . . . The reasons for this . . . [are] sentimental: the urge to recreate what had been destroyed, to rebuild the world we knew" (Dunlap 2005). This desire may be particularly strong in Gentilly because its pre-Katrina population was significantly older than the city average, so the living mnemonic community here is typically older than elsewhere. Commenting on this mnemonic divide, Jessie Perry, a resident of Gentilly for over forty years, points out the central battle in Gentilly: "The older people all want to come back, but the younger people don't want to come back and deal with the hassle" (Ritea 2006). For Perry and other Gentilly residents, bridging the memory of pre- and post-Katrina will be difficult, but not as difficult as it would be for those who do not feel that they are part of the mnemonic community.

Those involved with the rebuilding of Gentilly want the neighborhood to be remembered (and thus rebuilt) as the quintessential New Orleans neighborhood. While many other neighborhoods that have received attention in the media were predominantly white (such as Lakeview) or black (such as the Lower Ninth Ward), those familiar with Gentilly claim that its importance lies in that pre-Katrina it mirrored the socioeconomic demographics of New Orleans (Gentilly Project). They thus want to rebuild Gentilly so that the future and the past are mnemonically connected.

Part of establishing the mnemonic continuity of the neighborhood is recognizing the asemiotic spaces. For Harry Eves, a resident of Gentilly for nearly fifty years, the memory of Gentilly revolves around the sights and sounds of the neighborhood — practices that could perhaps describe many American communities, but for Eves and other residents set Gentilly apart. For Eves the memory of Gentilly coalesces around sweet peppers, beans, and flowers: "[I] used to pass them out all over the neighborhood," he remembers (Ritea 2006). It is not the memory of the peppers or beans or flowers themselves, however, that marks Gentilly, but the practice of exchanging them with neighbors. Eves goes on to note other neighborhood practices, such as collecting money for flowers when someone in the community dies. For Eves, it is not so much objects but asemiotic practices and relationships that serve as "scaffolds for memory" (see the following chapter in this book by Elizabeth Spelman).

BROADMOOR

Mayor Nagin and the now-aborted rebuilding plans of the Bring New Orleans Back Commission originally envisioned Broadmoor being reborn as a park. During an unveiling of future New Orleans neighborhoods, they presented a map that featured Broadmoor partially covered by a green dot (G. Russell 2006). Essentially Nagin and the commission were asking former residents to try and forget Broadmoor by putting something new in its place. In an attempt to save Broadmoor from becoming a space of anamnesis, the Broadmoor Improvement Association rallied residents by the hundreds for community meetings (G. Russell 2006).

As in Gentilly, however, spaces of memory in Broadmoor are in flux. "For Sale" signs are creeping reminders of forgetting, but are countered by "Rebuilding to stay" signs marking memory (*Times Picayune* July 28, 2006). As we ride through Broadmoor Jen reminds us that FEMA trailers are actually a welcomed sight — as they also signify a desire to return and hence not forget. As in Gentilly, part of the mnemonic battle is between "newcomers and natives" (J. Russell 2006). Longtime Broadmoor resident and community activist Hal Roark, commenting on the difference between those who are new to Broadmoor and those who have called it home for some time, says, "We see the neighborhood differently. . . . They see the blight, and we see what will be — the gardens and palm trees that will come back" (J. Russell 2006). Roark and others want to use the memory of Broadmoor as a guide for the future. One of the mottos of the neighborhood is "Broadmoor, better than before" (J. Russell 2006).

Still the battle not to forget goes on in Broadmoor. When residents discovered that the estimate to repair the local branch of the New Orleans library was $3.7 million they took the inflated figure as a calculated message urging them to move on. Susan Ratterree, a resident of Broadmoor, says, "They're telling us we should just give up" (J. Russell 2006). Susan and other residents of Broadmoor do not want to give up or forget, nor do they want others to forget about them. When $5 million had been pledged to help rebuild the neighborhood of Broadmoor, the leaders of the Broadmoor Improvement Association tried to silence (which would most likely lead to forgetting) the news of the gift, fearing that wide publicity would keep other potential donors from focusing on their neighborhood (Nolan 2006).

Broadmoor itself has become the symbol for remembering and forgetting. Jen looks out onto the streets of Broadmoor and says, "Broadmoor is the bottom of the bowl that is New Orleans. A lot of people outside of Broadmoor think that if Broadmoor is being rebuilt, why not my neighborhood, and others think if Broadmoor is being rebuilt that we can [rebuild] too." Broadmoor is thus becoming both a source of conflict and identity. Josh McIlwain, who helped to craft the original plan for the Bring New Orleans Back Commission, notes that this mental ordering of space, which privileges certain spaces over others, while somewhat inevitable, might end up ruining both the city and the neighborhood of Broadmoor: "Rather than pull together to say how do we design a city that we can all live in . . . they're simply saying 'I want my neighborhood back, the hell with you'" (Goldberg 2006). The result, as McIlwain points out, is that "each of these little neighborhoods will Balkanize the city . . . and be left with a city that can't support them" (Goldberg 2006). Essentially Jen and Josh McIlwain are recognizing the same point. Mnemonic battles can easily become cognitive battles as conflicts over memory give way to conflicts over perception and focus.

Mnemonic Triage

What we remember and consequently forget is determined by social frames. Society, implicitly and explicitly, largely determines what is relevant and what is irrelevant. That which society deems relevant is framed, and that which is not relevant is pushed to the margins (or even out) of the frame. Although, as individuals, we can ultimately distort these frames, remembering that which we are encouraged to forget or what the collective seems to have forgotten, we tend to take for granted both the norms of remembering and the sociomental signposts that help us to remember (Gross 2000, Zerubavel 2003).

This process of social framing is essentially one of triage. Societies (and of course groups) sort out the past, present, and even future into categories of meaning, in a process of "mnemonic triage." Mnemonic triage involves cognitively matching our social schemata with the past. That which is not remembered is that which does not fit into the schemata and that which challenges the schemata. Although our social schemata are developed over generations (see Zerubavel's [2003] mnemonic traditions), traumas can alter schemata. Alongside the *spatial* triage that is now taking place in New Orleans, as the city decides which structures merit demolition and which merit repair, *mnemonic* triage is occurring. Families like the Perrys of Gentilly and the Roarks of Broadmoor are deciding whether or not to return; ultimately they are deciding whether or not to start new memories elsewhere or to establish mnemonic continuity with the past.

What I have tried to demonstrate in this chapter is that, first, space is important for constructing social frames. As Spelman also notes in the chapter that follows, space can work as both the framework and the repository for memory, through the mnemonic communities that are formed by spatial relationships. Second, urban trauma can both form and deform our schemata. The contours of the mnemonic communities and of the process of managing space in Gentilly and Broadmoor (and elsewhere in New Orleans) are slowly being revealed. Through blogs (like Gentilly Girl or Gentilly Project), community forums (GNOCDC.org, GCIA.us, nolarp.com, broadmoorimprovement.com), and town meetings, and, of course, on the ground, space is being constructed through memory. The way that we remember and think about New Orleans is dynamic, and this dynamism both reflects and impacts the dynamic space of the city.

As James Donald notes, "The city is not a problem that can be solved" (1997, 182), nor can we hope to solve all the problems of the city by rebuilding it. At best we can be mindful of the memories of the city and the spaces of memory in the city and use those as starting points for rebuilding. The memory of the city is fragmented and homogenous, fleeting and obdurate, memorialized and eschewed. We must realize that we are mnemonically socialized (Zerubavel 2003) both to remember and to forget. Marc Augé (2004) tells us that remembering and forgetting are the ways in which we manage time. In New

Orleans we are now seeing that they are also the ways in which we manage space.

Notes

1. For an excellent comparison of the political economy and postmodern approaches to urban theory, see Gotham (2001b) or Borer (2006).

2. Although I use individual voices and thus reference individual memories, it is the intersubjective or collective memory of neighborhood residents that I am interested in. In order to establish the intersubjective, this narrative weaves back and forth from discussions of space to members of specific communities.

3. The memory of the space as "Little Syria" — an Arab space within the United States — would have been particularly problematic as the site was being constructed as a quintessentially "American" (and hence non-Arab) space attacked by Arabs from the outside. Memories of the site as "Little Syria" were fading anyway, due to the 1960s urban development plan under which the World Trade Center was constructed, but it seems likely that, even if this memory had persisted, it would have been suppressed after the attacks because of its fundamental incompatibility with the memory of the site as one attacked by Arabs.

4. Although individual accounts are difficult to come by as they obviously constrain the space as it is commemorated today, the best-known case is that of Jean Saint Malo, who was hanged on June 19, 1784.

5. Wayne Brekhus's (1998) conceptualization of the marked and unmarked, while not spatial in its orientation, has a great deal of potential for spatial analysis. Brekhus calls for a sociology of the unmarked, an examination of default categories that are usually taken for granted, i.e., "whiteness" in race or "maleness" in gender studies.

6. Part of the data for this section comes from accounts of the neighborhoods in various newspapers. The decision to focus on these two neighborhoods comes from my knowledge of the area, as a New Orleans native, as someone who conducted research prior to Katrina in and around New Orleans, and as someone with relatives in New Orleans neighborhoods (some of whom were left homeless by Katrina). Additional data is from a bus tour I took of the city on February 3, 2007. Although the tour was designed to focus on the effects of and responses to Hurricane Katrina, it was nonetheless very similar to tours of the city I had previously taken as part of my ongoing research on representations and memories of New Orleans. Our driver and guide were both from New Orleans and still live in the city. In addition both had worked for the tour company before Hurricane Katrina. I spoke with the guide, Jen (not her real name), intermittently during the tour.

Repair and the Scaffold of Memory

Elizabeth V. Spelman

Belongings

In early December 2005, residents of New Orleans' Ninth Ward were allowed back into their neighborhoods long enough to take a look at what remained of their homes and their belongings. As has been well remarked, the pattern of damage left in the wake of Katrina was not simply a reflection of the way Nature took its course. The condition of the levees and drainage systems, along with the history of a skewed distribution of social and economic resources, clearly was a crucial factor. Still, the scenes of destruction and devastation offered raw evidence of the furious impersonality of the storm. Its broad leveling of homes and other dwellings has rendered almost unrecognizable not just one or two places, as would be the case in intentional bombing of a specific building, for example, but huge patches of the Gulf Coast.

At the same time, such relative impersonality hardly obscured the particularity of people's losses, or the intimacy of their relation to their belongings. Widely published photographs have allowed us to view, for example, the latex glove–covered hands of Mr. Louis Simmons, holding the mud-soaked wallet he had left behind in his rush to reach safety. We had a glimpse of Ms. Josephine Butler, who spent a good part of her allotted time looking through the rubble of what remained of her home for the stone "guardian angel" she had hoped might protect the house her husband had built. And we could see Ms. Sandy Pritchett as she returned to gaze upon what was left of the house in which she had spent the entire forty-five years of her life (Sontag 2005).

I've referred to the "intimacy" of people's relation to their belongings, and such a term might not seem quite right in this context. After all, a returning inhabitant — Mrs. Mary Molizone, who had lived the last forty of her seventy-eight years in what is now probably a toxic house — took a look at what was left and said, "It's all just material things" (Sontag 2005). Perhaps that is so. But under the circumstances such a response may well be a useful emergency

Mr. Louis Simmons and his mud-soaked wallet. Photograph by Vincent Laforet; image courtesy of *The New York Times*/Redux.

borrowing of stoicism that Mrs. Molizone only recently came to endorse, something that complements and underscores her relief at simply being alive. In any event her assessment—"It's all just material things"—is at odds with what we otherwise have reason to acknowledge to be the crucial relation between people and the place-defining objects by which they are surrounded — including, in that revealing term, their belongings.

Indeed, there are many powerful descriptions of the loss of a sense of belonging when one's belongings have been so damaged as to be unable to help maintain continuity with one's past. Among such accounts is that by Hans Erich Nossack in his book *The End*, only very recently published in English translation. The firebombing of Hamburg in July 1943 reduced the city to rubble, and that meant not simply that no familiar landmarks remained, but that Nossack and the others lost all their belongings and thereby irreplaceable precious links to their pasts (Anderson 2005). In Nossack's case this meant the utter lack of connection to his favorite musical recordings and twenty-five years' worth of diaries. Here is Nossack, on his return to the area where his house had been: "What surrounded us did not remind us in any way of what was lost. It had nothing to do with it. It was something else, it was strangeness itself, it was the essentially not possible" (Nossack 2004, 37). A statement like this illustrates not a fetishistic attachment to commodities but the bewilderment and confusion likely to occur in the complete absence of the kind of objects in one's world that provide a sense of place and orientation to that place over time.

One can, of course, be surrounded by things and by people and yet feel as if one is nowhere (sometimes that is just what one might desire, if offered the choice — for example, the impersonality and nowhere/anywhere feel of a motel, rather than the forced intimacy and cozy particularity of a bed-and-breakfast). Part of what makes us feel as if we are somewhere, some particular place, is our having an intimate relation not only to people but to things.[1] As we make place for and give place to things, they give place to us.

For example, as this poem by Richard Jones makes vivid, in our very use of things we make demands upon them and they in turn make certain demands upon us.

> "Things"
> I go to a dimly lit second-hand store
> to lift empty champagne glasses
> and open dusty drawers.
> I buy the broken chair
> and dedicate myself
> to its new life.
> I leave with the chipped vase,
> the cracked violin, the yellowed lace.
>
> I go to bright department stores
> where aisles of merchandise
> sing their songs
> beneath fluorescent lights —
> desks, sofas, picture frames
> asking for a reason to exist,
> demanding our secrets, our love,
> every thing demanding
> everything of my life. (Jones 2000, 83)

Jones's poem suggests a variety of ways in which things become our belongings and we become theirs. Unlike the unbought items in the department stores, objects in the secondhand store (note the reference to human relationship built into such a phrase) once had been among someone's *belongings*. We don't know why they ceased to be such. Maybe they were no longer important enough to their former owners to have seemed worth keeping, or maybe they were the last sweet possessions of someone who just had to have the cash that might have come from selling them. Perhaps the *demands* they put upon their former owners were too strong, or too weak, to be kept among the owners' belongings. In any event both the used and the new objects are presented as lacking the kind of life they would have were they among the current belongings of the narrator. Nossack speaks of such life in recalling irreplaceable photographs and dolls: "These things have their life from us, because at some time we bestowed our affection on them; they absorbed our warmth and harbored it gratefully in order to enrich us with it again in meager hours. We were responsible for them; they could only die with us. And now they stood on the other side of the abyss in the fire and cried after us, begging: Don't leave us!" (26).

What the Ninth Ward returnees were specifically searching for as they came back to the sites where they used to live were neither the discarded belongings of others, in need of renewed life, nor new things offering new demands (which, of course, is not to deny that returnees might welcome such new or secondhand objects). Still, Jones's poem, like Nossack's anguish, invites us to consider that what might be left of the evacuees' belongings — a wallet, a stone animal, a child's sports trophy — are now in the position of renewing life, of reviving people's connection to their lives before Katrina. That such objects have such potential speaks to our relationship to belongings we do have, to what happens to us and to them in the course of that relationship, and to what happens to us and to them when that relationship is ruptured.

This is what Dennis Hastert, Speaker of the U.S. House of Representatives, and Barbara Bush, wife of President George Bush and mother of President George W. Bush, refused to understand or insisted on denying (no doubt they would acknowledge it in their own lives) in their cruel casual comments about what they apparently saw only as the wasteland of New Orleans and the Gulf Coast. House Speaker Hastert figured that "a lot of that place could be bulldozed." According to Barbara Bush, First Lady turned First Mother, the mascot of compassionate conservatism, surely it was a kind of blessing to be able to assemble in the womb of the Houston Astrodome, away from what she apparently could only imagine to be all that mess, all that poverty (Biguenet 2005b).

Dennis Hastert and Barbara Bush spoke as if the evacuees were people who had pasts that were not worth preserving, as if for the evacuees starting *de novo* could only be something positive. Though it was not only African Americans about whose homes and belongings they spoke with such arrogant facility, one can hear in such remarks echoes of nineteenth-century attitudes among slavery's apologists and their abettors in the medical world about the harsh conditions of labor and the routine breaking up of slave families — that some people just don't suffer as much as others, are barely susceptible to physical or emotional pain, aren't really affected by the rupture of ties to people or place or things (Pernick 1985).

It does nothing to exculpate Hastert and Bush to point out that there are broader forces at work than mean-spiritedness and suspiciously selective lack of empathy behind the failure to appreciate the significance of place and of objects that orient us to place over time. The contributors to this anthology include some of the hearty and growing posse of anthropologists, geographers, and other assorted social theorists who have been laboring in recent years to bring attention to the role of place in human existence. The necessity for doing so stems in part from the fact that it has been useful for certain human purposes to be able to conceive of place in abstraction from our complex sensory and emotional connection to it — for example, to be able to describe New Orleans in terms of its location on a map or with the aid of other objective parameters. We can agree that its latitude and longitude are 30.07 N and 80.9 W (or thereabouts, depending on the source); that it is 1,937 miles, or 3,118 kilometers, or 1,684 nautical miles, as the crow flies, from San Francisco. We can produce comparable descriptions of Santiago or Nairobi or Shanghai. The kind of conceptual and theoretical grid that makes such description possible seems to depend upon a notion of place that empties it of any identifying properties except those that locate it on the grid. Early on in *Getting Back into Place: Toward a Renewed Understanding of the Place-World*, Edward Casey quotes Cisco Lassiter in this connection: "[I]n the uniform, homogeneous space of a Euclidean-Newtonian grid, all places are essentially interchangeable. Our places, even our places for homes, are defined by objective measures" (1993, 38). On such a view, Casey (1993) urges, space is conceived of simply as "a platform for places," each of which is in turn "a formal container of material objects" (74). To be somewhere in space is to occupy a place, but this tells us nothing at all so far about the experience of place for humans, carrying on their lives as embodied and affective beings. Our connection to place involves more than being dependent on the physical environment, important as that is. Who we are and how we live emerge in the context of our relation to the places we inhabit and the artifacts with which we surround ourselves.

> The power a place such as a mere room possesses determines not only *where* I am in the limited sense of cartographic location but *how* I am together with others (i.e., how I commingle and communicate with them) and even *who* we shall become together. The "how" and the "who" are intimately tied to the "where," which gives to them a specific content and a coloration not available from any

other source. Place bestows upon them "a local habitation and a name" by establishing a concrete situatedness in the common world. This implacement is as social as it is personal. (Casey 1993, 23)

As Nossack pointed out, we are oriented in and to place in part by things (as well as by people, of course; but again this is not our focus here); something of our life is in them and something of theirs is in us. That is why it is not simply a coincidence that our spirits may be broken when the places in which we have dwelled disappear or the things with which we have made place are damaged beyond recognition.

The situation of the returnees — and the callous and cavalier attitude of the likes of Dennis Hastert and Barbara Bush — provides vivid reminders of the importance of place and of place-orienting belongings. These are things that can sustain our relationship not just to "the past," but to *our pasts*. For them to be destroyed or to fall into serious disrepair is for our continuity with the past to become ragged and attenuated. For them to be repaired or restored or reconstructed or replicated is for us to try to maintain or renew such continuity.

But these terms — repair, restore, reconstruct, replicate, and the larger constellation of which they are a part — are not synonymous, and differences among them are part of what is being battled over in New Orleans and along the Gulf Coast. How and why do such differences matter?

Objects and Memory

Objects provide a scaffold for memory, in the sense that they provide a kind of platform through which memories are reached for, a guiding structure through which the past is recalled (the extent to which recollection involves reconstitution is a matter for another occasion). Or, to vary the metaphor a bit, we might say that objects offer nodes through which or beads along which narratives of past events and past experiences are strung. (Objects, of course, are not unique in this way; sounds and smells can serve similar functions.) Returning at last to his home in New Orleans, John Biguenet noted that the losses he found weighing most heavily on him were his books, each of which "had its own story of how it had come to rest on one of my shelves" (2005a). Of course just as scaffolding can be removed, and the building it enfolded remain standing, so one can continue to have memories in the absence of objects. People die or disappear, things are destroyed or damaged beyond recognition, and yet we still are able to remember them. But—returning for a moment to the case of Mr. Louis Simmons — think of the difference between "I remember leaving my wallet on the bureau" and "Here, mud-soaked and rank-smelling as it is, is the wallet I left on the bureau as I was rushing to safety." In this latter case the wallet is a link to the past in the sense that the past still exists in it: this thing, this wallet, existed in that time and in that place. Indeed the still-existing wallet constitutes a check against my claim to remember that I had a wallet of a certain description and that I left it in the house.

But objects provide scaffolding for the past in different ways, depending on the particular state of repair in which they greet us or into which we put them. For example, in his classic *Historic Preservation: Curatorial Management of the Built World*, James Marston Fitch (1990) helps to clarify some of the significant differences among repair projects in terms of how much of the past, and which moments in the past, are meant to continue. He lists seven forms of intervention, in increasing order of what he characterizes as their relative "radicality": preservation, restoration, conservation and consolidation, reconstitution, adaptive use, reconstruction, replication (46–47, 96). Think, for example, about the different reasons Mr. Louis Simmons, or someone documenting the widespread effects of Katrina, might have for wanting to preserve his wallet, that is, maintain it in the same condition as he (or they) found it; restore it, that is, put it back in the condition it would have been at some earlier time; or find a way to replicate it, to make or find a wallet just like it. A preserved object wears its history in quite a different way than it would were it to be restored to some earlier stage in its life: this is the thing damaged by Katrina, still showing that damage, not the thing as it would have looked had Katrina not occurred. And however useful a replica of a wallet, or a house, is as a way of sustaining a memory of what one had or what one went through, the continuity it provides with the past clearly is of a different order than that made possible by preservation or restoration. It is not the thing that I had before Katrina, but something just like what I had before Katrina.

Think, too, of the difference between what is called in the tailor's trade "invisible mending" and those forms of repair in which the repair is meant to be quite visible. In London there is a shop called "Invisible Menders of Knightsbridge," promising the customer with a torn jacket that the garment can be made to look as if it had never been ripped. On the other hand, someone influenced by a certain strand of Japanese aesthetics, or for some other reason a connoisseur of the imperfect, may be delighted to find that the crack in a teapot is soldered boldly and brightly with gold, its history of daily handling, and the inevitable breaking to which it is thus subject, highlighted and celebrated. Invisible mending attempts to sustain continuity with the past by destroying evidence of any break (there is a certain paradox in the fact that in the process of restoring something to a past condition one erases evidence of another past condition); visible mending sustains continuity with the past by acknowledging, even emphasizing, the history of rupture.

Sometimes there is concern that the scaffolding for memory provided by objects in their various states of repair or disrepair, restoration or ruin, constitutes, in the language of Mabel O. Wilson (2001), too eager an attempt to *orchestrate* memory. Wilson has argued that the National Civil Rights Museum in Memphis, which includes restored and replicated spaces from the Lorraine Motel, where Martin Luther King Jr. was murdered, is set up in such a way as to shape very closely and carefully the meaning of the commemorated events. In its aspiration to thoroughly and authoritatively tell the whole story of the civil rights movement, and Rev. King's role in it, "the museum unwittingly denies its public the possibility of articulating their own meanings and associations of this complex history. Thus the endeavor to memorialize encourages, albeit unintentionally, a static interpretation of African-American history. The design and exhibitions of the National Civil Rights Museum reinforce an unfortunate fixity of cultural meaning and memory" (Wilson 2001, 17). The suggestion here is that monuments and museums should provide to the viewing public not rules for correct interpretations, but invitations to think about and develop questions concerning the meaning of the persons and events they commemorate. Referring to James Young's work on Holocaust memorials, Wilson urges us to think of memory not as something fully created by and encased in monuments and museums, but as itself a matter of ongoing work "whereby events, their recollection, and the role the monuments play in our lives remain never completed" (19).

Wilson also detects a nervous, eager patriotism in the museum's depiction of the struggle for freedom, an anxious glossing over of the extent of the horrors of racism past and present, a denial of the country's still unfinished business: the "exhibits and full-scale recreations authenticate a sanitized, institutional account of the Civil Rights Movement" (18). And she wonders about the extent to which monuments and museums may be culturally dissonant forms of recollection for African Americans. It is perhaps no coincidence that people whose use of public space historically has been under such control, and whose life stories and works only recently have been included in American history, have created so many "non-monumental, ephemeral means" of memory, such as the blues (13).

In a photo essay on industrial ruins, Tim Edensor (2003) has argued that the context in which objects are presented has powerful implications for the ways we are invited to think about and reflect on the past.

> The form of knowing available in ruins is not like that of the heritage industry which collects and organises particular fragments. Selected and carefully arranged, these displays disguise the excess of matter and meaning of which they are a part. Conversely, ruins are sites where we can construct alternative stories which decentre commodified, official and sociological descriptions, producing an open-ended form of knowing which is sensual and imaginative, which resides in chaotic arrangements, fragments, indescribable sensations and inarticulate things. (267)

According to Edensor, ruins offer up a partial and, save the occasional interventions of trespassers, random selection of things. What they present lays no claim to coherence, makes no pretense to full knowledge ("The shreds and silent things that remain can conjure up only the half-known or imagined" [266]). They are vestigial and incomplete. On the other hand, the curatorial arrangement, while exhibiting the coherence of the intentionally selected and arranged, is occluding something, hiding something from us. What is that "excess of matter and meaning" which it "disguises"? It is as if, according to Edensor, ruins in their very proliferation of matter (objects "give up their solidity, becoming distributed in an indiscernible mulch" [266]) present a great deal of conceptual and semantic noise. If they are "inarticulate" it is in part because we can no longer tell an articulate story about them — unless we remove them from what once was an explanatory context but which now is only a source of opacity. This doesn't mean, Edensor insists, that we can know nothing about them as long as they remain ruins, but rather that the kind of knowledge we can come to have is bound to be markedly different from that made possible by the curatorial touch.

　　These examples from the menu of repair options — from restoration to leaving in ruin — make clear not only how objects in their various states of repair provide different kinds of links to the past. They also tell us that decisions about what, why, and how to repair are never based simply on technical considerations. Let us return briefly to an example that is much less complicated than post-Katrina New Orleans. Suppose you discover a large rip in your jacket. What if anything you decide to do about that is likely to vary according to many factors, such as cost; the sentimental value of the garment (perhaps it once belonged to a sibling, now deceased); the relative level of your comfort and discomfort with wearing torn clothing (perhaps you've long cultivated the "worn" look, or perhaps, having been raised in a family for whom wearing used clothing was a necessity, not a choice, donning ripped clothing is something you'd like to avoid). Even if you desire and can afford having it mended by a tailor, you may be asked to decide just how visible or invisible the patchwork should be.

The mix of historical, political, aesthetic, technical, and economic considerations that go into the mundane decision of an individual is all the more
complicated in a situation such as post-Katrina New Orleans. For here what
comes to the fore is not only a host of technical and nontechnical criteria but
jockeying for position to have the final say over whether and how individual
dwellings and other buildings and structures will be repaired. Not surprisingly,
there is pretty much an inverse relation between the amount and degree of
damage done to one's home and neighborhood, and one's place in the hierarchy of decision making. As the urbanist Mike Davis (2005) has suggested,
echoing the concerns of many others, the economic and social interests of the
politically more powerful can easily trump the social and historical interests of
the less powerful: in post-Katrina New Orleans there is

> a sinister consensus of powerful interests about the benefits of an urban "triage"
> that abandons historical centers of Black political power like the Ninth Ward while
> rebuilding million-dollar homes along the disaster-prone shores of Lake Pontchar-
> train and the Mississippi Sound.

Davis's comments can serve to remind us why houses and other buildings,
with their specific histories and physical attractions, matter to people. It is not
simply whether one will have a roof over one's head or whether a community
will have the buildings necessary to carry on its ordinary business. Like the
never-ending debate over what to do at Ground Zero in New York City, ongoing struggles over what to do in New Orleans and the Gulf Coast remind us
that preserving or restoring or reconstructing environments, buildings, and
other artifacts may simultaneously be part of a project to restore a community's
sense of its historical identity, or its wounded pride, or its tattered hope. To not
have a say in that project is to be without acknowledgment of having a past and
having a rightful stake in the interpretation of that past.

We have seen how objects — personal belongings, houses, familiar buildings — provide a scaffold for memory; we have noted how the scaffolding
comes in different shapes, depending on the state of repair the objects are in.
But as should also be clear from the examples above, just as the state of repair
of an object provides a scaffold for memory, so memories provide a scaffold
for repair. Even the simplest form of repair constitutes a means of continuity
with the past (a past function or state or condition), but the nature of the attempt to forge that continuity depends on remembering what the object was
or what it did.

Let us return for a moment to a case discussed by Fitch (1990) in his book
on historic preservation: When Colonial Williamsburg was "restored" to the

way it was in 1775, somebody had to figure out what historical memory tells us buildings there looked like then. Fitch points out that the "restoration" in fact is "a beguiling mixture of the preserved, the restored, and the reconstructed," and that at the same time the hearty brew includes "evasion": when Fitch published his book, Williamsburg had still managed to ignore the role of slavery in the historical moment to which the restoration is supposed to take us (96). In the case of Katrina, it is illuminating in this connection to mention Mississippi's Commission on Recovery, Rebuilding and Renewal (the name offers a reminder, by the way, that the terms are not synonymous), organized by the state's governor, Haley Barbour. This commission pressures returnees to reconstruct their homes according to quite specific notions of appropriate restoration (McKee 2005). Restoration is guided by memory, and the commission wants to provide that memory. Critics of the project have pointed out that the directive seems to presume that cities can "exist in a fixed point in historical time," and have argued that "what results is a fairy tale version of history, and the consequences could be particularly harsh for New Orleans, which was well on its way to becoming a picture-postcard vision of the past before the hurricane struck" (Ouroussoff 2005). Accurate memory is supposed to provide scaffolding for the particular kind of repair — in this case, not mere repair but restoration — which the governor and his advisors have in mind. There's considerable worry about a powerful "convergence between political traditionalism and architectural nostalgia" (Davis 2005) in an area where the meaning of slavery was so deeply etched in building styles.

Once in place, rebuilt and reconstructed environments function, weakly or strongly, to orchestrate memory, as we learned from Mabel Wilson; and that means that *somebody's* memory, *somebody's* version of the past, will have orchestrated the rebuilding and reconstruction. Those charged with the responsibility of drawing up plans for a post-Katrina New Orleans ought at the very least to carefully describe and explain the mix of preservation, renovation, restoration, and reconstruction their plans prescribe. They ought to state in clear and unequivocal detail what historical events or conditions will thereby be erased or evaded, what human footprints will thereby be effaced.

Residents and Tourists

So far, then, I have been suggesting that the particular plight of residents displaced by that potent combination of nature and culture referred to as Katrina has reminded us how and why place and place-defining objects matter. The reaction of evacuees also occasions a vivid revisiting of the various repair projects of *Homo reparans*: It invites us to consider the significant political, emotional, aesthetic, and economic differences among, for example, preservation, restoration, and reconstruction. It allows us to understand how the various forms of repair provide their characteristic scaffolds for memory, even as such forms of repair themselves require the guide, the scaffolding, of memory.

Furthermore, focus on the situation of displaced New Orleanians and the loss of so many of their belongings turns out to reveal some of the fault lines in the globalized tourist city. For it throws into stark relief the difference between scaffolding for the preservation of some people's memories or some community's history, and scaffolding for the creation of new experiences and memories of others.

The very meaning of tourism, and the distinction between resident and tourist, has been the focus of some lively debates about the cultural and economic impact of tourism on cities and their residents. In a review some twenty years ago, Erik Cohen (1984) outlined eight different (and somewhat overlapping) ways of conceptualizing tourism: as a commercialized form of hospitality, as a democratized version of travel formerly available only to the wealthy, as a modern form of leisure activity, as a modern variety of religious pilgrimage, as an expression of a variety of cultural views of the tourists, as a process by which outsiders acculturate the locals, as one type of ethnic relations, and as a powerful form of neocolonialism (374–375).

While there seems to be widespread agreement that there probably is no single satisfactory way to characterize tourists (and some doubt about whether the distinction between tourist and resident is as neat as it might seem [Ashworth and Tunbridge 2004, 219]), Dean MacCannell's description of affluent middle-class visitors as "scavengers" for "new experiences" (1976, 13) underscores one of tourism's powerful lures: the promise of experiences one would not have elsewhere, and then the memory of those experiences. That promise includes the implicit pledge that there are certain kinds of experiences you *won't* have: for example, being robbed or mugged or left to stand in the rain waiting for a bus or not having the toilet work. New Orleans perhaps has been an especially alluring tourist destination for middle-class visitors who want to have a sense of being near to but still a safe distance from the seedy and the dangerous. The experiences, like the food, are expected to be a little spicier than those at home. (In the months after the disaster many New Orleanians worried that as a result of post-Katrina images of mayhem and rumors of uncontrolled violence "their city ha[d] been scarred, unfairly and forever" [McClain 2005]. Will residents be cheered or worried by the tour buses that soon began to take camera-toting visitors to see the damage for themselves [Nossiter 2006]?)

Tourism has been the dominant sector of the New Orleans economy for several decades, and as Kevin Fox Gotham has put it, "The transition to a tourism-dominated economy has paralleled population decline, white flight to the suburbs, racial segregation, poverty and a host of other social problems including crime, fiscal austerity, poor schools and decaying infrastructure" (Gotham 2002, 1740) (writing this three years before Katrina, Gotham was not in a position to fully appreciate the understatement in the final phrase). The needs of the tourism industry in a post-Katrina New Orleans, eager to rebuild its image as it rebuilds its infrastructure, seem likely to strengthen the kind of decision making already taking place which favors salvage of better protected neighborhoods over those like the Ninth Ward. However blurry the distinction between residents and tourists may be becoming in some contexts, differences between them, particularly in terms of their relative relation to place, experience, and memory, appear in clearer outline after Katrina and the response to it.

Certainly one important difference between residents and tourists has emerged: Whatever other differences there are in their repertoire of experiences, tourists will be distinguished precisely by their not having to face in New Orleans what so many residents cannot avoid. Indeed especially for those evacuees who return to jobs in the tourism industry (figures are difficult to come by here, but it seems likely that among the blue-collar jobs held by Ninth Ward residents were those serving the tourism industry), the difference between looking for scaffolding for one's own memories and providing scaffolding for the promised memories of others, between preserving memories and selling them, will be very stark. And it surely is one thing to desperately hope to reestablish the setting of one's own life, and quite another to set the stage for tourists, to provide the dramatic backdrop for their adventures—even if, indeed especially if, the life one leads is on the tourists' menu of attractions.

The situation of those trying to patch together their lives and their belongings in post-Katrina New Orleans underscores another difference between the tourist's relation to place-defining things and that of the resident. True, as embodied beings both the tourist and the resident have relations to things that provide a sense of place. But the tourist has left behind most of her belongings. (Evacuees from New Orleans living in hotels have left behind theirs, too, but surely they did not come to those hotels as tourists.) While the tourist may return regularly to a favorite spot, and in that sense count on a kind of continuity of place and time, it is a different kind of continuity than the intimate relation of resident to place-defining objects. Indeed the brief respite from the demands of place-defining objects often is among the pleasures to which the tourist looks forward.

The Place of Things

The intimate relation between evacuated residents and their belongings — their homes, their wallets, their trophies, their guardian angels — invites our close examination for several reasons. For one thing, we have to think about what it means to be beings with belongings, things that crucially mediate our relation to place. For another, we are led to consider objects, in their various states of repair, as providing scaffolding for memory, even as memory provides needed scaffolding for projects of repair. Third, reflection on the relation of residents and tourists to their belongings, and on the ways in which belongings mediate belonging, helps us to understand some of the differences between residents and tourists as stakeholders in the globalized tourist city. Still, a haunting image from Hans Erich Nossack's return to Hamburg suggests that part of the horror was the very collapse of the distinction, or rather, the precipitous fall from one side of it to the other: "We were like a group of tourists; the only thing missing was a megaphone and a guide's informational chatter. And already we were perplexed and did not know how to explain the strangeness" (2004, 38). For all the differences between the bombing of Hamburg and the leveling of the Ninth Ward, both seem to have turned residents into unwilling tourists, who may have to learn to belong to other things, other places.

Note

1. In these comments I don't wish for a moment to deny the importance of connection to other human beings. However, prompted by the power of the images of bewilderment and displacement described above, I want to focus on our relation to things and their place-defining capacity. Many of the examples discussed also make clear how our relationships to things are mediated by our relationships to people and vice versa.

PART FIVE

DIVISIONS AND CONNECTIONS

The challenge and greatness of cities is that they bring disconnections and differences geographically together. Henri Lefebvre calls this "social centrality." To use the language of Lewis Mumford (see chapter 1 of this book), this feature is that quality of cities which "concentrates" flows, people, and objects in time and space even while simultaneously disseminating them.

For Lefebvre, social centrality emerges because the city is a node of identity and orientation in a wider landscape of dispersion (Shields 1993, 103). This is a way of characterizing the "intersectionality" that makes cities not just large in scale but qualitatively "urban" rather than "small town" in character.

Nodal sites of social centrality are not only seminal to the identity formation of communities, but they also come to represent these communities or social groups to outsiders and the world at large, especially at sites of ritual and festival, such as Mardi Gras and the French Quarter (see Hetherington 1996, 42, concerning Stonehenge). As symbols, such times and places acquire a metonymic quality and a vivid life beyond what is actually real: they become mythologized. That is, abstract representations and images, as well as virtual qualities (their reputed character),[1] may overshadow the material realities of a place, including its state of repair. New Orleans in ruins would still be the capital of creole culture and jazz.

Isotopia and Power

A striking element of the disaster that followed Hurricane Katrina was its different impact on different neighborhoods, with racial implications especially if one compares, for example, the Garden District with the Lower Ninth Ward. Cities are not only nodes of connection but complex matrices of separation and segregation. A paradoxical aspect of social centrality is that truly urban cities hold contrasts and oppositions together in a productive tension. Lefebvre refers to this articulation as *isotopia* (2003, 121), the ability to both accommodate and conjoin differences, the quality of holding heterogeneous elements together as well as linking homogeneous elements that are distant from each other. Cities are thus "informed" by difference (Lefebvre 2003, 133). To give a simple example, street networks function this way to link together both similar and highly different properties. How to operationalize approaches that acknowledge the differences and tensions that coexist in cities is the main preoccupation of C. Tabor Fisher in chapter 9.

If divisions in a city are, in part, produced and maintained through connections, then those divisions are neither natural nor stable. And if divisions are produced through connections, then how can anyone, any institution, or any neighborhood claim centrality? For example, social centrality can be understood to operate simultaneously at different scales, in a nested manner. Thus, playgrounds can be shown to fulfill the functions of social centrality, where children develop a sense of belonging within public space (Mannion 1999, 221). Neighborhoods within a city can operate as microcosms of wider, urban-scale social centrality. Connections and divisions thus reflect social *centralities*, plural. Intersecting orders of social centrality give different densities to the "social space" of the city.

Mayor Nagin's declaration that he would restore New Orleans as a "chocolate city" was, in one sense, an appeal to difference and division. However, it was also an appeal to the centrality that the city has for African Americans. A similar theme is taken up by Jacob Wagner in chapter 10, where he discusses New Orleans' identity as a creole city. On the one hand, the creole is a particular artifact of New Orleans' history. On the other hand, the creole — and the creole city — is a microcosm of the crossings that continually mark the urban landscape. Hence, the creole city, while marginal to any preidentified culture, is simultaneously a city of social centralities produced through divisions and connections.

Finally, just as the divisions of a city are overlain with axes of connection, so the connections are frequently hindered by divisions:

The communications infrastructure [during Hurricane Katrina] needed to support intergovernmental decision making to enable communities to respond effectively to such a wide-ranging, rapidly moving, destructive storm was not in place. Consequently, when communications failed totally for the City of New Orleans under the brunt of hurricane winds and subsequent flooding, managers of emergency service organizations, businesses, and nonprofit organizations such as schools, hospitals, and nursing homes lost their capacity to coordinate action in collective response to the spreading danger. Without timely updates and clear reports on the status of operations at different locations, the enormity of the problem was beyond the comprehension of the personnel on duty at city, state, and federal levels of responsibility. Personnel had no means by which to integrate reports from multiple locations to create a regionwide profile of the event or to assess accurately the escalating destruction, let alone mobilize coordinated action. (Comfort and Haase 2006, 329)

This was more than a technical problem of damage and power outages. Analyses of the network of relief agencies from the federal government down to local volunteer organizations revealed that some sets of agencies did not communicate with other relevant actors and that the loosely coupled network of responders relied on eight key agencies which represented "cut points" in the network. If (and when) they did not communicate, this caused groups of actors to lose their ability to work effectively within the overall effort (Comfort and Haase 2006; see also Robinson, Berrett, and Stone 2006).

In other words, New Orleans' communication network, which should have been forging connections, was itself beset by hierarchical divisions. As a result, disaster responders suffered from *dis*connection in their immediate response to Hurricane Katrina. But this probably was not the entire story. In chapter 2, Jordan Flaherty suggested that organic connections of community were prevailing beneath the surface during the Katrina disaster, even as the media focused on the disconnections that existed within official channels of (non)-communication. In the final chapter of this book, Jonathan Shapiro Anjaria provides an additional counterexample in his account of disaster response in Mumbai. Although Mumbai is certainly also a city of differences and divisions, informal connectivities prevailed, and the city survived through a series of informal, local initiatives.

Social Centralities

Hurricane Katrina thus provides us with an opportunity to reconsider the nature of divisions, connections, and centralities. Despite the much-quoted words of some federal politicians who disavowed the importance of New Orleans' black neighborhoods, in all its marginality New Orleans is culturally and symbolically "central" to American culture, a point not lost on anyone actually involved in the reconstruction of New Orleans, nor on the contributors to the final part of this book. The following chapters demonstrate the elements of a more inclusive vision that acknowledges the vital importance of social interaction, the interplay between the past and present, and the importance of informal social networks in mitigating disasters. They embrace grassroots and local organizations whose response stands in contrast with those of the government and the media, who, when faced with the prospect of losing control over the environment and population of New Orleans, failed the city so miserably.

Note

1. Abstractions and other ideations are intentionally distinguished from virtualities, which are intangible but real things. Ontologically, virtualities (including such "things" as community, society, economic markets, or trust) are thus part of the real in a way that purely cognitive ideas or discursive fictions are not (see Shields 2003, 2005).

CHAPTER NINE

Repositioning the Theorist in the Lower Ninth Ward

C. Tabor Fisher

The devastation of New Orleans' Lower Ninth Ward made clear to all of us that Hurricane Katrina was more than a natural disaster. The scope and disparate effects of the storm were socially and spatially produced. The Lower Ninth Ward is one of the poorest neighborhoods in New Orleans and almost entirely African American. These facts have turned the Lower Ninth into a symbol of the racism and classism that Hurricane Katrina has forced into public discussion. However, it is important that the social and spatial theories we mobilize to address this racism and classism not obscure the complexities of spatial production and unwittingly constrain our resistance to the oppressions we seek to redress.

We must remain aware, as Henri Lefebvre has argued, that the same society that produces our space(s) also produces our spatial understandings (1991). According to Lefebvre, space is produced in the confluence of three "moments": spatial practice, our conceptions or representations of space, and symbolically laden representational spaces. A reconstruction of New Orleans that attempts to resist racism and classism must address these oppressions in all three "moments." Our spatial theory plays a role in producing the spaces of New Orleans, not only by impacting future spatial practices, but also by representing those spaces both conceptually and symbolically. This interplay between spatial theory and spatial production is the topic of this chapter. Because our conceptual and symbolic spatial representations are formed in and through the social spaces we live in, our spatial theories can become part of the process that reproduces those spaces. Thus, our spatial thinking may reproduce the racist and classist structures of our society. I argue here that our spatial understandings are radically altered by how we are positioned in relation to the spaces we are trying to understand. A reproduction of the Lower

Ninth Ward in resistance to racism and classism requires a spatial practice of hanging-out and a tentative representation of space as concrete, dynamic, and multiple.

The Danger of Abstract Thinking

According to Lefebvre, the space(s) of late capitalism are abstract, and this abstraction undergirds oppression and alienation. Abstract space bulldozes differences, seeking to homogenize space and society. Through abstraction, persons, space, and social relations are viewed metonymically as passive, objectified images. In metonymy, we are represented by a *part* of who we are — as, for example, I am understood by the law to be a "person" and bearer of human rights, without any mention of my brunette hair, my love of crossword puzzles, the fact that I sing all the time, or my white, southern, middle-class upbringing. We become abstract "impersonal pseudo-subject[s], alienated from our lived, concrete, unique selves" (Lefebvre 1991, 51). This abstraction, according to Lefebvre, masks dominance. Through abstract representations of space and abstract representational spaces, the social forces that produce space are naturalized, "reduc[ing] reality in the interests of power" (Lefebvre 1991, 367).

Abstract representations of space hide power by abstracting space from the social forces that produce it. For example, an early plan for rebuilding New Orleans, released in November 2005 by the Urban Land Institute (ULI), ranked neighborhoods by considering scientific measurements of flood damage and vulnerability. The plan then called for sections of the city — including portions of the Lower Ninth Ward — to be restricted from rebuilding in the near future (Urban Land Institute 2005). The most recent rebuilding strategy, the Unified New Orleans Plan (2007), resulted in a similar designation of the Lower Ninth Ward as an area that has not been repopulated and is prone to heavy flooding. Thus, the categories used by the ULI remain a part of current representations of the city that inform the rebuilding effort.

The mapping performed by the Urban Land Institute has the advantage of being comprehensive and uniform, allowing policymakers to "see" the whole city at once. However, the map is far from objective and allows preexisting inequities based on race and class to be reproduced. First, the criteria used to determine the feasibility of neighborhood reconstruction were narrowly confined to flood data rather than social factors. The ULI examined elevation, the depth and duration of the flooding from Hurricanes Katrina and Rita, the amount of flooding caused by levee failure, and the extent of structural damage. Historical data about the frequency of past flooding and likelihood of future floods were included. This information is important and should be considered, but it must be pointed out that all of these criteria represent the space as affected by *natural* rather than *social* forces. The only social dimensions included were values placed on historic districts and homeownership. These data are abstracted from the politics around declaring a district "historical" or the social forces surrounding the building and maintenance of homes (not to mention levees). This abstract representation of space, while repeatedly calling for equity, produces a space in which the inhabitants of the Lower Ninth are less important than those in the French Quarter, both in the representations the plan produced and in the spatial practices it recommends.

Abstract space also hides the relational nature of space. An abstract representational space is produced when metonymic pseudo-subjects are symbolic representations that inhabit contained spaces, effacing their social and spatial relations. The Lower Ninth Ward has been repeatedly called poor, black, and crime-ridden, drawing on racist images of "ghetto" or "slum." Poor blacks become symbolic pseudo-subjects, spatially attached to the ward through a process Charles Mills has described as a "circular indictment" (1997, 42): if you live in the Lower Ninth, then you are poor and deprived, and if you are poor and deprived, you must live in the Lower Ninth. The connection elides the relation between predominantly African American neighborhoods and predominantly white neighborhoods. As bell hooks (1990) writes, "margin" and "center" are linked and mutually constitutive, but viewing the *space* as raced erases that connection. It begins to appear as if poverty and deprivation just spring up from the soil, as if living there, rather than white supremacy, is the problem.

What is lost when the space of the Lower Ninth Ward is represented abstractly, both conceptually and symbolically, is people as active subjects. When spaces are understood abstractly, people may be counted, resulting in a number such as "98.3 percent African American." But those counted people are not active subjects; we can count apples the same way. Along with the loss of people as active subjects comes a loss of an understanding of the relations between people and between spaces, the power that structures those relations, and, ultimately, resistance. The flood data used by the ULI does not include the active subjectivity of the people who built levees, bought homes, and formed communities, nor is an abstract pseudo-subject an active, complex, embodied human being.

Spaces do not resist; only active people do. Therefore, in order to represent space in resistance to racism and classism, spatial theory must enable, rather than obliterate, the active subjectivity of the people who live in the Lower

House in Tremé.
Photograph by Jacob A.
Wagner; image courtesy
of the photographer.

Ninth Ward, and it must include the relations among the people in the space
and between those people and people in other spaces. Such a representation
will be concrete, multiple, dynamic, and textured, and, therefore, less clean
and comprehensive than abstract representations; but this kind of spatial thinking is needed to enable resistance.

Resistant Spatial Practice

María Lugones (2003) poses a problem for resistant spatial theorists: if theory
is abstract and produced from an objective distance, but resistance is concrete,
embodied, and produced in the moment, in the midst of oppressive spaces,
then how can resistant theory exist? She begins by looking at the distinction
Michel de Certeau (1984) makes between the strategies a planner develops
from a "proper" position outside of the space being studied and the tactics a
resistor enacts immersed within a space that she does not comprehend. I use

"comprehend" here in both senses of the term: to understand and to encompass. Since the resistor is in the space, much of what is happening there is out of her grasp and, thus, out of her control. For de Certeau, practices are tactical and resistant; theory is strategic and oppressive. Hence, a theory of resistance is impossible.

This follows also from my analysis above. If people resist and abstract theory does not include embodied people as active subjects, then abstract theory cannot comprehend or express resistance. Abstract space produces "'users' who cannot recognize themselves within it, and a thought which cannot conceive of adopting a critical stance towards it" (Lefebvre 1991, 93). The erasure of active subjects from the abstracted position of de Certeau's strategist results in what Lefebvre calls "the *entire* problem": the "silence of the 'users'" (1991, 365). My claim is that the users are speaking, moving, and producing space(s). The problem is that their voices and movements and productions are not registered from the abstracted position.

According to Lugones, the solution to this problem is the creation of tactical strategies—a blend of theory and practice. Tactical strategies are positioned concretely, on the street. Lugones argues for streetwalker theorizing that sees the world close-up, street level, yet deeply. The streetwalking theorist is able to have a complex understanding of space and the relations that constitute it, not by looking at it from above (and thus gaining a breadth of understanding), but by experiencing the production from within the space produced and in company with others moving through and producing it (and thus gaining a depth of understanding).

To be positioned this way is to be an active subject in the midst of active subjects, producing space(s) and understandings of space(s) simultaneously. This places the streetwalking theorist on the same ground as those she may have "studied" if she had been in the strategist's position. Both "theorist" and "objects of study" become active subjects and are placed in relation; both become responsible and able to respond to their activities and relations.

From this street-level position, spatial practices, representations of space, and representational spaces are transformed. Lugones elaborates a resistant spatial practice which she calls hanging-out. To hang-out is to create open-ended and multiple spaces through a collective, resistant inhabitation of space. "The streetwalker theorist cultivates a multiplicity and depth of perception and connection and 'hangs-out' even in well-defined institutional spaces, troubling and subverting their logics, their intent" (Lugones 2003, 224). To hang-out is to participate in the multiplicitous, embodied production of space in the midst and against the grain of dominant intentions. Without consulting zoning maps, with awareness but in defiance of the dominant power's restrictions on living here or doing business there, hanging-out proliferates space. For example, when streetwalkers, in the literal sense of prostitutes, hang-out on a street corner, they proliferate spaces because the corner is still being produced as a public thoroughfare even as the streetwalkers produce it as a place of business.

The spatial practice of hanging-out requires new spatial representations. Hanging-out, according to Lugones, involves a careful attention to the spaces that are constantly emerging through collective, resistant movement. Signs appear in the Lower Ninth: hand-painted signs that read "People Live Here" or "We're Coming Back Home," printed signs that read "Not As Seen on TV" or "No Bulldozing." These are representations of space that trouble the dominant representations of the space found in red stickers marking houses as uninhabitable or newspaper articles that describe the ward as "part demolition zone, part graveyard for lost dreams" (Roberts 2006, A9). A streetwalker theorist "cultivates a . . . depth of perception" that sees these signs as part of the production of a resistant space in the ward, activated by other street-level spatial producers. The ward is actively being produced, and as the needs and movements of resistors shift, so does the production. Hanging-out is, then, a dynamic movement producing and conceiving of multiple layered, shifting spaces.

The Blue House on Deslonde Street, which serves as a base of operations for the Common Ground Collective's work in the Lower Ninth, can be understood as a hang-out. As Lugones recommends, the organizers and volunteers in the Common Ground Collective understand themselves to be supporting the resistant spatial productions of the ward's residents, working with other active subjects rather than imposing their plans from without. The Blue House is multiple, existing both as the private home of a Lower Ninth resident not yet able to return and as a community organizing center. Hanging-out in the Blue House, Common Ground organizers are ready to see the space transformed when necessary and to move on when residents of the Lower Ninth ask them to (Filosa 2006c). Thus, the Blue House is being produced with the fluidity, multiplicity, and attention to resistant active subjectivity that is characteristic of a hang-out.

Understanding the Blue House as a hang-out challenges the spatial concepts de Certeau associates with the strategy/tactic distinction. De Certeau (1984) maintains that the strategist is "a subject of will and power" separated from the environment where the strategies will be enacted. Placement in a "proper" removes the strategist from the "objects" she studies. The tactician, on the other hand, does not have a "base where it can capitalize on its advantages, prepare its expansions, and secure independence with respect to circumstances" because she does not have a "proper" (xix). The Blue House does serve these purposes, providing a space where volunteers can regroup, recharge, store supplies, and prepare future activities. The key difference between the Blue House, as a resistant location of hanging-out, and the "proper" is that the Blue House is not a closed-off territory but a permeable and changeable location, deeply enmeshed in the Lower Ninth rather than separated from it. The existence of such a place that is "neither the 'nowhere' of de Certeau's tactics nor the 'proper' of the strategist" affirms Lugones's claim that resistors can hang-out in a tentative third space or borderland that is not ephemeral (2003, 215; see also 229n28).

My reading of the Blue House reveals a transformation of theory implied by but not explicitly stated in Lugones's work. The active production of space is not an application or instantiation of theory, although people are guided by their spatial understandings as they produce space. To apply or to instantiate implies a one-way relationship, but the social production of the Blue House speaks back to and questions de Certeau's dichotomy. Here practice questions theory. This space is a source of representations not as a passive object to be mirrored by representations, but as an active component in the interplay between how we think about space, how we produce space, and the reality that is produced.

This interplay adds a new dimension to my concern that the spatial theory that emerges from our racist and classist society may replicate our society's racism and classism. It is my contention that spatial theory is both productive of and produced by social space. A radical implication of Lefebvre's thought is that there is no reality that serves as the substratum of our social production of space. Space, society, and (spatial) knowledge are co-constitutive, but none of them is foundational. What is constituted in the interplay between them is reality, but that means that reality is not a stable given object to be discovered as we produce (spatial) knowledge. Reality changes as we come to know it — just as what we come to know changes as we relate to reality.

This changes our responsibilities in relation to knowledge production, including the production of spatial theories. It is no longer a question of accurately describing a reality to be discovered; it is a question of putting out knowledge that will enter into the production of a reality that will rebound back on knowledge, space, and society. There is, thus, an ethical responsibility to consider not only whether what we claim as knowledge is *true* in relation to (at the time) existing reality, but also whether what we put out as knowledge is *just* in relation to a reality that it projects. Given that different spatial knowledges are possible from a strategist's proper or from a streetwalking theorist's hang-out, the question becomes: from what space will we generate our spatial theories?

These considerations return me with renewed vigor to a question hooks (1990) asks:

> Within complex and ever shifting realms of power relations, do we position our-
> selves on the side of colonizing mentality? Or do we continue to stand in political
> resistance with the oppressed, ready to offer our ways of seeing and theorizing, of
> making culture, towards that revolutionary effort which seeks to create space where
> there is unlimited access to the pleasure and power of knowing, where transforma-
> tion is possible? (145)

From the proper of de Certeau's strategist, a "colonizing mentality" erases the active subjectivity of the "users," rendering them mute and passive. At best, they can be viewed as victims of the deprivation found in the margin — as residents of the Lower Ninth have been viewed. From the streetwalking theorist's position, however, there is the possibility of transformation, as active subjects work together to produce space(s) and knowledge(s).

Of course, none of this erases the relationships of power that exist between the strategist and the streetwalking theorist. Along with an attention to the active subjectivity of the people producing space, a streetwalking theorist is responsive and responsible to the relations within the space and between the space coming into being and other spaces. The streetwalking theorist moves with other active subjects, *socially* producing space and attentive to the relations among active subjects that enter into that production. Further, she is aware of the ways in which the space is being produced from without — from strategists who impose their conceptions of space and from activities that cross or get blocked at strategic boundaries. The relations of power that enter into the social production of space are discernible in streetwalker theorizing in a way that was not possible from an abstracted position. A streetwalking theorist is aware of both the active subjectivity and the relations that produce space, making it possible for her to conceptualize and move with resistance.

A Resistant Spatial Representation

A theorist repositioned to the street level of the Lower Ninth Ward, moving with other active subjects, can produce spatial thinking that has the potential to re-create spaces in resistance to racism and classism. The spatial thinking she participates in producing is dramatically different from the spatial thinking found in dominant understandings of the Lower Ninth. In dominant understandings, the ward is barely inhabited and not worth reinhabiting. The Lower Ninth is categorized in the Unified New Orleans Plan (2007) as an "area with [a] very slow repopulation [rate] and high risk of future flooding" and by urban planners as a place that never was "fit for human habitation" (Rivlin 2006). But resistant productions of space in the Lower Ninth Ward reveal a chosen location of struggle, vibrantly inhabited and globally interconnected.

Before discussing this resistant spatial understanding of the Lower Ninth Ward, let me point out that such an understanding will not be comprehensive. It will be tentative for two reasons. First, streetwalker theorizing is necessarily partial, both in that it is not comprehensive and in that it advocates for a particular position. Located on the street, the streetwalking theorist can produce a rich and deeply textured conceptualization of space, but not a complete one. (Of course, the strategist's conceptualization is also incomplete, since all the people, relations, and life have been extracted from it.) Streetwalker theorizing is a corporate enterprise, a making of knowledge with others, and, therefore, is never complete for any one streetwalking theorist. Beyond this sense of "partial" as incomplete, the conceptualizations produced by streetwalker theorists are also partial because streetwalking theorists choose "to stand in political resistance with the oppressed." Located in resistance to oppression, streetwalker theorizing advocates with the marginalized. Aware that conceptualizations of space enter into the production of space, streetwalker theorists actively promote representations that advocate for social justice.

A second reason that streetwalker theorizing is tentative is that it is dynamic. The social production of space is constantly occurring, and therefore, any representation of it will not be able to capture that movement or be an enduringly accurate description of the space. To capture or to describe, however, is not the purpose of a streetwalking representation of space. Instead, the streetwalking theorist is searching out the ways that space and reality are being produced and she attempts to move with those productions that open up space for resistant inhabitation.

The Lower Ninth Ward is what hooks (1990) calls a chosen margin of radical openness. People choose to be here, like Edgar Lewis Taylor, who says:

> They talk so bad about us why would I want to be anywhere else? Why would I want to be in the company of somebody that — they made us look bad, *nationally*. Like we were just, ah, I mean we were the slum of the earth or we just didn't have nothing or whatever. But that wasn't true. That wasn't true. (quoted in Corley 2006)

In resistance to dominant productions of the Lower Ninth as a "margin of deprivation," Lewis chooses to inhabit the space in resistance, as a place that can nourish and enrich him in ways that inhabitation in a hostile center cannot. This choice — an act of active subjectivity — is constrained in many ways and enacted differently by different inhabitants of the ward. The repositioned theorist is open to the complexity of the inhabitation of the Lower Ninth, as a variety of reasons and possibilities bring people here. Here Albert Bass lives by candlelight and helps out at Common Ground, dreaming of Don Quixote bringing down the windmills of power (Badkhen 2006). There Joe Bramlett toils at his grandmother's house after a long day at the docks. But he commutes back to Simmesport for the weekend, where his fiancée has been relocated. He is rebuilding for his grandmother, not for himself (personal communication June 11, 2006). A third house is gutted by students on spring break, their connection to the Lower Ninth forged by the media coverage of Katrina. What will emerge from these multiplicitous efforts is not yet clear.

What is clear is that the space is emerging. For the repositioned theorist the question is not what could be produced here, but what is already in production. Focusing on the dynamic, continuing production of the Lower Ninth Ward, the repositioned theorist has a deep sense of a history of resisting oppression that is continuing to struggle. She is particularly interested in how the active subjects of the Lower Ninth Ward position themselves in relation to history. A number of interconnected histories emerge in the space. For example, Herbert Gettridge Sr. built his house himself in 1952 and then rebuilt it in 1965 after Hurricane Betsy. Now, at the age of eighty-three, he is rebuilding it again. For Gettridge this is just one more time that hard work and commitment to his wife and family propel him to shape the space he lives in and loves (Filosa 2006b). For others, the flooding and its aftermath were directed by the hand of God, who protected his children through a tragedy of "Biblical proportions" (Remnick 2005). For many, Katrina is just one more in a series of "natural" disasters that rich, powerful, white men have manipulated in order to try and eradicate the poor blacks in the Lower Ninth Ward, including the Great Mississippi Flood of 1927 and Hurricane Betsy in 1965. Some feel a deep resonance with an "ancient memory" of families sold away from each other on the auction block when they were sent, without information, to locations all over the United States when they were evacuated (Lee 2006). These histories of the Lower Ninth are not mutually exclusive but intertwined to varying degrees by different people in the ward. The repositioned theorist cannot study this history in a search for the one, true story of the Lower Ninth Ward. She must move among people who are writing their history — both past and future — and at the same time producing the space of the Lower Ninth Ward. The Lower Ninth is a space of hardworking homeowners, *and* of religious community, *and* of former slaves, *and* of deprivation and oppressions, *and* of resistance.

The repositioned theorist is responsible for entering into the production of the space in ways that do not erase the histories of the active subjects who live there. She is responsible for considering the historics and the futures they imply in terms of their potential for justice as much as in terms of their accuracy. The focus on history is not one of nostalgia, but of placing the space in a history of struggle that transforms the present (hooks 1990, 147–149).

The repositioned theorist enters into a complex production of spaces that are being produced in relation to spaces throughout the world. The Lower Ninth, at present, is stretched out long and wide — to Houston and Atlanta, to Simmesport and Albuquerque. A new spatiality emerges in the living room of a house in Hammond, where Rev. Franklin Burke and his wife Lori weave connections between the dispersed flock of Good Faith Baptist Church. Letters and late-night phone calls from church members are treasured as the Burkes serve as a hub for a stretched-out community. Rev. Burke anchors that community to 1703 Benton Street, where he returns a number of times each week to gut and rebuild the church (Haygood 2006). Another minister, Rev. Douglas Haywood, spends his days in the Lower Ninth Ward, overseeing the resurrection of New Israel Baptist Church. He says, "I live in New Orleans East now," but then corrects himself. "I sleep in New Orleans East, but I live down here" (Roberts 2006). To the repositioned theorist, Haywood and others remain residents of the ward despite their current geographic locations. Many Lower Ninth residents remain rooted to their neighborhood, a part of it, even as they are told they cannot or should not return. Robert Rocque explains this historical and global connection:

> My roots are tied firmly into this place. My parents and grandparents are buried here. So this is really my home. But it's hard to stay in a place that you feel that they don't really want you to be here. (quoted in Lee 2006)

The former residents who are in the midst of reproducing the Lower Ninth Ward are multiply located, connecting the spaces they currently inhabit with the Lower Ninth in defiance of dominant productions of the ward as a lost cause.

Another connection that residents of the Lower Ninth are producing in resistance to dominant productions of the ward is an ambivalent relation to Iraq. The repositioned theorist becomes aware of this relation when she sees the word "Baghdad" spray-painted on a house on Reynes Street. This sign marks an affinity with Baghdad as a place destroyed by the U.S. government. As National Guard troops recently deployed in Iraq patrol the ward, that affinity intersects with dominant productions of the Lower Ninth (Roberts 2006). But the connections between Iraq and the Lower Ninth are also resistant reproductions as they embody the continuing outcry about the diversion of federal funds from New Orleans to Iraq and the omission of New Orleans from President Bush's State of the Union address in January 2007. This global connection between the Lower Ninth and Iraq, asserted by residents of the ward, challenges the theorizing of resistance as local that is present in de Certeau's distinction and in other spatial theories, such as David Harvey's association of social movements with place rather than space (1990). Some resistant residents of New Orleans understand themselves to be in a relation of affinity with Iraqis as well as in competition with them for federal reconstruction efforts. The repositioned theorist seeks to integrate this complex relation into her understandings of the ward.

To summarize, the repositioned theorist steps into an already emerging and complex space, inhabited by people who choose the Lower Ninth as active subjects. She steps into a conflicting history that reaches toward a number of possible futures. The space produced is conflictual and multiple, not planned cohesively, but full of plans. She seeks ways that move with the movements of others so that plans that promote justice are enabled, and so that the multiplicity of possibilities is encouraged rather than reduced.

Urban Planning and Activism

Repositioning the theorist in the Lower Ninth Ward provides altered possibilities for reproducing the space. The neighborhood becomes peopled, vibrant, struggling, complex, moving forward in resistance to dominant representations of the ward — representations that are influencing the spatial practice of reconstruction. The Unified New Orleans Plan's designation of the Lower Ninth as an area with low repopulation is based on utility usage in November 2006. However, Gettridge's electricity was not restored until that November. He did not have gas service (Filosa 2006a). Many residents may have been reluctant to return to the ward until electricity was restored, and then they would have to have an electrician inspect their wiring and circuit boxes before Entergy would turn on the service. A year and a half after the storm, electricity has not been restored in a large portion of the Lower Ninth, from Derbigny north to Florida and from Forstall west to the canal, and gas service is unavailable north of Claiborne (according to Entergy, New Orleans' energy supplier). This abstract measurement based on utility usage finds a much more desolate ward than the repositioned theorist's assessment, which includes someone like Rev. Haywood who *lives* in the ward, wherever he may sleep. This altered understanding of the space leads to a different assessment of how (and whether) the ward should be rebuilt.

The questions that remain for me revolve around the obstacles that emerge when the repositioned theorist attempts to move not only with the "users" of a space, but with the planners. Planners need comprehensive information — not tentative and partial information. The advocacy that the repositioned theorist embodies can easily be dismissed as subjective and parochial in the objective realm of the strategist's proper. Lefebvre (1991) warns:

> The expert either works for himself alone or else he serves the interests of bureaucratic, financial or political forces. If ever he were truly to confront these forces in the name of the interested parties, his fate would be sealed. (365)

As an activist and not a planner, Lugones is not worried about making her spatial practice comprehensible to "bureaucratic, financial or political forces." However, in the wake of this unnatural disaster, we may need to try.

Note

I am indebted to the thoughtful and constructive comments from anonymous reviewers and from my colleague, Lynne Arnault.

CHAPTER TEN

Understanding New Orleans

Creole Urbanism

Jacob A. Wagner

New Orleans after Hurricane Katrina is not a "clean slate." In the months following the disaster there have been repeated claims that the city is a tabula rasa, and the rebuilding of New Orleans has been touted as a "great opportunity" to change the design of the city. Nothing could be further from the truth.

The image of New Orleans as a clean slate is fundamentally flawed and rooted in a deeply modernist impulse (Toulmin 1990) that reveals intentions as well as ignorance. Those who claim that the city is a clean slate are shapers of an image that goes hand in hand with physically creating it as such. The wide circulation of this myth suggests the great depth of misunderstanding about New Orleans in the aftermath of the disaster. The absence of the majority of the city's residents—reduced after the flooding to a fraction of its population—is critical to this ideology. A clear plan for resettlement would contradict the vision of the city as a clean slate, and neighborhoods full of people would complicate a process of rebuilding concerned more with future profit than with the safety and needs both of exiled residents and those who have returned.

If the city and its neighborhoods are treated as a clean slate by those with the power and wealth to transform them, then the United States will lose one of its most eclectic local cultures and most interesting cities, "one of the few places that American civilization has not remade, flattened, replaced" (Eco 1986, 29). In the wake of devastation, what we need in New Orleans are not the grand claims of those who would level the city and start from scratch, but a recovery program that is sensitive to local culture and that respects the basic urban fabric of creole New Orleans.

Broad Street Apothecary, flooded out.
Photograph by Jacob A. Wagner; image courtesy of the photographer.

This chapter introduces the concept of *creole urbanism* as a framework for understanding New Orleans and the specific features that define the city's urban culture. Its purpose is to provide a lens through which to view the historical development of the city and to develop a vocabulary that serves as a counterpoint to the dominant rhetoric of the clean slate. New Orleans is the product of a deep history of urbanism from the French and Spanish colonial eras of the eighteenth century through the nineteenth-century era of river-borne commerce and the rise of a populous American port city to the tragedy of the twentieth-century streetcar city obliterated by highway development. Despite having been battered by decades of disinvestment and insensitive development, New Orleans remains a mix of historical layers, the remnants of each era juxtaposed against one another throughout the city.

Understanding the city's creole urbanism — its urban spatial structure — as a central component of its cultural identity is critical to the recovery process. The term "creole" — explained below in more detail — suggests the long history of ethnic hybridity that has contributed to the city's sense of place and identity. The term "urbanism" is meant to express both the deep history of urban settlement and the ways in which historical cities are the product of complex inter-actions between space and culture — not as a matter of abstraction, but rather as a product of lived experiences. As a whole, the concept of creole urbanism suggests the characteristics of New Orleans as a way of life — as lived space — in an effort to resist the tendency to homogenize the city and its neighborhoods.

Troublesome Details

Every radical human disaster calls for a reappraisal of public memory. Mo-ments of crisis emerge from a long history of events, although on the surface they may appear dramatic, spontaneous, and unprecedented. Making sense of the disaster and the events preceding it opens a window of opportunity through which a very public process of reckoning can take place. How quickly the window is closed by forces seeking to maintain the status quo is a matter of struggle and collective memory (see part 4 of this book, where Daina Harvey and Elizabeth Spelman discuss these themes in greater detail).

Ralph Ellison captures a critical challenge revealed by the human disaster in New Orleans when he declares:

> Perhaps more than any other people, Americans have been locked in a deadly struggle with time, with history. We've fled the past and trained ourselves to sup-press, if not forget, troublesome details of the national memory, and a great part of our optimism, like our progress, has been bought at the cost of ignoring the pro-cesses through which we've arrived at any given moment in our national existence. (Ellison 2001, 124)

The "troublesome details" of which Ellison wrote more than forty years ago are still very much with the United States, as Hurricane Katrina revealed for those people not already aware of the persistence of poverty and structural rac-ism at the heart of the American political economy. As such, the suppression of critical memory must be understood as the crux of the entire debacle still unfolding in New Orleans.

For better or worse, Hurricane Katrina has challenged the nation to reen-gage with the historical and contemporary realities of New Orleans, a city that expresses the deep contradictions of American history, and to reckon with deeply ignored problems of poverty, disinvestment in the public sphere, ne-glect of human rights, and structural racism.

In order to link the New Orleans experience to a broader understanding of urban life, we should analyze its particular urbanism. As Andy Merrifield (2002) has suggested, we need to know "how big cities create and get created by particular kinds of people, by specific kinds of selfhoods and psychologies, by special interpersonal and social relationships, cultures and sensibilities" (8). New Orleans is a city known for its local color and characters — real, fictional, living, and dead. But Merrifield's quote points to the important task of moving beyond stereotypes and simple descriptions to dig down into the particularities of place that emerge from deep historical and cultural analysis to produce an urban ethnography, which is so vital at this moment in the city's history.

We can find the urban sensibilities and psychologies of New Orleans not only among the diaspora of dispossessed across the nation, but also in the streets of the city. What makes New Orleans rare among North American cities, and worth fighting for, is the city's creole urbanism: the everyday interplay between historic urban neighborhoods with a density of social life that promotes a unique street culture rooted in an ethos of diversity and assimilation (see also Fields 2004, Roach 1996).

Understanding "Creole"

What does it mean to refer to New Orleans as a creole city? The term "creole" is often used to describe the culture and people of New Orleans. It is a term verging on stereotype and suffering at times from overuse. But it is important and useful to our understanding not only of the people but also of the built space of the city, and as such we should grapple with its history and usage. In the past the term "creole" has been used in ways that were both exclusive and inclusive. Given this contradictory history it is important to be deliberate in the application of such a complicated term to represent the urbanism of New Orleans.

The social process of creolization directs our attention to the presence of characteristics from two or more cultures and how these characteristics are discernable among people and the urban built environment. From the mix of these multiple cultures, a new culture emerges that is distinct and recognizable as different from each of the "parent" cultures. However, even as the new type emerges, the lines between the contributing cultures become blurred and what remains is a strong presence of ambiguity. The answer to the question "Where does one culture begin and the other end?" is no longer clear.

The informal use of the term "creole" designates the diversity of the city's cultural identity and is often used to characterize everything and anything from south Louisiana. As a designation for local culture in the face of outside cultural influence, this use of the term has provided an encompassing umbrella for all things New Orleans.

This usage suggests the historical influence of cultural assimilation in French Louisiana. Historically, the ethos of assimilation at the core of French and Spanish colonization efforts stands in stark contrast to the culture of segregation at the core of Anglo-American society (see, e.g., Paz 1985, 363). In New Orleans, this ethic of assimilation helped fuel the political protests of Afro-Creoles who fought the imposition of de jure racial segregation in the 1890s. Their vision of citizenship was part of the political ethos of the French diaspora, which provided a value system in which "race" was not the defining feature of one's political identity and citizenship (Logsdon and Bell 1992, 204–205).

In contrast to the assimilationist perspective, "creole" was also used to signify the elite identity in the city defined in terms of social status, race, and family lineage. This "whites only" definition and usage of the term is linked to the history of racialized power in the city, even as it also suggests a myth of racial purity. As historian Joseph Tregle (1992) has shown, this definition of the term arose in the post–Civil War era when the imposition of racial boundaries of "black" and "white" became central to the political reorganization of the city and the state. In the context of heightened racial consciousness in the late nineteenth century, "creole" was redefined as a term of exclusion by the emerging white elite to enforce new levels of racial segregation and social class division while undermining working-class solidarity on the city's waterfront (see Arnesen 1991, Tregle 1992).

In New Orleans, the presence of ethnic diversity, racial ambiguity, and cultural hybridity within a context of increasingly rigid definitions of racialized identity characterizes much of the twentieth-century experience. At critical moments in the city's history, the presence of cultural and racial ambiguity has been met with elite violence, social control, and the use of state power to enforce socially constructed boundaries of racial hierarchy (Wagner 2004). The beauty of New Orleans and the American experience, however, is that racial violence has not had the last word. Instead, cultural reinvention, humor, and resistance have transformed systems of oppression and helped to realize the promise of American democracy.

The legacy of Afro-Creole resistance to the Americanization of the city—what historians Joseph Logsdon and Arnold Hirsch refer to as "creole radicalism"—is essential to an understanding of the long history of civil rights struggle and racial politics in the city (Hirsch and Logsdon 1992, 195). It is also critical to the concept of creole urbanism because ethnic differences within the black community have long shaped notions of territory and identity in the city's neighborhoods. As the complexities of the term "creole" reveal, New Orleans is a cultural hybrid, but not in the superficial manner in which city boosters like to refer to the city's diversity as a "gumbo."

Placing New Orleans: Creole Urbanism

Creole urbanism, like the term "creole" itself, has the potential to be a contentious concept. The use of the term to describe the city's urbanism is meant in an inclusive manner, seeking to represent the city's deep history of urbanism as a product of diverse influences. The fact of multiplicity and ambiguity at the core of creole urbanism suggests that there is more than one way to read the urban environment. It warns us that significant places bear multiple meanings, and the basis for different interpretations resides in sometimes conflicting, sometimes complementary experiences of cultural, ethnic, religious, racial, and class identities. In fact, the more important a particular place or symbol is to the production of particular social divisions or power hierarchies, the more likely the meanings associated with that space will be contested. Today it is the very meaning of the city as a whole that is at the center of great debate and dialogue as the basic structure of the city and its future are in question.

Perhaps as a result of its diversity and marginality, New Orleans has existed only in the peripheral vision of American scholars (see also the chapters in this book by Steinberg, Shields, and Harvey). As urban historians Hirsch and Logsdon (1992) report, "Few of the nation's urban experts, we discovered, had ever tried to place New Orleans within the framework of existing scholarship about American cities" (ix). According to these authors, the identity of New Orleans is the result of at least four key historical factors:

1. the city's diverse linguistic roots (French, but also African, Native American, Spanish, Sicilian, Irish, and German influences);
2. the city's Catholicism, which is distinctly Mediterranean in its outlook and spirit rather than northern European;
3. the emphasis and tolerance of "bawdy sensual delights"—indicative of a Latin culture based in carnival (e.g., the famed debauchery of Mardi Gras); and
4. the city's proud, free black population—referred to as "creoles of color" or "Afro-Creoles," whose identity is linked to the French Diaspora and central to the notion of creole radicalism at the root of the city's civil rights movement.

I would add to these four factors another aspect that is often overlooked by scholars of urban culture and cities: New Orleans' unique sense of humor, which is deeply linked with its political culture. In New Orleans, the power of humor is deeply appreciated, and no public figure is safe from a good comedic lambasting. A key aspect of carnival culture is the strong sense of parody that runs through the city's streets and its history. Certainly, this sense of humor — a gallows humor in the shadow of Katrina and the levee failure — is one of the few things that locals can count on in the face of such overwhelming tragedy and loss. Without a good sense of humor, life in the city would be unbearable (Rose 2006).

In addition to these historical-cultural features, we must view the city through a socio-spatial perspective to identify five key factors that contribute to what I call the creole urbanism of New Orleans:

1. The presence of a broad diversity of neighborhoods that span more than 280 years of urban settlement.
2. A particular urban morphology that is the product of historical settlement patterns in a tortuous geography.
3. A distinct architectural heritage composed of a diversity of historical and cultural influences and sustained by generations of master builders and artisans, from African shotgun houses to the wrought-iron balconies of the French Quarter to the palatial Victorian mansions of the Anglo-American Garden District (see essays in Hankins and Maklansky 2002 — especially Spitzer).
4. A tolerance for decay and aging, such that abandonment of historic structures was commonplace in many neighborhoods before the flood. This factor, combined with the city's inability to demolish "slum" and "blighted" properties during the urban renewal era (the state of Louisiana did not delegate the authority to the city), resulted in what one scholar has called a "phenomenal stock of 19th century structures" (Heard 1997).
5. The city's unique street culture, rooted in the practices of all classes and hues of citizenry, from the social aid and pleasure clubs of the late-twentieth-century black American ghetto to the Uptown mansions of the white Carnival elite. In New Orleans, the street is a place of social performance, not simply a traffic sewer.

Creole urbanism provides a concept that links the front stoop of a creole cottage to the urban fabric of streetcar neighborhoods. It reminds us that the culinary practices of the city's cooks in their kitchens are deeply connected to the bayous and wetlands beyond the floodwalls that provide the basic ingredients of the regional food culture (Beriss 2006). Thus, the idea of creole urbanism can serve as a bridge across the various divides to understanding and explaining New Orleans.

King Roger's Seafood before the flood, March 2005.
Photograph by Jacob A. Wagner; image courtesy of the photographer.

From the Front Stoop to the Back of Town: Neighborhoods and Urban Form

Questions of urban form are central to understanding and appreciating the sense of place in the city. The geographer Peirce Lewis (1976) was the first scholar to comprehensively observe and explain the underlying historical settlement patterns that shape the city's urban form. A basic rectangular street grid altered to provide access to the meandering banks of the Mississippi River created in New Orleans an urban structure of regularity broken rhythmically by triangular forms at the junction of grids with merging and diverging alignments. For newcomers the regularity of the grid in an irregular site makes it easy to lose one's sense of direction. Street names change across major thoroughfares such as Canal Street, marking historical and cultural divides as well as one's location in the city. Locals have their own language for direction in the city — shaped less by the cardinal directions of cartographers and more by the idiosyncrasies of the city's site, described as "uptown-downtown" and "riverside-lakeside."

Neighborhoods throughout New Orleans present a diversity of architectural types and styles that illustrate various historical phases of housing production. But the urban fabric as a whole is more important in the long run than the specific architectural styles of individual homes. The scale of houses and buildings gives shape to a low-rise city laid out on a flat delta plain. The steel and glass verticality of the city's central business district is a great exception to what is predominantly a tightly packed residential environment. The basic urban fabric of the city's neighborhoods still reflects the influence of the city's orientation to the waterfront as the driving feature of the nineteenth-century economy. For much of its development, New Orleans was a steamboat and streetcar city, and the basic structure of those systems still influences the spatial organization of its neighborhoods.

The beauty of the city's architectural heritage is not only the highly detailed buildings but the skilled traditions that sustain the historic structures from one generation to the next. Master craftspeople whose media are plaster, wood, masonry, and iron tend to the city's historic houses and cemeteries like gardeners in a grand urban landscape (Spitzer 2002). While great attention has been paid to the role of African-Americans in the development of jazz and the musical heritage of New Orleans, much less attention has been paid to the role of Black artisans in the city building process. Here, New Orleans provides a compelling case that challenges us to look more closely at the role of African-American art and labor in the development of historic cities (see the essays in Hankins and Maklansky 2002).

In the post-Katrina context, the survival of the skilled trades and the building arts must be at the center of rebuilding the city's neighborhoods as well as its public school system. It is not enough to preserve historic structures in isolation from the living traditions of the building trades that have kept neighborhoods full of historic homes for generations.

The Street as a Place

Of the socio-spatial features that contribute to the experience of lived space in New Orleans, the street culture is what sets the city apart from the dominant cultural landscape of American suburbia. Second-line organizer and community leader Norman Francis knew that. So did master craftsman and Mardi Gras Indian Chief Allison "Tootie" Montana, who passed away just a few months before Hurricane Katrina (see also chapter 2 in this book by Jordan Flaherty). So did jazz musician, educator, and cultural leader Danny

Barker. All of these people knew that the ability to sustain the city's unique cultural traditions relied on a particular relationship between urban space and cultural practice.

Each of these community elders embodied the city's urban traditions in practice while passing their particular skills on to a new generation. It is significant, for example, that Danny Barker returned to New Orleans to instigate the rebirth of local musical traditions in the late 1960s and early 1970s as museum curator at the New Orleans Jazz Museum and musical advisor to the youth band at the Fairview Baptist Church. Barker's return to his roots in New Orleans helped to sustain musical practices and parading traditions while providing the foundation for a new generation of jazz innovators (Jacobsen and Marquis 2006).

As a space of cultural performance, neighborhood streets in New Orleans serve a role that most other city cultures in the United States have long since abandoned as active and living traditions. While the automobile has had a tremendous impact on the restructuring of New Orleans' mostly nineteenth-century urban form, the people of the city in their performance of specific cultural traditions have retained practices of parading that have long been dropped as spatial practice in other North American cities.[1] The African roots of New Orleans' culture and the city's carnival traditions have much to do with this, as does the subtropical climate and dependency on tourism. However, deeply held cultural attitudes toward the meaning of life inform and provide the context for this performance of tradition.

The city's unique culture resides in the fact that the people have not given their streets up entirely to the automobile. Streets in New Orleans are very much public space:

> The streets of the French Quarter and of all New Orleans are more than a path for movement: they are places in themselves, scenes for a pageant. More than any building, they have provided the setting [for] what are surely the city's essential art forms — the early jazz music of the marching bands and the parades of Mardi Gras. (Heard 1997, 11)

This idea of the "street as a place" is evident on an everyday basis in New Orleans, but especially during carnival season, around jazz funerals and second-lines, and in the parade traditions of the Mardi Gras Indians and social aid and pleasure clubs. Each of these traditions has its own calendar that helps to mark the passage of time, as well as providing a context for the passage of individual lives within the context of the city's history.

The creole urbanism of New Orleans holds the promise of an alternative, and yet unrealized, modernism that is an exception to the dominant mode of life in the United States. The dependency on the automobile has produced disastrous results in the wake of Katrina. Thousands of residents were stranded without a way out of the city, and the automobiles that were left behind and flooded have leaked oil and gasoline into the soil and groundwater. As such, the tragedy of American dependency on cars has been exposed, and New Orleans must be rebuilt as a city less dependent on the automobile with a twenty-first-century version of the streetcar system that once made it one of the most extensive in the nation.

The Americanization of New Orleans has proceeded on two fronts: one spatial and one cultural — both with grave consequences for creole urbanism. These two dimensions of urban change have influenced each other: as the city was rebuilt to favor the automobile, it also became a more racially segregated metropolitan area (see also chapter 5 in this book by Hugh Bartling). This process has meant not only the privatization of public space but also the diminishment of the radical creole vision of a future based not on the color consciousness of American racism — what Albert Murray (1971) called the "folklore of white supremacy" — but rather on the celebration of difference that lies at the heart of the city's hybridity (see also chapter 4 in this book by Rob Shields).

Over the course of the twentieth century, the urban form of creole New Orleans began to unravel. Processes of suburbanization both within Orleans Parish and beyond resulted in a metropolitan spatial pattern similar to many U.S. cities. In the process, the historic center around which the metropolitan area developed began to show the signs of disinvestment and the racial isolation of African Americans typical of American apartheid. Although New Orleans was not among the sixteen U.S. cities identified by Massey and Denton (1993) as hyper-segregated, it had begun to exhibit key indicators of extreme segregation. As Hirsch and Logsdon (1992) wrote more than a decade before Hurricane Katrina: "Metropolitanization meant more than racial polarization. The destruction of the old city, the disappearance of its tightly knit, clustered, multicultural neighborhoods, also meant the disintegration of the residential base that had created, nurtured and sustained New Orleans' unique culture" (200). This process of suburbanization within and beyond Orleans Parish was facilitated by federal policies as well as the technological capacity to drain and settle areas that had long been avoided because of their low-lying character. The story of American urbanism in the twentieth century has been the loss of diversity and the rise of suburban homogeneity, and this trend is especially obvious in New Orleans.

The Politics of Return: Reviving Creole New Orleans

The challenge facing New Orleans now is complex and multifaceted. It centers on the question of what makes it distinct as a place, what makes the culture of the city and its region, and finally, how in the face of such devastation and displacement the city can revive itself in a manner that builds upon the best of the past while challenging the deeply rooted problems of poverty, violence, a dysfunctional school system (see Lauria and Miron 2005), and structural racism.

No set of issues is more contentious in post-Katrina New Orleans than the politics of return. Rising costs of living in the city and the transfer of real property to new owners intent upon maximizing their investment are the greatest challenges to the restoration of local culture. The federal commitment to the elimination of public housing is an intensification of an active pre-Katrina policy of devolution via demolition. This policy puts to rest any question about the administration's commitment to the city's most vulnerable population. As such, the politics of return are now the central front in the battle over the future of the city's neighborhoods and its culture. Without plans and policies that outline a strategy for resettlement, we should not be surprised if the majority of the city's working-class African American residents remain shut out of the city.

Author Leon Forrest's concept of "reinvention" suggests a deep cultural tradition and worldview that must inform the resettlement process in New Orleans. According to Forrest, this concept is critical to an understanding of black cultural production in the Americas:

> "Reinvention seems to me so much a part of the black ethos, of taking something that is available or maybe conversely, denied blacks and making it into something else for survival and then adding a kind of stamp and style and elegance. . . . We're not simply a repository nor a reflection of the African experience, but that we're constantly remaking everything that was left over from Africa, everything that we got from the Europeans, into something completely new that both the Africans couldn't do and the Europeans couldn't do. Europeans didn't create jazz and neither did the Africans. Black Americans did that." (quoting Forrest in Warren 1993, 397)

Reviving the cultural economy of the city requires an understanding of the role of craftspeople, artists, cooks, and musicians while making space for their return. If creole urbanism is to be useful to those working toward the reconstruction and rebuilding of the city, it must facilitate an understanding of the subtleties of the city's identity while providing clues to how we can rebuild in a manner that does not obliterate local culture.

Conclusion

Will New Orleans be flattened and replaced? In the post–levee failure era, the future of the city's cultural identity — the basic fabric of creole urbanism — hangs in the balance. Viewed through the lens of Henri Lefebvre, New Orleanians now find themselves at the center of a *trial by space* in which various competing ideologies are seeking dominance through the transformation of urban space (Lefebvre 1991, 416). Which vision of the future will be realized is a matter of practical politics unfolding daily in the city's neighborhoods, in Baton Rouge, on Wall Street, and in Washington, DC.

While the architects in their various ideological camps have claimed much of the airtime, the scope of their influence is clearly limited. Beyond the gaze of the national press, the politics of land-use decisions are unfolding in a highly volatile environment of uncertainty in which those with the resources to rebuild have already begun and those without the resources remain on the sidelines. Unfortunately this situation favors the mobile capital of corporate finance, the parties generally the least interested in cultivating local culture, at the expense of the local businesses that have endured the earliest and most difficult phase of the rebuilding process.

Despite several planning processes, no clear vision for the city's future has been articulated by the people in positions of leadership. Against the grain of "clean slate" thinking, creole urbanism provides a conceptual framework that can be used to weave together the various constituent elements of the city's identity into a clear vision for rebuilding neighborhoods. The guiding spirit of the reconstruction must be the preservation and enhancement of creole urbanism in New Orleans.

Nothing could be more antithetical to the city's identity than the dominant mode of suburban-style, big-box construction. In the face of greater visual, cultural, and commercial monotony, the creole urbanism of New Orleans asks us to find what is distinct about each city we inhabit and to cultivate those features in ways that inform a renewed sense of dwelling. Creole urbanism suggests that New Orleans has its own culture, its own sense of time, and its own experience of broader historical trends at work in other places. Rather than attracting us to New Orleans as some exceptional case, however, the idea of creole urbanism should send all of us back to our own neighborhoods in search of the forgotten place identities in whatever location we call home.

Note

1. This is not to suggest that other American cities were influenced by African parading traditions to the same degree as New Orleans. It is rather to suggest that many ethnic groups in the nineteenth century used the parade as spatial practice to sustain cultural traditions and identities. Over time these practices have been abandoned in other cities, while New Orleans' particular traditions have been sustained, although transformed.

CHAPTER ELEVEN

On Street Life and Urban Disasters

Lessons from a "Third World" City

Jonathan Shapiro Anjaria

One month prior to Hurricane Katrina, the city of Mumbai, India, experienced a similar calamity. On July 26, 2005, thirty-seven inches of rain fell on Mumbai, resulting in massive flooding, destruction, and an unprecedented interruption to the functioning of the city. The physical appearance of the two flooded cities was so similar that, following Katrina, Mumbai newspapers clarified pictures of submerged cars in New Orleans with tongue-in-cheek captions such as: "This is not Mumbai." There was, however, a notable difference in the aftermath of the disasters in the collective imagination of these cities. In contrast to New Orleans, the aftermath of the Mumbai floods was not marked by stories of panic, social disorder, violence, or looting but by stories of widespread acts of generosity, selflessness, and kindness. This was especially remarkable considering the conventional rhetoric that constructs Mumbai as a paradigmatic dystopic Third World city, marked by underdevelopment, infrastructural failure, squalor, and despair. In this chapter I argue that, paradoxically, it was the very resistance of Mumbai's open spaces to modernist ideals of city planning that prevented it from experiencing the chaos and social breakdown witnessed in New Orleans. This was, in part, due to the fact that during and following the Mumbai floods it was the "unruly" crowds — those who, much to the frustration of city planners and civic activists, engage in multifarious uses of open spaces — who took on the social responsibility abdicated by the state.[1]

As even a cursory glance at the media accounts of New Orleans shows, a globally scaled imagination of cities informed the way the disaster was interpreted. In Mumbai, as in the United States, the scenes of desperation and chaos in New Orleans, as well as the stories of government inaction and ineptitude, were met with disbelief. The mere fact of the disaster was not remark-able; it was the fact that a disaster of this kind was happening in the United States. Like Americans, Mumbaikars were shocked that the scenes of despair and anger shown on television could come from a country that represented such enormous wealth and power. Indeed, what such reactions showed, on one level, is that the imagination of a globe divided into a First World (that works) and a Third World (that doesn't) has been internalized by those at the bottom of this hierarchy as much as by those at the top.

This chapter attempts to interrogate the imagination of the world as divided into functional First World urban spaces on the one hand and dysfunctional Third World urban spaces on the other, and proposes, in place of such an imagination, the possibility of a transnational study of cities that does not have the Euro-American urban experience as its central referent (cf. Robinson 2002). To this end, I argue that Mumbai's response to the formal infrastruc-tural breakdown caused by the July 26 floods demonstrates the need to recon-sider the assumptions that cities in the global South necessarily represent fail-ure. This need was made apparent by the writings emerging from the Katrina experience which relied on the trope of the "Third World" to make sense of images of post-Katrina New Orleans.

Unfortunately, absent in these writings is an inquiry into what the Third World might actually be. Rather, in the post-Katrina commentary, the "Third World" came to signify all that is bad, with the unproductive implication that the Third World can offer lessons only on what directions cities ought *not* to take as they try to avoid similar disasters in the future. By contrast, I propose that a study of the lived experience of cities in the global South, including the lived experience of urban disasters, outside developmentalist or apocalyptic narratives, might serve to disrupt the continued one-way travel of urban theory by providing crucial lessons not only for the future of the Third World city, but for cities in the United States and Europe as well.

Katrina's Third World

An image of the desperate and hopeless Third World figured prominently in the deluge of commentary on the unprecedented scenes of destruction and chaos following Katrina's wrath in New Orleans. Indeed, in the absence of specific referents, a language of the Third-World-as-urban-dystopia was de-ployed, with the assumption of its universal intelligibility among speaker and audience. The mainstream newspapers were most explicit in this regard. For instance, a writer for *The New York Times* reported, "It was left to reporters embedded in the mayhem to let Americans know that a Third World country had suddenly appeared on the Gulf Coast" (quoted in Brooks 2005);[2] CNN announced that "Interstate 10 in New Orleans was 'very Third World,' with people wandering around 'like nomads' and streets filled with water that 'just looks unhealthy'" (quoted in Brooks 2005); *U.S. News & World Report* referred to "Third World images of death and devastation" (quoted in Brooks 2005); Fox News declared that the viewing public will be "forever scarred by Third World horrors unthinkable in this nation until now" (quoted in Brooks 2005); and CNN quoted an AP source as saying, "'It's like being in a Third World country'" (CNN 2005).

Yet it was not only the mainstream media, whose facile use of stereotypes is relatively unremarkable, who were guilty of constructing the Third World in this dystopic cast. Similar Third World imagery dominated more critical writings as well. For instance, in a piece critical of the media representation in the wake of the disaster, Rosa Brooks writes, "In New Orleans last week, scores of reporters experienced firsthand some of the miseries of America's Third World" (Brooks 2005). A number of other writers followed suit: "Having failed to respond to Hurricane Katrina in the manner expected of the world's leading nation . . . the United States has finally gained membership in the third world" (Schanberg 2005); "Ironically, America's response to the predicament and suffering of Katrina's victims has been eerily reminiscent of that of a Third World country" (Sarvate 2005); "It is truer to say we discovered that New Orleans, like any other city, had been in the Third World all along. These faces of terror and want and despair and menace and stoicism are faces from the third world" (Rodriguez 2005); "What Katrina laid bare to the world, as well as to U.S. viewers . . . is that the United States . . . has a great deal in common with the Third World, and increasingly so" (Lobe 2005).

What is remarkable in this sampling of quotations is the way in which the idea that the Third World is a paradigmatic signifier of urban dystopia remains uninterrogated by even the most sophisticated and critical scholars writing on the coverage of the Katrina aftermath. For instance, in an article on U.S. audience response to scenes of New Orleans in the media, Virginia Dominguez (2005) argues that references to the Third World to describe the events demonstrates a lack of awareness of the poverty and inequalities that already exist throughout the United States. Dominguez argues that equating distraught non-white faces with the Third World "allows people to think that poverty and non-whiteness are non-American things, even when they are present in the U.S. in significant numbers." For Dominguez, the danger of describing the scenes as "looking like the third world" is that it encourages viewers to see the disaster as not affecting the "real America," whereas in fact, "New Orleans is no more and no less 'Third World' than the country as a whole."

Dominguez rightly notes that most Americans imagine the United States as uniquely untouched by global problems of poverty and inequality, which makes her critique especially salient in an increasingly solipsistic public sphere. However, and not to diminish its importance, implicit in her critique is an acceptance of what the "Third World" refers to. While Dominguez questions the popular and social-scientific assumptions of what constitutes "home," assumptions regarding "away" are still taken for granted. Like other critics of U.S. self-fantasies, Dominguez suggests that the First World is not really the First World, yet her article does not subject the imagination of the Third World to similar scrutiny. As I hope to show, there may also be something to gain if we at least entertain the possibility that the Third World is also not as it appears.

Slums, Crowds, and Urban Disorder

It is often the case that the imagination of the Third World city as marked by the abysmal failure of infrastructure and state and social order is derived from the development expert's and lay traveler's firsthand accounts of the *aesthetic* failures of these cities (Chakrabarty 2002, 66). They are exemplified by their crowds, their dilapidated buildings, and, inevitably, their slums, which are invariably first observed from an airplane window during the descent to the international airport.[3] Indeed, it is through these aesthetic failures that the foreign observer comes into awareness of self-evident realities of Third World poverty.

This fact is much to the consternation of Mumbai's business elite and their ideologues, who realize that it is the very visible and physical presence of the poor that, in contributing to its appearance of chaos and disorder, relegates Mumbai to the bottom of the heap of the world's cities. In fact, the visible appearance of Mumbai and other Indian cities' public spaces has been a cause of concern for two centuries. Throughout its history Mumbai has frustrated bourgeois, or modernist, ideals of urban space. It continues to do so today despite the talk of the city's supposed new entry into circuits of global capital — its new shopping malls, luxury residential complexes, and entertainment centers, for instance. The ideal characteristics of cities taken for granted since the mid-nineteenth century — wide open roads, empty sidewalks, swift flows of vehicular and pedestrian traffic, and segregation of activities — are largely absent in Mumbai.

In fact, Mumbai is a city that seems to wholeheartedly reject such ideals.

Thoroughfares are in a perpetual state of dense congestion, and sidewalks, when they exist, are used for a wide variety of activities, which rarely include walking. Indeed, the multifarious use of sidewalks (or, more appropriately, the space on the side of the road) is the characteristic most observers of Mumbai find particularly jarring, and yet this characteristic may also contain the key to understanding the alternative functioning of cities in the seemingly failed Third World. As Chakrabarty (2002) writes, to the Europeans and the national-ist elite who viewed Indian cities through a modernist lens, "The many different uses to which [the street] was put . . . presented, as it were, a total confusion of the private and the public. People washed, changed, slept, and even urinated and defecated in the open" (66). There is much to be gained for scholars of cities once they overcome the "particular way of seeing" (Chakrabarty 2002, 66) that sees such spaces for what they lack rather than for what they add to the functioning of the city as a whole. Instead of seeing such scenes as fail-ure, "Can one read this as a refusal to become citizens of an ideal, bourgeois order?" (Chakrabarty 2002, 77).

The current intellectual climate seems to include a structural blindness that disallows Third World cities, and the visually jarring urban spaces found within them, from being understood as anything but failures. In fact, this imagination is found in the writings of contemporary writers of diverse po-litical positions, as evinced by the shared apocalyptic imagery of Mike Da-vis's "Planet of Slums" and the conservative writer Robert Kaplan's "Coming Anarchy."[4] However, is the Third World city really on the brink, "bursting at the seams," or facing "imminent catastrophe," as many of these writ-ers would have us believe? Social and economic indicators in many places may support this claim. And yet, this doomsday rhetoric should not satisfy urban scholars interested in the plenitude of urban life. For this story of im-minent collapse rarely ever corresponds with the everyday realities of cities. Indeed, despite dilapidated physical appearances, failed local governments, abysmal "human development" statistics, and inadequate infrastructure, life continues. As AbdouMaliq Simone (2004) writes of African cities, which are the paradigmatic "failed" urban spaces of the First World social-scientific imaginary:

> In city after city, one can witness an incessant throbbing produced by the intense proximity of hundreds of activities: cooking, reciting, selling, loading and unload-ing, fighting, praying, relaxing, pounding, and buying, all side by side on stages too cramped, too deteriorated, too clogged with waste, history, and disparate energy, and sweat to sustain all of them. And yet they persist. (1)

Analyses funneled through the narrative of Third World crises miss this vast richness of human activity, as well as the simple fact that amid all the outward signs of failure, there just may be an alternative logic at work.

This is what the protagonist — an Australian escaped convict — in Gregory Roberts's popular novel, *Shantaram* (2004), observes shortly after his arrival in Mumbai. Watching the urban landscape unfold as he travels to his downtown hotel from the airport, he experiences the familiar reaction upon seeing the Third World city for the first time: "My first impression was that some catastrophe had taken place, and that the slums were refugee camps for the shambling survivors. . . . If you feel it at all, it's a lacerating guilt, that first confrontation with the wretched of the earth" (7). But as his journey through the city continues, he slowly experiences a change.

> I began to look beyond the immensity of the slum societies, and to see the people who lived within them. A woman stooped to brush forward the black satin psalm of her hair. Another bathed her children with water from a copper dish. . . . Men carried water in buckets. Men made repairs to one of the huts. And everywhere that I looked, people smiled and laughed. . . . I looked at the people, then, and I saw how *busy* they were — how much industry and energy described their lives. Occasional sudden glimpses inside the huts revealed the astonishing cleanliness of that poverty: the spotless floors, and glistening metal pots in neat, tapering towers. (7–8)

Indeed, only after watching the mundane activities of life does the narrator overcome initial reactions of horror and condemnation to realize the simple realities of the slum — that people "smiled and laughed" and lived lives of "industry and energy" — and only thus does he manage to reject the powerful metanarrative of the Third World city.

Unfortunately, banal feelings such as pleasure and happiness fail to have a place in many First World social scientists' imaginaries of the Third World city. This was made strikingly evident by a recent incident recounted by a Mumbai-based sociologist. While attending a conference on informal labor in Dakar, he and two other professors, one from the Philippines and the other from Belgium, took a drive around the city. At one point they drove past a large slum with groups of people sitting outside their small huts doing daily chores, chatting, laughing, and having a good time. Upon seeing this, the Belgian professor told his colleagues how surprised he was to see smiling people living in such poor conditions; he found it difficult to accept the simple fact that people, despite poverty and harsh living conditions, do not glumly sit all day in misery, ruing their fate or otherwise demonstrating their impoverishment.

192 Jonathan Shapiro Anjaria

What might we make of this well-meaning Belgian professor's surprise upon seeing smiling faces in a slum? For one, it demonstrates the presumed relationship between *infrastructural* failure and *social* failure, a presumption shared by a wide spectrum of people. The inability to see economically poor areas as anything but failures extends to U.S. cities as well, as became apparent during the Katrina disaster and subsequent relief and reconstruction efforts. Insensitive attitudes toward people displaced by Katrina — the most glaring example being Barbara Bush's comments that New Orleans residents were better off living on cots in sports arenas because they had been rescued from abject poverty (*New York Times* 2005) — are some of the consequences of preconceived notions regarding the lived experience of poverty.

In both New Orleans and Mumbai, then, there is an imperative to recognize what *works* in impoverished neighborhoods, without losing sight of economic inequalities and government failures to meet residents' infrastructural needs. Whereas to some, the African Americans living in the Texas sports arena that Barbara Bush referred to represent a certain kind of failure — of economic inequalities and government response in the face of natural disaster, for instance — to others they might represent the very characteristic that makes New Orleans a functioning urban space. As a number of scholars have noted, the pre-Katrina vibrancy of New Orleans is in no small part due to the great variety of purposes for which the street is put to use — including parades, second lines, and jazz funerals (Sakakeeny 2006; see also the preceding chapter in this book by Wagner) — all of which take place in the predominantly African American, and relatively poor, "failed" urban space of planners' imaginations. So, if we are to move beyond superficial responses to outward signs of urban failure such as tenements, slums, and crowds, we must look at how the wide diversity of urban spaces are actually lived. With this in mind, I return to the July 26 Mumbai floods and their aftermath.

Mumbai Floods: Disaster

Throughout the afternoon and evening of July 26, torrential rain fell on Mumbai. The city's drainage system — large parts of which are over one hundred years old — was quickly overwhelmed, and in a very brief period of time huge swathes of the city were under water. In the northern part of the city, nearly every ground-floor apartment and home was flooded, while large blocks of slums were completely inundated. In some places, water rose to a height of ten feet. By the late afternoon of the same day, the entire city was paralyzed. Communications and electricity were cut, all trains were stopped, all roads became impassable, and the airports were closed, severing the city's connections with the rest of India (Concerned Citizens' Commission 2005, 6).

While there had been other instances of abnormally heavy rainfall in the past, recent unsustainable development practices led in significant part to this unprecedented destruction. Rampant construction over natural water catchment areas, as well as encroachments on natural drainage systems, prevented the rainwater from flowing out of the city. A study conducted shortly after the disaster by the Concerned Citizens' Commission (CCC) — a coalition comprising housing rights activists, journalists, and union leaders — reported that the areas of the city worst affected by the floods were those that had experienced the greatest amount of recent construction over mangroves (which had earlier served as a buffer zone in times of heavy rain) or were located near the Mithi River. The Mithi River runs through the city from north to south and had for decades been ignored, seen more as a foul swamp than a vital natural mechanism for the evacuation of water. According to the CCC report, two large-scale development projects — the expansion of a runway for the international airport and massive land reclamation for the Bandra-Kurla complex (a new business district) — narrowed the river's width as well as radically altered its course, much as the flooding that occurred in New Orleans a month later similarly was exacerbated by hydrological engineering that had been undertaken to foster commercial development. As a result, and as the findings of the CCC show, people living in these areas experienced the worst effects of the flooding. Most notably, in large parts of Kalina, located near the airport, the water was eight to ten feet deep in many places, and did not fully drain for nearly a week.[5]

People living in the city's slums were worst affected by the flooding. By "slums," I refer to areas dominated by small, two-level semipermanent structures (called *jhopadpattis* in Mumbai), usually with one room on each level. For the most part, these "slums," like the poorer areas inundated by Hurricane Katrina, were not (and still are not) fly-by-night squatter settlements, but well-established residential and work areas. People living in slums in the northern suburbs of Andheri, Santa Cruz, and Kandivali, for instance, experienced devastating losses, as the water level in many places reached above people's heads. The worst incident occurred in Saki Naka, where a section of a hill collapsed, destroying dozens of shanties and killing over one hundred people. In other areas in the suburbs, less sturdily built shanties were simply washed away along with their contents, which sometimes included small children. And, as the CCC documented, for tens of thousands of people the floods resulted in great physical hardship — in some cases people could not eat, sleep, or bathe for days because of the floodwaters — and huge financial losses due to the de-struction of property, as well as general disruptions of everyday life due to the loss of documents and children's schoolbooks.

Moreover, the unusual intensity of the July 26 rains caused an unprece-dented disruption in the functioning of the city. For the first time in recent memory, the city's vast transportation system was rendered completely inoper-able, which had dramatic consequences for the hundreds of thousands of people who work in south Mumbai offices and live in the northern suburbs. The rains and flooding reached their peak in the late afternoon of the twenty-sixth, so that by the start of the commute the entire rail network, including the local lines that serve as the lifeline of the city, had stopped, stranding hundreds of thou-sands of people who were attempting to travel back home. Finally, once the drainage system had been overwhelmed by the torrential rain, huge volumes of water flowed into the roads and highways, making them impassable. Many roads took on the function of canals, turning into raging rivers and trapping tens of thousands of people in cars and buses. By the early evening, major thoroughfares and highways were littered with tens of thousands of vehicles abandoned by people who left their cars to finish their journey home on foot.

And so as dusk settled, the rain continued to pour, and it became clear that there was to be no motorized movement, hundreds of thousands of residents — both rich and poor — slowly made their way back to their homes through the waterlogged roads. Throughout the evening and night of July 26, huge crowds of people quietly walked, often in single file, sometimes through water as high as their waist, eager to get home to their families who had little knowledge of their safety or whereabouts.

Mumbai Floods: Response and Aftermath

As in New Orleans, the Mumbai floods resulted in a complete failure of the city's infrastructure and formal institutions. As the CCC report extensively documents, the state abdicated its responsibilities during the floods and the fol-lowing day. Most notably, police and workers of the Brihanmumbai Municipal Corporation (BMC) — officially responsible for disaster management in the city — were completely absent. However, while Mumbai's formal institutions failed, the city's informal institutions did not. Although the police and munici-pal government were entirely nonfunctional, there was no looting, theft, physi-cal assaults, or sexual violence. Instead, the public showed a huge outpouring of spontaneous acts of kindness and generosity. Indeed, despite the wide-scale destruction and infrastructural failure, something in the city worked.

Amid the catastrophe, chaos did not ensue, nor did social order "break down." In fact, quite the opposite occurred: much of the usual chaos diminished, as main arteries became eerily quiet. Blaring car and truck horns were replaced by the quiet swish of thousands of people slowly making their long, wet journey home by foot. But something else even more remarkable happened in this moment of radical infrastructural failure: Mumbai's infamous crowds became helpful, caring, and genuinely self-sacrificing. After centuries of being the marker of the city's backwardness and the object of fear and fascination by those in power, the crowd, it seemed, proved itself as far more than an engine for chaos and disorder. The hundreds of thousands of stranded people on the flooded streets walked slowly, calmly, sometimes even in a single-file line, with a genuine sense of cooperation.

In addition, throughout the city, through the night of the twenty-sixth and the following day, people came out of their homes to hand out biscuits, bananas, bottled water, and cooked rice and lentils to those who had spent the day and night walking through the flooded roads. Countless anonymous strangers handed out medicine to the elderly. Restaurants and street vendors gave out free food to the hungry. Other remarkable stories included slum residents handing out food and water to drivers stranded in their luxury cars; middle-class families opened their two-room apartments to groups of strangers for days; one rickshaw driver who found a lost, mentally challenged boy fed him for two days and finally located his parents' home. Throughout the devastated northern suburbs, residents put aside religious and ethnic differences to help each other. Even in areas with histories of horrific interreligious violence, there was widespread generosity, with people opening their homes to others regardless of community affiliation (Concerned Citizens' Commission 2005, 7).

Perhaps most importantly, in the days following the floods, stories also proliferated about the selfless acts of young men conventionally seen by the middle classes as loafers who threaten the security of themselves and their families. In one area near one of the city's largest slums, young men, having been flooded out of their one-room shanties, spent the night swimming through the raging water saving schoolchildren stranded in buses. Another group made a rope and carried hungry passengers to safety from the roof of another bus engulfed in floodwaters. There were also many stories of young men tying ropes to trees to help strangers cross flooded roads (Badam 2005), providing large plastic containers to help people stay afloat, and standing on the side of the road warning passersby of potholes, manholes, open drains, or other dangers hidden beneath the water (Rediff.com 2005).[6]

These young men were from the city's *jhopadpattis*, and they constitute the city's vast population of unemployed or, more commonly, underemployed youth. With little work and much time, their main activity is simply to "roam about"[7] to watch, and to be a part of the spectacle of the street. In sum, they constitute the notorious crowd and chaos of the Indian city's streets — for centuries feared and denigrated. Their contribution was so significant that, uncharacteristically, in the days following the floods, the upper classes briefly acknowledged the positive potential of this crowd. Slum residents and the young people who provided help to strangers, who as recently as a few days earlier had been declared the greatest impediment to Mumbai's achieving its global dreams, were now declared to represent the "true spirit" of Mumbai that saved the city in the time of crisis.[8]

The crowd's actions during the floods should, for one, force a rethinking of the disorderly public space as emblematic of Third World urban failure. According to the logic of modernist city planning, congestion, crowds, and the visible presence of the poor have been treated as urban diseases to be eradicated. In much scholarly writing on South Asia as well, the crowd has not fared well. For instance, in the past two decades, researchers of urban violence have attributed interreligious riots and political violence in India to this mobile, underemployed population. With little or no work, they are eager to be part of the action, and are thus susceptible to political or religious leaders' calls for often violent reprisals against a perceived enemy. However, little scholarly attention has been paid to the nonviolent, unspectacular crowd. For there is *always* an immanent crowd on Mumbai's streets — waiting disguised as individuals and pairs for a small accident, a fistfight, a policeman chasing a thief, a film shoot of a policeman chasing a thief, or another spectacle to effect its coalescence. In this case, for instance, groups of hungry and thirsty women, men, and children stranded on the roof of a bus amid swirling floodwaters provided the necessary catalyst. Until now, researchers have only understood this mobile population for its capacity for violence, but what July 26 and its aftermath revealed were its capacity for incredible acts of generosity and selflessness as well.[9]

The July 26 floods showed that Mumbai's vibrantly used public spaces are a valuable resource for the city. And, despite vast and growing inequalities in wealth and living standards, the selfless acts of kindness the poor and working classes in Mumbai provided strangers on flooded streets and open areas demonstrate that the poor still feel that they have a stake in the city. Nevertheless, as in post-Katrina New Orleans, few visions for the city's future development take into account this resource that the city already has. Instead, as I discuss below, most development projects continue to encourage the erasure of the crowd or the visible presence of the poor from the city's public spaces. The persistent dominance of modernist ideals is revealed most directly in the context of the intense debates over the reconfiguration of Mumbai's streets and sidewalks, as well as in plans to "redevelop" the city's slums that are taking place in the city at the present time. In these discussions we can clearly see the unintended consequences of facile ideas regarding failed Third World urban spaces.

Unruly Spaces

Whereas the stories following Katrina shocked the world by showing the horror of the Third World that lurks within a First World country, the stories that followed the Mumbai floods surprised upper-class Mumbaikars by showing them the kindness and humanity that lurks within their supposed dystopic, Third World city. Mumbaikars' surprise at this new picture of their city demonstrated, for one, the power of a global imagination that divides the world's cities into the livable and unlivable, the functional and dysfunctional, the successful and failed. This transnationally circulating imaginary of urban spaces encourages a disregard for how cities in the Third World actually work in favor of abstract models based on "concrete" economic and human development indicators.

As noted above, this blindness to the inherent possibilities offered by diverse urban configurations is not restricted to commentators ensconced in the rarified spaces of European or North American cities, but also informs how people elsewhere conceptualize the supposed failed cities in which they live. The day after Hurricane Katrina struck New Orleans, an editorial by Anish Trivedi, a well-known columnist and media personality, appeared in the Mumbai newspaper *Mid-Day*. Without being aware of what was, in fact, unfolding in New Orleans at the time, Trivedi compared the quick, efficient, and effective response of the American government to the New Orleans disaster with the inept response of the Mumbai government, concluding that the Mumbai municipality had a lot to learn from the Americans. Needless to say, the following week the author acknowledged his grievous error and admitted he had come to this conclusion without knowing what was actually happening in New Orleans (Trivedi 2005).

More than the mistake itself, significant about the article was the confidence with which Trivedi could assume that the American response to Katrina would *necessarily* be more efficient than that of the Mumbai municipality. My point is not simply to critique this individual writer, but to highlight the larger imagination of a world divided into functional and dysfunctional cities, or cities that work and cities on the brink of disaster — a way of conceptualizing the world that has concrete manifestations for the city's residents. Trivedi's mistake is indicative of the global flow of ideas regarding urban development and governance, as the columnist unreflexively expressed a commonly held blind faith in the idea of the First World city as a model for the Third.

There is, in Mumbai, a stream of U.S. consultancy firms and development and city "experts" who, at tremendous cost, "advise" the local government and other local bodies on issues of urban governance and development. More often than not, these recommendations for urban development disregard how the city actually functions in favor of an abstract ideal. An example of this is the report of the American consultancy firm McKinsey and Co., produced in coordination with and for the local business lobby group Bombay First. The report, "Vision Mumbai" (McKinsey and Co. 2003), is one of the better-known documents promoting the remaking of Mumbai in the image of ideal "global" or "world class" cities such as Singapore or Shanghai. Vision Mumbai has been touted as a landmark study of Mumbai's development prospects by foreign consultants who are experts in the field.[10] The report calls for the elimination of most building restrictions and encourages a remaking of the city's image through beautification schemes (read: elimination of the visible presence of the poor) and slum redevelopment (read: eradication). Elsewhere, Bombay First argues that the visible presence of the poor is an impediment to Mumbai's global aspirations.[11] The poor's disorderly presence on the streets is said to hinder the city efforts to woo foreign investors, visiting professionals, and tourists. It is in reports such as these that we can see how assumptions of a functional First World and an inherently dysfunctional Third have profound consequences for the future of cities such as Mumbai or New Orleans, which have long functioned as vibrant arenas of community and commerce despite their refusal to conform to contemporary models of the modernist or "global" city.

Despite the radical disjunctures between their visions for Mumbai and the reality of how the city works, Bombay First and other elite NGOs draw rhetorical power from the imaginary of the failed Third World city inhabited by a hapless, poverty-stricken population. Moreover, the fantasy of the slum as the site of hopelessness and despair, all too often propagated by well-meaning commentators and scholars, often results in perverse responses by the local authorities. The massive, incredibly violent, slum demolitions that have occurred in the past two years, for instance, were in part fueled by the myth of the slum as a useless site of hapless misery and despair, just as the occupation of New Orleans and the resettlement of its residents on cots laid out in neat rows in sporting arenas were justified by the need to bring order to the chaotic spaces and chaotic lives of that city's urban underclass. The fantasy of the miserable slum fails to acknowledge the reality. These are productive, lively spaces, entailing their own systems of safety, work, and democracy.[12]

The disjuncture between the fantasy of the slum and how it actually works is perhaps most striking in regard to Dharavi, which has acquired transnational fame as "Asia's largest slum." Despite this dubious moniker, Dharavi in fact is home to vast and sophisticated sites of disaggregated production of a wide variety of goods, including pottery, prepared foods, leather items, and clothing (Sharma 2000), which provide employment for tens of thousands of people. Nevertheless, in the imagination of many development experts who see slums only as failure, Dharavi remains nothing but a blot on the city's landscape. Thus, the most recent plan for its "redevelopment," proposed by a U.S.-based real estate developer of Indian origin, dismisses the sophisticated system of production already contained in this site, encouraging instead the building of large production units for multinational firms, along with the requisite luxury high-rises alongside them (Deshmukh 2006).

The inability to see the outward signs of underdevelopment as anything but failure is most striking in the current debates regarding street vendors in Mumbai. The city's elite civic organizations and NGOs (locally referred to as Advanced Locality Management groups, residents' associations, and citizens' groups) are engaging in a relentless campaign in the courts, police stations, municipal offices, and even the streets to rid the city of the visible presence of the poor. These NGOs — the self-declared guardians of the city's public spaces — explicitly fear street vendors and others living and working on the street for what they consider their illegitimate claims to public space. These groups fail to see street vending as anything but a failure, despite the fact that the advantages of lively, mixed-use public spaces are clear, not to mention the fact that street vending employs nearly three hundred thousand people. Instead, in meetings with the municipality on the necessity for more intense action against street vendors, for instance, the so-called citizens' groups draw on city planning discourses that see congestion and multifunctional public spaces as inherently undesirable.[13]

Moreover, as these campaigns demonstrate, preexisting systems of urban life are rarely ever utilized as the basis for future plans for the city. Rarely, as Simone writes of the African context, are activities such as informal economic exchange seen "as a platform for the creation of a very different kind of sustainable urban configuration than we have yet generally to know" (Simone 2004, 9). Instead, as we have seen, preexisting urban configurations are viewed through a narrow narrative of progress in which, for instance, street vendors are to be inevitably replaced by shopping malls, vegetable markets by air-conditioned supermarkets, and disaggregated, home-based production by centralized factories located far outside city limits.

A similar logic of urban development is currently at work in New Orleans, where the dominant vision for the future city is predicated on the erasure of preexisting urban forms. The alternative U.S. urbanism that New Orleans has forged over the centuries, characterized by a vibrant and democratic use of streets, is precisely what is being targeted for redevelopment. As Wagner notes in the previous chapter, this unique street culture — and "the fact that the people have not given their streets up entirely to the automobile" — offers "the promise of an alternative, and yet unrealized, modernism that is an exception to the dominant mode of life in the United States." However, currently dominant visions for the future of the city preclude this alternative. Due to associations with urban failure, poverty, and the "Third World," as well as to blatant racism, long-term African American residents of the city's poorer neighborhoods are not a part of the formal planning process, even though they would have the best idea of how the city could be rebuilt in a way sensitive to local history and cultural practices (Gibson 2006, 46). Instead, as has been well documented, the dominant vision for the future of New Orleans largely consists of "razing poor neighborhoods, incubating an urban middle class, and turning tenements into water-absorbing parks" (Gibson 2006, 46). The dream is to create a "digital" city that is clean, orderly, and white. As a person involved in planning the redevelopment of New Orleans aptly put it: "Those who want to see this city rebuilt want to see it done in a completely different way: demographically, geographically and politically. . . . The way we've been living is not going to happen again" (quoted in Gibson 2006, 46).

As the aftermaths of the two disasters show, there is an imperative to rethink common assumptions of what signifies failed or successful urban spaces. As we see in the case of the July 26 floods in Mumbai, the crowded, chaotic street — emblematic of the "teeming" Third World city — turned out to be Mumbai's savior. In fact, as in New Orleans, the chaotic street is what makes the city thrive. Among other things, this reflects a need to envision cities from the perspective of alternatives to modernist planning already existing in *all* the world's cities. It is time for urban planners to recognize that, amid the outward signs of urban failure in Mumbai, as well as in New Orleans, there is something very much at work. It is time to discard preconceived notions of successful cities in order to appreciate the vast possibilities for healthy, livable, and democratic urban spaces.

Notes

I thank Phil Steinberg, Colin McFarlane, and the anonymous reviewers at the University of Georgia Press for generous comments on this paper. The American Institute of Indian Studies provided research funding that made this paper possible.

1. To be clear, I am not suggesting in this paper that the residents of Mumbai exhibited a unique capacity for generosity, kindness, or sympathy toward helpless strangers. Nor am I suggesting that complete chaos or social breakdown accurately characterizes the situation in New Orleans after the city flooded. Amid disasters, the residents of each city proved themselves equally capable of incredible acts of selflessness. What I do wish to focus on are the divergent meanings of the two events — and how this difference might enable an understanding of the possibilities offered by the diverse kinds of urban configurations found around the world.

2. The following Brooks citations are also quoted in Dominguez (2005).

3. Chakrabarty makes a similar observation through V. S. Naipaul's *India: A Million Mutinies Now*: "Naipaul's travelogue begins by offering the reader a path that has been beaten into familiarity now for at least a century and a half: 'Bombay is a crowd. . . . Traffic into the city moved slowly because of the crowd. . . . With me, in the taxi, were fumes and heat and din. . . . The shops, even when small, even when dingy, had big, bright signboards. . . . Often, in front of these shops, and below those signboards, was just dirt; from time to time depressed-looking, dark people could be seen sitting down on this dirt and eating, indifferent to everything but their food'" (Chakrabarty 2002, 65–66). As Chakrabarty emphasizes, such a view is not "simply Western," but "speaks . . . the language of modernity, of civic consciousness and public health, even of certain ideas of beauty related to the management of public space and interests, an order of aesthetics from which the ideals of public health and hygiene cannot be separated" (66).

4. For a critique of the apocalyptic narrative found in Davis and its consequences, see Angotti (2005).

5. According to the logic of urban development in Mumbai, "encroachments" refers not to office buildings housing multinational companies, even if they illegally occupy space, but only to slums and informally operating, small-scale production units. In the year following the floods, hundreds of such small structures located along the banks of the Mithi were demolished, while the airport and the Bandra-Kurla office complex were left untouched.

6. Similar stories of poor residents providing selfless help to strangers emerged after the July 2006 multiple train bombings in Mumbai. It was widely reported that people living in shanties lining the train tracks were the first to provide sheets to help carry injured passengers (Fernandes 2006).

7. This is a translation of the male-gendered act of *"ghumna-phirna,"* what Chakrabarty (2002), citing Nita Kumar's *Artisans of Banaras*, identifies as one of the pleasures of disorderly public space denied by modernist city planning.

8. There is also an argument to be made that invocations of Mumbai's "indomitable spirit," heard following the July 2005 floods and the July 2006 train bombings, can also become a government excuse to abdicate its responsibilities. However, as Naresh Fernandes (2006) writes, both claims are true. The city residents have a remarkable resilience, and this resilience is something the government can use as an excuse for inaction.

9. This potential of the immanent crowd was first recognized by Jane Jacobs (1992) in her seminal critique of modernist city planning in the United States. In this work, she argues that spaces

deemed a failure from the perspective of planning—characterized by congestion, crowds, and multifarious activities—are in fact the healthiest, safest, and most vibrant, in large part because they offer the visual spectacle necessary to attract the continuous attention of a wide variety of people.

10. In fact, brief probing by local environmental activists (concerned over the report's recommendation that the coastal development restrictions should be eliminated) revealed that the report was based on a series of conversations with Mumbai business leaders rather than on any original research (Shekhar 2003).

11. "If we want to make Mumbai a world-class city, the slums have to go," says Bombay First's Vijay Mahajan (Nair 2005).

12. This is not to neglect the fact that there are very real, and vast, infrastructural problems found in slums, including the lack of basic necessities such as water and sanitation; efforts to eradicate these problems have been well documented elsewhere (Appadurai 2002, McFarlane 2004). My point, however, is that the way slums function internally is rarely incorporated into slum redevelopment plans. This has resulted in failed schemes to "rehabilitate" slum dwellers. As the report by Contractor, Madhiwalla, and Gopal (2006) documents, in Mumbai housing complexes where slum residents have been rehabilitated were found to be dangerous, alienating living spaces. This was especially the case for women, whose mobility was severely restricted in these new living environments. As a result, there are many incidences of Mumbaikars moving *out* of the new housing complexes and back into slums.

13. I have gone into more depth elsewhere (Anjaria 2006) regarding the politics of street vendors' claims on public space in Mumbai.

REFERENCES

Acomb, D. 2005. Hurricane Katrina. *National Journal*, September 10, 37(37), 2774.

Ahmed, Ashfaq. 2006. Dh81.5m bridge to be ready in March. *Gulf News*, May 30.

American Progress Action Fund, and commenters. 2006. Main author of New Orleans reconstruction plan. Think Progress Blog, January 11, http://thinkprogress.org/2006/01/11/main-author-of-new-orleans-reconstruction-plan/ (accessed January 22, 2007).

Anderson, Mark. 2005. Crime and punishment. *The Nation*, October 17, 34.

Angotti, Tom. 2005. New anti-urban theories of the metropolitan region: 'Planet of slums' and apocalyptic regionalism. Paper presented at the Conference of the Association of Collegiate School of Planners, October 27, in Kansas City, MO.

Anjaria, Jonathan Shapiro. 2006. Street hawkers and public space in Mumbai. *Economic and Political Weekly* 41(21), 2140–2146.

Ansell-Pearson, K. 2002. *Philosophy and the adventure of the virtual: Bergson and the time of life*. London and New York: Routledge.

Apostropher. 2005. There is no New Orleans. Apostropher blog, September 27, http://www.apostropher.com/blog/archives/002743.html (accessed January 23, 2007).

Appadurai, Arjun. 1996. *Modernity at large: Cultural dimensions of globalization*. Minneapolis: University of Minnesota Press.

——. 2002. Deep democracy: Urban governmentality and the horizon of politics. *Public Culture* 14(1), 21–47.

Armstrong, Louis. 1992. Growing up in New Orleans. In *New Orleans stories: Great writers on the city*, ed. John Miller and Genevieve Anderson, 23–38. San Francisco: Chronicle Books.

Arnesen, Eric. 1991. *Waterfront workers of New Orleans: Race, class and politics, 1863–1923*. New York: Oxford University Press.

Ashworth, Gregory J., and John E. Tunbridge. 2004. Whose tourist city? Localizing the global and globalising the local. In *A companion to tourism*, ed. Alan A. Lew, C. Michael Hall, and Allan M. Williams, 210–222. Malden, MA: Blackwell.

Associated Press. 2006. Lawmakers call Road Home program a failure. *KATC3 Acadiana's Newschannel* Web site, December 11, http://www.katc.com/Global/story.asp?s=5785497.

Audubon, John J. 1992. New Orleans journal. In *New Orleans stories: Great writers on the city*, ed. John Miller and Genevieve Anderson, 82–85. San Francisco: Chronicle Books.

Augé, Marc. 2004. *Oblivion*. Minneapolis: University of Minnesota Press.

Avila, Eric. 1998. The folklore of the freeway: Space, culture, and identity in postwar Los Angeles. *Aztlan* 23(1), 15–31.

Bachelard, Gaston. 1958. *The poetics of space*, trans. Maria Jolas. Boston: Beacon.

Badam, Ramola Talwar. 2005. Mumbaikars risked lives to reach out. http://in.rediff.com/news/2005/jul/29rain.htm.

Badkhen, A. 2006. Poor still stunned by Katrina. *San Francisco Chronicle*, August 20, A1.

Ballard, J. G. 1999. *The drowned world*. London: Gollancz. Originally published in 1962.

Barry, Patrick. 2006. Storm surges threaten U.S. economic heartlands. *New Scientist*, June 5.

Barsky, Lauren, Joseph Trainor, and Manuel Torres. 2006. Disaster realities in the aftermath of Hurricane Katrina: Revisiting the looting myth. Quick Response Research Report 184. Boulder: University of Colorado Natural Hazards Center. http://www.colorado.edu/hazards/research/qr/qr184/qr184.html.

Baudrillard, Jean. 1998. *The consumer society: Myths and structures*. London: Sage.

Baum, Rachel N. 2000. Never to forget: Pedagogical memory and second generation witness. In *Between hope and despair: Pedagogy and the remembrance of historical trauma*, ed. Roger I. Simon, Sharon Rosenberg and Claudia Eppert, 91–115. New York: Rowman and Littlefield.

Bauman, Z. 2000. *Liquid modernity*. Cambridge: Polity.

Baumbach, Richard O., Jr., and William E. Borah. 1981. *The second battle of New Orleans*. Tuscaloosa: University of Alabama Press.

BBC News. 2004. Iraq war illegal, says Annan, September 16, http://news.bbc.co.uk/2/hi/middle_east/3661134.stm.

———. 2005. Bush insists help is on the way, September 1, http://news.bbc.co.uk/go/pr/fr/-/2/hi/americas/4204754.stm.

———. 2006. New Orleans 'sinking even faster,' June 1, http://news.bbc.co.uk/2/hi/americas/5035728.stm.

Behar, Michael. 2006. 5 bold ideas for a hurricane-proof New Orleans. *Popular Science*, February.

Bergson, H. 1998. *Creative evolution* [Evolution créatrice.]. Mineola, NY: Dover.

Beriss, David. 2006. Back in the kitchen: Restaurants and the rebuilding of New Orleans' cultural economy. Paper presented at the Interdisciplinary Faculty Workshop, University of Missouri, February 24, in Kansas City, MO.

Betsky, Aaron. 1997. *Queer space: Architecture and same-sex desire*. New York: William Morrow.

Bhabha, Homi K. 1994. *The location of culture*. New York: Routledge.

Bierria, Alisa, Mayaba Liebenthal, and INCITE! Women of Color Against Violence. 2007. To render ourselves visible: Women of color organizing and Hurricane Katrina. In *What lies beneath: Katrina, race, and the state of the nation*, 31–47, South End Press Collective, ed. Cambridge, MA: South End Press.

Biguenet, John. 2005a. Pulp fiction. *The New York Times*, October 24, http://biguenet.page.nytimes.com/b/a/213131.htm?p=1.

———. 2005b. What have we learned? *The New York Times*, October 30, http://biguenet.page.nytimes.com/b/a/214898.htm.

Birch, Eugenie L., and Susan M. Wachter, eds. 2006. *Rebuilding urban places after disaster*. Philadelphia: University of Pennsylvania Press.

Blomley, N. 1994. *Law, space, and the geographies of power*. New York: Guilford.

Bondesan, M., G. B. Castiglioni, C. Elmi, G. Gabbianelli, R. Marocco, P. A. Pirazzoli, and A. Tomasin. 1995. Coastal areas at risk from storm surges and sea-level rise in Northeastern Italy. *Journal of Coastal Research* 11(4), 1354–1379.

Bordelon, E. 2003. Images of New Orleans: The relationship between motion pictures and tourists' expectations of a travel destination. TTRA South Central States 2003. http://www.latour.lsu.edu/presentations/Bordelon_TTRA2003BatonRouge.pdf (accessed January 22, 2007).

Borer, Michael. 2006. The location of culture: The urban culturalist perspective. *City and Community* 5(2), 173–197.

Brekhus, Wayne. 1998. A sociology of the unmarked: Redirecting our focus. *Sociological Theory* 16(1), 34–51.

Bring New Orleans Back Commission. 2006. *Rebuilding New Orleans*. New Orleans: City of New Orleans.

Brinkley, Douglas G. 2006. *The great deluge*. New York: William & Morrow.

Brookings Institution. 2006. New Orleans after the storm: Lessons from the past, a plan for the future. New York: Brookings Institution Metropolitan Policy Program. http://www.brookings.edu/metro/katrina.htm.

Brooks, Rosa. 2005. Our homegrown third world. *Los Angeles Times*, September 7.

Bryant-Davis, T. 2007. Healing requires recognition: The case for race-based traumatic stress. *The Counseling Psychologist* 35(1), 135–143.

Bunch, W., and commenters. 2005. How the poor got trapped in hellish New Orleans. Daily News Attytood Blog, September 1, http://www.attytood.com/2005/09/how_the _poor_got_trapped_in_he.html (accessed January 22, 2007).

Burgin, V. 1996. *In/different spaces: Place and memory in visual culture*. Berkeley: University of California Press.

Burkeman, Oliver. 2005. Water world. *The Guardian*, June 30.

Byrne, David. 2001. *Understanding the urban*. London: Palgrave.

Campanella, Richard. 2002. *Time and place in New Orleans: Past geographies in the present day*. Gretna, LA: Pelican.

Capote, Truman. 1980. *Music for chameleons*. New York: Random House.

Carter, R. T. 2007. Racism and psychological and emotional injury: Recognizing and assessing race-based traumatic stress. *The Counseling Psychologist* 35(1), 13–105.

Caruth, C. 1995. *Trauma: Explorations in memory*. Baltimore: John Hopkins University Press.

Casey, Edward. 1993. *Getting back into place: Toward a renewed understanding of the place-world*. Bloomington and Indianapolis: Indiana University Press.

———. 1996. How to get from space to place in a fairly short stretch of time: Phenomenological prolegomena. In *Sense of Place*, ed. Steven Feld and Keith H. Basso, 13–52. Santa Fe, NM: School of American Research Press.

Castells, Manuel. 1977. *The urban question*. London: Edward Arnold.

———. 1996. *The rise of the network society*. Oxford: Blackwell.

Center for Arts and Culture and Creative Industries, the Contemporary Arts Center, Tulane University School of Architecture, Xavier University, and the University of New Orleans Arts Administration. 2003. Creative investments in New Orleans: Cultural policy at the grassroots, December 11–12, forum summary. http://www.culturalpolicy .org/pdf/NewOrleansProceedings.pdf.

Chakrabarty, Dipesh. 2002. Of garbage, modernity, and the citizen's gaze. In *Habitations of modernity: Essays in the wake of subaltern studies*, 65–79. Chicago: University of Chicago Press.

Chambers, Iain. 1994. *Migrancy, culture, identity*. London: Routledge.

Chen, X., and Y. Zong. 1999. Major impacts of sea-level rise on agriculture in the Yangtze delta area around Shanghai. *Applied Geography* 19(1), 69–84.

Childs, John B., ed. 2005. *Hurricane Katrina: Response and responsibilities*. Santa Cruz, CA: New Pacific.

City of New Orleans. 2006. *City of New Orleans GIS files, 2006*. New Orleans: City of New Orleans.

City Planning Commission. 2004. *New century New Orleans master plan: Transportation plan*. New Orleans: New Orleans City Planning Commission.

Clark, John G. 1970. *New Orleans 1718–1812: An economic history*. Baton Rouge: Louisiana State University.

Clarke, David. 1997. Consumption and the city, modern and postmodern. *International Journal of Urban and Regional Research* 21(2), 218–237.

CNN. 2005. Harrowing tales of loss emerge in Katrina's wake, August 31, http://www.cnn .com/2005/WEATHER/08/31/katrina.people/index.html.

Codrescu, Andrei. 1992. Introduction to *New Orleans stories: Great writers on the city*, ed. John Miller and Genevieve Anderson, v–vii. San Francisco: Chronicle Books.

Cohen, Erik. 1984. The sociology of tourism: Approaches, issues, and findings. *Annual Review of Sociology* 10, 373–392.

Collins, Carvel. 1958. About the sketches. In *New Orleans sketches*, William Faulkner, 7–34. New Brunswick, NJ: Rutgers University Press.

Colten, Craig E. 2005. *An unnatural metropolis: Wresting New Orleans from nature*. Baton Rouge: Louisiana State University Press.

Colten, Craig E., ed. 2000. *Transforming New Orleans and its environs: Centuries of change*. Pittsburgh: University of Pittsburgh Press.

Comfort, Louise K. 2006. Cities at risk: Hurricane Katrina and the drowning of New Orleans. *Urban Affairs Review* 41(4): 501–516.

Comfort, Louise K., and Thomas W. Haase. 2006. Communication, coherence, and collective action: The impact of Hurricane Katrina on communications infrastructure. *Public Works Management Policy* 10(4), 328–343.

Common Dreams News Center. 2005. People's Hurricane Relief Fund and Oversight Coalition and National Lawyers Guild file Freedom of Information Act and Louisiana Open Records Act, September 26. http://www.commondreams.org/news2005/ 0926–03.htm.

Concerned Citizens' Commission. 2005. *Mumbai marooned: An inquiry into Mumbai floods 2005*, Draft final report. Mumbai.

Connolly, Ceci. 2005. 9th Ward: History, yes, but a future? *Washington Post*, October 3.

Contractor, Qudsiya, Neha Madhiwalla, and Meena Gopal. 2006. *Uprooted homes, uprooted lives: A study of the impact of involuntary resettlement of a slum community in Mumbai*. Mumbai: CEHAT (Centre for Enquiry into Health and Allied Themes).

Corley, C. 2006. Some Ninth Ward families allowed to return, May 19. *Morning Edition*, prod. National Public Radio. New York: Public Broadcasting Service.

Crang, Mike, and Penny S. Travlou. 2001. The city and topologies of memory. *Environment and Planning D — Society and Space* 19(2), 161.

Crinson, Mark. 2005. *Urban memory: History and amnesia in the modern city*. New York: Routledge.

Curtis, Neal. 2004. Spaces of anamnesis: Art and the immemorial. *Space and Culture* 7(3), 302–312.

Daniels, Ronald J., Donald F. Kettl, and Howard Kunreuther, eds. 2006. *On risk and disaster*. Philadelphia: University of Pennsylvania Press.

Dartmouth News. 2006. Project color-codes New Orleans neighborhood for recovery status. Press release, 05 June, http://www.dartmouth.edu/~news/releases/2006/06/05 .html.

Davis, Kevin. 2006. State of the parish. St. Tammany Parish, June 13, http://www2.stpgov .org/news/2006/06132006-StateoftheParish.html (accessed June 25, 2006).

Davis, Mike. 1990. *City of quartz: Excavating the future in Los Angeles*. Verso: London.

——. 2004a. Planet of slums: Urban involution and the informal proletariat. *New Left Review* 26, 5–34.

——. 2004b. Poor, black, and left behind. *Mother Jones*, September 24.

——. 2005. Gentrifying disaster. *Mother Jones*, October 25, http://www.motherjones .com/commentary/columns/10/gentrifying_disaster.html.

Dean, Cornelia, and Andrew C. Revkin. 2005. Geography complicates levee repair. *The New York Times*, August 31.

Dear, Michael, ed. 2002a. *From Chicago to L.A.: Re-visioning urban theory*. Thousand Oaks, CA: Sage.

——. 2002b. Los Angeles and the Chicago School: Invitation to a debate. *City and Community* 1(1), 1–32.

de Certeau, Michel. 1984. *The practice of everyday life*, trans. S. Rendall. Berkeley: University of California Press. Original work published in 1974.

De Landa, Manuel. 1997. *A thousand years of nonlinear history*. New York: Zone Books.

——. 2002. *Intensive science and virtual philosophy*. London and New York: Continuum.

Deleuze, Gilles. 2004. Capitalism and schizophrenia. In *Desert islands and other texts 1953–1974: Gilles Deleuze*, ed. David Lapoujade, trans. Mike Taormina, 232–241. New York: Semiotext(e).

Deleuze, Gilles, and Felix Guattari. 1987. *A thousand plateaus: Capitalism and schizo-phrenia*, trans. Brian Massumi. Minneapolis: University of Minnesota Press. Original work published in 1980.

DeParle, Jason. 2005. Broken levees, unbroken barriers. *New York Times*, September 4, sec. 4, 1.

Deshmukh, Smita. 2006. Dharavi slum is now realty goldmine. *Daily News and Analysis*, January 30.

Dominguez, Virginia R. 2005. Seeing and not seeing: Complicity in surprise. http://understandingkatrina.ssrc.org/Dominguez (accessed June 24, 2006).

Donald, James. 1997. This, here, now: Imaging the modern city. In *Imagining cities: Scripts, signs, memories*, ed. Sallie Westwood and John Williams, 181–201. New York: Routledge.

Donze, Frank. 2006. Buses roll through the summer in N.O. *Times-Picayune*, June 23, 1.

Doyle, Richard. 2002. *Flood*. London: Arrow Books.

———. Flood London Web site. http://www.floodlondon.com/.

Dreier, Peter. 2006. Katrina and power in America. *Urban Affairs Review* 41(4): 528–549.

Dreier, Peter, John Mollenkopf, and Todd Swanstrom. 2004. *Place matters: Metropolitics for the twenty-first century*. Lawrence: University of Kansas Press.

Duany, Andres, Elizabeth Plater-Zyberk, and Jeff Speck. 2000. *Suburban nation: The rise of sprawl and the decline of the American dream*. New York: North Point.

Dunlap, David. 2005. Future face of New Orleans has an uncertain look for now. *The New York Times*, October 1.

Dunne, Mike. 2005. *America's wetland: Louisiana's vanishing coast*. Baton Rouge: Louisiana State University Press.

Dvorak, Petula. 2006. Hurricane victims demand more help: Federal government not doing enough to aid rebuilding, survivors say. *Washington Post*, February 9, http://www.washingtonpost.com/wp-dyn/content/article/2006/02/08/AR2006020801826.html.

Dyson, Michael E. 2006. *Come hell or high water*. New York: Basic Books.

Eco, Umberto. 1986. *Travels in hyperreality: Essays*. New York: Harcourt.

Edensor, Tim. 2003. Haunting the city: Industrial ruins and their ghosts. In *Deterritorialisations . . . Revisioning landscapes and politics*, ed. Mark Dorrian and Gillian Rose, 264–267. London: Black Dog Publishing.

Edney, Hazel T. 2007. Nagin: "Tragedy Is Still Not Over." *Sacramento Observer*, March 25, http://www.sacobserver.com/government/032507/nagin_katrina.shtml.

Eggler, B. 2006. East N.O. tours of ruins banned. Councilwoman cites victim 'exploitation'. *Times Picayune*, January 7.

Eichstedt, Jennifer, and Stephen Small. 2002. *Representations of slavery: Race and ideology on southern plantation museums*. Washington: Smithsonian Institution Press.

Eisenberg, Pablo. 2006. After Katrina: What foundations should do, January 26. *Chronicle of Philanthropy*, http://www.nng.org/news_detail.html?news_id=61.

Ellin, Nan. 1996. *Postmodern urbanism*. Cambridge, MA: Blackwell.

Ellison, Ralph. 2001. Review of *Blues People* by LeRoi Jones. In *Living with music: Ralph Ellison's jazz writings*, ed. Robert G. O. Meally, 124. New York: Random House. Original work published in 1964.

Entergy. Electric and gas service in New Orleans. http://www.entergy-neworleans.com/ your_home/storm_center/storms_katrina.aspx (accessed February 10, 2007).

Environment Agency, The. 2007. The Thames Barrier: A description of flooding risks in London, June 15, http://www.environment-agency.gov.uk/regions/thames/323150/ 335688/341764/341767/.

Ericson, M., A. Tse, and J. Wilgoren. 2005. Katrina's diaspora. *New York Times*, October 2, http://www.nytimes.com/imagepages/2005/10/02/national/nationalspecial/ 20051002diaspora_graphic.html.

Escobedo, Jodie. 2005. Blog of Jodie Escobedo, MD - Peak Health Medical Group —9/05 Katrina medical relief trip. Medmusings Blog, October 18, http://www.enochchoi .com/thoughts/archives/001796.html.

Faulkner, William. 1958. The tourist. In *New Orleans Sketches*, 49–50. New Brunswick, NJ: Rutgers University Press.

Faux, William V., II, and Heeman Kim. 2006. Visual representation of the victims of Hurricane Katrina: A dialectical approach to content analysis and discourse. *Space and Culture* 9(1), 55–59.

Fernandes, Naresh. 2006. India's indestructible heart. *The New York Times*, July 12.

Fields, Willard. 2004. *Urban landscape change in New Orleans, LA: The case of the lost neighborhood of Louis Armstrong*. Diss., University of New Orleans.

Filosa, Gwen. 2006a. The lonely Lower 9: 16 months after Hurricane Katrina, hope is as rare as people on the streets of the Lower 9th Ward. *The Times-Picayune*, December 18, 1.

———. 2006b. The Lower 9th Ward lies in ruins. *The Times-Picayune*, August 25, 1.

———. 2006c. Group lays foundation to rebuild Lower 9th: Idealistic youth are committed to area. *The Times-Picayune*, May 1, Metro 1.

Fischetti, Mark. 2001. Drowning New Orleans. *Scientific American*, October, http://www .sciam.com/article.cfm?chanID=sa006&articleID=00060286-CB58-1315-8B58834 14B7F0000&pageNumber=1&catID=2.

Fitch, James M. 1990. *Historic preservation: Curatorial management of the built world*. Charlottesville: University Press of Virginia.

Flaherty, Jordan. 2006. Dispatches From the Gulf Region. *WireTap Magazine*, April 25, http://www.alternet.org/wiretap/35389/.

Florida, Richard. 2002. Bohemia and economic geography. *Journal of Economic Geography* 2, 55–71.

———. 2003. Cities and the creative class. *City and Community* 2(1), 3–26.

———. 2004. *Cities and the creative class*. New York: Routledge.

Foley, John, and Mickey Lauria. 2003. Historic preservation in New Orleans' French Quarter: Unresolved racial tensions. In *Knights and castles: Minorities and urban re-*

generation, ed. Huw Thomas and Francesco L. Piccolo, 67–89. Burlington, VT: Ashgate.

Fra Paleo, Urbano. 2006. Impossible but inevitable cities. *Space and Culture* 9(1), 20–22.

Freemantle, Tony. 2006. New Orleans struggles to its feet. *Houston Chronicle*, August 27, http://www.chron.com/disp/story.mpl/front/4142554.html.

Garreau, Joel. 1991. *Edge cities: Life on the new frontier.* New York: Doubleday.

Gentilly Project, The. Why Gentilly? http://www.mosaic-nola.org/mc/page.do?sitePageId =37142.

Gibson, Timothy. 2006. New Orleans and the wisdom of lived space. *Space and Culture* 9(1), 45–47.

Gilloch, Graeme, and Jane Kilby. 2005. Trauma and memory in the city: From Auster to Austerlitz. In *Urban memory: History and amnesia in the modern city*, ed. Mark Crinson, 1–19. New York: Routledge.

Gilmore, H. W. 1944. The old New Orleans and the new: A case for ecology. *American Sociological Review* 9(4), 385–394.

Gilroy, Paul. 1993. *The black Atlantic: Double consciousness and modernity.* Cambridge: Harvard University Press.

Glaeser, Edward L. 2005. Should the government rebuild New Orleans, or just give residents checks? The Economists' Voice 2(4): art. 4, http://www.bepress.com/ev/vol2/iss4/art4.

Godschalk, David R., David J. Brower, and Timothy Beatley. 1989. *Catastrophic coastal storms.* Durham, NC: Duke University Press.

Goldberg, Michelle. 2006. Saving the neighborhood, February 24, http://www.salon.com/news/feature/2006/02/24/broadmoor/.

Goodfriend, Glenn A., and Daniel Jean Stanley. 1999. Rapid strand-plain accretion in the northeastern Nile Delta in the 9th century AD and the demise of the port of Pelusium. *Geology* 27(2), 147–150.

Gordon, John. 2005. Inmates find and give comfort through hospice ministry. Circle of Hope Web site, May, http://umcom.org/foundation/Circle_of_Hope/Newsletter/archive/MayIssue.htm.

Gotham, Kevin F. 2001a. Redevelopment for whom and for what purpose. In *Critical perspectives on urban redevelopment*, vol. 6 (Research in Urban Sociology), ed. Kevin Fox Gotham, 429–452. New York: JAI Press.

———. 2001b. Urban redevelopment, past and present. In *Critical perspectives on urban redevelopment*, vol. 6 (Research in Urban Sociology), ed. Kevin Fox Gotham, 1–31. New York: JAI Press.

———. 2002. Marketing Mardi Gras: Commodification, spectacle, and the political economy of tourism in New Orleans. *Urban Studies* 39(10), 1735–1756.

———. 2003. Toward an understanding of the spatiality of urban poverty: The urban poor as spatial actors. *International Journal of Urban and Regional Research* 27(3), 723–737.

——. 2005. Tourism gentrification: The case of New Orleans' Vieux Carré (French Quarter). *Urban Studies* 42(7), 1099–1121.

Gotham, Kevin F., and Krista Brumley. 2002. Using space: Agency and identity in a public-housing development. *City and Community* 1(3), 267–289.

Gottdiener, Mark. 1985. *The social production of urban space.* Austin: University of Texas Press.

Graham, Stephen. 2006. "Homeland" insecurities? Katrina and the politics of "security" in metropolitan America. *Space and Culture* 9(1), 63–67.

Greater New Orleans Community Data Center. 2007. *Demographic estimates: Breakdowns by age, race, ethnicity, income, homeownership.* New Orleans: Greater New Orleans Community Data Center, http://www.gnocdc.org/demographic_estimates .html (accessed February 5, 2007).

Gross, Davis. 2000. *Lost time: On remembering and forgetting in late modern culture.* Amherst: University of Massachusetts Press.

Gruesz, Kirsten S. 2006. The Gulf of Mexico system and the "Latinness" of New Orleans. *American Literary History* 18, 468–495.

Hankins, J. E., and S. Maklansky, eds. 2002. *Raised to the trade: Creole building arts of New Orleans.* New Orleans: New Orleans Museum of Art.

Hartman, Chester, and Gregory D. Squires, eds. 2006. *There is no such thing as a natural disaster.* London: Routledge.

Harvey, Daina C. 2006a. 'Mis en Fiction du Monde': Les Lieux de Mémoire and New Orleans. *Space and Culture* 9(1), 92–94.

——. 2006b. (Re)Creating culture through tourism: Black heritage space in New Jersey. In *Tourism, Culture and Regeneration,* ed. M. K. Smith, 59–68. London: CABI.

Harvey, David. 1973. *Social justice and the city.* Baltimore: Johns Hopkins University Press.

——. 1982. *The limits to capital.* Cambridge: Massachusetts Institute of Technology Press.

——. 1985. *The urbanization of capital.* Oxford: Blackwell.

——. 1990. *The condition of postmodernity: An enquiry into the origins of cultural change.* Cambridge, MA: Blackwell.

——. 2001. *Spaces of capital.* Edinburgh: Edinburgh University Press.

——. 2005. *A brief history of neoliberalism.* New York: Oxford University Press.

Haydel, Jennifer. 1995–1996. The wood screw pump: A study of the drainage development of New Orleans. http://www.loyno.edu/historyt/journal/1995–6/haydel.htm.

Hayes, Brian. 2005. Natural and unnatural disasters. *American Scientist* 98(6), 496–499.

Haygood, Wil. 2006. Scattered by Katrina, linked by a church. *The Washington Post,* August 5, A1.

Hayles, N Katherine. 1999 *How we became posthuman: Virtual bodies in cybernetics, literature, and informatics.* Chicago: University of Chicago Press.

Heard, Malcolm. 1997. *French Quarter manual: An architectural guide to New Orleans' Vieux Carré.* Jackson: University Press of Mississippi.

Hearn, Lafcadio. 2001. *Inventing New Orleans: Writings of Lafcadio Hearn.* Jackson: University Press of Mississippi.

Henderson, P. 2006. New Orleans population whiter, smaller post-storm. *Reuters Alert-Net,* June 7, http://www.alertnet.org/thenews/newsdesk/N07185461.htm.

Hesse, Barnor. 1997. White governmentality: Urbanism, nationalism, racism. In *Imagining cities: Scripts, signs, memories,* ed. Sallie Westwood and John Williams, 80–103. London: Routledge.

Hetherington, K. 1996. Identity formation, space and social centrality. *Theory, Culture and Society* 13(4), 33–52.

Hirsch, Arnold R. 1983. New Orleans: Sunbelt in the swamp. In *Sunbelt cities: Politics and growth since World War II,* ed. Richard M. Bernard and Bradley R. Rice, 100–137. Austin: University of Texas Press.

Hirsch, Arnold R., and Joseph Logsdon, eds. 1992. *Creole New Orleans: Race and Americanization.* Baton Rouge: Louisiana State University Press.

Hirsch, Marianne. 1996. Past lives: Postmemories in exile. *Poetics Today* 17(4), 659–686.

Holt, William, III. 2000. Distinguishing metropolises: The production of urban imagery. In *Constructions of urban space,* vol. 5 (Research in Urban Sociology), ed. Ray Hutchinson, 225–252. New York: JAI Press.

hooks, bell. 1990. *Yearning: Race, gender, and cultural politics.* Boston: South End Press.

Horne, Jed. 2006. *Breach of faith.* New York: Random House.

Hurston, Zora N. 1935. *Mules and men.* New York: HarperCollins.

Intergovernmental Panel on Climate Change. 2007. *Climate change 2007: The physical science basis.* Geneva: Intergovernmental Panel on Climate Change, World Meteorological Organization.

Jackson, Kenneth. 1985. *Crabgrass frontier.* Oxford: Oxford University Press.

Jackson, Michael. 2002. *Politics of storytelling: Violence, transgression and subjection.* Copenhagen: Museum of Tusculanum Press.

Jacobs, Claude F. 2001. Folk for whom? Tourist guidebooks, local color, and the spiritual churches of New Orleans. *Journal of American Folklore* 114, 309–330.

Jacobs, Jane. 1992. *The death and life of great American cities.* New York: Vintage Books. Originally published in 1961.

Jacobsen, Tom, and Don Marquis. 2006. Danny's boys grow up. *The Mississippi Rag,* May 1–11.

Jha, Alok. 2003. Who needs Essex anyway? *The Guardian,* June 12.

Jones, Richard. 2000. *The blessing: New and selected poems.* Port Townsend, WA: Copper Canyon Press.

Judd, Dennis R., and Susan S. Fainstein, eds. 1999. *The tourist city.* New Haven, CT: Yale University Press.

Juvenile Justice Project of Louisiana Web site. Growing up in Louisiana: Putting our kids at risk. http://www.jjpl.org/WhatsHappeningToOurKids/GrowingUpInLouisiana/growingup.html.

Kamenetz, Anya. 2005. After Katrina: The smell in dry New Orleans now. *Village Voice*, September 19, http://www.villagevoice.com/news/0538,kamenetzweb2,67967,2.html.

Kaplan, Robert D. 1994. The coming anarchy: How scarcity, crime, overpopulation, tribalism, and disease are rapidly destroying the social fabric of our planet. *The Atlantic Monthly*, February.

Kelman, Ari. 2003. *A River and its city: The nature of landscape in New Orleans*. Berkeley: University of California Press.

Kent, Joshua D. 2005. *2005 Louisiana hurricane impact atlas, volume 1*. Baton Rouge: Louisiana Geographic Information Center, http://lagic.lsu.edu/lgisc/publications/2005/LGISC-PUB-20051116–00_2005_HURRICANE_ATLAS.pdf.

Kerouac, Jack. 1976. *On the Road*. New York: Penguin.

Kessler, Kristina. 2006. Bobbing buildings. *Urban Land*, May.

King, Anthony. 1990. *Global cities: Post-imperialism and the internationalization of London*. London: Routledge.

Kirmayer, L. 1996. Landscapes of memory: Trauma, narrative and dissociation. In *Tense Past*, 153–198. New York: Routledge.

Kirp, David, John Dwyer, and Larry Rosenthal. 1995. *Our town: Race, housing and the soul of suburbia*. New Brunswick, NJ: Rutgers University Press.

Knabb, Richard D., Jamie R. Rhome, and Daniel P. Brown. 2006. *Tropical cyclone report: Hurricane Katrina*, August 10, 2006, revision. Miami: National Hurricane Center, http://www.nhc.noaa.gov/pdf/TCR-AL122005_Katrina.pdf.

Kolbert, Elizabeth. 2005. The climate of man – III. *The New Yorker*, May 9.

———. 2006. Watermark. *The New Yorker*, February 27.

Lal, Prita. 2007. The great flood of 1927 through a post-Katrina lens. *Left Turn*, January 1, http://www.leftturn.org/?q=node/628.

Lash, Scott, and J. Urry. 1994. *Economies of signs and spaces*. Thousand Oaks, CA: Sage.

Lauria, Mickey, and Luis F. Miron. 2005. *Urban schools: The new social spaces of resistance*. New York: Peter Lang.

Lawrence, Steven. 2006. Snapshot of philanthropy's response to the gulf coast hurricanes, February. Foundation Center, http://foundationcenter.org/gainknowledge/research/pdf/katrina snap.pdf.

Leake, Jonathan. 2005. Ten-mile barrier to stop London flood. *Times* (UK), January 1.

Leavitt, William M., and John J. Kiefer. 2006. Infrastructure interdependency and the creation of a normal disaster: The case of Hurricane Katrina and the City of New Orleans. *Public Works Management Policy* 10(4), 306–314.

Lee, Spike, dir. 2006. *When the levees broke: A requiem in four acts*. HBO Home Video.

Lefebvre, Henri. 1968. *Le droit à la ville*, 2nd ed. Paris: Anthropos.

———. 1991. *The production of space*, trans. Donald Nicholson-Smith. Oxford: Blackwell. Original work published in 1974.

———. 1996. *Writings on cities*, ed. and trans. Eleonore Kofman and Elizabeth Lebas. Malden, MA: Blackwell.

———. 2003. *Urban revolution*, trans. Robert Bononno, Minneapolis: Minnesota University Press. Original work published in 1970.

Leibniz, G. W. 1965a. Monadology. In *Monadology, and other philosophical essays*, ed. P. Schrecker and A. M. Schrecker, 148–163. Indianapolis: Bobbs-Merrill Co.

———. 1965b. What is nature? In *Monadology, and other philosophical essays*, ed. P. Schrecker and A. M. Schrecker, 95–113. Indianapolis: Bobbs-Merrill Co.

Lemley, J. K. 1996. Image versus reality: Channel Tunnel image management. *Proceedings of the Institution of Civil Engineers. Civil Engineering* 114(1), 12–17.

Levy, Clifford J. 2005. Seeing life outside New Orleans alters life inside it. *The New York Times*, November 20.

Lewis, Peirce F. 1976. *New Orleans: The making of an urban landscape*, 1st ed. Santa Fe, NM: Center for American Places.

Leyden, K. 1985. *Recovery and reconstruction after Hurricane Camille: Post storm hazard mitigation on the Mississippi Gulf Coast.* Chapel Hill: University of North Carolina, Center for Urban and Regional Studies.

Liss, Andrea. 2000. Artifactual testimonies and the staging of holocaust memories. In *Between hope and despair: Pedagogy and the remembrance of historical trauma*, ed. Roger I. Simon, Sharon Rosenberg and Claudia Eppert, 117–133. New York: Rowman and Littlefield.

Lobe, Jim. 2005. Katrina exposes the 'Third World' at home. http://www.ipsnews.net/news.asp?idnews=30125.

Logsdon, Joseph, and Caryn Cossé Bell. 1992. The Americanization of black New Orleans, 1850–1900. In *Creole New Orleans: Race and Americanization*, ed. Arnold Hirsch and Joseph Logsdon, 201–261. Baton Rouge: Louisiana State University Press.

Lomax, Alan. 1939. *The John and Ruby Lomax 1939 southern states record trip.* Washington, DC: Special Collection, American Folklife Center, Library of Congress.

Loo, C. M., J. A. Fairbank, R. M. Scurfield, L. O. Ruch, D. W. King, L. J. Adams, and C. M. Chemtob. 2001. Measuring exposure to racism: development and validation of a Race-Related Stressor Scale (RRSS) for Asian American Vietnam veterans. *Psychological Assessment* 13(4), 503–520.

Louisiana Geographic Information Center. 2002. *Louisiana GIS CD: A digital map of the state, version 2.0.* Baton Rouge: Louisiana Geographic Information Center.

Louisiana Recovery Authority. 2007. *2006 Louisiana health and population survey*, January 17. Baton Rouge: Louisiana Recovery Authority, http://popest.org/popestla2006/files/PopEst_Orleans_SurveyReport.pdf.

Lugones, M. 2003. *Pilgrimages/peregrinajes: Theorizing coalition against multiple oppressions.* Lanham, MD: Rowman and Littlefield.

Lundvall, Bengt-Ake, ed. 1992. *National systems of innovation: towards a theory of innovation and interactive learning.* London: Pinter.

Lyotard, Jean-François. 2004. Anamnesis: Of the visible. *Theory, Culture and Society* 21(1), 107–119.

MacCannell, Dean. 1976. *The tourist: A new theory of the leisure class.* New York: Schocken.

Mannion, Gregory B. 1999. Childrens' participation in changing school grounds and public play areas in Scotland. Unpublished Ph.D. diss., University of Sterling, http://dspace .stir.ac.uk/dspace/bitstream/1893/88/1/Children'sParticipation+inChangingSchool GroundsAndPlayParks.PDF.

Massey, Doreen. 1994. *Space, place, and gender.* Minneapolis: University of Minnesota Press.

———. 2005. *For space.* London: Sage.

Massey, Douglas S., and Nancy A. Denton. 1993. *American apartheid: Segregation and the making of the underclass.* Cambridge: Harvard University Press.

Massumi, Brian. 2002. *Parables for the virtual: Movement, affect, sensation.* Durham, NC: Duke University Press.

May, Peter J., Raymond J. Burby, Neil J. Ericksen, John W. Handmer, Jennifer E. Dixon, Sarah Michaels, and D. Ingle Smith. 1996. *Environmental management and governance: Intergovernmental approaches to hazards and sustainability.* London: Routledge.

Maygarden, Benjamin, Jill-Karen Yakubik, Ellen Weiss, Chester Peyronnin, and Kenneth R. Jones. 1999. *National register evaluation of New Orleans drainage system, Orleans Parish, Louisiana.* New Orleans: U.S. Army Corps of Engineers, New Orleans District.

McClam, Erin. 2005. New Orleans frets about image. Efforts underway to counter tales of post-Katrina chaos. *The Boston Globe*, December 27, http://www.boston.com/news/ nation/articles/2005/12/27/new_orleans_frets_about_image/.

McFarlane, Colin. 2004. Geographical imaginations and spaces of political engagement: Examples from the Indian Alliance. *Antipode*, 891–916.

McKee, Bradford. 2005. To restore or reinvent? *The New York Times*, November 24, http://select.nytimes.com/gst/abstract.html?res=F50C12FA3D550C778EDDA80994 DD404482.

McKinsey and Company, Inc. 2003. Vision Mumbai: Transforming Mumbai into a world-class city: A summary of recommendations, http://www.bombayfirst.org/McKinsey Report.pdf.

McPhee, John. 1990. *The control of nature.* New York: Farrar Straus & Giroux.

Medina, Jennifer. 2005. In New Orleans, the trashman will have to move mountains. *New York Times*, October 16, 1, http://www.nytimes.com/2005/10/16/national/national special/16garbage.html?ex=1287115200&en=8a05b6f861297adc&ei=5088&partner =rssnyt&emc=rss.

Medley, Keith Weldon. 2000. American legacy: Black New Orleans. *American Heritage Magazine*, Summer.

Melish, Joanne. 1998. *Disowning slavery: Gradual emancipation and "race" in New England, 1780–1860*. Ithaca, NY: Cornell University Press.

Merrifield, Andy. 2002. *Dialectical urbanism: Social struggles in the capitalist city*. New York: Monthly Review Press.

Metropolitan Crime Commission, The. 2005. Performance of the New Orleans criminal justice system 2003–2004: A research report. http://www.metropolitancrimecommission .org/html/2Perf_of_the_NO_Criminal_Justice_System_2003–20041.pdf.

Miéville, China. 2003. *The scar*. London: Pan Books.

Mills, Charles W. 1997. *The racial contract*. Ithaca, NY: Cornell University Press.

Mississippi Renewal Forum. 2005. *The Mississippi renewal forum summary report: Recommendations for rebuilding the Gulf Coast*. Gaithersburg, MD: The Town Paper.

Moe, Richard, and Carter Wilkie. 1997. *Changing places: rebuilding community in the age of sprawl*. New York: Henry Holt.

Molotch, Harvey. 1976. The city as a growth machine. *American Journal of Sociology* 82, 309–332.

Mosher, Anne E., Barry D. Keim, and Susan A. Franques. 1995. Downtown dynamics. *Geographical Review* 85(4), 497–517.

Mumford, Lewis. 1961. *The city in history*. San Diego: Harcourt Brace.

———. 1970. *The culture of cities*. New York: Harvest. Originally published in 1938.

Murdock, Deroy. 2005. Multi-layered failures: Government responses to Katrina. *National Review*, September 13, http://www.nationalreview.com/murdock/murdock2005 09130839.asp.

Murray, Albert. 1971. *South to a very old place*. New York: Vintage Books.

Nair, Binoo. 2005. Mumbai bigwigs to sway Sonia on slums. *Mid-Day*, February 17.

Netherlands Architecture Institute. Polders: The scene of land and water. http://www.nai .nl/polders/e/index.html.

New Orleans Convention and Visitors Bureau. *Facts and statistics*. New Orleans: New Orleans Convention and Visitors Bureau, http://www.neworleanscvb.com/static/index .cfm/contentID/443 (accessed June 11, 2006).

New York Times, The. 2005. Barbara Bush calls evacuees better off, September 7, http://www.nytimes.com/2005/09/07/national/nationalspecial/07barbara.html?ex =1182052800&en=a061c153fd29c8cd&ei=5070.

Nolan, Bruce. 2006. Broadmoor plan gets boost. *The Times-Picayune*, September 28.

Nossack, Hans Erich. 2004. *The end*. Chicago and London: University of Chicago Press.

Nossiter, Adam. 2006. A big government fix-it plan for New Orleans. *The New York Times*, January 5, A1 and A21.

———. 2007. New Orleans of future may stay half its old size. *The New York Times*, January 21.

Olick, Jeffrey. 2005. *In the house of the hangman: The agonies of German defeat, 1943–1949*. Chicago: University of Chicago Press.

Omi, Michael, and Howard Winant. 1994. *Racial formation in the United States: From the 1960s to the 1990s*. New York: Routledge.

Ong, Aihwa. 1999. *Flexible citizenship: The cultural logics of transnationality.* Durham, NC: Duke University Press.

Ouroussoff, Nicolai. 2005. Katrina's legacy: Theme park or cookie cutter? *The New York Times,* October 18, B1.

Park, Robert E. 1925. The city: Suggestions for the investigation of human behavior in the urban environment. In *The city,* ed. Robert E. Park, Ernest W. Burgess, and Roderick D. McKenzie, 1–46. Chicago: University of Chicago Press.

Parsons, Talcott. 1949. *The structure of social action.* Glencoe, IL: Free Press.

Paz, Octavio. 1985. *The labyrinth of solitude.* New York: Grove Weidenfeld.

Peirce, Charles S. 1958. *Collected papers of Charles Sanders Peirce,* 8 volumes. Cambridge, MA: Harvard University Press.

Peirce, Neil. 2005. How Katrina keeps on hurting. http://www.alternet.org/katrina/27635/.

People's Hurricane Relief Fund and Oversight Coalition website. http://www.peopleshurricane.org.

Pernick, Martin. 1985. *A calculus of suffering: Pain, professionalism, and anesthesia in nineteenth century America.* New York: Columbia University Press.

Perret, William S., and Mark F. Chatry. 1991. Coastal Louisiana: Abundant renewable natural resources — in peril. Paper presented at Coastal Zone '91, the Seventh Symposium on Coastal and Ocean Management, July 8–12, in Long Beach, CA.

Piazza, Tom. 2005. Why New Orleans matters. Houston: Regan Books.

Pielke, Roger, Sr. 2007. Comments on "Comments by Herbert S. Saffir on Hurricane Katrina." Climate Science: Roger Pielke Sr. Research Group Weblog, February 13, http://climatesci.colorado.edu/2007/02/13/comments-by-herbert-s-saffir-on-hurricane-katrina/ (accessed February 26, 2007).

Post, Robert C. 2006. The machine in the Garden District. *Technology and Culture* 47(1), 91–94.

Reckdahl, Katy. 2005. Long road to freedom. *Gambit Weekly,* July 26, http://www.bestofneworleans.com/dispatch/2005–07–26/cover_story.php.

Rediff.com. 2005. "Nothing stops the Mumbai spirit," July 27. http://in.rediff.com/news/2005/jul/27rain6.htm.

Reed, Adolph, Jr. 2006. New Orleans: Undone by neoliberalism. *The Nation,* September 18.

Reiss, Spencer. 2006. His space. *Wired Magazine* 14(7), http://www.wired.com/wired/archive/14.07/murdoch.html.

Remnick, David. 2005. High water: Letter from Louisiana. *The New Yorker,* October 3, 48.

Rice, Anne. 1992. *The Vampire Lestat.* New York: Ballantine.

Ritea, Steve. 2006. Gentilly. *The Times Picayune,* August 27.

Rivlin, Gary. 2006. All parts of city in rebuild plan of New Orleans. *The New York Times,* January 8, 1.

Roach, Joseph. 1996. *Cities of the dead.* New York: Columbia University Press.

Roberts, Gregory D. 2004. *Shantaram.* New York: St. Martin's Press.

Roberts, M. 2006. In Lower Ninth Ward, demolition and desolation. *The Washington Post*, November 12, A9.

Robinson, Jennifer. 2002. Global and world cities: A view from off the map. *International Journal of Urban and Regional Research* 26(3), 531–554.

———. 2004. A world of cities. *The British Journal of Sociology* 55(4), 569–578.

Robinson, Scott E., Britt Berrett, and Kelley Stone. 2006. The development of collaboration of response to Hurricane Katrina in the Dallas Area. *Public Works Management and Policy* 10(4), 315–327.

Rodriguez, Richard. 2005. Essay: The third world. http://www.pbs.org/newshour/essays/july-dec05/rodriguez_9–06.html.

Rose, Chris. 2006. *One dead in attic*. New Orleans: Chris Rose Books.

Rostow, Walt W. 1960. *The stages of economic growth: A non-communist manifesto*. Cambridge: Cambridge University Press.

Russell, Gordon. 2006. Broadmoor. *The Times Picayune*, August 17.

Russell, Jenna. 2006. Planning a comeback. *Boston Globe*, July 30.

Sakakeeny, Matt. 2006. Resounding silence in the streets of a musical city. *Space and Culture* 9(1), 41–44.

Sarvate, Sarita. 2005. Welcome to the 'Third World,' America. http://www.alternet.org/katrina/25112.

Sassen, Saskia. 1991. *The global city: New York, London, Tokyo*. Princeton, NJ: Princeton University Press.

———. 2006. *Cities in a world economy*, 3rd ed. Thousand Oaks, CA: Pine Forge Press.

Sassen, Saskia, ed. 2002. *Global networks, linked cities*. London: Routledge.

Savage, Mike, and Alan Warde. 1993. *Urban sociology, capitalism and modernity*. London: Macmillan.

Schanberg, Sydney H. 2005. Katrina puts us — and the press — in a different place. *Village Voice*, September 13.

Schwartz, Barry. 2000. *Abraham Lincoln and the forge of national memory*. Chicago: The University of Chicago Press.

Schwartz, John. 2006. Army builders accept blame over flooding. *The New York Times*, June 2.

Sharma, Kalpana. 2000. *Rediscovering Dharavi: Stories from Asia's largest slum*. New Delhi: Penguin.

Shekhar, Vaishnavi. 2003. McKinsey blueprint is only a summary. *Times of India*, October 10.

Shields, Rob. 1990. The system of pleasure. Liminality and the carnivalesque at Brighton. *Theory, Culture and Society* 7(1), 32–79.

———. 1991. *Places on the margin: Alternative geographies of modernity*. London: Routledge Chapman Hall.

———. 1997. Flow as a new paradigm. *Space and Culture* 1(1), 1–7.

———. 2003. *The virtual*. London: Routledge.

———. 2005. The virtuality of urban culture: Blanks, dark moments and blind fields. In *Soziale Welte: Die Wirklichkeit der Stadte* (Vol. 16), ed. H. Berking and M. Löw, 377–386. Baden-Baden: Nomos Verlagsgessellschaft.

Shields, R., ed. 1993. *Life style shopping: The subject of consumption.* London: Routledge.

Shipler, D. 2005. Monkey see, monkey do. *Columbia Journalism Review* 6, November/December, http://www.cjr.org/issues/2005/6/shipler.asp.

Simmel, Georg. 1950. The metropolis and mental life. In *The sociology of Georg Simmel*, ed. Kurt H. Wolff, 409–424. New York: New Press. Original work published in 1903.

Simone, AbdouMaliq. 2004. *For the city yet to come: Changing African life in four cities.* Durham, NC: Duke University Press.

Smith, Neil. 1990. *Uneven development*, 2nd ed. Oxford: Blackwell.

———. 1996. *The new urban frontier: Gentrification and the revanchist city.* London: Routledge.

Soja, Edward. 1989. *Postmodern geographies: The reassertion of space in critical social theory.* New York: Verso.

———. 1997. Six discourses on the postmetropolis. In *Imagining cities: Scripts, signs, memories*, ed. Sallie Westwood and John Williams, 19–30. New York: Routledge.

———. 2000. *Postmetropolis: Critical studies of cities and regions.* Malden, MA: Blackwell.

Sontag, Deborah. 2005. Months after Katrina, bittersweet homecoming in the 9th Ward. *The New York Times*, December 2, A20.

South End Press Collective, ed. 2007. *What lies beneath: Katrina, race, and the state of the nation.* Cambridge, MA: South End Press.

Souther, Jonathan M. 2006. *New Orleans on parade: Tourism and the transformation of the Crescent City.* Baton Rouge: Louisiana State University Press.

Spain, Daphne. 1979. Race relations and residential segregation in New Orleans: Two centuries of paradox. *Annals of the American Academy of Political and Social Science* 441, 82–96.

Spitzer, Nick. 2002. The aesthetics of work and play in Creole New Orleans. In *Raised to the trade: Creole building arts of New Orleans*, ed. J. E. Hankins and S. Maklansky, 96–130. New Orleans: New Orleans Museum of Art.

Stanley, Jean-Daniel, and Thomas F. Jorstad. 2006. Short contribution: Buried canopic channel identified near Egypt's Nile Delta Coast with radar (SRTM) imagery. *Geoarchaeology* 21(5), 503–514.

State of Louisiana. 2005. *Emergency operations plan.* Baton Rouge: Office of Homeland Security and Emergency Preparedness.

Street, Paul. 2005. Framing Katrina: Dominant media and damage control in the wake of a not-so-natural disaster. *The Black Commentator* 152, http://www.blackcommentator.com/152/152_street_katrina.html.

Sundeen, Matt, James B. Reed, and Melissa Savage. 2005. *Coordinated human service transportation: State legislative approaches.* Denver: National Conference of State Legislatures.

Taimerica Management Company. 2006. *Future directions for St. Tammany Parish, post-Katrina*. Covington, LA: St. Tammany Parish.

Thackeray, William. 1992. A Mississippi bubble. In *New Orleans stories: Great writers on the city*, ed. John Miller and Genevieve Anderson, 116–118. San Francisco: Chronicle Books.

Thevenot, Brian. 2006. New Orleans reporting. *American Journal Review*, December/January, http://ajr.org/article.asp?id=3998.

Timber Piling Council. 2004. History of Piling. http://www.timberpilingcouncil.org/history.html.

Times Picayune, The. 2006. *Katrina: The ruin and recovery of New Orleans*. Champaign, IL: Spotlight Press.

Tisserand, M. 2006. Linking to New Orleans. *The Nation*, September 1, http://www.thenation.com/doc/20060918/nola_links.

Toole, John K. 1992. A confederacy of dunces. In *New Orleans stories: Great writers on the city*, ed. John Miller and Genevieve Anderson, 70–81. San Francisco: Chronicle Books.

Toulmin, Stephen. 1990. *Cosmopolis: The hidden agenda of modernity*. Chicago: University of Chicago Press.

Tregle, Joseph. 1992. Creoles and Americans. In *Creole New Orleans: Race and Americanization*, ed. Arnold Hirsch and Joseph Logsdon, 131–185. Baton Rouge: Louisiana State University Press.

Trivedi, Anish. 2005. Egg on Sunday. *Mid-Day*, September 11.

Trollope, Fanny M. F. 2006. *Domestic manners of the Americans*. Retrieved from http://etext.library.adelaide.edu.au/. Originally published in 1832.

Uhlenbeck, Max. 2005. The revolution will not be funded: Beyond the non-profit industrial complex, November 1. *Left Turn* 18, 25.

Unified New Orleans Plan. 2007. *Final draft of the citywide strategic recovery and rebuilding plan*, January 29, http://www.unifiedneworleansplan.

Union of Concerned Scientists. 2005. *Global warming: Hurricanes and climate change*, revised November 17, 2005. Boston: Union of Concerned Scientists, http://www.ucsusa.org/global_warming/science/hurricanes-and-climate-change.

Urban Land Institute. 2005. *New Orleans: A strategy for rebuilding*, November 12–18, http://www.uli.org/AM/Template .cfm?Section=Search&section=Reports_PDF_files_&template=/CM/ContentDisplay.cfm&ContentFileID=22500.

Urry, John. 2000. Mobile sociology. *British Journal of Sociology* 51(1), 185–203.

———. 2002. Mobility and proximity. *Sociology* 36(2), 255–274.

U.S. Army Corps of Engineers. 1992. *National register evaluation of Sewerage Pumping Station B*. New Orleans: Earth Search Inc.

U.S. Census Bureau. 1990. Various pages. Washington, DC: U.S. Census Bureau, http://quickfacts.census.gov.

———. 2000. Various pages. Washington, DC: U.S. Census Bureau, http://quickfacts.census.gov.

U.S. Department of Housing and Urban Development. 2006. *Current housing unit damage estimates: Hurricanes Katrina, Rita, and Wilma, February 12, 2006. (Revised April 7, 2006).* Washington, DC: Department of Housing and Urban Development, http://www.gnocdc.org/reports/Katrina_Rita_Wilma_Damage_2_12_06___revised.pdf.

U.S. Federal Bureau of Investigation. 2005. *Crime in the United States, 2004: Uniform crime reports.* Washington, DC: Federal Bureau of Investigation, http://www.fbi.gov/ucr/cius_04/documents/CIUS2004.pdf.

U.S. Federal Emergency Management Agency. 2005. *FEMA-1603-DR: Hurricane Katrina.* Washington, DC: Federal Emergency Management Agency, http://www.fema.gov/news/event.fema?id=4808.

———. 2007. *Reported mailing addresses of Katrina IA applicants,* January 26. Washington, DC: Federal Emergency Management Agency, http://www.fema.gov/pdf/hazard/hurricane/2005katrina/metro_stats.pdf.

U.S. National Hurricane Center. *The Saffir-Simpson Hurricane Scale.* Miami: National Hurricane Center, National Oceanographic and Atmospheric Administration, http://www.nhc.noaa.gov/aboutsshs.shtml.

Viosca, Percy, Jr. 1928. Louisiana wetlands and the value of their wildlife and fishery resources. *Ecology* 9(2), 216–229.

Virilio, P. 1997. *Open sky.* New York: Verso.

———. 1999. *Politics of the very worst.* New York: Semiotext(e).

Virilio, P., and John Armitage. 1999. From modernism to hypermodernism and beyond: An interview with Paul Virilio. *Theory, Culture and Society* 16(5–6), 25–55.

Wacquant, Loïc, and William Julius Wilson. 1989. The cost of racial and class exclusion in the inner city. *Annals of the American Academy of Political and Social Science* 501, 8–25.

Wagner, Jacob A. 2004. The myth of Liberty Place: Race and public memory in New Orleans, 1874–1993. Diss., University of New Orleans.

Walters, Joanna. 2005. Cornel West on Katrina. *Tikkun Magazine,* http://www.tikkun.org/rabbi_lerner/news_item.2005–09–12.2271273974.

Ward, Andrew. 2006. Main Street or main chance? *Financial Times,* 24 June.

Warner, Sam Bass. 1962. *Streetcar suburbs: The process of growth in Boston, 1870–1900.* Cambridge: Harvard University Press.

Warren, Kenneth W. 1993. The mythic city: An interview with Leon Forrest. *Callaloo* 16(2), Leon Forrest, fiction writer: A special section, 392–408.

Watson, Douglas J., and L. Douglas Kiel. 2006. Introduction: Special issue on natural disasters and public works management and policy. *Public Works Management Policy* 10(4), 280–283.

Westwood, Sallie, and John Williams. 1997. *Imagining cities: Scripts, signs, memories.* New York: Routledge.

Whelan, Robert K., Alma H. Young, and Mickey Lauria. 1994. Urban regimes and racial politics in New Orleans. *Journal of Urban Affairs* 16(1), 1–21.

White House, The. 2005. President discusses hurricane relief in address to the nation. Press release, September 15, http://www.whitehouse.gov/news/releases/2005/09/20050915-8.html.

Whoriskey, P. 2006. New Orleans' population remains low. *Contra Costa Times*, June 11, http://www.contracostatimes.com/mld/cctimes/news/nation/14793901.htm?source=rss&channel=cctimes_nation (accessed June 24, 2006).

Whyte, William F. 1993. *Street corner society: The social structure of an Italian slum*, 4th ed. Chicago: University of Chicago Press. Originally published in 1943.

Williams, S. Jeffress, Shea Penland, and Asbury Sallenger. 1991. Results of geologic processes studies of barrier island erosion and wetlands loss in coastal Louisiana. Paper presented at Coastal Zone '91, the Seventh Symposium on Coastal and Ocean Management, July 8–12, in Long Beach, CA.

Williams, Tennessee. 1947. *A streetcar named Desire*. New York: New Directions.

Wilson, Mabel O. 2001. Between rooms 307: Spaces of memory at the national civil rights museum. In *Sites of memory: Perspectives on architecture and race*, ed. Craig E. Barton, 13–26. New York: Princeton Architectural Press.

Wilson, William Julius. 1987. *The truly disadvantaged*. Chicago: University of Chicago Press.

Wirth, Louis. 1938. Urbanism as a way of life. *American Journal of Sociology* 44(1), 1–24.

Wittfogel, Karl 1957. *Oriental despotism*. New Haven, CT: Yale University Press.

Woods, Clyde A. 2005. Do you know what it means to miss New Orleans? Katrina, trap economics, and the rebirth of the blues. *American Quarterly* 57(4), 1005–1018.

Woodward, C. Vann. 1951. *Origins of the new South 1877–1913*. Baton Rouge: Louisiana State University Press.

Zerubavel, Eviatar. 1997. *Social mindscapes: An invitation to cognitive sociology*. Cambridge, MA: Harvard University Press.

———. 2003. *Time maps: Collective memory and the social shape of the past*. Chicago: University of Chicago Press.

CONTRIBUTORS

Jonathan Shapiro Anjaria is a doctoral student in the Department of Anthropology, University of California, Santa Cruz.

Hugh Bartling is an associate professor in the Department of Public Policy Studies, DePaul University.

C. Tabor Fisher is an assistant professor in the Department of Philosophy, LeMoyne College.

Jordan Flaherty is a writer and community organizer based in New Orleans and an editor of *Left Turn Magazine*.

Daina Cheyenne Harvey is a doctoral student in the Department of Sociology, Rutgers University.

Fernando Lara is an assistant professor of architecture in the Taubman College of Architecture and Urban Planning, University of Michigan.

Geoff Manaugh is an architectural critic, founding editor of BLDGBLOG, and Senior Editor at *Dwell Magazine*.

Rob Shields is the Henry Marshall Tory Chair and Professor in the Departments of Sociology and Art and Design, University of Alberta.

Elizabeth V. Spelman is the Barbara Richmond Chair in the Humanities and Professor in the Departments of Philosophy and Women and Gender Studies, Smith College.

Phil Steinberg is an associate professor in the Department of Geography, Florida State University.

Matthew Tiessen is a doctoral student in the Departments of Sociology and Art & Design, University of Alberta.

Nicola Twilley is an independent scholar and writer based in Los Angeles.

Jacob A. Wagner is an assistant professor in the Department of Urban Planning and Design, University of Missouri–Kansas City.

INDEX

Numbers in *italics* indicate figures.

Bush, George W., 44–45, 132
Bush-Clinton Katrina Fund, 48
Butler, Josephine, 140

Camille, Hurricane, 18–20
Casey, Edward, 144–45
charter schools, 42
Chicago School of urban sociology, 7
circular indictment, 161
cities, 5–8, 18, 61; abstracting themselves
    from nature, 23–24; as arenas of
    asemiotic spaces, 62; capacity of,
    to amaze, 112–13; as collections of
    individuals, 23; divisions in, 156; as
    human sites of remembering, 125;
    mobility of, 113–14; as nodes for
    the concentration and dissemination
    of flows, people, and objects, 7–8,
    155; rootedness of, 25–26; as sites
    for circulating capital, people, and
    information, 102; tensions present in,
    4; understanding the space of, 129–30;
    value of, 8–9
City in History, The (Mumford), 100
civil rights movement, 35
Coast 2050 plan, 67
Codrescu, Andrei, 85, 86–87, 91, 92
Cohen, Erik, 151
Colonial Williamsburg, 149–50
Colten, Craig, 6, 102–3
Commission on Recovery, Rebuilding
    and Renewal (Mississippi), 150
Common Ground Relief Collective, 52,
    53–54, 164
Community Labor United, 52–53
Compass, Eddie, 44
Concerned Citizens' Commission
    (Mumbai), 193
Confederacy of Dunces, A (Toole), 87
Congress for New Urbanism, 108
control, illusion of, 60

Control of Nature, The (McPhee), 63–66
co-presence, 115
corporate left, involvement of, in New
    Orleans, 47
Corps of Engineers. *See* U.S. Army Corps
    of Engineers
cosmopolitan hub, as element defining
    cities, 7–8
creole, defining, 175–77
creole city, 156
creole population, 16
creole radicalism, 176–77
creole urbanism, 130, 177–78; New
    Orleans and, 173, 175; preserving and
    enhancing, 184–85
Critical Resistance, 54
Cruz, Rosana, 51
culture, smell of, 90–92
Culture of Cities, The (Mumford), 5–8
culture hearth, as element defining cities,
    6–7

Davis, Kevin, 110
Davis, Mike, 149, 150, 190
Deacons for Defense, 35
de Certeau, Michel, 162–63, 164–65
Deleuze, Gilles, 120, 122
delta cities, 24, 80, 81; cultural aspects
    of, 84–88, 89–90; engineering, 81–84;
    liminality of, 88–90; natural features
    of, 79–81; navigating, 78–79; as type,
    78
density, as element defining cities, 6
design: landscape, 66; New Urbanist,
    108–9; urban, 60, 61, 71
Dharavi (Mumbai), 199
disaster response, political repercussions
    of, 44–45
displacement: resistance to, 45–46;
    trauma of, 127
Dominguez, Paul, 85

hooks, bell, 161, 166, 167
Houston, and Hurricane Rita, 111
hub city, New Orleans as, 9–13, 15
hurricane activity, rise in, 20
hurricanes. *See entries for specific storms*
Hurston, Zora Neale, 88, 92

ideology of mobility, 99
images: mobility of, 96; struggles over,
   96–97
immanent crowd, potential of, 201–2n9
INCITE! Women of Color Against
   Violence, 49, 50–51, 54
India, cities' public spaces in, 189
information technology, and shaping of
   cities, 101–2
information transmission, speed of,
   118–19
intersectionality, 155
Interstate 10, effect of, on New Orleans
   neighborhood, 105
intervention, forms of, 146
isotopia, 156

Jefferson, Thomas, 79
Jha, Alok, 74
Jones, Richard, 142, 143

Kaplan, Robert, 190
Katrina, Hurricane: aftermath of,
   22–23; criminalizing survivors of,
   39–40; deaths from, 20; dominant
   narrative following, 3; expectations
   about, 20–21; false stories circulating
   during, 96–97; and governmental
   neglect, 22; landscape design and,
   66; meteorological characteristics of,
   18–20; neighborhoods and, 155–56;
   and nonprofit professionals, 49–50; as
   regional disaster, 110–11; and urban
   social or policy problems, 3–4
Kayden, Jerold S., 134

Keppard, Freddie, 85
Kerouac, Jack, 89
Kessler, Kristina, 70
King, Martin Luther, Jr., 147
knowledge production, ethical
   responsibility of, 165–66
Kolbert, Elizabeth, 64–65, 69, 72
Kucera, Christina, 38

Landa, Manuel De, 114
Landrieu, Mary, 134
Lassiter, Cisco, 144
Latin American population, 16
Le Corbusier, 100
Lefebvre, Henri, 7, 23, 28, 155, 165, 171;
   on abstractness of the space(s) of late
   capitalism, 160; on cities informed by
   difference, 156; on the silence of the
   users, 163; on spatial understandings,
   159; trial by space, 184
Leibniz, Gottfried Wilhelm, 114
levees, 65–66, 82–83; collapse of, 21
Lewis, Peirce, 5, 24, 88–89, 168, 179; on
   siting of New Orleans, 78–79, 81
Liebenthal, Mayaba, 52
liquid modernity, 114–15
Little Venice (London), 72–73
Logsdon, Joseph, 176, 177, 182
Lomax, Alan, 85
London (England, UK): Little Venice,
   72–73; sea wall proposed for, 73
Long, Huey P., 44
Louisiana, education spending in, 35
Louisiana, southeastern, evacuation plans
   for, 106–7
Louisiana, southern: disappearing, 72; soil
   consistency of, 65
Louisiana Road Home program, 44
low-density development, privileging of,
   in New Orleans, 103–4
Lower Ninth Ward (New Orleans
   neighborhood): declared not "fit for

Love
in a
Blue
Time

HANIF KUREISHI

SCRIBNER PAPERBACK FICTION
PUBLISHED BY SIMON & SCHUSTER

SCRIBNER PAPERBACK FICTION
Simon & Schuster Inc.
Rockefeller Center
1230 Avenue of the Americas
New York, NY 10020

First published in Great Britain by Faber and Faber Limited.
First Scribner Paperback Fiction edition 1999
SCRIBNER PAPERBACK FICTION *and design are trademarks of*
Jossey-Bass, Inc., used under license by
Simon & Schuster, the publisher of this work.

3   5   7   9   10   8   6   4   2

The Library of Congress cataloged the Scribner edition as follows:
Kureishi, Hanif.
Love in a blue time / Hanif Kureishi.
p.   cm.
I. Title.
PR6061.U68L66   1997
823'.914—dc21   97-19118
CIP

ISBN 978-0-684-84818-1

"In a Blue Time" and *"With Your Tongue down My Throat"* first
appeared in Granta; *"We're Not Jews"* first appeared in the London
Review of Books; *"D'accord, Baby"* appeared in Atlantic Monthly
and the Independent Magazine; *"My Son the Fanatic"* first appeared
in The New Yorker, and subsequently in New Writing 4 (ed. A. S.
Byatt and Alan Hollinghurst); *"The Tale of the Turd"* appeared in em
writing & music and The Word.

Contents

Love
in a
Blue
Time

In a Blue Time

When the phone rings, who would you most like it to be? And who would you hate it to be? Who is the first person that comes into your mind, Roy liked to ask people, at that moment?

The phone rang and Roy jumped. He had thought, during supper in their new house, with most of their clothes and books in boxes they were too weary to unpack, that it would be pleasant to try their new bed early. He looked across the table at Clara and hoped she'd let the phone run on to the answering machine so he could tell who it was. He disliked talking to his friends in front of her; she seemed to scrutinise him. Somehow he had caused her to resent any life he might have outside her.

She picked up the phone, saying 'Hallo' suspiciously. Someone was speaking but didn't require or merit a reply. Roy mouthed at her, 'Is it Munday? Is it him?'

She shook her head.

At last she said, 'Oh God,' and waved the receiver at Roy. In the hall he was putting on his jacket.

'Are you going to him?'

'He's in trouble.'

She said, 'We're in trouble, and what will you do about that?'

'Go inside. You'll get cold standing there.'

She clung to him. 'Will you be long?'

'I'll get back as soon as I can. I'm exhausted. You should go to bed.'

'Thank you. Aren't you going to kiss me?'

He put his mouth to hers, and she grunted. He said, 'But I don't even want to go.'

'You'd rather be anywhere else.'

At the gate he called, 'If Munday rings, please take his number. Say that otherwise I'll go to his office first thing tomorrow morning.'

She knew this call from the producer Munday was important to him, indeed to both of them. She nodded and then waved.

It wouldn't take him more than fifteen minutes to drive to the house in Chelsea where his old friend Jimmy had been staying the last few months. But Roy was tired, and parked at the side of the road to think. To think! Apprehension and dread swept through him.

Roy had met Jimmy in the mid-seventies in the back row of their university class on Wittgenstein. Being four years older than the other students, Jimmy appeared ironically knowing compared to Roy's first friends, who had just left school. After lectures Jimmy never merely retired to the library with a volume of Spinoza, or, as Roy did, go disappointedly home and study, while dreaming of the adventures he might have, were he less fearful. No – Jimmy did the college a favour by popping in for an hour or so after lunch. Then he'd hang out impressing some girls he was considering for his stage adaptation of *Remembrance of Things Past*.

After he'd auditioned them at length, and as the sky darkened over the river and the stream of commuters across Blackfriars Bridge thinned, Jimmy would saunter forth into the city's pleasures. He knew the happenin' cinemas, jazz clubs, parties. Or, since he ran his own magazine, *Blurred Edges*, he'd interview theatre directors, photographers, tattooists and performance artists who, to Roy's surprise, rarely refused. At that time students were still considered by some people to be of consequence, and Jimmy would light a joint, sit on the floor and let the recorder run. He would print only the trifling parts of the tape – the gossip and requests for drinks – satisfying his theory that what people were was more interesting than their opinions.

Tonight Jimmy had said he needed Roy more than he'd ever needed him. Or rather, Jimmy's companions had relayed that message. Jimmy himself hadn't made it to the phone or even to his feet. He was, nevertheless, audible in the background.

On the doorstep Roy hesitated. Next morning he had a critical breakfast meeting with Munday about the movie Roy had written and was, after two years of preparation, going to direct. He was also, for the first time, living with Clara. This had been a sort of choice, but its consequences – a child on the way – had somehow surprised them both.

He couldn't turn back. Jimmy's was the voice Roy most wanted to hear on the phone. Their friendship had survived even the mid-eighties, that vital and churning period when everything had been forced forward with a remorseless velocity. Roy had cancelled his debts to anyone whose affection failed to yield interest. At that time, when Roy lived alone, Jimmy would turn up late at night, just to talk. This was welcome and unusual in Roy's world, as they didn't work together and there was no question of loss or gain between them. Jimmy wasn't impressed by Roy's diligence. While Roy rushed between meetings Jimmy was, after all, idling in bars and the front of girls' shirts. But though Jimmy disappeared for weeks – one time he was in prison – when Roy had a free day, Jimmy was the person Roy wanted to spend it with. The two of them would lurch from pub to pub from lunchtime until midnight, laughing at everything. He had no other friends like this, because there are some conversations you can only have with certain people.

Roy pushed the door and cautiously made his way down the uncarpeted stairs, grasping the banister with feeble determination as, he realised, his father used to do. Someone seemed to have been clawing at the wallpaper with their fingernails. A freezing wind blew across the basement: a broken chair must have travelled through a window.

There was Jimmy, then, on the floor, with a broken bottle beside him. The only object intact was a yellowing photograph of Keith Richards pinned to the wall.

Not that Jimmy would have been able to get into his bed. It was occupied by a cloudy-faced middle-aged woman with well-cut hair who, though appearing otherwise healthy, kept nodding out. Cradled into her was a boy of around sixteen with a sly scared look, naked apart from a Lacoste crocodile tattooed onto his chest. Now and again the woman seemed to achieve a dim consciousness and tried shoving him away, but she couldn't shift him.

Jimmy lay on the floor like a child in the playground, with the foot of a bully on his chest. The foot belonged to Marco, the owner of the house, a wealthy junkie with a blood-stained white scarf tied around his throat. Another man, Jake, stood beside them.

'The cavalry's arrived,' Jake said to Marco, who lifted his boot.

Jimmy's eyes were shut. His twenty-one-year-old girl-friend Kara, the daughter of a notable bohemian family, who had been seeing Jimmy for a year, ran and kissed Roy gratefully. She was accompanied by an equally young friend, with vivid lips, leopard-skin hat and short skirt. If Roy regretted coming, he particularly regretted his black velvet jacket. Cut tight around the waist, it was long and shining and flared out over the thighs. The designer, a friend for whom Roy had shot a video, had said that ageing could only improve it. But wherever he wore it, Roy understood now, it sang of style and money, and made him look as if he had a job.

Kara and the girl took Roy to one side and explained that Jimmy had been drinking. Kara had found him in Brompton Cemetery with a smack dealer, though he claimed to have given that up. This time she was definitely leaving him until he sorted himself out.

'They're animals,' murmured Jimmy.

Marco replaced his foot on his chest.

The kid in the bed, who had now mounted the woman, glared over his shoulder, saying to Jimmy, 'What the fuck, you don't never sleep here no more. You got smarter people to be with than us.'

Jimmy shouted, 'It's my bed! And stop fucking that woman, she's overdosing!'

There was nothing in the woman's eyes.

'Is she all right?' Roy asked.

'She still alive,' the boy explained. 'My finger on her pulse.'

Jimmy cried, 'They stole my fucking booze and drunk it, found my speed and took it, and stole my money and spent it. I'm not having these bastards in my basement, they're bastards.'

Jake said to Roy: 'Number one, he's evicted right now this minute. He went berserk. Tried to punch us around, and then tried to kill himself.'

Jimmy winked up at Roy. 'Did I interrupt your evening, man? Were you talking about film concepts?'

For years Roy had made music videos and commercials, and directed episodes of soap operas. Sometimes he taught at the film school. He had also made a sixty-minute film for the BBC, a story about a black girl singer. He had imagined that this would be the start of something considerable, but although the film received decent reviews, it had taken him no further. In the mid-eighties he'd been considered for a couple of features, but like most films, they'd fallen through. He'd seen his contemporaries make films in Britain, move to LA and buy houses with pools. An acquaintance had been nominated for an Oscar.

Now at last his own movie was in place, apart from a third of the money and therefore the essential signed contracts and final go-ahead, which were imminent. In the past week Munday had been to LA and New York. He had been told that with a project of this quality he wouldn't have trouble raising the money.

Kara said, 'I expect Roy was doing some hard work.' She turned to him. 'He's too much. Bye-bye, Jimmy, I love you.'

While she bent down and kissed Jimmy, and he rubbed his hand between her legs, Roy looked at the picture of Keith Richards and considered how he'd longed for the uncontrolled life, seeking only pleasure and avoiding the ponderous difficulties of keeping everything together. He wondered if that was what he still wanted, or if he were still capable of it.

When Kara had gone, Roy stood over Jimmy and asked, 'What d'you want me to do?'

'Quote the lyrics of "Tumblin' Dice".'

The girl in the hat touched Roy's arm. 'We're going clubbing. Aren't you taking Jimmy to your place tonight?'

'What? Is that the idea?'

'He tells everyone you're his best friend. He can't stay here.' The girl went on. 'I'm Candy. Jimmy said you work with Munday.'

'That's right.'

'What are you doing with him, a promo?'

From the floor Jimmy threw up his protracted cackle.

Roy said, 'I'm going to direct a feature I've written.'

'Can I work on it with you?' she asked. 'I'll do anything.'

'You'd better ring me to discuss it,' he said.

Jimmy called, 'How's the pregnant wife?'

'Fine.'

'And that young girl who liked to sit on your face?'

Roy made a sign at Candy and led her into an unlit room next door. He cut out some coke, turned to the waiting girl and kissed her against the wall, smelling this stranger and running his hands over her. She inhaled her line, but before he could dispose of his and hold her again, she had gone.

Marco and Jake had carted Jimmy out, stashed him in Roy's car and instructed him to fuck off for good.

Roy drove Jimmy along the King's Road. As always now, Jimmy was dressed for outdoors, in sweaters, boots and heavy coat. In contrast, Roy's colleagues dressed in light clothes and would never inadvertently enter the open air: when they wanted weather they would fly to a place that had the right kind. An over-ripe gutter odour rose from Jimmy, and Roy noticed the dusty imprint of Marco's foot on his chest. Jimmy pulled a pair of black lace-trimmed panties from his pocket and sniffed at them like a duchess mourning a relative.

This was an opportunity, Roy decided, to use on Jimmy some of the honest directness he had been practising at work. Surely it would be instructive and improving for Jimmy to survive without constant assistance. Besides, Roy couldn't be sucked into another emotional maelstrom.

He said, 'Isn't there anywhere you can go?'

'What for?' said Jimmy.

'To rest. To sleep. At night.'

'To sleep? Oh I see. It's okay. Leave me on the corner.'

'I didn't mean that.'

'I've slept out before.'

'I meant you've usually got someone. Some girl.'

'Sometimes I stay with Candy.'

'Really?'

Jimmy said, 'You liked her, yeah? I'll try and arrange something. Did I tell you she likes to stand on her head with her legs open?'

'You should have mentioned it to Clara on the phone.'

'It's a very convenient position for cunnilingus.'

'Particularly at our age when unusual postures can be a strain,' added Roy.

Jimmy put his hand in Roy's hair. 'You're going grey, you know.'

'I know.'

'But I'm not. Isn't that strange?' Jimmy mused a few seconds. 'But I can't stay with her. Kara wouldn't like it.'

'What about your parents?'

'I'm over forty! They're dying, they make me take my

7

shoes off! They weep when they see me! They – '

Jimmy's parents were political refugees from Eastern Europe who'd suffered badly in the war, left their families, and lived in Britain since 1949. They'd expected, in this city full of people who lived elsewhere in their minds, to be able to return home, but they never could. Britain hadn't engaged them; they barely spoke the language. Meanwhile Jimmy fell in love with pop. When he played the blues on his piano his parents had it locked in the garden shed. Jimmy and his parents had never understood one another, but he had remained as rootless as they had been, never even acquiring a permanent flat.

He was rummaging in his pockets where he kept his phone numbers on torn pieces of cigarette packet and ragged tube tickets. 'You remember when I brought that girl round one afternoon – '

'The eighteen-year-old?'

'She wanted your advice on getting into the media. You fucked her on the table in front of me.'

'The media got into her.'

'Indeed. Can you remember what you wore, who you pretended to be, and what you said?'

'What did I say?'

'It was your happiest moment.'

'It was a laugh.'

'One of our best.'

'One of many.'

They slapped hands.

Jimmy said, 'The next day she left me.'

'Sensible girl.'

'We'd exploited her. She had a soul which you were disrespectful to.' Jimmy reached over and stroked Roy's face. 'I just wanted to say, I love you, man, even if you are a bastard.'

Jimmy started clapping to the music. He could revive as quickly as a child. Nevertheless, Roy determined to beware of his friend's manipulations; this was how Jimmy had survived since leaving university without ever working. For years women had fallen at Jimmy's feet; now he collapsed at theirs. Yet even as he descended they liked him as much. Many were convinced of his lost genius, which had been perfectly preserved for years, by procrastination. Jimmy got away with things; he didn't earn what he received. This was delicious but also a provocation, mocking justice.

Roy had pondered all this, not without incomprehension and envy, until he grasped how much Jimmy gave the women. Alcoholism, unhappiness, failure, ill-health, he showered them with despair, and guiltlessly extracted as much concern as they might proffer. They admired, Roy guessed, his having made a darkness to inhabit. Not everyone was brave enough to fall so far out of the light. To Roy it also demonstrated how many women still saw sacrifice as their purpose.

Friendship was the recurring idea in Roy's mind. He recalled some remarks of Montaigne. 'If I were pressed to say why I love him, I feel that my only reply could be, "because it was he, because it was I".' Also, 'Friendship is enjoyed even as it is desired; it is bred, nourished and increased only by enjoyment, since it is a spiritual thing and the soul is purified by its practice.' However, Montaigne had said nothing about the friend staying with you, as Jimmy seemed set on doing; or about dealing with someone who couldn't believe that, given the choice, anyone would rather be sober than drunk, and that once someone had started drinking they would not stop voluntarily before passing out – the only way of going to sleep that Jimmy found natural.

Roy no longer had any clue what social or political obligations he had, nor much idea where such duties could come from. At university he'd been a charged conscience, acquiring dozens of attitudes wholesale, which, over the years, he had let drop, rather as people stopped wearing certain clothes one by one and started wearing others, until they transformed themselves without deciding to. Since then Roy hadn't settled in any of the worlds he inhabited, but only stepped through them like hotel rooms, and, in the process, hadn't considered what he might owe others. Tonight, what love did this lying, drunken, raggedy-arsed bastard demand?

'Hey.' Roy noticed that Jimmy's fingers were tightening around the handbrake.

'Stop.'

'Now?' Roy said.

'Yes!'

Jimmy was already clambering out of the car and making for an off-licence a few steps away. He wasn't sober but he knew where he was. Roy had no choice but to follow. Jimmy was asking for a bottle of vodka. Then, as Jimmy noticed Roy extracting a £50 note – which was all, to his annoyance, that he was carrying – he added a bottle of whisky to his order. When the assistant turned his back Jimmy swiped four beer cans and concealed them inside his jacket. He also collected Roy's change.

Outside, a beggar extended his cap and mumbled some words of a song. Jimmy squatted down at the man's level and stuffed the change from the £50 into his cap.

'I've got nothing else,' Jimmy said. 'Literally fuck-all. But take this. I'll be dead soon.'

The man held the notes up to the light. This was too much. Roy went to snatch them back. But the bum had disappeared them and was repeating, 'On yer way, on yer way . . .'

Roy turned to Jimmy. 'It's my money.'

'It's nothing to you, is it?'

'That doesn't make it yours.'

'Who cares whose it is? He needs it more than us.'

'. . . on yer way . . .'

'He's not our responsibility.'

Jimmy looked at Roy curiously. 'What makes you say that? He's pitiful.'

Roy noticed two more derelicts shuffling forward. Further up the street others had gathered, anticipating generosity.

'. . . on yer way . . .'

Roy pulled Jimmy into the car and locked the doors from inside.

Along from Roy's house, lounging by a wall with up-to-something looks on their faces, were two white boys who occupied a nearby basement. The police were often outside, and their mother begging them to take them away; but the authorities could do nothing until the lads were older. Most mornings when Roy went out to get his *Independent* he walked across glass where cars had been broken into. Several times he had greeted the boys. They nodded at him now; one day he would refuse his fear and speak properly. He didn't like to think there was anyone it was impossible to contact in some way, but he didn't know where to begin. Meanwhile he could hardly see out of his house for the bars and latticed slats. Beside his bed he kept a knife and hammer, and was mindful of not turning over too strenuously for fear of whacking the red alarm button adjacent to his pillow.

'This the new house? Looks comfortable,' said Jimmy. 'You didn't invite me to the house-warming, but Clara's gonna be delighted to see me now. Wished I owned a couple of suitcases so I could stand at the door and tell her I'm here for a while.'

'Don't make too much noise.'

Roy led Jimmy into the living room. Then he ran upstairs, opened the bedroom door and listened to Clara breathing in the darkness. He had wanted to fuck her that night. When the phone rang he was initiating the painstaking preparatory work. It was essential not to offend her in any way since a thumbs-down was easy, and agreeable, to her. He had been sitting close by her and sending, telepathically – his preferred method of communication – loving sensual messages. As they rarely touched one another gratuitously, immediate physical contact – his hand in her hair – would be a risk. But if he did manage to touch her without a setback and even if, perhaps, he persuaded her to pull her skirt up a little – this made him feel as if he had reached the starting-gate, at least – he knew success was a possibility. Bearing this in mind he would rush upstairs to bed, changing into his pyjamas so as not to alarm her with uncovered flesh. He had, scrupulously, to avoid her getting the right idea.

He tried to anticipate which mood would carry her through the bedroom door. If there was something he'd neglected to do, like lock the back door or empty the dishwasher, arduous diplomacy would be imperative. Otherwise he would observe her undressing as she watched TV, knowing it would be only moments before his nails were in the bitch's fat arse.

But wait: she had perched on the end of the bed to inspect her corns while sucking on a throat pastille and discussing the cost of having the front of the house repointed. His desire was boiling, and he wanted to strike down his penis, which by now was through the front of his pyjamas, with a ruler.

As she watched TV beside him and he played with her breasts, she continued to pretend that this was not happening; perhaps, for her, it wasn't. She did, though, appear to believe in foreplay, at least for herself. After a time she would even remove all her clothes, though not without a histrionic shiver to demonstrate that sex altered one's temperature. At this encouragement he would scoot across the floor and hunt, in the back of a drawer, for a pair of crumpled black nylon French knickers. Rolling her eyes at the tawdry foolishness of men she might, if his luck was in, pull them on. He knew she was finally conquered when she stopped watching television. Unfortunately, she used this opportunity, while she had his attention, to scold him for minor offences. He could, with pleasure, have taped over her mouth.

In all this there must have been, despite their efforts, a unifying pleasure, for next morning she liked to hold him, and wanted to be kissed.

Roy could only close the door now. Before returning to Jimmy he went into the room next door. Clara had bought a changing table on which lay pairs of mittens, baby boots, little red hats, cardigans smaller than handkerchiefs. The curtains were printed with airborne elephants; on the wall was a picture of a farmyard.

What had he done? She puzzled him still. Never had a woman pursued him as passionately as Clara over the past five years. Not a day would pass, at the beginning, when she didn't send him flowers and books, invite him to concerts and the cinema, or cook for him. Perhaps she had been attempting, by example, to kindle in him the romantic feeling she herself desired. He had accepted it like a pasha. At other times he'd attempted to brush her away, and had always kept other women. He saw now what a jejune protest that was. Her love had been an onslaught. She wanted a family. He, who liked to plan everything, but had really only known what sort of work he sought, had complied in order to see what might occur. He had been easily overrun; the child was coming; it gave him vertigo.

He was tugging at a mattress leaning against the wall. Jimmy would be cosy here, perhaps too cosy, reflected Roy, going downstairs without it.

Jimmy was lying with his feet on the sofa. Beside him he had arranged a beer, a glass and a bottle of Jack Daniels taken from the drinks cupboard. He was lighting a cigarette from the matches Roy had collected from the Royalton and the Odeon, smart New York restaurants, and kept to impress people.

There was no note from Clara about Munday, and no message on the machine.

Roy said, 'All right, pal?' He decided he loved his friend, envied his easy complacency, and was glad to have him here.

Jimmy said, 'Got everything I need.'

'Take it easy with the Jack. What about the bottle we bought?'

'Don't start getting queenie. I didn't want to break into them straight away. So – here we are together again.' Jimmy presented his glass. 'What the fuck?'

'Yeah, what the fuck!'

'Fuck everything!'

'Fuck it!'

The rest of the Jack went and they were halfway through the vodka the next time Roy pitched towards the clock. The records had come out, including Black Sabbath. A German porn film was playing with the sound turned off. The room became dense with marijuana smoke. They must have got hungry. After smashing into a tin of baked beans with a hammer and spraying the walls, Roy climbed on Jimmy's shoulders to buff the mottled ceiling with a cushion cover and then stuffed it in Jimmy's mouth to calm him down. Roy didn't know what time the two of them stripped in order to demonstrate the Skinhead Moonstomp or whether he had imagined their neighbour banging on the wall and then at the front door.

It seemed not long after that Roy hurried into Soho for buttered toast and coffee in the Patisserie Valerie. In his business, getting up early had become so habitual that if, by mistake, he woke up after seven, he panicked, fearing life had left without him.

Before ten he was at Munday's office where teams of girls with Home Counties accents, most of whom appeared to be wearing cocktail dresses, were striding across the vast spaces waving contracts. Roy's arrival surprised them; they had no idea whether Munday was in New York, Los

Angeles or Paris, or when he'd be back. He was 'raising money'. Because it had been on his mind, Roy asked seven people if they could recall the name of Harry Lime's English friend in *The Third Man*. But only two of them had seen the film and neither could remember.

There was nothing to do. He had cleared a year of other work to make this film. The previous night had sapped him, but he felt only as if he'd taken a sweet narcotic. Today he should have few worries. Soon he'd be hearing from Munday.

He drifted around Covent Garden, where, since the mid-eighties, he rarely ventured without buying. His parents had not been badly off but their attitude to money had been, if you want something think whether you really need it and if you can do without it. Well, he could do without most things, if pushed. But at the height of the decade money had gushed through his account. If he drank champagne rather than beer, if he used cocaine and took taxis from one end of Soho to the other five times a day, it barely dented the balance. It had been a poetic multiplication; the more he made the more he admired his own life.

He had loved that time. The manic entrepreneurialism, prancing individualism, self-indulgence and cynicism appealed to him as nothing had for ten years. Pretence was discarded. Punk disorder and nihilism ruled. Knowledge, tradition, decency and the lip-service paid to equality; socialist holiness, talk of 'principle', student clothes, feminist absurdities, and arguments defending regimes – 'flawed experiments' – that his friends wouldn't have been able to live under for five minutes: such pieties were trampled with a Nietzschean pitilessness. It was galvanising.

He would see something absurdly expensive – a suit, computers, cameras, cars, apartments – and dare himself to buy it, simply to discover what the consequences of such recklessness might be. How much fun could you have before everything went mad? He loved returning from the shops and opening the designer carrier bags, removing the tissue paper, and trying on different combinations of clothes while playing the new CDs in their cute slim boxes. He adored the new restaurants, bars, clubs, shops, galleries, made of black metal, chrome or neon, each remaining fashionable for a month, if it was lucky.

Life had become like a party at the end of the world. He was sick of it, as one may grow sick of champagne or of kicking a dead body. It was over, and there was nothing. If there was to be anything it had to be made anew.

He had lived through an age when men and women with energy and ruthlessness but without much ability or persistence excelled. And even though most of them had gone under, their ignorance had confused Roy, making him wonder whether the things he had striven to learn, and thought of as 'culture', were irrelevant. Everything was supposed to be the same: commercials, Beethoven's late quartets, pop records, shopfronts, Freud, multi-coloured hair. Greatness, comparison, value, depth: gone, gone, gone. Anything could give some pleasure; he saw that. But not everything provided the sustenance of a deeper understanding.

His work had gone stale months ago. Whether making commercials, music videos or training films, Roy had always done his best. But now he would go along with whatever the client wanted, provided he could leave early.

Around the time he had begun to write his film, he started checking the age of the director or author if he saw a good movie or read a good book. He felt increasingly ashamed of his still active hope of being some sort of artist. The word itself sounded effete; and his wish seemed weakly adolescent, affected, awkward.

Once, in a restaurant in Vienna during a film festival, Roy saw that Fellini had come in with several friends. The maestro went to every table with his hands outstretched. Then the tall man with the head of an emperor sat down and ate in peace. And what peace it would be! Roy thought often of how a man might feel had he made, for instance, *La Dolce Vita*, not to speak of *8½*. What insulating spirit this would give him, during breakfast, or waiting to see his doctor about a worrying complaint, enduring the empty spaces that boundary life's occasional rousing events!

Bergman, Fellini, Ozu, Wilder, Cassavetes, Rosi, Renoir: the radiance! Often Roy would rise at five in the morning to suck the essential vitamin of poetry in front of the video. A few minutes of *Amarcord*, in which Fellini's whole life was present, could give him perspective all day. Certain sequences he examined scores of times, studying the writing, acting, lighting and camera movements. In commercials he was able to replicate certain shots or the tone of entire scenes. 'Bit more Bergman?' he'd say. 'Or do you fancy some Fellini here?'

In New York he went to see *Hearts Of Darkness*, the documentary about Coppola's making of *Apocalypse Now*. He was becoming aware of what he wouldn't do now: parachute from a plane or fight in a war or revolution; travel across Indonesia with a backpack; go to bed with three women at once, or even two; learn Russian, or even French, properly; or be taught the principles of architecture. But for days he craved remarkable and noble schemes on which everything was risked.

What would they be? For most of his adult life he'd striven to keep up with the latest thing in cinema, music, literature and even the theatre, ensuring that no one mentioned an event without his having heard of it. But now he had lost the thread and didn't mind. What he wanted was to extend himself. He tormented himself with his own mediocrity. And he saw that, apart from dreams, the most imaginative activity most people allowed themselves was sexual fantasy. To live what you did – somehow – was surely the point.

In his garden in the mornings, he began to write, laying

out the scenes on index cards on the grass, as if he were playing patience. The concentration was difficult. He was unused to such a sustained effort of dreaming, particularly when the outcome was distant, uncertain and not immediately convertible into a cheque or interest from colleagues. Why not begin next year?

After a few days' persistence his mind focused and began to run in unstrained motion. In these moments – reminded of himself even as he got lost in what he was doing – the questions he had asked about life, its meaning and direction, if any, about how best to live, could receive only one reply. To be here now, doing this.

That was done. He was in a hurry to begin shooting. Private satisfactions were immaterial. The film had to make money. When he was growing up, the media wasn't considered a bright boy's beat. Like pop, television was disparaged. But it had turned out to be the jackpot. Compared to his contemporaries at school, he had prospered. Yet the way things were getting set up at home he had to achieve until he expired. He and Clara would live well: nannies, expensive schools, holidays, dinner parties, clothes. After setting off in the grand style, how could you retreat to less without anguish?

All morning his mind had whirled. Finally he phoned Clara. She'd been sick, and had come downstairs to discover Jimmy asleep on the floor amid the night's debris, wrapped in the tablecloth and the curtains, which had become detached from the rail. He had pissed in a pint glass and placed it on the table.

To Roy's surprise she was amused. She had, it was true, always liked Jimmy, who flirted with her. But he couldn't imagine her wanting him in her house. She wasn't a cool or loose hippie. She taught at a university and could be formidable. Most things could interest her, though, and she was able to make others interested. She was enthusiastic and took pleasure in being alive, always a boon in others, Roy felt. Like Roy, she adored gossip. The misfortunes and vanity of others gave them pleasure. But it was still a mostly cerebral and calculating intelligence that she had. She lacked Jimmy's preferred kind of sentimental self-observation. It had been her clarity that had attracted Roy, at a time when they were both concerned with advancement.

Cheered by her friendliness towards Jimmy, Roy wanted to be with him today.

Jimmy came out of the bathroom in Roy's bathrobe and sat at the table with scrambled eggs, the newspaper, his cigarettes and 'Let It Bleed' on loud. Roy was reminded of their time at university, when, after a party, they would stay up all night and the next morning sit in a pub garden, or take LSD and walk along the river to the bridge at Hammersmith, which Jimmy, afraid of heights, would have to run across with his eyes closed.

Roy read his paper while surreptitiously watching Jimmy eat, drink and move about the room as if he'd inhabited it for years. He was amazed by the lengthy periods between minor tasks that Jimmy spent staring into space, as if each action set off another train of memory, regret and speculation. Then Jimmy would search his pockets for phone numbers and shuffle them repeatedly. Finally, Jimmy licked his plate and gave a satisfied burp. When Roy had brushed the crumbs from the floor, he decided to give Jimmy a little start.

'What are you going to do today?'

'Do? In what sense?'

'In the sense of . . . to do something.'

Jimmy laughed.

Roy went on, 'Maybe you should think of looking for work. The structure might do you good.'

'Structure?'

Jimmy raised himself to talk. There was a beer can from the previous night beside the sofa; he swigged from it and then spat out, having forgotten he'd used it as an ashtray. He fetched another beer from the fridge and resumed his position.

Jimmy said, 'What sort of work is it that you're talking about here?'

'Paying work. You must have heard of it. You do something all day – '

'Usually something you don't like to do – '

'Whatever. Though you might like it.' Jimmy snorted. 'And at the end of the week they give you money with which you can buy things, instead of having to scrounge them.'

This idea forced Jimmy back in his seat. 'You used to revere the surrealists.'

'Shooting into a crowd! Yes, I adored it when – '

'D'you think they'd have done anything but kill themselves laughing at the idea of salaried work? You know it's serfdom.'

Roy lay down on the floor and giggled. Jimmy's views had become almost a novelty to Roy. Listening to him reminded Roy of the pleasures of failure, a satisfaction he considered to be unjustly unappreciated now he had time to think about it. In the republic of accumulation and accountancy there was no doubt Jimmy was a failure artist of ability. To enlarge a talent to disappoint, it was no good creeping into a corner and dying dismally. It was essential to raise, repeatedly, hope and expectation in both the gullible and the knowing, and then to shatter them. Jimmy was intelligent, alertly bright-eyed, convincing. With him there was always the possibility of things working out. It was an achievement, therefore, after a calculated build-up, to bring off a resounding fuck-up. Fortunately Jimmy would always, on the big occasion, let you down: hopelessness, impotence, disaster, all manner of wretchedness – he could bring them on like a regular nightmare.

Not that it hadn't cost him. It took resolution, organisation, and a measure of creativity to drink hard day and night; to insult friends and strangers; to go to parties uninvited and attempt to have sex with teenage girls; to borrow money and never pay it back; to lie, make feeble excuses, be evasive, shifty and selfish. He had had many advantages to overcome. But finally, after years of application, he had made a success, indeed a triumph, of failure.

Jimmy said, 'The rich love the poor to work, and the harder the better. It keeps them out of trouble while they're ripped off. Everyone knows that.' He picked up a porn magazine, *Peaches*, and flipped through the pages. 'You don't think I'm going to fall for that shit, do you?'

Roy's eyes felt heavy. He was falling asleep in the morning! To wake himself up he paced the carpet and strained to recall the virtues of employment.

'Jimmy, there's something I don't understand about this.'

'What?'

'Don't you ever wake up possessed by a feeling of things not done? Of time and possibility lost, wasted? And failure . . . failure in most things – that could be overcome. Don't you?'

Jimmy said, 'That's different. Of mundane work you know nothing. The worst jobs are impossible to get. You've lived for years in the enclosed world of the privileged with no idea what it's like outside. But the real work you mention, I tell you, every damn morning I wake up and feel time rushing past me. And it's not even light. Loneliness . . . fear. My heart vibrates.'

'Yes! and don't you think, this is a new morning, maybe this day I can redeem the past? Today something real might be done?'

'Sometimes I do think that,' Jimmy said. 'But most of the time . . . to tell you the truth, Roy, I know nothing will get done. Nothing, because that time is past.'

When the beer was gone they went out, putting their arms around one another. On the corner of Roy's street was a rough

21

pub with benches outside, where many local men gathered between March and September, usually wearing just shorts. They'd clamber from their basements at half past ten and by eleven they'd be in place, chewing a piece of bread with their beer, smoking dope and shouting above the traffic. Their women, who passed by in groups, pushing prams laden with shopping, were both angrier and more vital.

One time Roy walked past and heard Springsteen's hypodermic cry 'Hungry Heart' blaring from inside. He'd lingered apprehensively: surely the song would rouse the men to some sudden recklessness, the desire to move or hunt down experience? But they merely mouthed the words.

He thought of the books which had spoken to him as a teenager and how concerned they were with young men fleeing home and domesticity, to hurl themselves at different boundaries. But where had it led except to self-destruction and madness? And how could you do that kind of thing now? Where could you run?

Roy's preferred local was a low-ceilinged place with a semicircular oak bar. Beyond, it was long and deep, broken up by booths, corners and turns. Men sat alone, reading, staring, talking to themselves, as if modelling for a picture entitled 'The Afternoon Drinkers'. There was a comfortable aimlessness; in here nothing had to happen.

Jimmy raised his glass. Roy saw that his hand trembled, and that his skin looked bruised and discoloured, the knuckles raw, fingers bitten.

'By the way, how was Clara this morning?'

'That was her, right?' said Jimmy.

'Yeah.'

'She's big outfront but looking great. A bit like Jean Shrimpton.'

'You told her that?'

Jimmy nodded.

Roy said, 'That's what did the trick. You'll be in with her for a couple of days now.'

'Still fuck her?'

'When I can't help myself,' said Roy. 'You'd think she'd appreciate the interest but instead she says that lying beside me is like sleeping next to a bag of rubbish that hasn't been collected for a fortnight.'

'She's lucky to have you,' said Jimmy.

'Me?'

'Oh yes. And she knows it too. Still, thank Christ there's plenty of pussy back on stream now that that Aids frenzy has worn off.'

Roy said, 'All the same, it's easy to underestimate how casual and reassuring married love can be. You can talk about other things while you're doing it. It isn't athletic. You can drift. It's an amicable way of confirming that everything is all right.'

'I've never had that,' said Jimmy.

'You're not likely to, either.'

'Thanks.'

After a time Jimmy said, 'Did I mention there was a phone call this morning. Someone's office. Tuesday?'

'Tuesday?'

'Or was it Wednesday?'

'Munday!'

'Munday? Yeah, maybe it was . . . one of those early days.'

Roy grasped him by the back of the neck and vibrated him a little. 'Tell me what he said.'

Jimmy said, 'Gone. Everything vaporises into eternity – all thoughts and conversations.'

'Not this one.'

Jimmy sniggered, 'The person said he's in the air. Or was. And he's popping round for a drink.'

'When?'

'I think it was . . . today.'

'Christ,' said Roy. 'Finish your pint.'

'A quick one, I think, to improve our temper.'

'Get up. This is the big one. It's my film, man.'

'Film? When's it on?'

'Couple of years.'

'What? Where's the hurry? How can you think in those kinda time distances?'

Roy held Jimmy's glass to his lips. 'Drink.'

Munday might, Roy knew, swing by for a few minutes and treat Roy as if he were a mere employee; or he might hang out for five hours, discussing politics, books, life.

Munday embodied his age, particularly in his puritanism. He was surrounded by girls; he was rich and in the film business; everywhere there were decadent opportunities. But work was his only vice, with the emphasis on negotiating contracts. His greatest pleasure was to roar, after concluding a deal: 'Course, if you'd persisted, or had a better agent, I'd have paid far more.'

He did like cocaine. He didn't like to be offered it, for this might suggest he took it, which he didn't, since it was passé. He did, nevertheless, like to notice a few lines laid accidentally out on the table, into which he might dip his nose in passing.

Cocaine would surely help things go better. As Roy guided Jimmy back, he considered the problem. There was a man – Upton Turner – who was that rare thing, a fairly reliable dealer who made home visits and occasionally arrived on the stated day. Roy had been so grateful for this – and his need so urgent – that when Turner had visited in the past, Roy had inquired after his health and family, giving Turner, he was afraid, the misapprehension that he was a person as well as a vendor. He had become a nuisance. The last time Roy phoned him, Turner had flung the phone to one side, screaming that the cops were at the door and he was 'lookin' at twenty years!' As Roy listened, Turner was dumping thousands of pounds worth of powder down the toilet, only to discover that the person at the door was a neighbour who wanted to borrow a shovel.

Despite Turner's instability, Roy called him. Turner said he'd come round. At once Munday's office then rang.

'He's coming to you,' they said. 'Don't go anywhere.'

'But when?' Roy whined.

'Expect him in the near future,' the cool girl replied, and added, with a giggle, 'This century, definitely.'

'Ha, ha.'

They had some time at least. While listening for Upton's car, Roy and Jimmy had a few more drinks. At last Roy called Jimmy over to the window.

'There.'

'No!' Jimmy seized the curtain to give him strength. 'It's a wind-up. That isn't Turner. Maybe it's Munday.'

'It is our man, without a doubt.'

'Doesn't he feel a little conspicuous – in his profession?'

'Wouldn't you think so?'

'Jesus, Roy, and you're letting this guy into your new home?'

They watched Turner trying to land the old black Rolls in a space, his pit-bull sitting up front and music booming from the windows. He couldn't get the car in anywhere, and finally left it double-parked in the road with the traffic backing up around it, and rushed into the house with the noisy dog. Turner was small, balding and middle-aged, in a white shirt and grey suit that clung to his backside and flared at the ankles. He saw Jimmy drinking at the table and came to an abrupt standstill.

'Roy, son, you're all fucking pissed. You should have said we're having a bit of a laugh, I'd have brought the party acid.'

'This is Jimmy.'

Turner sat down, parting his legs and sweeping back his jacket, exposing his genitals outlined by tight trousers as if he anticipated applause. He reached into his pocket and tossed a plastic bag onto the table containing fifty or sixty small envelopes. Jimmy was rubbing his hands together in anticipation.

Turner said, 'How many of these are you having? Eh?'

'Not sure yet.'

'Not sure? What d'you mean?'

'Just that.'

'All right,' Turner conceded. 'Try it, try it.'

Roy opened one of the envelopes.

'Never seen so many books an' videos as you got in these boxes,' Turner said, pacing about. He halted by a pile and said, 'Alphabetical. A mind well ordered. As a salesman I evaluate the people from looking at their houses. Read 'em all?'

'It's surprising how many people ask that,' Roy said with relaxed enjoyment. 'It really is. Turner, d'you want a drink or something else?'

'You must know a lot then.' Turner insisted.

'Not necessarily,' Jimmy said. 'It doesn't follow.'

'I know what you mean.' Turner winked at Jimmy and they laughed. 'But the boy must know something. I'm gonna offer credit where it's due, I'm generous like that.' He lit a cigarette in his cupped hand and surveyed the kitchen. 'Nice place. You an' the wife getting the builders in?'

'Yeah.'

'Course. I bet you have a pretty nice life, all in all. Plays, travel, posh friends. The police aren't looking for you, are they?'

'Not like they are for you, Turner.'

'No. That's right.'

'Turner's looking at fifteen. Isn't that right, man?'

'Yeah,' said Turner. 'Sometimes twenty. I'm looking at –' He noticed Jimmy suppressing a giggle and turned to see Roy smirking. He said, 'I'm looking at a lot of shit. Now, Mister Roy, if you know so fucking much I'll try and think if there's something I need to ask you, while I'm here.'

Jimmy said to Roy, 'Are you ready for Mr Turner's questions?'

Roy tapped his razor blade on the table and organised the

powder into thick lines. He and Jimmy hunched over to inhale. Turner sat down at last and pointed at the envelopes.

'How many of them d'you want?'

'Three.'

'How many?'

'Three, I said.'

'Fuck.' Turner banged his fist on the table. 'Slags.'

Roy said, 'You want a piece of pie?'

'That I could go for.'

Roy cut a piece of Clara's cherry pie and gave it to Turner. Turner took two large bites and it was inside him. Roy cut another piece. This time Turner leaned back in his chair, raised his arm and hurled it across the kitchen as if he were trying to smash it through the wall. The dog thrashed after it like a shoal of piranhas. It was an aged creature and its eating was slobbery and breathless. The second it had finished, the dog ran back to Turner's feet and planted itself there, waiting for more.

Turner said to Roy, 'Three, did you say?'

'Yeah.'

'So I have come some considerable miles at your instant command for fuck-all. You know,' he said sarcastically, 'I'm looking at eighteen.'

'In that case four. All right. Four g's. Might as well, eh, Jimmy?'

Turner slapped the dog. 'You'll get another go in a minute,' he told it. He looked at Jimmy. 'What about ten?'

'Go for it,' said Jimmy to Roy. 'We'll be all right tomorrow. Ten should see us through.'

'Smart,' said Turner. 'Planning ahead.'

'Ten?' Roy said. 'No way. I don't think you should hustle people.'

Turner's voice became shrill. 'You saying I hustle you?'

Roy hesitated. 'I mean by that . . . it's not a good business idea.'

Turner raised his voice. 'I'm doing this to pay off my

brother's debts. My brother who was killed by scum. It's all for him.'

'Quite right,' murmured Jimmy.

'Hey, I've got a fucking question for you,' Turner said. 'Little Roy.'

'Yes?'

'Do you know how to love life?'

Jimmy and Roy looked at one another.

Turner said, 'That's stumped you, right? I'm saying here, is it a skill? Or a talent? Who can acquire it?' He was settling into his rap. 'I deal to the stars, you know.'

'Most of them introduced to you by me,' Roy murmured.

'And they the unhappiest people I seen.'

'It's still a difficult question,' said Roy.

He looked at Turner, who was so edgy and complicated it was hard to think of him as a child. But you could always see the light of childhood in Jimmy, he was luminous with curiosity.

'But a good one,' said Jimmy.

'You're pleased with that one,' Roy said to Turner.

'Yeah, I am.' Turner looked at Jimmy. 'You're right. It's a difficult question.'

Roy put his hand in his jeans pocket and dragged out a wad of £20 notes.

'Hallo,' Turner said.

'Jesus,' said Jimmy.

'What?' Roy said.

'I'll take a tenner off.' Turner said. 'As we're friends – if you buy six.'

'I told you, not six,' said Roy, counting the money. There was plenty of it, but he thumbed through it rapidly.

Turner reached out to take the whole wad and held it in his fist, looking down at the dog as his foot played on its stomach.

'Hey,' Roy said and turned to Jimmy who was laughing.

'What?' said Turner, crumpling the money in his hand.

Roy pulled the cherry pie towards him and cut a slice. His hand was shaking now. 'You are in a state,' Turner said. He took the mobile phone out of his pocket and turned it off.

'Am I?' Roy said. 'What are you going to do with that money?'

Turner got up and took a step towards Roy. 'Answer the fucking question!'

Roy put up his hands. 'I can't.'

Turner pushed three small envelopes towards Jimmy, put all the money in his pocket, yanked away his drug bag, and, pursued by the dog, charged to the door. Roy ran to the window and watched the Rolls take off down the street.

'You wanker,' he said to Jimmy. 'You fucking wanker.'

'Me?'

'Christ. We should have done something.'

'Like what?'

'Where's the knife! You should have stuck it in the bastard's fucking throat! That pig's run off with my money!'

'Thing is, you can't trust them proles, man. Sit down.'

'I can't!'

'Here's the knife. Go after him then.'

'Fuck, fuck!'

'This will calm you down,' said Jimmy.

They started into the stuff straight away and there was no going back. Roy attempted to put one gram aside for Munday but Jimmy said, why worry, they could get more later. Roy didn't ask him where from.

Roy was glad to see Upton go. He'd be glad, too, to see the end of the chaos that Jimmy had brought with him.

'What are your plans?' he asked. 'I mean, what are you going to doing in the next few days?'

Jimmy shook his head. He knew what Roy was on about, but ignored him, as Roy sat there thinking that if he was capable of love he had to love all of Jimmy now, at this moment.

It was imperative, though, that he clear his mind for

Munday. The drug got him moving. He fetched a jersey and clean socks for Jimmy, thrust Jimmy's old clothes into a plastic bag, and, holding them at arm's length, pushed them deep into the rubbish. He showered, got changed, opened the windows and prepared coffee.

It was only when Munday, who was ten years younger than him and Jimmy and far taller, came through the door, that Roy realised how spaced he and Jimmy were. Fortunately Clara had said she'd be out that evening. Munday, who had just got off the plane, wanted to relax and talk.

Roy forced his concentration as Munday explained his latest good news. His business, for which Roy had made many music videos, was in the process of being sold to a conglomerate. Munday would to able to make more films and with bigger budgets. He would be managing director and rich.

'Excellent,' said Roy.

'In some ways,' Munday said.

'What do you mean?'

'Let's have another drink.'

'Yes, we must celebrate.' Roy got up. 'I won't be a moment.'

At the door he heard Jimmy say, 'You might be interested to hear that I myself have attempted a bit of writing in my time . . .'

It was that 'I myself' that got him out.

Roy went to buy champagne. He was hurrying around the block. Powerful forces were keeping him from his house. His body ached and fluttered with anxiety; he had Aids at least, and, without a doubt, cancer. A heart attack was imminent. On the verge of panic, he feared he might run yelling into the road but was, at that moment, unable to take another step. He couldn't, though, stay where he was, for fear he might lie down and weep. In a pub he ordered a half but took only two sips. He didn't know how long he'd been sitting there, but he didn't want to go home.

Munday and Jimmy were sitting head to head. Jimmy was telling him a 'scenario' for a film about a famous ageing film director and a drifting young couple who visit him, to pay homage. After they've eaten with him, praised his percipience and vision, admired his awards and heard his Brando stories, they enquire if there is anything they can do for him. The director says he wants to witness the passion of their love-making, hear their conversation, see their bodies, hear their cries and look at them sleeping. The girl and her earnest young man co-operate until . . . They become his secretaries; they take him prisoner; maybe they murder him. Jimmy couldn't remember the rest. It was written down somewhere.

'It's a decent premise,' said Munday.

'Yes,' agreed Jimmy.

Munday turned to Roy, who had rejoined them. 'Where's this guy been hiding?'

He was durable and unsubtle, Munday; and, in spite of his efforts, kindness and concern for others were obvious.

'In the pub,' said Roy.

'Artist on the edge,' said Jimmy.

'Right,' said Munday. 'Too much comfort takes away the hunger. I'll do this . . .' he said.

He would advance Jimmy the money to prepare a draft.

'How much?' asked Jimmy.

'Sufficient.'

Jimmy raised his glass. 'Sufficient. Brilliant – don't you think, Roy?'

Roy said he had to talk to Munday in the kitchen.

'OK,' said Munday. Roy closed the door behind them. Munday said, 'Terrific guy.'

'He used to be remarkable,' said Roy in a low voice, realising he'd left the champagne in the pub. 'Shame he's so fucked now.'

'He has some nice ideas.'

'How can he get them down? He's been dried out three times but always goes back on.'

'Anyhow, I'll see what I can do for him.'

'Good.'

'I meet so few interesting people these days. But I'm sorry to hear about your condition.'

'Pardon?'

'It happens to so many.'

'What happens?'

'I see. You don't want it to get around. But we've worked together for years. You're safe with me.'

'Is that right? Please tell me,' Roy said, 'what you're talking about.'

Munday explained that Jimmy had told him of Roy's addiction to cocaine as well as alcohol.

'You don't believe that, do you?' Roy said.

Munday put his arm around him. 'Don't fuck about, pal, you're one of my best video directors. It's tough enough as it is out there.'

'But you don't, do you?'

'He predicted you'd be in denial.'

'I'm not in fucking denial!'

Munday's eyes widened. 'Maybe not.'

'But I'm not – really!'

Nevertheless, Munday wouldn't stop regarding him as if he were contriving how to fit these startling new pieces into the puzzle that Roy had become.

He said, 'What's that white smear under your nose? and the blade on the table? You will always work, but not if you lie to my face. Roy, you're degrading yourself! I can't have you falling apart on a shoot. You haven't been giving one hundred per cent and you look like shit.'

'Do I?'

'Sure you feel okay now? Your face seems to be twitching. Better take some of these.'

'What are they?'

'Vitamins.'

'Munday –'

'Go on, swallow.'

'Please –'

'Here's some water. Get them down. Christ, you're choking. Lean forward so I can smack you on the back. Jesus, you won't work for me again until you've come out of the clinic. I'll get the office to make a booking tonight. Just think, you might meet some exciting people there.'

'Who?'

'Guitarists. Have you discussed it with Clara?'

'Not yet.'

'If you don't, I will.'

'Thank you. But I need to know what's happening with the film.'

'Listen up then. Just sip the water and concentrate – if you can.'

Later, at the front door Munday shook Jimmy's hand and said he'd be in touch. He said, 'You guys. Sitting around here, music, conversation, bit of dope. I'm going back to the airport now. Another plane, another hotel room. I'm not complaining. But you know.'

The moment Munday got in his Jag and started up the street, Roy screamed at Jimmy. Jimmy covered his face and swore, through his sobs, that he couldn't recall what he'd told Munday. Roy turned away. There was nothing to grasp or punish in Jimmy.

They stopped at an off-licence and drank on a bench in Kensington High Street. A young kid calling himself a traveller sat beside them and gave them a hit on some dope. Roy considered how enjoyably instructive it could be to take up such a position in the High Street, and how much one noticed about people, whereas to passers-by one was invisible, pitied or feared. After a while they went morosely into a pub where the barman served everyone else first and then was rude.

Roy's film would be delayed for at least eighteen months, until Munday was in a stronger position to argue for 'unconventional' projects. Roy doubted it would happen now.

For most of his adult years he'd wanted success, and thought he knew what it was. But now he didn't. He would have to live with himself as he was and without the old hope. Clara would be ashamed of him. As his financial burdens increased his resources had, in a few minutes, shrunk.

As the dark drew in and the street lights came on and people rushed through the tube stations, he and Jimmy walked about, stopping here and there. There seemed, in London, to be a pub on every corner, with many men on red plush seats drinking concentratedly, having nothing better to do. Occasionally they passed restaurants where, in the old days, Roy was greeted warmly and had passed much time, too much – sometimes four or five hours – with business acquaintances, now forgotten. Soon Roy was lost, fleeing with the energy of the frustrated and distressed, while Jimmy moved beside him with his customary cough, stumble and giggle, fuelled by the elation of unaccustomed success, and a beer glass under his coat.

At one point Jimmy suddenly pulled Roy towards a phone box. Jimmy ran in, waited crouching down, and shot out again, pulling Roy by his jacket across the road, where they shrank down beside a hedge.

'What are you doing?'

'We were going to get beaten up.' Though shuddering and looking about wildly, Jimmy didn't stop his drink. 'Didn't you hear them swearing at us? Poofs, poofs, they said.'

'Who, who?'

'Don't worry. But keep your head down!' After a while he said, 'Now come on. This way!'

Roy couldn't believe that anyone would attempt such a thing on the street, but how would he know? He and Jimmy hastened through crowds of young people queuing for a concert; and along streets lined with posters advertising groups and comedians whose names he didn't recognise.

There was a burst of laughter behind them. Roy wheeled round, but saw no one. The noise was coming from a parked car – no, from across the road. Then it seemed to disappear down the street like the tail of a typhoon. Now his name was being called. Assuming it was a spook, he pressed on, only to see a young actor he'd given work to, and to whom he'd promised a part in the film. Roy was aware of his swampy loafers and stained jacket that stank of pubs. Jimmy stood beside him, leaning on his shoulder, and they regarded the boy insolently.

'I'll wait to hear, shall I?' said the actor, after a time, having muttered some other things that neither of them understood.

They settled in a pub from which Roy refused to move. At last he was able to tell Jimmy what Munday had said, and explain what it meant. Jimmy listened. There was a silence.

'Tell me something, man,' Jimmy said. 'When you prepared your shooting scripts and stuff – '

'I suppose you're a big film writer now.'

'Give me a chance. That guy Munday seemed okay.'

'Did he?'

'He saw something good in me, didn't he?'

'Yes, yes. Perhaps he did.'

'Right. It's started, brother. I'm on the up. I need to get a room – a bedsitter with a table – to get things moving in the literary department. Lend me some money until Munday pays me.'

'There you go.'

Roy laid a £20 note on the table. It was all the cash he had now. Jimmy slid it away.

'What's that? It's got to be a grand.'

'A grand?'

Jimmy said, 'That's how expensive it is – a month's rent in advance, a deposit, phone. You've avoided the real world for ten years. You don't know how harsh it is. You'll get the money back – at least from him.'

Roy shook his head. 'I've got a family now, and I haven't got an income.'

'You're a jealous bastard – an' I just saved your life. It's a mistake to begrudge me my optimism. Lend me your pen.' Jimmy made a note on the back of a bus ticket, crossed it out and rejigged it. 'Wait and see. Soon you'll be coming to my office an' asking me for work. I'm gonna have to examine your CV to ensure it ain't too low-class. Now, do you do it every day?'

'Do what?'

'Work.'

'Of course.'

'Every single day?'

'Yes. I've worked every day since I left university. Many nights too.'

'Really?' Jimmy read back what he'd scrawled on the ticket, folded it up, and stuck it in his top pocket. 'That's what I must do.' But he sounded unconvinced by what he'd heard, as if, out of spite, Roy had made it sound gratuitously laborious.

Roy said, 'I feel a failure. It's hard to live with. Most people do it. I s'pose they have to find other sources of pride. But what – gardening? Christ. Everything's suddenly gone down. How am I going to cheer myself up?'

'Pride?' Jimmy sneered. 'It's a privilege of the complacent. What a stupid illusion.'

'You would think that.'

'Why would I?'

'You've always been a failure. You've never had any expectations to feel let down about.'

36

'Me?' Jimmy was incredulous. 'But I have.'

'They're alcoholic fantasies.'

Jimmy was staring at him. 'You cunt! You've never had a kind word for me or my talents!'

'Lifting a glass isn't a talent.'

'You could encourage me! You don't know how indifferent people can be when you're down.'

'Didn't I pick you up and invite you to stay in my house?'

'You been trying to shove me out. Everything about me is wrong or despised. You threw my clothes away. I tell you, you're shutting the door on everyone. It's bourgeois snobbery, and it is ugly.'

'You're difficult, Jimmy.'

'At least I'm a friend who loves you.'

'You don't give me anything but a load of trouble.'

'I've got nothing, you know that! Now you've stolen my hope! Thanks for robbing me!' Jimmy finished his drink and jumped up. 'You're safe. Whatever happens, you ain't really going down, but I am!'

Jimmy walked out. Roy had never before seen Jimmy leave a pub so decisively. Roy sat there another hour, until he knew Clara would be home.

He opened the front door and heard voices. Clara was showing the house to two couples, old friends, and was describing the conservatory she wanted built. Roy greeted them and made for the stairs.

'Roy.'

He joined them at the table. They drank wine and discussed the villa near Perugia they would take in the summer. He could see them wearing old linen and ancient straw hats, fanning themselves haughtily.

He tilted his head to get different perspectives, rubbed his forehead and studied his hands, which were trembling, but couldn't think of anything to say. Clara's friends were well off, and of unimaginative and unchallenged intelligence.

About most things, by now, they had some picked-up opinion, sufficient to aid party conversation. They were set and protected; Roy couldn't imagine them overdosing on their knees, howling.

The problem was that at the back of Roy's world-view lay the Rolling Stones, and the delinquent dream of his adolescence – the idea that vigour and spirit existed in excess, authenticity and the romantic unleashed self: a bourgeois idea that was strictly anti-bourgeois. It had never, finally, been Roy's way, though he'd played at it. But Jimmy had lived it to the end, for both of them.

The complacent talk made Roy weary. He went upstairs. As he undressed, a cat tripped the security lamps and he could see the sodden garden. He'd barely stepped into it, but there were trees and grass and bushes out there. Soon he would get a table and chair for the lawn. With the kid in its pram, he'd sit under the tree, brightened by the sun, eating Vignotte and sliced pear. What did one do when there was nothing to do?

He'd fallen asleep; Clara was standing over him, hissing. She ordered him to come down. He was being rude; he didn't know how to behave. He had 'let her down'. But he needed five minutes to think. The next thing he heard was her saying goodnight at the door.

He awoke abruptly. The front door bell was ringing. It was six in the morning. Roy tiptoed downstairs with a hammer in his hand. Jimmy's stringy body was soaked through and he was coughing uncontrollably. He had gone to Kara's house but she'd been out, so he'd decided to lie down in her doorway until she returned. At about five there had been a storm, and he'd realised she wasn't coming back.

Jimmy was delirious and Roy persuaded him to lie him on the sofa, where he covered him with a blanket. When he brought up blood Clara called the doctor. The ambulance took him away not long after, fearing a clot on the lung.

Roy got back into bed beside Clara and rested his drink on her hard stomach. Clara went to work but Roy couldn't get up. He stayed in bed all morning and thought he couldn't ever sleep enough to recover. At lunchtime he walked around town, lacking even the desire to buy anything. In the afternoon he visited Jimmy in the hospital.

'How you feeling, pal?'

A man in his pyjamas can only seem disabled. No amount of puffing-up can exchange the blue and white stripes for the daily dignity which has been put to bed with him. Jimmy hardly said hallo. He was wailing for a drink and a cigarette.

'It'll do you good, being here,' Roy patted Jimmy's hand. 'Time to sort yourself out.'

Jimmy almost leapt out of bed. 'Change places!'

'No thanks.'

'You smug bastard – if you'd looked after me I wouldn't be in this shit!'

A fine-suited consultant, pursued by white-coated disciples, entered the ward. A nurse drew the curtain across Jimmy's wounded face.

'Make no mistake, I'll be back!' Jimmy cried.

Roy walked past the withered, ashen patients, and towards the lift. Two men in lightweight uniforms were pushing a high bed to the doors on their way to the operating theatre. Roy slotted in behind them as they talked across a dumb patient who blinked up at the roof of the lift. They were discussing where they'd go drinking later. Roy hoped Jimmy wouldn't want him to return the next day.

Downstairs the wide revolving door swept people into the hospital and pushed him out into the town. From the corner of the building, where dressing-gowned patients had gathered to smoke, Roy turned to make a farewell gesture at the building where his friend lay. Then he saw the girl in the leopard-skin hat, Kara's friend.

He called out. Smiling, she came over, holding a bunch of

flowers. He asked her if she was working and when she shook her head, said, 'Give me your number. I'll call you tomorrow. I've got a couple of things on the go.'

Before, he hadn't seen her in daylight. What, now, might there be time for?

She said, 'When's the baby due?'

'Any day now.'

'You're going to have your hands full.'

He asked her if she wanted a drink.

'Jimmy's expecting me,' she said. 'But ring me.'

He joined the robust street. Jimmy couldn't walk here, but he, Roy, could trip along light-headed and singing to himself – as if it were he who'd been taken to hospital, and at the last moment, as the anaesthetic was inserted, a voice had shouted, 'No, not him!', and he'd been reprieved.

Nearby was a coffee shop where he used to go. The manager waved at him, brought over hot chocolate and a cake, and, as usual, complained about the boredom and said he wished for a job like Roy's. When he'd gone, Roy opened his bag and extracted his newspaper, book, notebook and pens. But he just watched the passers-by. He couldn't stay long because he remembered that he and Clara had an ante-natal class. He wanted to get back, to see what was between them and learn what it might give him. Some people you couldn't erase from your life.

We're Not Jews

Azhar's mother led him to the front of the lower deck, sat him down with his satchel, hurried back to retrieve her shopping, and took her place beside him. As the bus pulled away Azhar spotted Big Billy and his son Little Billy racing alongside, yelling and waving at the driver. Azhar closed his eyes and hoped it was moving too rapidly for them to get on. But they not only flung themselves onto the platform, they charged up the almost empty vehicle hooting and panting as if they were on a fairground ride. They settled directly across the aisle from where they could stare at Azhar and his mother.

At this his mother made to rise. So did Big Billy. Little Billy sprang up. They would follow her and Azhar. With a sigh she sank back down. The conductor came, holding the arm of his ticket machine. He knew the Billys, and had a laugh with them. He let them ride for nothing.

Mother's grey perfumed glove took some pennies from her purse. She handed them to Azhar who held them up as she had shown him.

'One and a half to the Three Kings,' he said.

'Please,' whispered Mother, making a sign of exasperation.

'Please,' he repeated.

The conductor passed over the tickets and went away.

'Hold onto them tightly,' said Mother. 'In case the inspector gets on.'

Big Billy said, 'Look, he's a big boy.'

'Big boy,' echoed Little Billy.

'So grown up he has to run to teacher,' said Big Billy.

'Cry baby!' trumpeted Little Billy.

41

Mother was looking straight ahead, through the window. Her voice was almost normal, but subdued. 'Pity we didn't have time to get to the library. Still, there's tomorrow. Are you still the best reader in the class?' She nudged him. 'Are you?'

'S'pose so,' he mumbled.

Every evening after school Mother took him to the tiny library nearby where he exchanged the previous day's books. Tonight, though, there hadn't been time. She didn't want Father asking why they were late. She wouldn't want him to know they had been in to complain.

Big Billy had been called to the headmistress's stuffy room and been sharply informed – so she told Mother – that she took a 'dim view'. Mother was glad. She had objected to Little Billy bullying her boy. Azhar had had Little Billy sitting behind him in class. For weeks Little Billy had called him names and clipped him round the head with his ruler. Now some of the other boys, mates of Little Billy, had also started to pick on Azhar.

'I eat nuts!'

Big Billy was hooting like an orang-utan, jumping up and down and scratching himself under the arms – one of the things Little Billy had been castigated for. But it didn't restrain his father. His face looked horrible.

Big Billy lived a few doors away from them. Mother had known him and his family since she was a child. They had shared the same air-raid shelter during the war. Big Billy had been a Ted and still wore a drape coat and his hair in a sculpted quiff. He had black bitten-down fingernails and a smear of grease across his forehead. He was known as Motorbike Bill because he repeatedly built and rebuilt his Triumph. 'Triumph of the Bill,' Father liked to murmur as they passed. Sometimes numerous lumps of metal stood on rags around the skeleton of the bike, and in the late evening Big Bill revved up the machine while his record player balanced on the windowsill repeatedly blared out a 45 called

'Rave On'. Then everyone knew Big Billy was preparing for the annual bank holiday run to the coast. Mother and the other neighbours were forced to shut their windows to exclude the noise and fumes.

Mother had begun to notice not only Azhar's dejection but also his exhausted and dishevelled appearance on his return from school. He looked as if he'd been flung into a hedge and rolled in a puddle – which he had. Unburdening with difficulty, he confessed the abuse the boys gave him, Little Billy in particular.

At first Mother appeared amused by such pranks. She was surprised that Azhar took it so hard. He should ignore the childish remarks: a lot of children were cruel. Yet he couldn't make out what it was with him that made people say such things, or why, after so many contented hours at home with his mother, such violence had entered his world.

Mother had taken Azhar's hand and instructed him to reply, 'Little Billy, you're common – common as muck!'

Azhar held onto the words and repeated them continuously to himself. Next day, in a corner with his enemy's taunts going at him, he closed his eyes and hollered them out. 'Muck, muck, muck – common as muck you!'

Little Billy was as perplexed as Azhar by the epithet. Like magic it shut his mouth. But the next day Little Billy came back with the renewed might of names new to Azhar: sambo, wog, little coon. Azhar returned to his mother for more words but they had run out.

Big Billy was saying across the bus, 'Common! Why don't you say it out loud to me face, eh? Won't say it, eh?'

'Nah,' said Little Billy. 'Won't!'

'But we ain't as common as a slut who marries a darkie.'

'Darkie, darkie,' Little Billy repeated. 'Monkey, monkey!'

Mother's look didn't deviate. But, perhaps anxious that her shaking would upset Azhar, she pulled her hand from his and pointed at a shop.

'Look.'

'What?' said Azhar, distracted by Little Billy murmuring his name.

The instant Azhar turned his head, Big Billy called, 'Hey! Why don't you look at us, little lady?'

She twisted round and waved at the conductor standing on his platform. But a passenger got on and the conductor followed him upstairs. The few other passengers, sitting like statues, were unaware or unconcerned.

Mother turned back. Azhar had never seen her like this, ashen, with wet eyes, her body stiff as a tree. Azhar sensed what an effort she was making to keep still. When she wept at home she threw herself on the bed, shook convulsively and thumped the pillow. Now all that moved was a bulb of snot shivering on the end of her nose. She sniffed determinedly, before opening her bag and extracting the scented handkerchief with which she usually wiped Azhar's face, or, screwing up a corner, dislodged any stray eyelashes around his eye. She blew her nose vigorously but he heard a sob.

Now she knew what went on and how it felt. How he wished he'd said nothing and protected her, for Big Billy was using her name: 'Yvonne, Yvonne, hey, Yvonne, didn't I give you a good time that time?'

'Evie, a good time, right?' sang Little Billy.

Big Billy smirked. 'Thing is,' he said, holding his nose, 'there's a smell on this bus.'

'Pooh!'

'How many of them are there living in that flat, all squashed together like, and stinkin' the road out, eatin' curry and rice!'

There was no doubt that their flat was jammed. Grandpop, a retired doctor, slept in one bedroom, Azhar, his sister and parents in another, and two uncles in the living room. All day big pans of Indian food simmered in the kitchen so people could eat when they wanted. The kitchen wallpaper bubbled and cracked and hung down like ancient scrolls. But Mother always denied that they were 'like that'. She refused to allow the word 'immigrant' to be used about Father, since in her eyes it applied only to illiterate tiny men with downcast eyes and mismatched clothes.

Mother's lips were moving but her throat must have been dry: no words came, until she managed to say, 'We're not Jews.'

There was a silence. This gave Big Billy an opportunity. 'What you say?' He cupped his ear and his long dark sideburn. With his other hand he cuffed Little Billy, who had begun hissing. 'Speak up. Hey, tart, we can't hear you!'

Mother repeated the remark but could make her voice no louder.

Azhar wasn't sure what she meant. In his confusion he recalled a recent conversation about South Africa, where his best friend's family had just emigrated. Azhar had asked why, if they were to go somewhere – and there had been such talk – they too couldn't choose Cape Town. Painfully she replied that there the people with white skins were cruel to the black and brown people who were considered inferior and were forbidden to go where the whites went. The coloureds had separate entrances and were prohibited from sitting with the whites.

This peculiar fact of living history, vertiginously irrational and not taught in his school, struck his head like a hammer and echoed through his dreams night after night. How could such a thing be possible? What did it mean? How then should he act?

'Nah,' said Big Billy. 'You no Yid, Yvonne. You us. But worse. Goin' with the Paki.'

All the while Little Billy was hissing and twisting his head in imitation of a spastic.

Azhar had heard his father say that there had been 'gassing' not long ago. Neighbour had slaughtered neighbour, and such evil hadn't died. Father would poke his finger at his wife, son and baby daughter, and state, 'We're in the front line!'

These conversations were often a prelude to his announcing that they were going 'home' to Pakistan. There they wouldn't have these problems. At this point Azhar's mother would become uneasy. How could she go 'home' when she was at home already? Hot weather made her swelter; spicy food upset her stomach; being surrounded by people who didn't speak English made her feel lonely. As it was, Azhar's grandfather and uncle chattered away in Urdu, and when Uncle Asif's wife had been in the country, she had, without prompting, walked several paces behind them in the street. Not wanting to side with either camp, Mother had had to position herself, with Azhar, somewhere in the middle of this curious procession as it made its way to the shops.

Not that the idea of 'home' didn't trouble Father. He himself had never been there. His family had lived in China and India; but since he'd left, the remainder of his family had moved, along with hundreds of thousands of others, to Pakistan. How could he know if the new country would suit him, or if he could succeed there? While Mother wailed, he would smack his hand against his forehead and cry, 'Oh God, I am trying to think in all directions at the same time!'

He had taken to parading about the flat in Wellington boots with a net curtain over his head, swinging his portable typewriter and saying he expected to be called to Vietnam as a war correspondent, and was preparing for jungle combat.

It made them laugh. For two years Father had been working as a packer in a factory that manufactured shoe polish. It was hard physical labour, which drained and infuriated him. He loved books and wanted to write them. He got up at five every morning; at night he wrote for as long as he could keep his eyes open. Even as they ate he scribbled over the backs of envelopes, rejection slips and factory stationery, trying to sell articles to magazines and newspapers. At the same time he was studying for a correspondence course on 'How To Be A Published Author'. The sound of his frenetic typing drummed into their heads like gunfire. They were forbidden to complain. Father was determined to make money from the articles on sport, politics and literature which he posted off most days, each accompanied by a letter that began, 'Dear Sir, Please find enclosed . . .'

But Father didn't have a sure grasp of the English language which was his, but not entirely, being 'Bombay variety, mish and mash'. Their neighbour, a retired schoolteacher, was kind enough to correct Father's spelling and grammar, suggesting that he sometimes used 'the right words in the wrong place, and vice versa'. His pieces were regularly returned in the self-addressed stamped envelope that the *Writers' and Artists' Yearbook* advised. Lately, when they plopped through the letter box, Father didn't open them, but tore them up, stamped on the pieces and swore in Urdu, cursing the English who, he was convinced, were barring him. Or were they? Mother once suggested he was doing something wrong and should study something more profitable. But this didn't get a good response.

In the morning now Mother sent Azhar out to intercept the postman and collect the returned manuscripts. The envelopes and parcels were concealed around the garden like an alcoholic's bottles, behind the dustbins, in the bike shed, even under buckets, where, mouldering in secret, they sustained hope and kept away disaster.

At every stop Azhar hoped someone might get on who would discourage or arrest the Billys. But no one did, and as they moved forward the bus emptied. Little Billy took to jumping up and twanging the bell, at which the conductor only laughed.

Then Azhar saw that Little Billy had taken a marble from his pocket, and, standing with his arm back, was preparing to fling it. When Big Billy noticed this even his eyes widened. He reached for Billy's wrist. But the marble was released: it cracked into the window between Azhar and his mother's head, chipping the glass.

She was screaming. 'Stop it, stop it! Won't anyone help! We'll be murdered!'

The noise she made came from hell or eternity. Little Billy blanched and shifted closer to his father; they went quiet.

Azhar got out of his seat to fight them but the conductor blocked his way.

Their familiar stop was ahead. Before the bus braked Mother was up, clutching her bags; she gave Azhar two carriers to hold, and nudged him towards the platform. As he went past he wasn't going to look at the Billys, but he did give them the eye, straight on, stare to stare, so he could see them and not be so afraid. They could hate him but he would know them. But if he couldn't fight them, what could he do with his anger?

They stumbled off and didn't need to check if the crêpe-soled Billys were behind, for they were already calling out, though not as loud as before.

As they approached the top of their street the retired teacher who assisted Father came out of his house, wearing a three-piece suit and trilby hat and leading his Scottie. He looked over his garden, picked up a scrap of paper which had blown over the fence, and sniffed the evening air. Azhar wanted to laugh: he resembled a phantom; in a deranged world the normal appeared the most bizarre. Mother immediately pulled Azhar towards his gate.

Their neighbour raised his hat and said in a friendly way, 'How's it all going?'

At first Azhar didn't understand what his mother was talking about. But it was Father she was referring to. 'They send them back, his writings, every day, and he gets so angry . . . so angry . . . Can't you help him?'

'I do help him, where I can,' he replied.

'Make him stop, then!'

She choked into her handkerchief and shook her head when he asked what the matter was.

The Billys hesitated a moment and then passed on silently.

Azhar watched them go. It was all right, for now. But tomorrow Azhar would be for it, and the next day, and the next. No mother could prevent it.

'He's a good little chap,' the teacher was saying, of Father.

'But will he get anywhere?'

'Perhaps,' he said. 'Perhaps. But he may be a touch –'

Azhar stood on tiptoe to listen. 'Over hopeful. Over hopeful.'

'Yes,' she said, biting her lip.

'Tell him to read more Gibbon and Macaulay,' he said. 'That should set him straight.'

'Right.'

'Are you feeling better?'

'Yes, yes,' Mother insisted.

He said, concerned, 'Let me walk you back.'

'That's all right, thank you.'

Instead of going home, mother and son went in the opposite direction. They passed a bomb site and left the road for a narrow path. When they could no longer feel anything firm beneath their feet, they crossed a nearby rutted muddy playing field in the dark. The strong wind, buffeting them sideways, nearly had them tangled in the slimy nets of a soccer goal. He had no idea she knew this place.

At last they halted outside a dismal shed, the public toilet, rife with spiders and insects, where he and his friends often played. He looked up but couldn't see her face. She pushed the door and stepped across the wet floor. When he hesitated she tugged him into the stall with her. She wasn't going to let him go now. He dug into the wall with his penknife and practised holding his breath until she finished, and wiped herself on the scratchy paper. Then she sat there with her eyes closed, as if she were saying a prayer. His teeth were clicking; ghosts whispered in his ears; outside there were footsteps; dead fingers seemed to be clutching at him.

For a long time she examined herself in the mirror, powdering her face, replacing her lipstick and combing her hair. There were no human voices, only rain on the metal roof, which dripped through onto their heads.

'Mum,' he cried.

'Don't you whine!'

He wanted his tea. He couldn't wait to get away. Her eyes were scorching his face in the yellow light. He knew she wanted to tell him not to mention any of this. Recognising at last that it wasn't necessary, she suddenly dragged him by his arm, as if it had been his fault they were held up, and hurried him home without another word.

The flat was lighted and warm. Father, having worked the early shift, was home. Mother went into the kitchen and Azhar helped her unpack the shopping. She was trying to be normal, but the very effort betrayed her, and she didn't kiss Father as she usually did.

Now, beside Grandpop and Uncle Asif, Father was listening to the cricket commentary on the big radio, which had an illuminated panel printed with the names of cities they could never pick up, Brussels, Stockholm, Hilversum, Berlin, Budapest. Father's typewriter, with its curled paper tongue, sat on the table surrounded by empty beer bottles.

'Come, boy.'

Azhar ran to his father who poured some beer into a glass for him, mixing it with lemonade.

The men were smoking pipes, peering into the ashy bowls, tapping them on the table, poking them with pipe cleaners, and relighting them. They were talking loudly in Urdu or Punjabi, using some English words but gesticulating and slapping one another in a way English people never did. Then one of them would suddenly leap up, clapping his hands and shouting, 'Yes – out – out!'

Azhar was accustomed to being with his family while grasping only fragments of what they said. He endeavoured to decipher the gist of it, laughing, as he always did, when the men laughed, and silently moving his lips without knowing what the words meant, whirling, all the while, in incomprehension.

D'accord, Baby

All week Bill had been looking forward to this moment. He was about to fuck the daughter of the man who had fucked his wife. Lying in her bed, he could hear Celestine humming in the bathroom as she prepared for him.

It had been a long time since he'd been in a room so cold, with no heating. After a while he ventured to put his arms out over the covers, tore open a condom and laid the rubber on the cardboard box which served as a bedside table. He was about to prepare another, but didn't want to appear over optimistic. One would achieve his objective. He would clear out then. Already there had been too many delays. The waltz, for instance, though it made him giggle. Nevertheless he had told Nicola, his pregnant wife, that he would be back by midnight. What could Celestine be doing in there? There wasn't even a shower; and the wind cut viciously through the broken window.

His wife had met Celestine's father, Vincent Ertel, the French ex-Maoist intellectual, in Paris. He had certainly impressed her. She had talked about him continually, which was bad enough, and then rarely mentioned him, which, as he understood now, was worse.

Nicola worked on a late-night TV discussion programme. For two years she had been eager to profile Vincent's progress from revolutionary to Catholic reactionary. It was, she liked to inform Bill – using a phrase that stayed in his mind – indicative of the age. Several times she went to see Vincent in Paris; then she was invited to his country place near Auxerre. Finally she brought him to London to record the interview. When it was done, to celebrate, she took him to Le Caprice for champagne, fishcakes and chips.

That night Bill had put aside the script he was directing and gone to bed early with a ruler, pencil and *The Brothers Karamazov*. Around the time that Nicola was becoming particularly enthusiastic about Vincent, Bill had made up his mind not only to study the great books – the most dense and intransigent, the ones from which he'd always flinched – but to underline parts of and even to memorise certain passages. The effort to concentrate was a torment, as his mind flew about. Yet most nights – even during the period when Nicola was preparing for her encounter with Vincent – he kept his light on long after she had put hers out. Determined to swallow the thickest pills of understanding, he would lie there muttering phrases he wanted to retain. One of his favourites was Emerson's: 'We but half express ourselves, and are ashamed of that divine idea which each of us represents.'

One night Nicola opened her eyes and with a quizzical look said, 'Can't you be easier on yourself?'

Why? He wouldn't give up. He had read biology at university. Surely he couldn't be such a fool as to find these books beyond him? His need for knowledge, wisdom, nourishment was more than his need for sleep. How could a man have come to the middle of his life with barely a clue about who he was or where he might go? The heavy volumes surely represented the highest point to which man's thought had flown; they had to include guidance.

The close, leisurely contemplation afforded him some satisfaction – usually because the books started him thinking about other things. It was the part of the day he preferred. He slept well, usually. But at four, on the long night of the fishcakes, he awoke and felt for Nicola across the bed. She wasn't there. Shivering, he walked through the house until dawn, imagining she'd crashed the car. After an hour he remembered she hadn't taken it. Maybe she and Vincent had gone on to a late-night place. She had never done anything like this before.

He could neither sleep nor go to work. He decided to sit at the kitchen table until she returned, whenever it was. He was drinking brandy, and normally he never drank before eight in the evening. If anyone offered him a drink before this time, he claimed it was like saying goodbye to the whole day. In the mid-eighties he'd gone to the gym in the early evening. For some days, though, goodbye was surely the most suitable word.

It was late afternoon before his wife returned, wearing the clothes she'd gone out in, looking dishevelled and uncertain. She couldn't meet his eye. He asked her what she'd been doing. She said 'What d'you think?' and went into the shower.

He had considered several options, including punching her. But instead he fled the house and made it to a pub. For the first time since he'd been a student he sat alone with nothing to do. He was expected nowhere. He had no newspaper with him, and he liked papers; he could swallow the most banal and incredible thing provided it was on newsprint. He watched the passing faces and thought how pitiless the world was if you didn't have a safe place in it.

He made himself consider how unrewarding it was to constrain people. Infidelities would occur in most relationships. These days every man and woman was a cuckold. And why not, when marriage was insufficient to satisfy most human need? Nicola had needed something and she had taken it. How bold and stylish. How petty to blame someone for pursuing any kind of love!

He was humiliated. The feeling increased over the weeks in a strange way. At work or waiting for the tube, or having dinner with Nicola – who had gained, he could see, a bustling, dismissive intensity of will or concentration – he found himself becoming angry with Vincent. For days on end he couldn't really think of anything else. It was as if the man were inhabiting him.

As he walked around Soho where he worked, Bill

entertained himself by think of how someone might get even with a type like Vincent, were he so inclined. The possibility was quite remote but this didn't prevent him imagining stories from which he emerged with some satisfaction, if not credit. What incentive, distraction, energy and interest Vincent provided him with! This was almost the only creative work he got to do now.

A few days later he was presented with Celestine. She was sitting with a man in a newly opened café, drinking cappuccino. Life was giving him a chance. It was awful. He stood in the doorway pretending to look for someone and wondered whether he should take it.

Vincent's eldest daughter lived in London. She wanted to be an actress and Bill had auditioned her for a commercial a couple of years ago. He knew she'd obtained a small part in a film directed by an acquaintance of his. On this basis he went over to her, introduced himself, made the pleasantest conversation he could, and was invited to sit down. The man turned out to be a gay friend of hers. They all chatted. After some timorous vacillation Bill asked Celestine in a cool tone whether she'd have a drink with him later, in a couple of hours.

He didn't go home but walked about the streets. When he was tired he sat in a pub with the first volume of *Remembrance of Things Past*. He had decided that if he could read to the end of the whole book he would deserve a great deal of praise. He did a little underlining, which since school he had considered a sign of seriousness, but his mind wandered even more than usual, until it was time to meet her.

To his pleasure Bill saw that men glanced at Celestine when they could; others openly stared. When she fetched a drink they turned to examine her legs. This would not have happened with Nicola; only Vincent Ertel had taken an interest in her. Later, as he and Celestine strolled up the street looking for cabs, she agreed that he could come to her place at the end of the week.

It was a triumphant few days of gratification anticipated. He would do more of this. He had obviously been missing out on life's meaner pleasures. As Nicola walked about the flat, dressing, cooking, reading, searching for her glasses, he could enjoy despising her. He informed his two closest friends that the pleasures of revenge were considerable. Now his pals were waiting to hear of his coup.

Celestine flung the keys, wrapped in a tea-towel, out of the window. It was a hard climb: her flat was at the top of a run-down five-storey building in West London, an area of bedsits, students and itinerants. Coming into the living room he saw it had a view across a square. Wind and rain were sweeping into the cracked windows stuffed with newspaper. The walls were yellow, the carpet brown and stained. Several pairs of jeans were suspended on a clothes horse in front of a gas fire which gave off an odour and heated parts of the room while leaving others cold.

She persuaded him to remove his overcoat but not his scarf. Then she took him into the tiny kitchen with bare floorboards where, between an old sink and the boiler, there was hardly room for the two of them.

'I will be having us some dinner.' She pointed to two shopping bags. 'Do you like troot?'

'Sorry?'

It was trout. There were potatoes and green beans. After, they would have apple strudel with cream. She had been to the shops and gone to some trouble. It would take ages to prepare. He hadn't anticipated this. He left her there, saying he would fetch drink.

In the rain he went to the off-licence and was paying for the wine when he noticed through the window that a taxi had stopped at traffic lights. He ran out of the shop to hail the cab, but as he opened the door couldn't go through with it. He collected the wine and carried it back.

He waited in her living room while she cooked, pacing and drinking. She didn't have a TV. Wintry gales battered the window. Her place reminded him of rooms he'd shared as a student. He was about to say to himself, thank God I'll never have to live like this again, when it occurred to him that if he left Nicola, he might, for a time, end up in some unfamiliar place like this, with its stained carpet and old, broken fittings. How fastidious he'd become! How had it happened? What other changes had there been while he was looking in the other direction?

He noticed a curled photograph of a man tacked to the wall. It looked as though it had been taken at the end of the sixties. Bill concluded it was the hopeful radical who'd fucked his wife. He had been a handsome man, and with his pipe in his hand, long hair and open-necked shirt, he had an engaging look of self-belief and raffish pleasure. Bill recalled the slogans that had decorated Paris in those days. 'Everything Is Possible', 'Take Your Desires for Realities', 'It Is Forbidden to Forbid'. He'd once used them in a TV commercial. What optimism that generation had had! With his life given over to literature, ideas, conversation, writing and political commitment, ol' Vincent must have had quite a time. He wouldn't have been working constantly, like Bill and his friends.

The food was good. Bill leaned across the table to kiss Celestine. His lips brushed her cheek. She turned her head and looked out across the dark square to the lights beyond, as if trying to locate something.

He talked about the film industry and what the actors, directors and producers of the movies were really like. Not that he knew them personally, but they were gossiped about by other actors and technicians. She asked questions and laughed easily.

Things should have been moving along. He had to get up at 5.30 the next day to direct a commercial for a bank. He was becoming known for such well-paid but journeyman work. Now that Nicola was pregnant he would have to do more of it. It would be a struggle to find time for the screenwriting he wanted to do. It was beginning to dawn on him that if he was going to do anything worthwhile at his age, he had to be serious in a new way. And yet when he considered his ambitions, which he no longer mentioned to anyone – to travel overland to Burma while reading Proust, and other, more 'internal' things – he felt a surge of shame, as if it was immature and obscene to harbour such hopes; as if, in some ways, it was already too late.

He shuffled his chair around the table until he and Celestine were sitting side by side. He attempted another kiss.

She stood up and offered him her hands. 'Shall we dance?'

He looked at her in surprise. 'Dance?'

'It will 'ot you up. Don't you . . . dance?'

'Not really.'

'Why?'

'Why? We always danced like this.' He shut his eyes and nodded his head as if attempting to bang in a nail with his forehead.

She kicked off her shoes.

'We dance like this. I'll illustrate you.' She looked at him. 'Take it off.'

'What?'

'This stupid thing.'

She pulled off his scarf. She shoved the chairs against the wall and put on a Chopin waltz, took his hand and placed her other hand on his back. He looked down at her dancing feet even as he trod on them, but she didn't object. Gently but firmly she turned and turned him across the room, until he was dizzy, her hair tickling his face. Whenever he glanced up she was looking into his eyes. Each time they crossed the room she trotted back, pulling him, amused. She seemed determined that he should learn, certain that this would benefit him.

'You require some practice,' she said at last. He fell back into his chair, blowing and laughing. 'But after a week, who knows, we could be having you work as a gigolo!'

It was midnight. Celestine came naked out of the bathroom smoking a cigarette. She got into bed and lay beside him. He thought of a time in New York when the company sent a white limousine to the airport. Once inside it, drinking whisky and watching TV as the limo passed over the East River towards Manhattan, he wanted nothing more than for his friends to see him.

She was on him vigorously and the earth was moving: either that, or the two single beds, on the juncture of which he was lying, were separating. He stuck out his arms to secure them, but with each lurch his head was being forced down into the fissure. He felt as if his ears were going to be torn off. The two of them were about to crash through onto the floor.

He rolled her over onto one bed. Then he sat up and showed her what would have happened. She started to laugh, she couldn't stop.

The gas meter ticked; she was dozing. He had never lain beside a lovelier face. He thought of what Nicola might have sought that night with Celestine's father. Affection, attention, serious talk, honesty, distraction. Did he give her that now? Could they give it to one another, and with a kid on the way?

Celestine was nudging him and trying to say something in his ear.

'You want what?' he said. Then, 'Surely . . . no . . . no.'

'Bill, yes.'

He liked to think he was willing to try anything. A black eye would certainly send a convincing message to her father. She smiled when he raised his hand.

'I deserve to be hurt.'

'No one deserves that.'

'But you see . . . I do.'

That night, in that freezing room, he did everything she asked, for as long as she wanted. He praised her beauty and her intelligence. He had never kissed anyone for so long, until he forgot where he was, or who they both were, until there was nothing they wanted, and there was only the most satisfactory peace.

He got up and dressed. He was shivering. He wanted to wash, he smelled of her, but he wasn't prepared for a cold bath.

'Why are you leaving?' She leaped up and held him. 'Stay, stay, I haven't finished with you yet.'

He put on his coat and went into the living room. Without looking back he hurried out and down the stairs. He pulled the front door, anticipating the fresh damp night air. But the door held. He had forgotten: the door was locked. He stood there.

Upstairs she was wrapped in a fur coat, looking out of the window.

'The key,' he said.

'Old man,' she said, laughing. 'You are.'

She accompanied him barefoot down the stairs. While she unlocked the door he mumbled, 'Will you tell your father I saw you?'

'But why?'

He touched her face. She drew back. 'You should put something on that,' he said. 'I met him once. He knows my wife.'

'I rarely see him now,' she said.

She was holding out her arms. They danced a few steps across the hall. He was better at it now. He went out into the street. Several cabs passed him but he didn't hail them. He kept walking. There was comfort in the rain. He put his head back and looked up into the sky. He had some impression that happiness was beyond him and everything was coming down, and that life could not be grasped but only lived.

With Your Tongue down My Throat

1

I tell you, I feel tired and dirty, but I was told no baths allowed for a few days, so I'll stay dirty. Yesterday morning I was crying a lot and the woman asked me to give an address in case of emergencies and I made one up. I had to undress and get in a white smock and they took my temperature and blood pressure five times. Then a nurse pushed me in a wheelchair into a green room where I met the doctor. He called us all 'ladies' and told jokes. I could see some people getting annoyed. He was Indian, unfortunately, and he looked at me strangely as if to say, 'What are you doing here?' But maybe it was just my imagination.

I had to lie on a table and they put a needle or two into my left arm. Heat rushed over my face and I tried to speak. The next thing I know I'm in the recovery room with a nurse saying, 'Wake up, dear, it's all over.' The doctor poked me in the stomach and said, 'Fine.' I found myself feeling aggressive. 'Do you do this all the time?' I asked. He said he did nothing else.

They woke us at six and there were several awkward-looking, sleepy boyfriends outside. I got the bus and went back to the squat.

A few months later we got kicked out and I had to go back to Ma's place. So I'm back here now, writing this with my foot up on the table, reckoning I look like a painter. I sip water with a slice of lemon in it. I'm at Ma's kitchen table and there are herbs growing in pots around me. At least the place is clean, though it's shabby and all falling apart. There are photographs of Ma's women friends from the Labour Party and the Women's Support Group and there is Blake's picture of Newton next to drawings by her kids from school. There are books everywhere, on the Alexander Method and the Suzuki Method and all the other methods in the world. And then there's her boyfriend.

Yes, the radical (ha!) television writer and well-known toss-pot Howard Coleman sits opposite me as I record him with my biro. He's reading one of his scripts, smoking and slowly turning the pages, but the awful thing is, he keeps giggling at them. Thank Christ Ma should be back any minute now from the Catholic girls' school where she teaches.

It's Howard who asked me to write this diary, who said write down some of the things that happen. My half-sister Nadia is about to come over from Pakistan to stay with us. Get it all down, he said.

If you could see Howard now like I can, you'd really laugh. I mean it. He's about forty-three and he's got on a squeaky leather jacket and jeans with the arse round his knees and these trainers with soles that look like mattresses. He looks like he's never bought anything new. Or if he has, when he gets it back from the shop, he throws it on the floor, empties the dustbin over it and walks up and down on it in a pair of dirty Dr Marten's. For him dirty clothes are a political act.

But this is the coup. Howard's smoking a roll-up. He's got this tin, his fag papers and the stubby yellow fingers with which he rolls, licks, fiddles, taps, lights, extinguishes and relights all day. This rigmarole goes on when he's in bed with Ma, presumably on her chest. I've gone in there in the morning for a snoop and found his ashtray by the bed, condom on top.

Christ, he's nodding at me as I write! It's because he's so keen on ordinary riff-raff expressing itself, especially no-hoper girls like me. One day we're writing, the next we're on the barricades.

Every Friday Howard comes over to see Ma.

To your credit, Howard the hero, you always take her somewhere a bit jazzy, maybe to the latest club (a big deal for a poverty-stricken teacher). When you get back you undo her bra and hoick your hands up her jumper and she warms hers down your trousers. I've walked in on this! Soon after this teenage game, mother and lover go to bed and rattle the room for half an hour. I light a candle, turn off the radio and lie there, ears flapping. It's strange, hearing your ma doing it. There are momentous cries and gasps and grunts, as if Howard's trying to bang a nail into a brick wall. Ma sounds like she's having an operation. Sometimes I feel like running in with the first-aid kit.

Does this Friday thing sound remarkable or not? It's only Fridays he will see Ma. If Howard has to collect an award for his writing or go to a smart dinner with a critic he won't come to see us until the next Friday. Saturdays are definitely out!

We're on the ninth floor. I say to Howard: 'Hey, clever boots. Tear your eyes away from yourself a minute. Look out the window.'

The estate looks like a building site. There's planks and window frames everywhere – poles, cement mixers, sand, grit, men with mouths and disintegrating brick underfoot.

'So?' he says.

'It's rubbish, isn't it? Nadia will think we're right trash.'

'My little Nina,' he says. This is how he talks to me.

'Yes, my big Howard?'

'Why be ashamed of what you are?'

'Because compared with Nadia we're not much, are we?'

'I'm much. You're much. Now get on with your writing.'

He touches my face with his finger. 'You're excited, aren't you? This is a big thing for you.'

It is, I suppose.

All my life I've been this only child living here in a council place with Ma, the drama teacher. I was an only child, that is, until I was eleven, when Ma says she has a surprise for

63

me, one of the nicest I've ever had. I have a half-sister the same age, living in another country.

'Your father had a wife in India,' Ma says, wincing every time she says *father*. 'They married when they were fifteen, which is the custom over there. When he decided to leave me because I was too strong a woman for him, he went right back to India and right back to Wifey. That's when I discovered I was pregnant with you. His other daughter Nadia was conceived a few days later but she was actually born the day after you. Imagine that, darling. Since then I've discovered that he's even got two other daughters as well!'

I don't give my same-age half-sister in another country another thought except to dislike her in general for suddenly deciding to exist. Until one night, suddenly, I write to Dad and ask if he'll send her to stay with us. I get up and go down the lift and out in the street and post the letter before I change my mind. That night was one of my worst and I wanted Nadia to save me.

On some Friday afternoons, if I'm not busy writing ten-page hate letters to DJs, Howard does imagination exercises with me. I have to lie on my back on the floor, imagine things like mad and describe them. It's so sixties. But then I've heard him say of people: 'Oh, she had a wonderful sixties!'

'Nina,' he says during one of these gigs, 'you've got to work out this relationship with your sister. I want you to describe Nadia.'

I zap through my head's TV channels – Howard squatting beside me, hand on my forehead, sending loving signals. A girl materialises sitting under a palm tree, reading a Brontë novel and drinking yogurt. I see a girl being cuddled by my father. He tells stories of tigers and elephants and rickshaw wallahs. I see . . .

'I can't see any more!'

Because I can't visualise Nadia, I have to see her.

*

So. This is how it all comes about. Ma and I are sitting at breakfast, Ma chewing her vegetarian cheese. She's dressed for work in a long, baggy, purple pinafore dress with black stockings and a black band in her hair, and she looks like a 1950s teenager. Recently Ma's gone blonde and she keeps looking in the mirror. Me still in my T-shirt and pants. Ma tense about work as usual, talking about school for hours on the phone last night to friends. She tries to interest me in child abuse, incest and its relation to the GCSE. I say how much I hate eating, how boring it is and how I'd like to do it once a week and forget about it.

'But the palate is a sensitive organ,' Ma says. 'You should cultivate yours instead of –'

'Just stop talking if you've got to fucking lecture.'

The mail arrives. Ma cuts open an airmail letter. She reads it twice. I know it's from Dad. I snatch it out of her hand and walk round the room taking it in.

Dear You Both,

It's a good idea. Nadia will be arriving on the 5th. Please meet her at the airport. So generous of you to offer. Look after her, she is the most precious thing in the entire world to me.

Much love.

At the bottom Nadia has written: 'Looking forward to seeing you both soon.'

Hummmm . . .

Ma pours herself more coffee and considers everything. She has these terrible coffee jags. Her stomach must be like distressed leather. She is determined to be businesslike, not emotional. She says I have to cancel the visit.

'It's simple. Just write a little note and say there's been a misunderstanding.'

And this is how I react: 'I don't believe it! Why? No way! But why?' Christ, don't I deserve to die, though God knows I've tried to die enough times.

'Because, Nina, I'm not at all prepared for this. I really don't know that I want to see this sister of yours. She symbolises my betrayal by your father.'

I clear the table of our sugar-free jam (no additives).

'Symbolises?' I say. 'But she's a person.'

Ma gets on her raincoat and collects last night's marking. You look very plain, I'm about to say. She kisses me on the head. The girls at school adore her. There, she's a star.

But I'm very severe. Get this: 'Ma. Nadia's coming. Or I'm going. I'm walking right out that door and it'll be junk and prostitution just like the old days.'

She drops her bag. She sits down. She slams her car keys on the table. 'Nina, I beg you.'

2

Heathrow. Three hours we've been here, Ma and I, burying our faces in doughnuts. People pour from the exit like released prisoners to walk the gauntlet of jumping relatives and chauffeurs holding cards: Welcome Ngogi of Nigeria.

But no Nadia. 'My day off,' Ma says, 'and I spend it in an airport.'

But then. It's her. Here she comes now. It is her! I know it is! I jump up and down waving like mad! Yes, yes, no, yes! At last! My sister! My mirror.

We both hug Nadia, and Ma suddenly cries and her nose runs and she can't control her mouth. I cry too and I don't even know who the hell I'm squashing so close to me. Until I sneak a good look at the girl.

You. Every day I've woken up trying to see your face, and now you're here, your head jerking nervously, saying little, with us drenching you. I can see you're someone I know nothing about. You make me very nervous.

You're smaller than me. Less pretty, if I can say that. Bigger nose. Darker, of course, with a glorious slab of hair like a piece of chocolate attached to your back. I imagined, I don't know why (pure prejudice, I suppose), that you'd be wearing the national dress, the baggy pants, the long top and light scarf flung all over. But you have on FU jeans and a faded blue sweatshirt – you look as if you live in Enfield. We'll fix that.

Nadia sits in the front of the car. Ma glances at her whenever she can. She has to ask how Nadia's father is.

'Oh yes,' Nadia replies. 'Dad. The same as usual, thank you. No change really, Debbie.'

'But we rarely see him,' Ma says.

'I see,' Nadia says at last.

'So we don't,' Ma says, her voice rising, 'actually know what "same as usual" means.'

Nadia looks out of the window at green and grey old England. I don't want Ma getting in one of her resentful states.

After this not another peep for about a decade and then road euphoria just bursts from Nadia.

'What good roads you have here! So smooth, so wide, so long!'

'Yes, they go all over,' I say.

'Wow. All over.'

Christ, don't they even have fucking roads over there?

Nadia whispers. We lean towards her to hear about her dear father's health. How often the old man pisses now, running for the pot clutching his crotch. The sad state of his old gums and his obnoxious breath. Ma and I watch this sweetie compulsively, wondering who she is: so close to us and made from my substance, and yet so other, telling us about Dad with an outrageous intimacy we can never share. We arrive home, and she says in an accent as thick as treacle (which makes me hoot to myself when I first hear it): 'I'm so tired now. If I could rest for a little while.'

'Sleep in my bed!' I cry.

Earlier I'd said to Ma I'd never give it up. But the moment

my sister walks across the estate with us and finally stands there in our flat above the building site, drinking in all the oddness, picking up Ma's method books and her opera programmes, I melt, I melt. I'll have to kip in the living room from now on. But I'd kip in the toilet for her.

'In return for your bed,' she says, 'let me, I must, yes, give you something.'

She pulls a rug from her suitcase and presents it to Ma. 'This is from Dad.' Ma puts it on the floor, studies it and then treads on it.

And to me? I've always been a fan of crêpe paper and wrapped in it is the Pakistani dress I'm wearing now (with open-toed sandals – handmade). It's gorgeous: yellow and green, threaded with gold, thin summer material.

I'm due a trip to the dole office any minute now and I'm bracing myself for the looks I'll get in this gear. I'll keep you informed.

I write this outside my room waiting for Nadia to wake. Every fifteen minutes I tap lightly on the door like a worried nurse.

'Are you awake?' I whisper. And: 'Sister, sister.' I adore these new words. 'Do you want anything?'

I think I'm in love. At last.

Ma's gone out to take back her library books, leaving me to it. Ma's all heart, I expect you can see that. She's good and gentle and can't understand unkindness and violence. She thinks everyone's just waiting to be brought round to decency. 'This way we'll change the world a little bit,' she'd say, holding my hand and knocking on doors at elections. But she's lived on the edge of a nervous breakdown for as long as I can remember. She's had boyfriends before Howard but none of them lasted. Most of them were married because she was on this liberated kick of using men. There was one middle-class Labour Party smoothie I called Chubbie.

'Are you married?' I'd hiss when Ma went out of the room, sitting next to him and fingering his nylon tie.

'Yes.'

'You have to admit it, don't you? Where's your wife, then? She knows you're here? Get what you want this afternoon?'

You could see the men fleeing when they saw the deep needy well that Ma is, crying out to be filled with their love. And this monster kid with green hair glaring at them. Howard's too selfish and arrogant to be frightened of my ma's demands. He just ignores them.

What a job it is, walking round in this Paki gear!

I stop off at the chemist's to grab my drugs, my trancs. Jeanette, my friend on the estate, used to my eccentricities – the coonskin hat with the long rabbit tail, for example – comes along with me. The chemist woman in the white coat says to Jeanette, nodding at me when I hand over my script: 'Does she speak English?'

Becoming enthralled by this new me now, exotic and interior. With the scarf over my head I step into the Community Centre and look like a lost woman with village ways and chickens in the garden.

In a second, the communists and worthies are all over me. I mumble into my scarf. They give me leaflets and phone numbers. I'm oppressed, you see, beaten up, pig-ignorant with an arranged marriage and certain suttee ahead. But I get fed up and have a game of darts, a game of snooker and a couple of beers with a nice lesbian.

Home again I make my Nadia some pasta with red pepper, grated carrot, cheese and parsley. I run out to buy a bottle of white wine. Chasing along I see some kids on a passing bus. They eyeball me from the top deck, one of them black. They make a special journey down to the platform where the little monkeys swing on the pole and throw racial abuse from their gobs.

'Curry breath, curry breath, curry breath!'
The bus rushes on. I'm flummoxed.

She emerges at last, my Nadia, sleepy, creased around the
eyes and dark. She sits at the table, eyelashes barely apart,
not ready for small talk. I bring her the food and a glass of
wine which she refuses with an upraised hand. I press my
eyes into her, but she doesn't look at me. To puncture the
silence I play her a jazz record – Wynton Marsalis's first. I
ask her how she likes the record and she says nothing.
Probably doesn't do much for her on first hearing. I watch
her eating. She will not be interfered with.

She leaves most of the food and sits. I hand her a pair of
black Levi 501s with the button fly. Plus a large cashmere
polo-neck (stolen) and a black leather jacket.

'Try them on.'

She looks puzzled. 'It's the look I want you to have. You
can wear any of my clothes.'

Still she doesn't move. I give her a little shove into the
bedroom and shut the door. She should be so lucky. That's
my best damn jacket. I wait. She comes out not wearing the
clothes.

'Nina, I don't think so.'

I know how to get things done. I push her back in. She
comes out, backwards, hands over her face.

'Show me, please.'

She spins round, arms out, hair jumping.

'Well?'

'The black suits your hair,' I manage to say. What a vast
improvement on me, is all I can think. Stunning she is,
dangerous, vulnerable, superior, with a jewel in her nose.

'But doesn't it . . . doesn't it make me look a little rough?'

'Oh yes! Now we're all ready to go. For a walk, yes? To see
the sights and everything.'

'Is it safe?'

'Of course not. But I've got this.'

I show her.

'Oh, God, Nina. You would.'

Oh, this worries and ruins me. Already she has made up her mind about me and I haven't started on my excuses.

'Have you used it?'

'Only twice. Once on a racist in a pub. Once on some mugger who asked if I could spare him some jewellery.'

Her face becomes determined. She looks away. 'I'm training to be a doctor, you see. My life is set against human harm.'

She walks towards the door. I pack the switch-blade.

Daddy, these are the sights I show my sister. I tow her out of the flat and along the walkway. She sees the wind blaring through the busted windows. She catches her breath at the humming bad smells. Trapped dogs bark. She sees that one idiot's got on his door: *Dont burglar me theres nothin to steel ive got rid of it all.* She sees that some pig's sprayed on the wall: *Nina's a slag dog.* I push the lift button.

I've just about got her out of the building when the worst thing happens. There's three boys, ten or eleven years old, climbing out through a door they've kicked in. Neighbours stand and grumble. The kids've got a fat TV, a microwave oven and someone's favourite trainers under a little arm. The kid drops the trainers.

'Hey,' he says to Nadia (it's her first day here). Nadia stiffens. 'Hey, won't yer pick them up for me?'

She looks at me. I'm humming a tune. The tune is 'Just My Imagination'. I'm not scared of the little jerks. It's the bad impression that breaks my heart. Nadia picks up the trainers.

'Just tuck them right in there,' the little kid says, exposing his armpit.

'Won't they be a little large for you?' Nadia says.

'Eat shit.'

Soon we're out of there and into the air. We make for

71

South Africa Road and the General Smuts pub. Kids play football behind wire. The old women in thick overcoats look like lagged boilers on little feet. They huff and shove carts full of chocolate and cat food.

I'm all tense now and ready to say anything. I feel such a need to say everything in the hope of explaining all that I give a guided tour of my heart and days.

I explain (I can't help myself): this happened here, that happened there. I got pregnant in that squat. I bought bad smack from that geezer in the yellow T-shirt and straw hat. I got attacked there and legged it through that park. I stole pens from that shop, dropping them into my motorcycle helmet. (A motorcycle helmet is very good for shoplifting, if you're interested.) Standing on that corner I cared for nothing and no one and couldn't walk on or stay where I was or go back. My gears had stopped engaging with my motor. Then I had a nervous breakdown.

Without comment she listens and nods and shakes her head sometimes. Is anyone in? I take her arm and move my cheek close to hers.

'I tell you this stuff which I haven't told anyone before. I want us to know each other inside out.'

She stops there in the street and covers her face with her hands.

'But my father told me of such gorgeous places!'

'Nadia, what d'you mean?'

'And you show me filth!' she cries. She touches my arm. 'Oh, Nina, it would be so lovely if you could make the effort to show me something attractive.'

Something attractive. We'll have to get the bus and go east, to Holland Park and round Ladbroke Grove. This is now honeyed London for the rich. Here there are *La* restaurants, wine bars, bookshops, estate agents more prolific than doctors, and attractive people in black, few of them ageing. Here there are health food shops where you buy tofu, nuts, live-culture yoghurt and organic toothpaste.

Here the sweet little black kids practise on steel drums under the motorway for the Carnival and old blacks sit out in the open on orange boxes shouting. Here the dope dealers in Versace suits travel in from the suburbs on commuter trains, carrying briefcases, trying to sell slummers bits of old car tyre to smoke.

And there are more stars than beggars. For example? Van Morrison in a big overcoat is hurrying towards somewhere in a nervous mood.

'Hiya, Van! Van? Won't ya even say hello!' I scream across the street. At my words Van the Man accelerates like a dog with a winklepicker up its anus.

She looks tired so I take her into Julie's Bar where they have the newspapers and we sit on well-woven cushions on long benches. Christ only know how much they have the cheek to charge for a cup of tea. Nadia looks better now. We sit there all friendly and she starts off.

'How often have you met our father?'

'I see him every two or three years. When he comes on business, he makes it his business to see me.'

'That's nice of him.'

'Yes, that's what he thinks. Can you tell me something, Nadia?' I move closer to her. 'When he'd get home, our father, what would he tell you about me?'

If only I wouldn't tempt everything so. But you know me: can't live on life with slack in it.

'Oh, he was worried, worried, worried.'

'Christ. Worried three times.'

'He said you . . . no.'

'He said what?'

'No, no, he didn't say it.'

'Yes, he did, Nadia.'

She sits there looking at badly dressed television producers in linen suits with her gob firmly closed.

'Tell me what my father said or I'll pour this pot of tea over my head.'

I pick up the teapot and open the lid for pouring-over-the-head convenience. Nadia says nothing; in fact she looks away. So what choice do I have but to let go a stream of tea over the top of my noddle? It drips down my face and off my chin. It's pretty scalding, I can tell you.

'He said, all right, he said you were like a wild animal!'

'Like a wild animal?' I say.

'Yes. And sometimes he wished he could shoot you to put you out of your misery.' She looks straight ahead of her. 'You asked for it. You made me say it.'

'The bastard. His own daughter.'

She holds my hand. For the first time, she looks at me, with wide-open eyes and urgent mouth. 'It's terrible, just terrible there in the house. Nina, I had to get away! And I'm in love with someone! Someone who's indifferent to me!'

'And?'

And nothing. She says no more except: 'It's too cruel, too cruel.'

I glance around. Now this is exactly the kind of place suitable for doing a runner from. You could be out the door, halfway up the street and on the tube before they'd blink. I'm about to suggest it to Nadia, but, as I've already told her about my smack addiction, my two abortions and poured a pot of tea over my head, I wouldn't want her to get a bad impression of me.

'I hope,' I say to her, 'I hope to God we can be friends as well as relations.'

Well, what a bastard my dad turned out to be! Wild animal! He's no angel himself. How could he say that? I was always on my best behaviour and always covered my wrists and arms. Now I can't stop thinking about him. It makes me cry.

This is how he used to arrive at our place, my daddy, in the days when he used to visit us.

First there's a whole day's terror and anticipation and getting ready. When Ma and I are exhausted, having practically cleaned the flat with our tongues, a black taxi slides over the horizon of the estate, rarer than an ambulance, with presents cheering on the back seat: champagne, bicycles, dresses that don't fit, books, dreams in boxes. Dad glows in a £3,000 suit and silk tie. Neighbours lean over the balconies to pleasure their eyeballs on the prince. It takes two or three of them working in shifts to hump the loot upstairs.

Then we're off in the taxi, speeding to restaurants with menus in French where Dad knows the manager. Dad tells us stories of extreme religion and hilarious corruption and when Ma catches herself laughing she bites her lip hard – why? I suppose she finds herself flying to the magnet of his charm once more.

After the grub we go to see a big show and Mum and Dad hold hands. All of these shows are written, on the later occasions, by Andrew Lloyd Webber.

This is all the best of life, except that, when Dad has gone and we have to slot back into our lives, we don't always feel like it. We're pretty uncomfortable, looking at each other and shuffling our ordinary feet once more in the mundane. Why does he always have to be leaving us?

After one of these occasions I go out, missing him. When alone, I talk to him. At five in the morning I get back. At eight Ma comes into my room and stands there, a woman alone and everything like that, in fury and despair.

'Are you involved in drugs and prostitution?'

I'd been going with guys for money. At the massage parlour you do as little as you can. None of them has disgusted me, and we have a laugh with them. Ma finds out because I've always got so much money. She knows the state of things. She stands over me.

'Yes.' No escape. I just say it. Yes, yes, yes.

'That's what I thought.'

'Yes, that is my life at the moment. Can I go back to sleep now? I'm expected at work at twelve.'

'Don't call it work, Nina. There are other words.'

She goes. Before her car has failed to start in the courtyard, I've run to the bathroom, filled the sink, taken Ma's lousy leg razor and jabbed into my wrists, first one, then the other, under water, digging for veins. (You should try it sometime; it's more difficult than you think: skin tough, throat contracting with vomit acid sour disgust.) The nerves in my hands went and they had to operate and everyone was annoyed that I'd caused such trouble.

Weeks later I vary the trick and swallow thirty pills and fly myself to a Surrey mental hospital where I do puzzles, make baskets and am fucked regularly for medicinal reasons by the art therapist who has a long nail on his little finger.

Suicide is one way of saying you're sorry.

With Nadia to the Tower of London, the Monument, Hyde Park, Buckingham Palace and something cultured with a lot of wigs at the National Theatre. Nadia keeps me from confession by small talk which wears into my shell like sugar into a tooth.

Ma sullen but doing a workmanlike hospitality job. Difficult to get Nadia out of her room most of the time. Hours she spends in the bathroom every day experimenting with make-up. And then Howard the hero decides to show up.

Ma not home yet. Early evening. Guess what? Nadia is sitting across the room on the sofa with Howard. This is their first meeting and they're practically on each other's laps. (I almost wrote lips.) All afternoon I've had to witness this meeting of minds. They're on politics. The words that ping off the walls are: pluralism, democracy, theocracy and Benazir! Howard's senses are on their toes! The little turd can't believe the same body (in a black cashmere sweater and black leather jacket) can contain such intelligence, such beauty, and yet jingle so brightly with facts about the Third World! There in her bangles and perfume I see her speak to

WITH YOUR TONGUE DOWN MY THROAT

him as she hasn't spoken to me once – gesticulating!

'Howard. I say this to you from my heart, it is a corrupt country! Even the revolutionaries are corrupt! No one has any hope!'

In return he asks, surfacing through the Niagara of her conversation: 'Nadia, can I show you something? Videos of the TV stuff I've written?'

She can't wait.

None of us has seen her come in. Ma is here now, coat on, bags in her hands, looking at Nadia and Howard sitting so close their elbows keep knocking together.

'Hello,' she says to Howard, eventually. 'Hiya,' to Nadia. Ma has bought herself some flowers, which she has under her arm – carnations. Howard doesn't get up to kiss her. He's touching no one but Nadia and he's very pleased with himself. Nadia nods at Ma but her eyes rush back to Howard the hero.

Nadia says to Howard: 'The West doesn't care if we're an undemocratic country.'

'I'm exhausted,' Ma says.

'Well,' I say to her. 'Hello, anyway.'

Ma and I unpack the shopping in the kitchen. Howard calls through to Ma, asking her school questions which she ignores. The damage has been done. Oh yes. Nadia has virtually ignored Ma in her own house. Howard, I can see, is pretty uncomfortable at this. He is about to lift himself out of the seat when Nadia puts her hand on his arm and asks him: 'How do you create?'

'How do I create?'

How does Howard create? With four word-kisses she has induced in Howard a Nelson's Column of excitement. 'How do you create?' is the last thing you should ever ask one of these guys.

'They get along well, don't they?' Ma says, watching them through the crack of the door. I lean against the fridge.

'Why shouldn't they?'

'No reason,' she says. 'Except that this is my home. Everything I do outside here is a waste of time and no one thanks me for it and no one cares for me, and now I'm excluded from my own flat!'

'Hey, Ma, don't get –'

'Pour me a bloody whisky, will you?'

I pour her one right away. 'Your supper's in the oven, Ma.' I give her the whisky. My ma cups her hands round the glass. Always been a struggle for her. Her dad in the army; white trash. She had to fight to learn. 'It's fish pie. And I did the washing and ironing.'

'You've always been good in that way, I'll give you that. Even when you were sick you'd do the cooking. I'd come home and there it would be. I'd eat it alone and leave the rest outside your door. It was like feeding a hamster. You can be nice.'

'Are you sure?'

'Only your niceness has to live among so many other wild elements. Women that I know. Their children are the same. A tragedy or a disappointment. Their passions are too strong. It is our era in England. I only wish, I only wish you could have some kind of career or something.'

I watch her and she turns away to look at Howard all snug with the sister I brought here. Sad Ma is, and gentle. I could take her in my arms to console her now for what I am, but I don't want to indulge her. A strange question occurs to me. 'Ma, why do you keep Howard on?'

She sits on the kitchen stool and sips her drink. She looks at the lino for about three minutes, without saying anything, gathering herself up, punching her fist against her leg, like someone who's just swallowed a depth charge. Howard's explaining voice drifts through to us.

Ma gets up and kick-slams the door.

'Because I love him even if he doesn't love me!'

Her tumbler smashes on the floor and glass skids around our feet.

'Because I need sex and why shouldn't I! Because I'm lonely, I'm lonely, okay, and I need someone bright to talk to! D'you think I can talk to you? D'you think you'd ever be interested in me for one minute?'

'Ma –'

'You've never cared for me! And then you brought Nadia here against my wishes to be all sweet and hypercritical and remind me of all the terrible past and the struggle of being alone for so long!'

Ma sobbing in her room. Howard in with her. Nadia and me sit together at the two ends of the sofa. My ears are scarlet with the hearing of Ma's plain sorrow through the walls. 'Yes, I care for you,' Howard's voice rises. 'I love you, baby. And I love Nina, too. Both of you.'

'I don't know, Howard. You don't ever show it.'

'But I'm blocked as a human being!'

I say to Nadia: 'Men are pretty selfish bastards who don't understand us. That's all I know.'

'Howard's an interesting type,' she says coolly. 'Very open-minded in an artistic way.'

I'm getting protective in my old age and very pissed off.

'He's my mother's boyfriend and long-standing lover.'

'Yes, I know that.'

'So lay off him. Please, Nadia. Please understand.'

'What are you, of all people, accusing me of?'

I'm not too keen on this 'of all people' business. But get this.

'I thought you advanced Western people believed in the free intermingling of the sexes?'

'Yes, we do. We intermingle all the time.'

'What then, Nina, is your point?'

'It's him,' I explain, moving in. 'He has all the weaknesses. One kind word from a woman and he thinks they want to sleep with him. Two kind words and he thinks he's the only man in the world. It's a form of mental illness, of delusion. I

wouldn't tangle with that deluded man if I were you!'
All right!

A few days later.
Here I am slouching at Howard's place. Howard's hole, or
'sock' as he calls it, is a red-brick mansion block with public-
school, stately dark oak corridors, off Kensington High
Street. Things have been getting grimmer and grimmer.
Nadia stays in her room or else goes out and pops her little
camera at 'history'. Ma goes to every meeting she hears of.
I'm just about ready for artery road.

I've just done you a favour. I could have described every
moment of us sitting through Howard's television *œuvre*
(which I always thought meant *egg*). But no – on to the juicy
bits!

There they are in front of me, Howard and Nadia cheek to
cheek, within breath-inhaling distance of each other, going
through the script.

Earlier this morning we went shopping in Covent Garden.
Nadia wanted my advice on what clothes to buy. So we
went for a couple of sharp dogtooth jackets, distinctly city,
fine brown and white wool, the jacket caught in at the waist
with a black leather belt; short panelled skirt; white silk
polo-neck shirt; plus black pillbox, suede gloves, high heels.
If she likes something, if she wants it, she buys it. The rich.
Nadia bought me a linen jacket.

Maybe I'm sighing too much. They glance at me with un-
delight.

'I can take Nadia home if you like,' Howard says.
'I'll take care of my sister,' I say. 'But I'm out for a stroll
now. I'll be back at any time.'

I stroll towards a café in Rotting Hill. I head up through
Holland Park, past the blue sloping roof of the Common-
wealth Institute (or Nigger's Corner as we used to call it) in
which on a school trip I pissed into a wastepaper basket.
Past modern nannies – young women like me with dyed

black hair – walking dogs and kids.

The park's full of hip kids from Holland Park School, smoking on the grass; black guys with flat-tops and muscles; yuppies skimming frisbees and stuff; white boys playing Madonna and Prince. There are cruising turd-burglars with active eyes, and the usual London liggers, hang-gliders and no-goodies waiting to sign on. I feel outside everything, so up I go, through the flower-verged alley at the end of the park, where the fudge-packers used to line up at night for fucking. On the wall it says: *Gay solidarity is class solidarity.*

Outside the café is a police van with grilles over the windows full of little piggies giggling with their helmets off. It's a common sight around here, but the streets are a little quieter than usual. I walk past an Asian policewoman standing in the street who says hello to me. 'Auntie Tom,' I whisper and go into the café.

In this place they play the latest calypso and soca and the new Eric Satie recording. A white Rasta sits at the table with me. He pays for my tea. I have chilli with a baked potato and grated cheese, with tomato salad on the side, followed by Polish cheesecake. People in the café are more subdued than normal; all the pigs making everyone nervous. But what a nice guy the Rasta is. Even nicer, he takes my hand under the table and drops something in my palm. A chunky chocolate lozenge of dope.

'Hey. I'd like to buy some of this,' I say, wrapping my swooning nostrils round it.

'Sweetheart, it's all I've got,' he says. 'You take it. My last lump of blow.'

He leaves. I watch him go. As he walks across the street in his jumble-sale clothes, his hair jabbing out from his head like tiny bedsprings, the police get out of their van and stop him. He waves his arms at them. The van unpacks. There's about six of them surrounding him. There's an argument. He's giving them some heavy lip. They search him. One of them is pulling his hair. Everyone in the café is watching. I pop the dope into my mouth and swallow it. Yum yum.

I go out into the street now. I don't care. My friend shouts across to me: 'They're planting me. I've got nothing.'

I tell the bastard pigs to leave him alone. 'It's true! The man's got nothing!' I give them a good shouting at. One of them comes at me.

'You wanna be arrested too!' he says, shoving me in the chest.

'I don't mind,' I say. And I don't, really. Ma would visit me.

Some kids gather round, watching the rumpus. They look really straggly and pathetic and dignified and individual and defiant at the same time. I feel sorry for us all. The pigs pull my friend into the van. It's the last I ever see of him. He's got two years of trouble ahead of him, I know.

When I get back from my walk they're sitting on Howard's Habitat sofa. Something is definitely going on, and it ain't cultural. They're too far apart for comfort. Beadily I shove my aerial into the air and take the temperature. Yeah, can't I just smell humming dodginess in the atmosphere?

'Come on,' I say to Nadia. 'Ma will be waiting.'

'Yes, that's true,' Howard says, getting up. 'Give her my love.'

I give him one of my looks. 'All of it or just a touch?'

We're on the bus, sitting there nice and quiet, the bus going along past the shops and people and the dole office when these bad things start to happen that I can't explain. The seats in front of me, the entire top deck of the bus in fact, keeps rising up. I turn my head to the window expecting that the street at least will be anchored to the earth, but it's not. The whole street is throwing itself up at my head and heaving about and bending like a high rise in a tornado. The shops are dashing at me, at an angle. The world has turned into a monster. For God's sake, nothing will keep still, but

I've made up my mind to have it out. So I tie myself to the seat by my fists and say to Nadia, at least I think I say, 'You kiss him?'

She looks straight ahead as if she's been importuned by a beggar. I'm about to be hurled out of the bus, I know. But I go right ahead.

'Nadia. You did, right? You did.'

'But it's not important.'

Wasn't I right? Can't I sniff a kiss in the air at a hundred yards?

'Kissing's not important?'

'No,' she says. 'It's not, Nina. It's just affection. That's normal. But Howard and I have much to say to each other.' She seems depressed suddenly. 'He knows I'm in love with somebody.'

'I'm not against talking. But it's possible to talk without r-r-rubbing your tongues against each other's tonsils.'

'You have a crude way of putting things,' she replies, turning sharply to me and rising up to the roof of the bus. 'It's a shame you'll never understand passion.'

I am crude, yeah. And I'm about to be crushed into the corner of the bus by two hundred brown balloons. Oh, sister.

'Are you feeling sick?' she says, getting up.

The next thing I know we're stumbling off the moving bus and I lie down on an unusual piece of damp pavement outside the Albert Hall. The sky swings above me. Nadia's face hovers over mine like ectoplasm. Then she has her hand flat on my forehead in a doctory way. I give it a good hard slap.

'Why are you crying?'

If our father could see us now.

'Your bad behaviour with Howard makes me cry for my ma.'

'Bad behaviour? Wait till I tell my father –'

'Our father –'

'About you.'

'What will you say?'

'I'll tell him you've been a prostitute and a drug addict.'

'Would you say that, Nadia?'

'No,' she says, eventually. 'I suppose not.'

She offers me her hand and I take it.

'It's time I went home,' she says.

'Me, too,' I say.

3

It's not Friday, but Howard comes with us to Heathrow. Nadia flicks through fashion magazines, looking at clothes she won't be able to buy now. Her pride and dignity today is monstrous. Howard hands me a pile of books and writing pads and about twelve pens.

'Don't they have pens over there?' I say.

'It's a Third World country,' he says. 'They lack the basic necessities.'

Nadia slaps his arm. 'Howard, of course we have pens, you stupid idiot!'

'I was joking,' he says. 'They're for me.' He tries to stuff them all into the top pocket of his jacket. They spill on the floor. 'I'm writing something that might interest you all.'

'Everything you write interests us,' Nadia says.

'Not necessarily,' Ma says.

'But this is especially . . . relevant,' he says.

Ma takes me aside: 'If you must go, do write, Nina. And don't tell your father one thing about me!'

Nadia distracts everyone by raising her arms and putting her head back and shouting out in the middle of the airport: 'No, no, no, I don't want to go!'

My room, this cell, this safe, bare box stuck on the side of my father's house, has a stone floor and whitewashed walls. It has a single bed, my open suitcase, no wardrobe, no music. Not a frill in the grill. On everything there's a veil of khaki dust waiting to irritate my nostrils. The window is tiny, just twice the size of my head. So it's pretty gloomy here. Next door there's a smaller room with an amateur shower, a sink and a hole in the ground over which you have to get used to squatting if you want to piss and shit.

Despite my moans, all this suits me fine. In fact, I requested this room. At first Dad wanted Nadia and me to share. But here I'm out of everyone's way, especially my two other half-sisters: Gloomie and Moonie I call them.

I wake up and the air is hot, hot, hot, and the noise and petrol fumes rise around me. I kick into my jeans and pull my Keith Haring T-shirt on. Once, on the King's Road, two separate people came up to me and said: 'Is that a Keith Haring T-shirt?'

Outside, the sun wants to burn you up. The light is different too: you can really see things. I put my shades on. These are cool shades. There aren't many women you see in shades here.

The driver is revving up one of Dad's three cars outside my room. I open the door of a car and jump in, except that it's like throwing your arse into a fire, and I jiggle around, the driver laughing, his teeth jutting as if he never saw anything funny before.

'Drive me,' I say. 'Drive me somewhere in all this sunlight. Please. Please.' I touch him and he pulls away from me. Well, he is rather handsome. 'These cars don't need to be revved. Drive!'

He turns the wheel back and forth, pretending to drive and hit the horn. He's youngish and thin – they all look undernourished here – and he always teases me.

'You stupid bugger.'

See, ain't I just getting the knack of speaking to servants? It's taken me at least a week to erase my natural politeness to the poor.

'Get going! Get us out of this drive!'

'No shoes, no shoes, Nina!' He's pointing at my feet.

'No bananas, no pineapples,' I say. 'No job for you either, Lulu. You'll be down the Job Centre if you don't shift it.'

Off we go then, the few yards to the end of the drive. The guard at the gate waves. I turn to look back and there you are standing on the porch of your house in your pyjamas, face covered with shaving cream, a piece of white sheet wrapped around your head because you've just oiled your hair. Your arms are waving not goodbye. Gloomie, my suddenly acquired sister, runs out behind you and shakes her fists, the dogs barking in their cage, the chickens screaming in theirs. Ha, ha.

We drive slowly through the estate on which Dad lives with all the other army and navy and air force people: big houses and big bungalows set back from the road, with sprinklers on the lawn, some with swimming pools, all with guards.

We move out on to the Superhighway, among the painted trucks, gaudier than Chinese dolls, a sparrow among peacocks. What a crappy road and no fun, like driving on the moon. Dad says the builders steal the materials, flog them and then there's not enough left to finish the road. So they just stop and leave whole stretches incomplete.

The thing about this place is that there's always something happening. Good or bad it's a happening place. And I'm thinking this, how cheerful I am and everything, when bouncing along in the opposite direction is a taxi, an old yellow and black Morris Minor stuck together with sellotape. It's swerving in and out of the traffic very fast until the driver loses it, and the taxi bangs the back of the car in front, glances off another and shoots off across the Superhighway and is coming straight for us. I can see the driver's face when Lulu finally brakes. Three feet from us the taxi flies into a wall that runs alongside the road. The two men keep travelling, and their heads crushed into their chests pull their bodies through the windscreen and out into the morning air. They look like Christmas puddings.

Lulu accelerates. I grab him and scream at him to stop but

we go faster and faster.

'Damn dead,' he says, when I've finished clawing him. 'A wild country. This kind of thing happen in England, yes?'

'Yes, I suppose so.'

Eventually I persuade him to stop and I get out of the car.

I'm alone in the bazaar, handling jewellery and carpets and pots and I'm confused. I know I have to get people presents. Especially Howard the hero who's paying for this. Ah, there's just the thing: a cage the size of a big paint tin, with three chickens inside. The owner sees me looking. He jerks a chicken out, decapitates it on a block and holds it up to my face, feathers flying into my hair.

I walk away and dodge a legless brat on a four-wheeled trolley made out of a door, who hurls herself at me and then disappears through an alley and across the sewers. Everywhere the sick and the uncured, and I'm just about ready for lunch when everyone starts running. They're jumping out of the road and pulling their kids away. There is a tidal wave of activity, generated by three big covered trucks full of soldiers crashing through the bazaar, the men standing still and nonchalant with rifles in the back. I'm half knocked to hell by some prick tossed off a bike. I am tiptoeing my way out along the edge of a fucking sewer, shit lapping against my shoes. I've just about had enough of this country, I'm just about to call for South Africa Road, when –

'Lulu,' I shout. 'Lulu.'

'I take care of you,' he says. 'Sorry for touching.'

He takes me back to the car. Fat, black buffalo snort and shift in the mud. I don't like these animals being everywhere, chickens and dogs and stuff, with sores and bleeding and threats and fear.

'You know?' I say. 'I'm lonely. There's no one I can talk to. No one to laugh with here, Lulu. And I think they hate me, my family. Does your family hate you?'

*

I stretch and bend and twist in the front garden in T-shirt and shorts. I pull sheets of air into my lungs. I open my eyes a moment and the world amazes me, its brightness. A servant is watching me, peeping round a tree.

'Hey, peeper!' I call, and carry on. When I look again, I notice the cook and the sweeper have joined him and they shake and trill.

'What am I doing?' I say. 'Giving a concert?'

In the morning papers I notice that potential wives are advertised as being 'virtuous and fair-skinned'. Why would I want to be unvirtuous and brown? But I do, I do!

I take a shower in my room and stroll across to the house. I stand outside your room, Dad, where the men always meet in the early evenings. I look through the wire mesh of the screen door and there you are, my father for all these years. And this is what you were doing while I sat in the back of the class at my school in Shepherd's Bush, pregnant, wondering why you didn't love me.

In the morning when I'm having my breakfast we meet in the living room by the bar and you ride on your exercise bicycle. You pant and look at me now and again, your stringy body sways and tightens, but you say fuck all. If I speak, you don't hear. You're one of those old-fashioned romantic men for whom women aren't really there unless you decide we are.

Now you lie on your bed and pluck up food with one hand and read an American comic with the other. A servant, a young boy, presses one of those fat vibrating electric instruments you see advertised in the *Observer* Magazine on to your short legs. You look up and see me. The sight of me angers you. You wave furiously for me to come in. No. Not yet. I walk on.

In the women's area of the house, where visitors rarely visit, Dad's wife sits sewing.

'Hello,' I say. 'I think I'll have a piece of sugar cane.'

I want to ask the names of the other pieces of fruit on the table, but Wifey is crabby inside and out, doesn't speak English and disapproves of me in all languages. She has two servants with her, squatting there watching Indian movies on the video. An old woman who was once, I can see, a screen goddess, now sweeps the floor on her knees with a handful of twigs. Accidentally, sitting there swinging my leg, I touch her back with my foot, leaving a dusty mark on her clothes.

'Imagine,' I say to Wifey.

I slip the sugar cane into my mouth. The squirting juice bounces off my taste buds. I gob out the sucked detritus and chuck it in front of the screen goddess's twigs. You can really enjoy talking to someone who doesn't understand you.

'Imagine my dad leaving my ma for you! And you don't ever leave that seat there. Except once a month you go to the bank to check up on your jewellery.'

Wifey keeps all her possessions on the floor around her. She is definitely mad. But I like the mad here: they just wander around the place with everyone else and no one bothers you and people give you food.

'You look like a bag lady. D'you know what a bag lady is?'

Moonie comes into the room. She's obviously heard every word I've said. She starts to yell at me. Wifey's beaky nozzle turns to me with interest now. Something's happening that's even more interesting than TV. They want to crush me. I think they like me here for that reason. If you could see, Ma, what they're doing to me just because you met a man at a dance in the Old Kent Road and his French letter burst as you lay in front of a gas fire with your legs up!

'You took the car when we had to go out to work!' yells Moonie. 'You forced the driver to take you! We had to sack him!'

'Why sack him?'

'He's naughty! Naughty! You said he drives you badly! Nearly killed! You're always causing trouble, Nina, doing some stupid thing, some very stupid thing!'

Gloomie and Moonie are older than Nadia and me. Both have been married, kicked around by husbands arranged by Dad, and separated. That was their small chance in life. Now they've come back to Daddy. Now they're secretaries. Now they're blaming me for everything.

'By the way. Here.' I reach into my pocket. 'Take this.'

Moonie's eyes bulge at my open palm. Her eyes quieten her mouth. She starts fatly towards me. She sways. She comes on. Her hand snatches at the lipstick.

'Now you'll be able to come out with me. We'll go to the Holiday Inn.'

'Yes, but you've been naughty.' She is distracted by the lipstick. 'What colour is it?'

'Can't you leave her alone for God's sake? Always picking on her!' This is Nadia coming into the room after work. She throws herself into a chair. 'I'm so tired.' To the servant she says: 'Bring me some tea.' At me she smiles. 'Hello, Nina. Good day? You were doing some exercises, I hear. They rang me at work to tell me.'

'Yes, Nadia.'

'Oh, sister, they have such priorities.'

For the others I am 'cousin'. From the start there's been embarrassment about how I am to be described. Usually, if it's Moonie or Gloomie they say: 'This is our distant cousin from England.' It amuses me to see my father deal with this. He can't bring himself to say either 'cousin' or 'daughter' so he just says Nina and leaves it. But of course everyone knows I am his illegitimate daughter. But Nadia is the real 'daughter' here. 'Nadia is an impressive person,' my father says, on my first day here, making it clear that I am diminished, the sort with dirt under her nails. Yes, she is clever, soon to be doctor, life-saver. Looking at her now she seems less small than she did in London. I'd say she has enough dignity for the entire government.

'They tear-gassed the hospital.'

'Who?'

'The clever police. Some people were demonstrating outside. The police broke it up. When they chased the demonstrators inside they tear-gassed them! What a day! What a country! I must wash my face.' She goes out.

'See, see!' Moonie trills. 'She is better than you! Yes, yes, yes!'

'I expect so. It's not difficult.'

'We know she is better than you for certain!'

I walk out of all this and into my father's room. It's like moving from one play to another. What is happening on this set? The room is perfumed with incense from a green coiled creation which burns outside the doors, causing mosquitoes to drop dead. Advanced telephones connect him to Paris, Dubai, London. On the video is an American movie. Five youths rape a woman. Father – what do I call him, Dad? – sits on the edge of the bed with his little legs sticking out. The servant teases father's feet into his socks.

'You'll get sunstroke,' he says, as if he's known me all my life and has the right to be high-handed. 'Cavorting naked in the garden.'

'Naked is it now?'

'We had to sack the driver, too. Sit down.'

I sit in the row of chairs beside him. It's like visiting someone in hospital. He lies on his side in his favourite mocking-me-for-sport position.

'Now –'

The lights go out. The TV goes off. I shut my eyes and laugh. Power cut. Father bounces up and down on the bed. 'Fuck this motherfucking country!' The servant rushes for candles and lights them. As it's Friday I sit here and think of Ma and Howard meeting today for food, talk and sex. I think Howard's not so bad after all, and even slightly good-looking. He's never deliberately hurt Ma. He has other women – but that's only vanity, a weakness, not a crime –

and he sees her only on Friday, but he hasn't undermined her. What more can you expect from men? Ma loves him a lot – from the first moment, she says; she couldn't help herself. She's still trusting and open, despite everything.

Never happen to me.

Dad turns to me: 'What do you do in England for God's sake?'

'Nadia has already given you a full report, hasn't she?'

A full report? For two days I gaped through the window lip-reading desperately as nose to nose, whispering and giggling, eyebrows shooting up, jaws dropping like guillotines, hands rubbing, Father and Nadia conducted my prosecution. The two rotund salt and pepper pots, Moonie and Gloomie, guarded the separate entrances to this room.

'Yes, but I want the full confession from your mouth.'

He loves to tease. But he is a dangerous person. Tell him something and soon everyone knows about it.

'Confess to what?'

'That you just roam around here and there. You do fuck all full time, in other words.'

'Everyone in England does fuck all except for the yuppies.'

'And do you go with one boy or with many?' I say nothing. 'But your mother has a boy, yes? Some dud writer, complete failure and playboy with unnatural eyebrows that cross in the middle?'

'Is that how Nadia described the man she tried to –'

'What?'

'Be rather close friends with?'

The servant has a pair of scissors. He trims Father's hair, he snips in Father's ear, he investigates Father's nostrils with the clipping steel shafts. He attaches a tea-cloth to Father's collar, lathers Father's face, sharpens the razor on the strop and shaves Father clean and reddish.

'Not necessarily,' says Father, spitting foam. 'I use my imagination. Nadia says eyebrows and I see bushes.'

He says to his servant and indicates me: 'An Englisher born and bred, eh?'

The servant falls about with the open razor.

'But you belong with us,' Dad says. 'Don't worry, I'll put you on the right track. But first there must be a strict course of discipline.'

The room is full of dressed-up people sitting around Dad's bed looking at him lying there in his best clothes. Dad yells out cheerful slanders about the tax evaders, bribe-takers and general scumbags who can't make it this evening. Father obviously a most popular man here. It's better to be entertaining than good. Ma would be drinking bleach by now.

At last Dad gives the order they've been waiting for.

'Bring the booze.'

The servant unlocks the cabinet and brings out the whisky.

'Give everyone a drink except Nina. She has to get used to the pure way of life!' he says, and everyone laughs at me.

The people here are tractor dealers (my first tractor dealer!), journalists, landowners and a newspaper tycoon aged thirty-one who inherited a bunch of papers. He's immensely cultured and massively fat. I suggest you look at him from the front and tell me if he doesn't look like a flounder. I look up to see my sister standing at the window of Dad's room, straining her heart's wet eyes at the Flounder who doesn't want to marry her because he already has the most pleasant life there is in the world.

Now here's a message for you fuckers back home. The men here invite Nadia and me to their houses, take us to their club, play tennis with us. They're chauvinistic as hell, but they put on a great show. They're funny and spend money and take you to their farms and show you their guns and kill a snake in front of your eyes. They flirt and want to poke their things in you, but they don't expect it.

Billy slides into the room in his puffy baseball jacket and pink plimsolls and patched jeans. He stands there and puts his hands in his pockets and takes them out again.

'Hey, Billy, have a drink.'

'OK. Thanks . . . Yeah. OK.'

'Don't be shy,' Dad says. 'Nina's not shy.'

So the entire room looks at shy Billy and Billy looks at the ground.

'No, well, I could do with a drink. Just one. Thanks.'

The servant gets Billy a drink. Someone says to someone else: 'He looks better since he had that break in Lahore.'

'It did him the whole world of damn good.'

'Terrible what happened to the boy.'

'Yes. Yes. Ghastly rotten.'

Billy comes and sits next to me. Their loud talking goes on.

'I've heard about you,' he says under the talking. 'They talk about you non-stop.'

'Goody.'

'Yeah. Juicy Fruit?' he says.

He sits down on the bed and I open my case and give him all my tapes.

'Latest stuff from England.'

He goes through them eagerly. 'You can't get any of this stuff here. This is the best thing that has ever happened to me.' He looks at me. 'Can I? Can I borrow them? Would you mind, you know?' I nod. 'My room is on top of the house. I'll never be far away.'

Oh, kiss me now! Though I can see that's a little premature, especially in a country where they cut off your arms or something for adultery. I like your black jeans.

'What's your accent?' I say.

'Canadian.' He gets up. No, don't leave now. Not yet. 'Wanna ride?' he says.

In the drive the chauffeurs smoke and talk. They stop

talking. They watch us. Billy puts his baseball cap on my head and touches my hair.

'Billy, push the bike out into the street so no one hears us leave.'

I ask him about himself. His mother was Canadian. She died. His father was Pakistani, though Billy was brought up in Vancouver. I turn and Moonie is yelling at me. 'Nina, Nina, it's late. Your father must see you now about a strict discipline business he has to discuss!'

'Billy, keep going.'

He just keeps pushing the bike, oblivious of Moonie. He glances at me now and again, as if he can't believe his luck. I can't believe mine, baby!

'So Pop and I came home to live. Home. This place isn't my home. But he always wanted to come home.'

We push the bike up the street till we get to the main road.

'This country was a shock after Vancouver,' he says.

'Same for me.'

'Yeah?' He gets sharp. 'But I'd been brought here to live. How can you ever understand what that's like?'

'I can't. All right, I fucking can't.'

He goes on. 'We were converting a house in 'Pindi, Pop and me. Digging the foundations, plastering the walls, doing the plumbing . . .'

We get on the bike and I hold him.

'Out by the beach, Billy.'

'Yeah. But it's not simple. You know the cops stop couples and ask to see their wedding certificates.'

It's true but fuck it. Slowly, stately, the two beige outlaws ride through the city of open fires. I shout an Aretha Franklin song into the night. Men squat by busted cars. Wild maimed pye-dogs run in our path. Traffic careers through dust, past hotels and airline buildings, past students squatting beside traffic lights to read, near where there are terrorist explosions and roads melt like plastic.

To the beach without showing our wedding certificate. It's

more a desert than a beach. There's just sand: no shops, no
hotels, no ice-creamers, no tattooists. Utterly dark. Your eyes
search for a light in panic, for safety. But the curtains of the
world are well and truly pulled here.

I guide Billy to the Flounder's beach hut. Hut – this place
is bigger than Ma's flat. We push against the back door and
we're in the large living room. Billy and I dance about and
chuck open the shutters. Enter moonlight and the beach as
Billy continues his Dad rap.

'Pop asked me to drill some holes in the kitchen. But I had
to empty the wheelbarrow. So he did the drilling. He hit a
cable or something. Anyway, he's dead, isn't he?'

We kiss for a long time, about forty minutes. There's not a
lot you can do in kissing; half an hour of someone's tongue
in your mouth could seem an eternity, but what there is to
do, we do. I take off all my clothes and listen to the sea and
almost cry for missing South Africa Road so. But at least
there is the light friction of our lips together, barely touching.
Harder. I pull the strong bulk of his head towards mine,
pressing my tongue to the corner of his mouth. Soon I pass
through the mouth's parting to trace the inside curve of his
lips. Suddenly his tongue fills my mouth, invading me, and I
clench it with my teeth. Oh, oh, oh. As he withdraws I follow
him, sliding my tongue into the oven of his gob and lie there
on the bench by the open shutters overlooking the Arabian
Sea, connected by tongue and saliva, my fingers in his ears
and hair, his finger inside my body, our bodies dissolving
until we forget ourselves and think of nothing, thank fuck.

It's still dark and no more than ninety minutes have passed,
when I hear a car pulling up outside the hut. I shake Billy
awake, push him off me and pull him across the hut and into
the kitchen. The fucking door's warped and won't shut so
we just lie down on the floor next to each other. I clam Billy
up with my hand over his gob. There's a shit smell right next
to my nose. I start to giggle. I stuff Billy's fingers into my

mouth. He's laughing all over the place too. But we shut up sharpish when a couple come into the hut and start to move around. For some reason I imagine we're going to be shot.

The man says: 'Curious, indeed. My sister must have left the shutters open last time she came here.'

The other person says it's lovely, the moonlight and so on. Then there's no talking. I can't see a sausage but my ears are at full stretch. Yes, kissing noises.

Nadia says: 'Here's the condoms, Bubble!'

My sister and the Flounder! Well. The Flounder lights a lantern. Yes, there they are now, I can see them: she's trying to pull his long shirt over his head, and he's resisting.

'Just my bottoms!' he squeals. 'My stomach! Oh, my God!'

I'm not surprised he's ashamed, looking in this low light at the size of the balcony over his toy shop.

I hear my name. Nadia starts to tell the Flounder – or 'Bubble' as she keeps calling him – how the Family Planning in London gave me condoms. The Flounder's clucking with disapproval and lying on the bench by the window looking like a hippo, with my sister squatting over his guts, rising and sitting, sighing and exclaiming sometimes, almost in surprise. They chat away quite naturally, fucking and gossiping and the Flounder talks about me. Am I promiscuous, he wants to know. Do I do it with just anyone? How is my father going to discipline me now he's got his hands on me? Billy shifts about. He could easily be believing this shit. I wish I had some paper and a pen to write him a note. I kiss him gently instead. When I kiss him I get a renewal of this strange sensation that I've never felt before today: I feel it's Billy I'm kissing, not just his lips or body, but some inside thing, as if his skin is just a representative of all of him, his past and his blood. Amour has never been this personal for me before!

Nadia and the Flounder are getting hotter. She keeps asking Bubble why they can't do this every day. He says, yes, yes, yes, and won't you tickle my balls? I wonder how she'll find them. Then the Flounder shudders and Nadia, moving in rhythm like someone doing a slow dance, has to stop. 'Bubble!' she says and slaps him, as if he's a naughty child that's just thrown up. A long fart escapes Bubble's behind. 'Oh, Bubble,' she says, and falls on to him, holding him closer.

Soon he is asleep. Nadia unstraddles him and moves to a chair and has a little cry as she sits looking at him. She only wants to be held and kissed and touched. I feel like going to her myself.

When I wake up it's daylight and they're sitting there together, talking about their favourite subject. The Flounder is smoking and she is trying to masturbate him.

'So why did she come here with you?' he is asking. Billy opens his eyes and doesn't know where he is. Then he sighs. I agree with him. What a place to be, what a thing to be doing! (But then, come to think of it, you always find me in the kitchen at parties.)

'Nina just asked me one day at breakfast. I had no choice and this man, Howard –'

'Yes, yes,' the Flounder laughs. 'You said he was handsome.'

'I only said he had nice hair,' she says.

But I'm in sympathy with the Flounder here, finding this compliment a little gratuitous. The Flounder gets up. He's ready to go.

And so is Billy. 'I can't stand much more of this,' he says. Nadia suddenly jerks her head towards us. For a moment I think she's seen us. But the Flounder distracts her.

I hear the tinkle of the car keys and the Flounder says: 'Here, put your panties on. Wouldn't want to leave your panties here on the floor. But let me kiss them first! I kiss them!'

There are sucky kissing noises. Billy is twitching badly and drumming his heels on the floor. Nadia looks at the

Flounder with his face buried in a handful of white cotton.

'And,' he says with a muffled voice, 'I'm getting lead in my pencil again, Nadia. Let us lie down, my pretty one.'

The Flounder takes her hand enthusiastically and jerks it towards his ding-dong. She smacks him away. She's not looking too pleased.

'I've got my pants on, you bloody fool!' Nadia says harshly. 'That pair of knickers you've sunk your nose in must belong to another woman you've had here!'

'What! But I've had no other woman here!' The Flounder glares at her furiously. He examines the panties, as if hoping to find a name inside. 'Marks & Spencers. How strange. I feel sick now.'

'Marks & Spencers! Fuck this!' says Billy, forcing my hands off his face. 'My arms and legs are going to fucking drop off in a minute!'

So up gets Billy. He combs his hair and turns up the collar of his shirt and then strolls into the living room singing a couple of choruses from The The. I get up and follow him, just in time to see Nadia open her mouth and let off a huge scream at the sight of us. The Flounder, who has no bottoms on, gives a frightened yelp and drops my pants which I pick up and, quite naturally, put on. I'm calm and completely resigned to the worst. Anyway, I've got my arm round Billy.

'Hi, everyone,' Billy says. 'We were just asleep in the other room. Don't worry, we didn't hear anything, not about the condoms or Nina's character or the panties or anything. Not a thing. How about a cup of tea or something?'

I get off Billy's bike midday. 'Baby,' he says.

'Happy,' I say, wearing his checked shirt, tail out. Across the lawn with its sprinkler I set off for Dad's club, a sun-loved white palace set in flowers.

White-uniformed bearers humble as undertakers set down trays of foaming yogurt. I could do with a proper drink myself. Colonels with generals and ladies with perms, fans and crossed legs sit in cane chairs. I wish I'd slept more.

The old man. There you are, blazer and slacks, turning the pages of *The Times* on an oak lectern overlooking the gardens. You look up. Well, well, well, say your eyes, not a dull day now. Her to play with.

You take me into the dining room. It's chill and smart and the tables have thick white cloths on them and silver cutlery. The men move chairs for the elegant thin women, and the waiters take the jackets of the plump men. I notice there are no young people here.

'Fill your plate,' you say, kindly. 'And come and sit with me. Bring me something too. A little meat and some dhal.'

I cover the plate with food from the copper pots at the buffet in the centre of the room and take it to you. And here we sit, father and daughter, all friendly and everything.

'How are you today, Daddy?' I say, touching your cheek.

Around us the sedate upper class fill their guts. You haven't heard me. I say once more, gently: 'How are you today?'

'You fucking bitch,' you say. You push away your food and light a cigarette.

'Goody,' I say, going a little cold. 'Now we know where we are with each other.'

'Where the fuck were you last night?' you inquire of me. You go on: 'You just fucked off and told no one. I was demented with worry. My blood pressure was through the roof. Anything could have happened to you.'

'It did.'

'That bloody boy's insane.'

'But Billy's pretty.'

'No, he's ugly like you. And a big pain in the arse.'

'Dad.'

'No, don't interrupt! A half-caste wastrel, a belong-nowhere, a problem to everyone, wandering around the face of the earth with no home like a stupid-mistake-mongrel dog that no one wants and everyone kicks in the backside.'

For those of you curious about the menu, I am drinking tear soup.

'You left us,' I say. I am shaking. You are shaking. 'Years ago, just look at it, you fucked us and left us and fucked off and never came back and never sent us money and instead made us sit through fucking *Jesus Christ Superstar* and *Evita*.'

Someone comes over, a smart judge who helped hang the Prime Minister. We all shake hands. Christ, I can't stop crying all over the place.

It's dusk and I'm sitting upstairs in a deckchair outside Billy's room on the roof. Billy's sitting on a pillow. We're wearing cut-off jeans and drinking iced water and reading old English newspapers that we pass between us. Our washing is hanging up on a piece of string we've tied between the corner of the room and the television aerial. The door to the room is open and we're listening again and again to 'Who's Loving You' – very loud – because it's our favourite record. Billy keeps saying: 'Let's hear it again, one mo' time, you know.' We're like an old couple sitting on a concrete patio in Shepherd's Bush, until we get up and dance with no shoes on and laugh and gasp because the roof burns our feet so we have to go inside to make love again.

Billy goes in to take a shower and I watch him go. I don't like being separated from him. I hear the shower start and I sit down and throw the papers aside. I go downstairs to Nadia's room and knock on her door. Wifey is sitting there and Moonie is behind her.

'She's not in,' Moonie says.

'Come in,' Nadia says, opening her door, I go in and sit on the stool by the dressing table. It's a pretty room. There is pink everywhere and her things are all laid out neatly and she sits on the bed brushing her hair and it shines. I tell her we should have a bit of a talk. She smiles at me. She's prepared to make an effort, I can see that, though it surprises me. She did go pretty berserk the other day, when we came out of the kitchen, trying to punch me and everything.

'It was an accident,' I tell her now.

'Well,' she says. 'But what impression d'you think it made on the man I want to marry?'

'Blame me. Say I'm just a sicko Westerner. Say I'm mad.'

'It's the whole family it reflects on,' she says.

She goes to a drawer and opens it. She takes out an envelope and gives it to me.

'It's a present for you,' she says kindly. When I slip my finger into the flap of the envelope she puts her hand over mine. 'Please. It's a surprise for later.'

Billy is standing on the roof in his underpants. I fetch a towel and dry his hair and legs and he holds me and we move a little together to imaginary music. When I remember the envelope Nadia gave me, I open it and find a shiny folder inside. It's a ticket to London.

I'd given my ticket home to my father for safe-keeping, an open ticket I can use any time. I can see that Nadia's been to the airline and specified the date, and booked the flight. I'm to leave tomorrow morning. I go to my dad and ask him what it's all about. He just looks at me and I realise I'm to go.

4

Hello, reader. As I'm sure you've noticed by now, I, Howard, have written this Nina and Nadia stuff in my sock, without leaving the country, sitting right here on my spreading arse and listening to John Coltrane. (And rolling cigarettes.) Do you think Nina could have managed phrases like 'an accent as thick as treacle' and 'But the curtains are well and truly pulled here' and especially 'Oh, oh, oh'? With her education? So all along, it's been me, pulling faces, speaking in tongues, posing and making an attempt on the truth through lies. And also, I just wanted to be Nina. The days Deborah and I have spent beating on her head, trying to twist her the right way round, read this, study dancing, here's a book about Balanchine and the rest of it. What does she make of all this force feeding? So I became her, entered her. Sorry.

Nina in fact has been back a week, though it wasn't until yesterday that I heard from her when she phoned to tell me that I am a bastard and that she had to see me. I leave straightaway.

At Nina's place. There she is, sitting at the kitchen table with her foot up on the table by her ashtray in the posture of a painter. Deborah not back from school.

'You look superb,' I tell her. She doesn't recoil in repulsion when I kiss her.

'Do I look superb?' She is interested.

'Yeah. Tanned. Fit. Rested.'

'Oh, is that all? She looks hard at me. 'I thought for a moment you were going to say something interesting. Like I'd changed or something. Like something had happened.'

We walk through the estate, Friday afternoon. How she walks above it all now, as if she's already left! She tells me everything in a soft voice: her father, the servants, the boy Billy, the kiss, the panties. She says: 'I was devastated to leave Billy in that country on his own. What will he do? What will happen to that boy? I sent him a pack of tapes. I sent him some videos. But he'll be so lonely.' She is upset.

The three of us have supper and Deborah tries to talk about school while Nina ignores her. It's just like the old days. But Nina ignores Deborah not out of cruelty but because she is elsewhere. Deborah is thinking that probably Nina has left her for good. I am worried that Debbie will expect more from me.

The next day I fly to my desk, put on an early Miles Davis tape and let it all go, tip it out, what Nina said, how she looked, what we did, and I write (and later cross out) how I like to put my little finger up Deborah's arse when we're fucking and how she does the same to me, when she can comfortably reach. I shove it all down shamelessly (and add bits) because it's my job to write down the things that happen round here and because I have a rule about no material being sacred.

What does that make me?

I once was in a cinema when the recently uncovered spy Anthony Blunt came in with a friend. The entire cinema (but not me) stood up and chanted 'Out, out, out' until the old queen got up and left. I feel like that old spy, a dirty betrayer with a loudspeaker, doing what I have to.

I offer this story to you, Deborah and Nina, to make of it what you will, before I send it to the publisher.

Dear Howard,

How very kind of you to leave your story on my kitchen table casually saying, 'I think you should read this before I publish it.' I was pleased: I gave you an extra kiss, thinking that at last you wanted me to share your work (I almost wrote world).

I could not believe you opened the story with an account of an abortion. As you know I know, it's lifted in its entirety from a letter written to you by your last girlfriend, Julie. You were conveniently in New York when she was having the abortion so that she had to spit out all the bits of her broken heart in a letter, and you put it into the story pretending it was written by my daughter.

The story does also concern me, our 'relationship' and even where we put our fingers. Your portrait of me as a miserable whiner let down by men would have desperately depressed me, but I've learned that unfeeling, blood-sucking men like you need to reduce women to manageable clichés, even to destroy them, for the sake of control.

I am only sorry it's taken me this long to realise what a low, corrupt and exploitative individual you are, who never deserved the love we both offered you. You have torn me apart. I hope the same thing happens to you one day. Please never attempt to get in touch again.

Deborah

Someone bangs on the door of the flat. I've been alone all day. I'm not expecting anyone, and how did whoever it is get into the building in the first place?

'Let me in, let me in!' Nina calls out. I open up and she's standing there soaked through with a sports bag full of things and a couple of plastic bags under her arm.

'Moving in?' I say.

'You should be so lucky,' she says, barging past me. 'I'm on me way somewhere and I thought I'd pop by to borrow some money.'

She comes into the kitchen. It's gloomy and the rain hammers into the courtyard outside. But Nina's cheerful, happy to be back in England and she has no illusions about her father now. Apparently he was rough with her, called her a half-caste and so on.

'Well, Howard, you're in the shit, aren't you?' Nina says. 'Ma's pissed off no end with you, man. She's crying all over the shop. I couldn't stand it. I've moved out. You can die of a broken heart, you know. And you can kill someone that way too.'

'Don't talk about it,' I say, breaking up the ice with a hammer and dropping it into the glasses. 'She wrote me a pissed-off letter. Wanna read it?'

'It's private, Howard.'

'Read it, for Christ's sake, Nina,' I say, shoving it at her. She reads it and I walk round the kitchen looking at her. I stand behind her a long time. I can't stop looking at her today.

She puts it down without emotion. She's not sentimental; she's always practical about things, because she knows what cunts people are.

'You've ripped Ma off before. She'll get over it, and no one reads the shit you write anyway except a lot of middle-class wankers. As long as you get paid and as long as you give me some of it you're all right with me.'

I was right. I knew she'd be flattered. I give her some money and she gathers up her things. I don't want her to go.

'Where are you off to?'

'Oh, a friend's place in Hackney. Someone I was in the loony bin with. I'll be living there. Oh, and Billy will be joining me.' She smiles broadly. 'I'm happy.'

'Wow. That's good. You and Billy.'

'Yeah, ain't it just!' She gets up and throws back the rest of the whisky. 'Be seeing ya!'

'Don't go yet.'

'Got to.'

At the door she says: 'Good luck with the writing and everything.'

I walk to the lift with her. We go down together. I go out to the front door of the building. As she goes out into the street running with sheets of rain, I say: 'I'll come with you to the corner,' and walk with her, even though I'm not dressed for it.

At the corner I can't let her go and I accompany her to the bus stop. I wait with her for fifteen minutes in my shirt and slippers. I'm soaked through holding all her bags but I think you can make too much of these things. 'Don't go,' I keep saying inside my head. Then the bus arrives and she takes her bags from me and gets on and I stand there watching her but she won't look at me because she is thinking of Billy. The bus moves off and I watch until it disappears and then I go inside the flat and take off my clothes and have a bath. Later. I write down the things she said but the place still smells of her.

Blue, Blue Pictures of You

I used to like talking about sex. All of life, I imagined – from politics to aesthetics – merged in passionate human conjunctions. A caress, not to speak of a kiss, could transport you from longing to Russia, on to Velazquez and ahead to anarchism. To illustrate this fancy, I did, at one time, consider collecting a 'book of desire', an anthology of outlandish, melancholy and droll stories about the subject. This particular story was one, had the project been finished – or even started – I would have included. It was an odd story. Eshan, the photographer who told it to me, used the word himself. At least he said it was the oddest request he'd had. When it was put to him by his pub companion, his first response was embarrassment and perplexity. But of course he was fascinated too.

At the end of the street where Eshan had a tiny office and small dark room, there was a pub where he'd go at half past six or seven, most days. He liked to work office hours, believing much discipline was required to do what he did, as if without it he would fly off into madness – though he had, in fact, never flown anywhere near madness, except to sit in that pub.

Eshan thought he liked routine, and for weeks would do exactly the same thing every day, while frequently loathing this decline into habit. In the pub he would smoke, drink and read the paper for an hour or longer, depending on his mood and on whether he felt sentimental, guilty or plain affectionate towards his wife and two children. Sometimes he'd get home before the children were asleep, and carry them around on his back, kick balls with them, and tell them stories of pigs with spiders on their heads. Other times he would turn up late so he could have his wife make supper, and be free of the feeling that the kids were devouring his life.

Daily, there were many hapless people in that bar: somnolent junkies from the local rehab, the unemployed and unemployable, pinball pillocks. Eshan nodded at many of them, but if one sat at his table without asking, he could become truculent. Often, however, he would chat to people as he passed to and fro, being more grateful than he knew for distracting conversation. He had become, without meaning to, one of the bar's characters.

Eshan's passion was to photograph people who had produced something of significance, whose work had 'meaning'. These were philosophers, novelists, painters, film and theatre directors. He used only minimal props and hard, direct lighting. The idea wasn't to conceal but to expose. The spectator could relate the face to what the subject did. He called it the moment of truth in the features of people seeking the truth.

He photographed 'artists' but also considered himself, in private only, to be 'some sort' of an artist. To represent oneself – a changing being, alive with virtues and idiocies – was, for Eshan, the task that entailed the most honesty and fulfilment. But although his work had been published and exhibited, he still had to send out his portfolio with introductory letters, and harass people about his abilities. This was demeaning. By now he should, he reckoned, have got further. But he accepted his condition, imagining that overall he possessed most of what he required to live a simple but not complacent life. His wife illustrated children's books, and could earn decent money, so they got by. To earn a reasonable living himself, Eshan photographed new groups for the pop press – not that he was stimulated by these callow faces, though occasionally he was moved by their ugliness, the stupidity of their innocence, and their crass hopes. But they wanted only clichés.

A young man called Brian, who always wore pink shades,

started to join Eshan regularly. The pub was his first stop of the day after breakfast. He was vague about what he did, though it seemed to involve trying to manage bands and set up businesses around music. His main occupation was dealing drugs, and he liked supplying Eshan with different kinds of grass that he claimed would make him 'creative'. Eshan replied that he took drugs in the evenings to stop himself getting creative. When Eshan talked about surrealism, or the great photographers, Brian listened with innocent enthusiasm, as if these were things he could get interested in were he a different person. It turned out that he did know a little about the music that Eshan particularly liked, West Coast psychedelic music of the mid-sixties, and the films, writing and politics that accompanied it. Eshan talked of the dream of freedom, rebellion and irresponsibility it had represented, and how he wished he'd had the courage to go there and join in.

'You make it sound like the past few years in London,' Brian said. 'Except the music is faster.'

A couple of months after Eshan started seeing him in the pub, Brian parted from his casual girlfriends. He went out regularly – it was like a job; and he was the sort of man that women were attracted to in public places. There was hope; every night could take you somewhere new. But Brian was nearly thirty; for a long time he had been part of everything new, living not for the present but for the next thing. He was beginning to see how little it had left him, and he was afraid.

One day he met a girl who used to play the drums in a trip-hop group. Any subject – the economy, the comparative merits of Paris, Rome or Berlin – would return him to this woman. Every day he went to some trouble to buy her something, even if it was only a pencil. Other times it might be a first-edition Elizabeth David, an art deco lamp from Prague, a tape of Five Easy Pieces, a bootleg of Lennon singing 'On The Road to Rishikesh'. These things he would anxiously bring to the pub to ask Eshan's opinion of. Eshan wondered if Brian imagined that because he was a photographer he had taste and judgement, and, being married, had some knowledge of romance.

After a few drinks Eshan would go home and Brian would start phoning to make his plans for the night ahead. In what Eshan considered to be the middle of the night, Brian and Laura would go to a club, to someone's house, and then on to another club. Eshan learned that there were some places that only opened at nine on Sunday morning.

Lying in bed with his wife as they watched TV and read nineteenth-century novels while drinking camomile tea, Eshan found himself trying to picture what Brian and Laura were doing, what sort of good time they were having. He looked forward to hearing next day where they'd been, what drugs they'd taken, what they wore and how the conversation had gone. He was particularly curious about her reaction to each gift; he wanted to know whether she was demanding more and better gifts, or if she appreciated the merits of each one. And what, Eshan inquired with some concern, was Brian getting in return?

'Enough,' Brian inevitably replied.

'So she's good to you?'

Unusually, Brian replied that no lover had ever shown him what she had. Then he leaned forward, glanced left and right, and felt compelled to say, despite his loving loyalty, what this was. Her touch, her words, her sensual art, not to mention her murmurs, gasps, cries; and her fine wrists, long fingers and dark fine-haired bush that stood out like a punk's back-combed mohican – all were an incomparable rapture. Only the previous evening she had taken him by the shoulders and said –

'Yes?' Eshan asked.

'Your face, your hands, you, all of you, you . . .'

Eshan dried his palms on his trousers. Sighing inwardly, he listened, while signalling a detached approval. He encouraged Brian to repeat everything, like a much-loved story, and Brian was delighted to do so, until they were no longer sure of the facts.

Perhaps Eshan envied Brian his lover and their pleasure, and Brian was beginning to envy Eshan his stability. Whatever it was between them, Brian involved Eshan in his new love. It was, Eshan was pleased to see, agonising. Laura drew out Brian's best impulses; tenderness, kindness, generosity. He became more fervent as a dealer so as to take her to restaurants most nights; he borrowed money and took her to Budapest for a week.

But in love each moment is magnified, and every gesture, word and syllable is examined like a speech by the President. Solid expectation, unfurled hope, immeasurable disappointment – all are hurled together like a cocktail of random drugs that, quaffed within the hour, make both lovers reel. If she dressed up and went to a party with a male friend, he spent the night catatonic with paranoia; if he saw an old girlfriend, she assumed they would never speak again. And surely she was seeing someone else, someone better in every way? Did she feel about him as he did her? To love her was to fear losing her. Brian would have locked her in a bare room to have everything hold still a minute.

One day when Eshan went to the bar he returned to see that Brian had picked up a folder Eshan had left on the table, opened it, and was holding up the photographs. Brian could be impudent, which was his charm, and Eshan liked charm, because it was rare and good to watch as a talent. But it also exposed Brian as a man who was afraid; his charm was charged with the task of disarming people before they damaged him.

'Hey,' said Eshan.

Brian placed his finger on a picture of Doris Lessing. Laura was reading *The Golden Notebook*; could he buy it for her? Eshan said, yes, and he wouldn't charge. But Brian insisted. They agreed on a price and on a black frame. They drank more and wondered what Laura would think. A few days later Brian reported that though Laura would never finish the book – she never finished any book, the satisfaction was too diffuse – she had been delighted by the picture. Could she visit his studio?

'Studio? If only it was. But yes, bring her over – it's time we met.'

'Tomorrow, then.'

They were more than two hours late. Eshan had been meditating, which he did whenever he was tense or angry. You couldn't beat those Eastern religions for putting the wet blanket on desire. When he was turning out the lights and ready to leave, Brian and Laura arrived at the door with wine. Eshan put out his work for Laura. She looked closely at everything. They smoked the dope he had grown on his balcony from Brian's seeds, lay on the floor with the tops of their heads touching, and watched a Kenneth Anger film. Brian and Laura rang some people and said they were going out. Would he like to come? Eshan almost agreed. He said he would like to have joined them, but that he got up early to work. And the music, an electronic blizzard of squeaks, bleeps and beats, had nothing human in it.

'Yes, that's right,' Laura said. 'Nothing human there. A bunch of robots on drugs.'

'You don't mean that,' said Brian.

A few days after the visit Brian made the strange request.

'She enjoyed meeting you,' he was saying, as Eshan read his newspaper in the pub.

'And me her,' Eshan murmured without raising his eyes. 'Anyone would.'

It cheered Brian to hear her praised. 'She's pretty, eh?'

'No, beautiful.'

'Yes, that's it, you've got the right word.'

He picked up his phone. 'She wants to ask you a favour. Can she join us?'

'I've got to go.'

'Of course, you've got to put the kids to bed, but I think you'll find it an interesting favour.'

Laura arrived within fifteen minutes. She sat down at their table and began.

'What we want is for you to photograph us.'

Eshan nodded. Laura glanced at Brian. 'Naked. Or we could wear things. Rings through our belly buttons or something. But anyway – making love.' Eshan looked at her. 'You photograph us fucking,' she concluded. 'Do you see?'

Eshan didn't know what to say.

She asked, 'What about it?'

'I am not a pornographer.'

It must have sounded pompous. She gave him an amused look.

'I've seen your stuff, and we haven't the nerve for pornography. It isn't even beauty we want. And I know you don't go for that.'

'No. What is it?'

'You see, we go to bed and eat crackers and drink wine and caress one another and chatter all day. We've both been through terrible things in our lives, you see. Now we want to capture this summer moment – I mean we want you to capture it for us.'

'To look back on?'

She said, 'I suppose that is it. We all know love doesn't last.'

'Is that right?' said Eshan.

Brian added, 'It might be replaced by something else.'

'But this terrible passion and suspicion . . . and the intensity of it . . . will get domesticated.' She went on, 'I think that when one has an idea, even if it is a queer one, one should follow it through, don't you?'

Eshan supposed he agreed with this.

Laura kissed Brian and said to him, 'Eshan's up for it.'

'I'm not sure,' said Brian.

Eshan had picked up his things, said goodbye and reached the door, before he returned.

'Why me?'

She was looking up at him.

'Why? Brian has run into you with your children. You're a kind father, a normal man, and you will surely understand what we want.' Eshan looked at Brian, who had maintained a neutral expression. She said, 'But . . . if it's all too much, let's forget it.'

It was an idea they'd conceived frivolously. He would give her the chance to drop the whole thing. She should call in the morning.

He thought it over in bed. When Laura made the request, though excited, she hadn't seemed mad or over-ebullient. It was vanity, of course, but a touching, naive vanity, not a grand one; and he was, more than ever, all for naivety. Laura was, too, a woman anyone would want to look at.

An old upright piano and guitar; painted canvases leaning against the wall; club fliers, rolling papers, pills, a razor blade, beer bottles empty and full, standing on a chest of drawers. Leaning against this, a long mirror. The bed, its linen white, was in the centre of the room.

Laura pulled the curtains, and then half-opened them again.

'Will you have enough light?'

'I'll manage,' Eshan whispered.

Brian went to shave. Then, while Eshan unpacked his things, he plucked at the guitar with his mouth open, and drank beer. The three of them spoke in low voices and were solicitous of one another, as if they were about to do something dangerous but delicate, like planting a bomb.

A young man, covered in spots, wandered into the room.

'Get out now and go to bed,' Laura said. 'You've got chickenpox. Everyone here had it?' she asked.

They all laughed. It was better then. She put a chair against the door. They watched her arrange herself on the bed. Eshan photographed her back; he photographed her face. She took her clothes off. The breeze from the open window caressed her. She stretched out her fingers to Brian.

He walked over to her and they pressed their faces together. Eshan photographed that. She undressed him. Eshan shot his discomfort.

Soon they were taking up different positions, adjusting their heads, putting their hands here and there for each shot. Brian began to smile as if he fancied himself as a model.

'It's very sweet, but it ain't going to work,' Eshan told them. 'There's nothing there. It's dead.'

'He might be right,' Laura told Brian. 'We're going to have to pretend he's not here.'

Eshan said, 'I'll put film in the camera now, then.'

Eshan didn't go to bed but carried his things through the dark city back to his studio. He developed the material as quickly as he could and when it was done went home. His wife and children were having breakfast, laughing and arguing as usual. He walked in and his children kept asking him to take off his coat. He felt like a criminal, though the only laws he'd broken were his own, and he wasn't sure which ones they were.

Unusually he had the pictures with him and he went through them several times as he ate his toast, keeping them away from the children.

'Please, can I see?' His wife put her hand on his shoulder. 'Don't hide them. It's a long time since you've shown me your work. You live such a secret life.'

'Do I?'

'Sometimes I think you're not doing anything at all over there but just sitting.'

She looked at the photographs and then closed the folder.

'You stayed out all night without getting in touch. What have you been doing?'

'Taking pictures.'

'Don't talk to me like that. Who are these people, Eshan?'

'People I met in the pub. They asked me to photograph them.'

They went into the kitchen and she closed the door. She could be very disapproving, and she didn't like mysteries.

'And you did this?'

'You know I like to start somewhere and finish somewhere else. It wasn't an orgy.'

'Are you going to publish or sell them?'

'No. They paid me. And that's it.'

He got up.

'Where are you going?'

'Back to work.'

'If this the same kind of thing you'll be doing today?'

'Ha ha ha.'

He tried to resume his routine but couldn't work, or even listen to music or read the papers. He could only look at the pictures. They were not pornography, being too crude and unembellished for that. He had omitted nothing human. All the same, the images gave him a dry mouth, exciting and distressing him at the same time. He wouldn't be able to start anything else until the material was out of the studio.

He thought Brian would have gone back to his place, but wasn't certain. However, he couldn't persuade himself to ring first. He took a chance and walked all the way back there again. He was exhausted but was careful to cross the road where he crossed it before.

She came to the door in her dressing gown, and was surprised to see him. He said he'd brought the stuff round, and proffered the folder as evidence.

He went past her and up the stairs. She tugged her dressing gown around herself, as if he hadn't seen her body before. Upstairs they sat on the broken sofa. She was reluctant to look at the stuff, but knew she had to. She held up the contact sheets, turning them this way and that, repeatedly.

'Is that what you wanted?' he asked.

'I don't know.'

'Is that what you do on a good day?'

'I should thank you for the lovely job you've done. I don't know what I can do in return.' He looked at her. She said, 'How about a drum lesson?'

'Why not?'

She took him into a larger room, where he noticed some of Brian's gifts. Set before a big window, with a view of the street and the square, was her red spangled kit. She showed him how she played, and demonstrated how he could. Soon this bored her and she made lunch. As he ate she returned to the photographs, glanced through them without comment, and went back to the table. He wasn't certain that she wanted him there. But she didn't ask him to go away and seemed to assume that he had nothing better to do. He didn't know what else he would do anyway, as if something had come to an end.

They started to watch television, but suddenly she switched it off and stood up and sat down. She started agitatedly asking him questions about the people he knew, how many friends he had, what he liked about them, and what they said to one another. At first he answered abruptly, afraid of boring her. But she said she'd never had any guidance, and for the past few years, like everyone else, had only wanted a good time. Now she wanted to find something important to do, wanted a reason to get out of bed before four. He murmured that fucking might be a good excuse for staying in bed, just as the need to wash was an excuse for lying in the bath. She understood that, she said. She hardly knew anyone with a job; London was full of drugged, useless people who didn't listen to one another but merely thought all the time of how to distract themselves and never spoke of anything serious. She was tired of it; she was even tired of being in love; it had become another narcotic. Now she wanted interesting difficulty, not pleasure or even ease.

'And look, look at the pictures . . .'

'What do they say?'

'Too much, my friend.'

She hurried from the room. After a time she returned with a bucket which she set down on the carpet. She held the photographs over it and invited him to set fire to them.

'Are you sure?' he said.

'Oh yes.'

They singed the carpet and burned their fingers, and then they threw handfuls of ash out of the window and cheered.

'Are you going to the pub now?' she asked as he said goodbye.

'I don't think I'll be going there for a while.'

He told her that the next day he was going to photograph a painter who had also done record covers. He asked her to come along, 'to have a look'. She said she would.

Leaving the house he crossed the street. He could see her sitting in the window playing. When he walked away he could hear her all the way to the end of the road.

My Son the Fanatic

Surreptitiously the father began going into his son's bed-room. He would sit there for hours, rousing himself only to seek clues. What bewildered him was that Ali was getting tidier. Instead of the usual tangle of clothes, books, cricket bats, video games, the room was becoming neat and ordered; spaces began appearing where before there had been only mess.

Initially Parvez had been pleased: his son was outgrowing his teenage attitudes. But one day, beside the dustbin, Parvez found a torn bag which contained not only old toys, but computer discs, video tapes, new books and fashionable clothes the boy had bought just a few months before. Also without explanation, Ali had parted from the English girlfriend who used to come often to the house. His old friends had stopped ringing.

For reasons he didn't himself understand, Parvez wasn't able to bring up the subject of Ali's unusual behaviour. He was aware that he had become slightly afraid of his son, who, alongside his silences, was developing a sharp tongue. One remark Parvez did make, 'You don't play your guitar any more,' elicited the mysterious but conclusive reply, 'There are more important things to be done.'

Yet Parvez felt his son's eccentricity as an injustice. He had always been aware of the pitfalls which other men's sons had fallen into in England. And so, for Ali, he had worked long hours and spent a lot of money paying for his education as an accountant. He had bought him good suits, all the books he required and a computer. And now the boy was throwing his possessions out!

The TV, video and sound system followed the guitar. Soon

the room was practically bare. Even the unhappy walls bore marks where Ali's pictures had been removed.

Parvez couldn't sleep; he went more to the whisky bottle, even when he was at work. He realised it was imperative to discuss the matter with someone sympathetic.

Parvez had been a taxi driver for twenty years. Half that time he'd worked for the same firm. Like him, most of the other drivers were Punjabis. They preferred to work at night, the roads were clearer and the money better. They slept during the day, avoiding their wives. Together they led almost a boy's life in the cabbies' office, playing cards and practical jokes, exchanging lewd stories, eating together and discussing politics and their problems.

But Parvez had been unable to bring this subject up with his friends. He was too ashamed. And he was afraid, too, that they would blame him for the wrong turning his boy had taken, just as he had blamed other fathers whose sons had taken to running around with bad girls, truanting from school and joining gangs.

For years Parvez had boasted to the other men about how Ali excelled at cricket, swimming and football, and how attentive a scholar he was, getting straight 'A's in most subjects. Was it asking too much for Ali to get a good job now, marry the right girl and start a family? Once this happened, Parvez would be happy. His dreams of doing well in England would have come true. Where had he gone wrong?

But one night, sitting in the taxi office on busted chairs with his two closest friends watching a Sylvester Stallone film, he broke his silence.

'I can't understand it!' he burst out. 'Everything is going from his room. And I can't talk to him any more. We were not father and son – we were brothers! Where has he gone? Why is he torturing me!'

And Parvez put his head in his hands.

Even as he poured out his account the men shook their

heads and gave one another knowing glances. From their grave looks Parvez realised they understood the situation.

'Tell me what is happening!' he demanded.

The reply was almost triumphant. They had guessed something was going wrong. Now it was clear. Ali was taking drugs and selling his possessions to pay for them. That was why his bedroom was emptying.

'What must I do then?'

Parvez's friends instructed him to watch Ali scrupulously and then be severe with him, before the boy went mad, overdosed or murdered someone.

Parvez staggered out into the early morning air, terrified they were right. His boy – the drug addict killer!

To his relief he found Bettina sitting in his car.

Usually the last customers of the night were local 'brasses' or prostitutes. The taxi drivers knew them well, often driving them to liaisons. At the end of the girls' shifts, the men would ferry them home, though sometimes the women would join them for a drinking session in the office. Occasionally the drivers would go with the girls. 'A ride in exchange for a ride,' it was called.

Bettina had known Parvez for three years. She lived outside the town and on the long drive home, where she sat not in the passenger seat but beside him, Parvez had talked to her about his life and hopes, just as she talked about hers. They saw each other most nights.

He could talk to her about things he'd never be able to discuss with his own wife. Bettina, in turn, always reported on her night's activities. He liked to know where she was and with whom. Once he had rescued her from a violent client, and since then they had come to care for one another.

Though Bettina had never met the boy, she heard about Ali continually. That late night, when he told Bettina that he suspected Ali was on drugs, she judged neither the boy nor his father, but became businesslike and told him what to watch for.

'It's all in the eyes,' she said. They might be bloodshot; the pupils might be dilated; he might look tired. He could be liable to sweats, or sudden mood changes. 'Okay?'

Parvez began his vigil gratefully. Now he knew what the problem might be, he felt better. And surely, he figured, things couldn't have gone too far? With Bettina's help he would soon sort it out.

He watched each mouthful the boy took. He sat beside him at every opportunity and looked into his eyes. When he could he took the boy's hand, checking his temperature. If the boy wasn't at home Parvez was active, looking under the carpet, in his drawers, behind the empty wardrobe, sniffing, inspecting, probing. He knew what to look for: Bettina had drawn pictures of capsules, syringes, pills, powders, rocks.

Every night she waited to hear news of what he'd witnessed.

After a few days of constant observation, Parvez was able to report that although the boy had given up sports, he seemed healthy, with clear eyes. He didn't, as his father expected, flinch guiltily from his gaze. In fact the boy's mood was alert and steady in this sense: as well as being sullen, he was very watchful. He returned his father's long looks with more than a hint of criticism, of reproach even, so much so that Parvez began to feel that it was he who was in the wrong, and not the boy!

'And there's nothing else physically different?' Bettina asked.

'No!' Parvez thought for a moment. 'But he is growing a beard.'

One night, after sitting with Bettina in an all-night coffee shop, Parvez came home particularly late. Reluctantly he and Bettina had abandoned their only explanation, the drug theory, for Parvez had found nothing resembling any drug in Ali's room. Besides, Ali wasn't selling his belongings. He threw them out, gave them away or donated them to charity shops.

Standing in the hall, Parvez heard his boy's alarm clock go off. Parvez hurried into his bedroom where his wife was still awake, sewing in bed. He ordered her to sit down and keep quiet, though she had neither stood up nor said a word. From this post, and with her watching him curiously, he observed his son through the crack in the door.

The boy went into the bathroom to wash. When he returned to his room Parvez sprang across the hall and set his ear at Ali's door. A muttering sound came from within. Parvez was puzzled but relieved.

Once this clue had been established, Parvez watched him at other times. The boy was praying. Without fail, when he was at home, he prayed five times a day.

Parvez had grown up in Lahore where all the boys had been taught the Koran. To stop him falling asleep when he studied, the Moulvi had attached a piece of string to the ceiling and tied it to Parvez's hair, so that if his head fell forward, he would instantly awake. After this indignity Parvez had avoided all religions. Not that the other taxi drivers had more respect. In fact they made jokes about the local mullahs walking around with their caps and beards, thinking they could tell people how to live, while their eyes roved over the boys and girls in their care.

Parvez described to Bettina what he had discovered. He informed the men in the taxi office. The friends, who had been so curious before, now became oddly silent. They could hardly condemn the boy for his devotions.

Parvez decided to take a night off and go out with the boy. They could talk things over. He wanted to hear how things were going at college; he wanted to tell him stories about their family in Pakistan. More than anything he yearned to understand how Ali had discovered the 'spiritual dimension', as Bettina described it.

To Parvez's surprise, the boy refused to accompany him. He claimed he had an appointment. Parvez had to insist that no appointment could be more important than that of a son with his father.

The next day, Parvez went immediately to the street where Bettina stood in the rain wearing high heels, a short skirt and a long mac on top, which she would open hopefully at passing cars.

'Get in, get in!' he said.

They drove out across the moors and parked at the spot where on better days, with a view unimpeded for many miles by nothing but wild deer and horses, they'd lie back, with their eyes half closed, saying 'This is the life.' This time Parvez was trembling. Bettina put her arms around him.

'What's happened?'

'I've just had the worst experience of my life.'

As Bettina rubbed his head Parvez told her that the previous evening he and Ali had gone to a restaurant. As they studied the menu, the waiter, whom Parvez knew, brought him his usual whisky and water. Parvez had been so nervous he had even prepared a question. He was going to ask Ali if he was worried about his imminent exams. But first, wanting to relax, he loosened his tie, crunched a popadom and took a long drink.

Before Parvez could speak, Ali made a face.

'Don't you know it's wrong to drink alcohol?' he said.

'He spoke to me very harshly,' Parvez told Bettina. 'I was about to castigate the boy for being insolent, but managed to control myself.'

He had explained patiently to Ali that for years he had worked more than ten hours a day, that he had few enjoyments or hobbies and never went on holiday. Surely it wasn't a crime to have a drink when he wanted one?

'But it is forbidden,' the boy said.

Parvez shrugged, 'I know.'

'And so is gambling, isn't it?'

'Yes. But surely we are only human?'

Each time Parvez took a drink, the boy winced, or made a

fastidious face as an accompaniment. This made Parvez drink more quickly. The waiter, wanting to please his friend, brought another glass of whisky. Parvez knew he was getting drunk, but he couldn't stop himself. Ali had a horrible look on his face, full of disgust and censure. It was as if he hated his father.

Halfway through the meal Parvez suddenly lost his temper and threw a plate on the floor. He had felt like ripping the cloth from the table, but the waiters and other customers were staring at him. Yet he wouldn't stand for his own son telling him the difference between right and wrong. He knew he wasn't a bad man. He had a conscience. There were a few things of which he was ashamed, but on the whole he had lived a decent life.

'When have I had time to be wicked?' he asked Ali.

In a low monotonous voice the boy explained that Parvez had not, in fact, lived a good life. He had broken countless rules of the Koran.

'For instance?' Parvez demanded.

Ali hadn't needed time to think. As if he had been waiting for this moment, he asked his father if he didn't relish pork pies?

'Well . . . '

Parvez couldn't deny that he loved crispy bacon smothered with mushrooms and mustard and sandwiched between slices of fried bread. In fact he ate this for breakfast every morning.

Ali then reminded Parvez that he had ordered his own wife to cook pork sausages, saying to her, 'You're not in the village now, this is England. We have to fit in!'

Parvez was so annoyed and perplexed by this attack that he called for more drink.

'The problem is this,' the boy said. He leaned across the table. For the first time that night his eyes were alive. 'You are too implicated in Western civilisation.'

Parvez burped; he thought he was going to choke.

'Implicated!' he said. 'But we live here!'

'The Western materialists hate us,' Ali said. 'Papa, how can you love something which hates you?'

'What is the answer then?' Parvez said miserably. 'According to you.'

Ali addressed his father fluently, as if Parvez were a rowdy crowd that had to be quelled and convinced. The Law of Islam would rule the world; the skin of the infidel would burn off again and again; the Jews and Christers would be routed. The West was a sink of hypocrites, adulterers, homosexuals, drug takers and prostitutes.

As Ali talked, Parvez looked out of the window as if to check that they were still in London.

'My people have taken enough. If the persecution doesn't stop there will be *jihad*. I, and millions of others, will gladly give our lives for the cause.'

'But why, why?' Parvez said.

'For us the reward will be in paradise.'

'Paradise!'

Finally, as Parvez's eyes filled with tears, the boy urged him to mend his ways.

'How is that possible?' Parvez asked.

'Pray,' Ali said. 'Pray beside me.'

Parvez called for the bill and ushered his boy out of the restaurant as soon as he was able. He couldn't take any more. Ali sounded as if he'd swallowed someone else's voice.

On the way home the boy sat in the back of the taxi, as if he were a customer.

'What has made you like this?' Parvez asked him, afraid that somehow he was to blame for all this. 'Is there a particular event which has influenced you?'

'Living in this country.'

'But I love England,' Parvez said, watching his boy in the mirror. 'They let you do almost anything here.'

'That is the problem,' he replied.

For the first time in years Parvez couldn't see straight. He knocked the side of the car against a lorry, ripping off the wing mirror. They were lucky not to have been stopped by the police: Parvez would have lost his licence and therefore his job.

Getting out of the car back at the house, Parvez stumbled and fell in the road, scraping his hands and ripping his trousers. He managed to haul himself up. The boy didn't even offer him his hand.

Parvez told Bettina he was now willing to pray, if that was what the boy wanted, if that would dislodge the pitiless look from his eyes.

'But what I object to,' he said, 'is being told by my own son that I am going to hell!'

What finished Parvez off was that the boy had said he was giving up accountancy. When Parvez had asked why, Ali had said sarcastically that it was obvious.

'Western education cultivates an anti-religious attitude.'

And, according to Ali, in the world of accountants it was usual to meet women, drink alcohol and practise usury.

'But it's well-paid work,' Parvez argued. 'For years you've been preparing!'

Ali said he was going to begin to work in prisons, with poor Muslims who were struggling to maintain their purity in the face of corruption. Finally, at the end of the evening, as Ali was going to bed, he had asked his father why he didn't have a beard, or at least a moustache.

'I feel as if I've lost my son,' Parvez told Bettina. 'I can't bear to be looked at as if I'm a criminal. I've decided what to do.'

'What is it?'

'I'm going to tell him to pick up his prayer mat and get out of my house. It will be the hardest thing I've ever done, but tonight I'm going to do it.'

'But you mustn't give up on him,' said Bettina. 'Many young people fall into cults and superstitious groups. It doesn't mean they'll always feel the same way.'

She said Parvez had to stick by his boy, giving him support, until he came through.

Parvez was persuaded that she was right, even though he didn't feel like giving his son more love when he had hardly been thanked for all he had already given.

Nevertheless, Parvez tried to endure his son's looks and reproaches. He attempted to make conversation about his beliefs. But if Parvez ventured any criticism, Ali always had a brusque reply. On one occasion Ali accused Parvez of 'grovelling' to the whites; in contrast, he explained, he was not 'inferior'; there was more to the world than the West, though the West always thought it was best.

'How is it you know that?' Parvez said, 'seeing as you've never left England?'

Ali replied with a look of contempt.

One night, having ensured there was no alcohol on his breath, Parvez sat down at the kitchen table with Ali. He hoped Ali would compliment him on the beard he was growing but Ali didn't appear to notice.

The previous day Parvez had been telling Bettina that he thought people in the West sometimes felt inwardly empty and that people needed a philosophy to live by.

'Yes,' said Bettina. 'That's the answer. You must tell him what your philosophy of life is. Then he will understand that there are other beliefs.'

After some fatiguing consideration, Parvez was ready to begin. The boy watched him as if he expected nothing.

Haltingly Parvez said that people had to treat one another with respect, particularly children their parents. This did seem, for a moment, to affect the boy. Heartened, Parvez continued. In his view this life was all there was and when you died you rotted in the earth. 'Grass and flowers will grow out of me, but something of me will live on –'

'How?'

'In other people. I will continue – in you.' At this the boy appeared a little distressed. 'And your grandchildren,' Parvez added for good measure. 'But while I am here on earth I want to make the best of it. And I want you to, as well!'

'What d'you mean by "make the best of it"?' asked the boy.

'Well,' said Parvez. 'For a start . . . you should enjoy yourself. Yes. Enjoy yourself without hurting others.'

Ali said that enjoyment was a 'bottomless pit'.

'But I don't mean enjoyment like that!' said Parvez. 'I mean the beauty of living!'

'All over the world our people are oppressed,' was the boy's reply.

'I know,' Parvez replied, not entirely sure who 'our people' were, 'but still – life is for living!'

Ali said, 'Real morality has existed for hundreds of years. Around the world millions and millions of people share my beliefs. Are you saying you are right and they are all wrong?'

Ali looked at his father with such aggressive confidence that Parvez could say no more.

One evening Bettina was sitting in Parvez's car, after visiting a client, when they passed a boy on the street.

'That's my son,' Parvez said suddenly. They were on the other side of town, in a poor district, where there were two mosques.

Parvez set his face hard.

Bettina turned to watch him. 'Slow down then, slow down!' She said, 'He's good-looking. Reminds me of you. But with a more determined face. Please, can't we stop?'

'What for?'

'I'd like to talk to him.'

Parvez turned the cab round and stopped beside the boy.

'Coming home?' Parvez asked. 'It's quite a way.'

The sullen boy shrugged and got into the back seat. Bettina sat in the front. Parvez became aware of Bettina's short skirt, gaudy rings and ice-blue eyeshadow. He became conscious that the smell of her perfume, which he loved, filled the cab. He opened the window.

While Parvez drove as fast as he could, Bettina said gently to Ali, 'Where have you been?'

'The mosque,' he said.

'And how are you getting on at college? Are you working hard?'

'Who are you to ask me these questions?' he said, looking out of the window. Then they hit bad traffic and the car came to a standstill.

By now Bettina had inadvertently laid her hand on Parvez's shoulder. She said, 'Your father, who is a good man, is very worried about you. You know he loves you more than his own life.'

'You say he loves me,' the boy said.

'Yes!' said Bettina.

'Then why is he letting a woman like you touch him like that?'

If Bettina looked at the boy in anger, he looked back at her with twice as much cold fury.

She said, 'What kind of woman am I that deserves to be spoken to like that?'

'You know,' he said. 'Now let me out.'

'Never,' Parvez replied.

'Don't worry, I'm getting out,' Bettina said.

'No, don't!' said Parvez. But even as the car moved she opened the door, threw herself out and ran away across the road. Parvez shouted after her several times, but she had gone.

Parvez took Ali back to the house, saying nothing more to him. Ali went straight to his room. Parvez was unable to read the paper, watch television or even sit down. He kept pouring himself drinks.

At last he went upstairs and paced up and down outside Ali's room. When, finally, he opened the door, Ali was praying. The boy didn't even glance his way.

Parvez kicked him over. Then he dragged the boy up by his shirt and hit him. The boy fell back. Parvez hit him again. The boy's face was bloody. Parvez was panting. He knew that the boy was unreachable, but he struck him nonetheless. The boy neither covered himself nor retaliated; there was no fear in his eyes. He only said, through his split lip: 'So who's the fanatic now?'

The Tale of the Turd

I'm at this dinner. She's eighteen. After knowing her six months I've been invited to meet her parents. I am, to my surprise, forty-four, same age as her dad, a professor – a man of some achievement, but not that much. He is looking at me or, as I imagine, looking me over. The girl-woman will always be his daughter, but for now she is my lover.

Her two younger sisters are at the table, also beautiful, but with a tendency to giggle, particularly when facing in my direction. The mother, a teacher, is putting a soft pink trout on the table. I think, for once, yes, this is the life, what they call a happy family, they've asked to meet me, why not settle down and enjoy it?

But what happens, the moment I'm comfortable I've got to have a crap. In all things I'm irregular. It's been two days now and not a dry pellet. And the moment I sit down in my better clothes with the family I've got to go.

These are good people but they're a little severe. I am accompanied by disadvantages – my age, no job, never had one, and my . . . tendencies. I like to say, though I won't tonight – unless things get out of hand – that my profession is failure. After years of practice, I'm quite a success at it.

On the way here I stopped off for a couple of drinks, otherwise I'd never have come through the door, and now I'm sipping wine and discussing the latest films not too facetiously and my hands aren't shaking and my little girl is down the table smiling at me warm and encouraging. Everything is normal, you see, except for this gut ache, which is getting worse, you know how it is when you've got to go. But I won't get upset, I'll have a crap, feel better and then eat.

I ask one of the sisters where the bathroom is and kindly she points at a door. It must be the nearest, thank Christ, and I get across the room stooping a little but no way the family's gonna see me as a hunchback.

I sit down concerned they're gonna hear every splash but it's too late: the knotty little head is already pushing out, a flower coming through the earth, but thick and long and I'm not even straining, I can feel its soft motion through my gut, in one piece. It's been awaiting its moment the way things do, like love. I close my eyes and appreciate the relief as the corpse of days past slides into its watery grave.

When I'm finished I can't resist glancing down – even the Queen does this – and the turd is complete, wide as an aubergine and purplish too. It's flecked with carrot, I notice, taking a closer look, but, ah, probably that's tomato, I remember now, practically the only thing I've eaten in twenty-four hours.

I flush the toilet and check my look. Tired and greying I am now, with a cut above my eye and a bruise on my cheek, but I've shaved and feel as okay as I ever will, still with the boyish smile that says I can't harm you. And waiting is the girl who loves me, the last of many, I hope, who sends me vibrations of confidence.

My hand is on the door when I glance down and see the prow of the turd turning the bend. Oh no, it's floating in the pan again and I'm bending over for a better look. It's one of the biggest turds I've ever seen. The flushing downpour has rinsed it and there is no doubt that as turds go it is exquisite, flecked and inlaid like a mosaic depicting, perhaps, a historical scene. I can make out large figures going at one another in argument. The faces I'm sure I've seen before. I can see some words but I haven't got my glasses to hand.

I could have photographed the turd, had I brought a camera, had I ever owned one. But now I can't hang around, the trout must be cooling and they're too polite to start eating without me. The problem is, the turd is bobbing.

I'm waiting for the cistern to refill and every drip is an eternity, I can feel the moments stretching out, and outside I can hear the murmuring voices of my love's family but I can't leave that submarine there for the mother to go in and see it wobbling about. She knows I've been in the clinic and can see I'm drinking again; I've been watching my consumption, as they say, but I can't stop and she's gonna take her daughter to one side and . . .

I've been injecting my little girl. 'What a lovely way to take drugs,' she says sweetly. She wants to try everything. I don't argue with that and I won't patronise her. Anyhow, she's a determined little blonde thing, and for her friends it's fashionably exciting. I can tell she's made up her mind to become an addict.

It took me days to hunt out the best stuff for her, pharmaceutical. It's been five years for me, but I took it with her to ensure she didn't make a mistake. Except an ex-boyfriend caught up with us, took me into a doorway and split my face for corrupting her. Yet she skips school to be with me and we take in Kensington Market and Chelsea. I explain their history of fashion and music. The records I tell her to listen to, the books I hold out, the bands I've played with, the creative people I tell her of, the deep talks we have, are worth as much as anything she hears at school, I know that.

At last I flush it again.

Girls like her . . . it is easy to speak of exploitation, and people do. But it is time and encouragement I give them. I know from experience, oh yes, how critical and diminishing parents can be, and I say try, I say yes, attempt anything. And I, in my turn, am someone for them to care for. It breaks my heart but I've got, maybe, two years with her before she sees I can't be helped and she will pass beyond me into attractive worlds I cannot enter.

I pray only that she isn't pulling up her sleeve and stroking her tracks, imagining her friends being impressed by those mascots, the self-inflicted scars of experience; those girls are dedicated to the truth, and like to show their parents how defiant they can be.

I'm reaching for the door, the water is clear and I imagine the turd swimming towards Ramsgate. But no, no, no, don't look down, what's that, the brown bomber must have an aversion to the open sea. The monstrous turd is going nowhere and nor am I while it remains an eternal recurrence. I flush it again and wait but it won't leave its port and what am I going to do, this must be an existential moment and all my days have converged here. I'm trembling and running with sweat but not yet lost.

I'm rolling up the sleeve of my Italian suit, it's an old suit, but it's my best jacket. I don't have a lot of clothes, I wear what people give me, what I find in the places I end up in, and what I steal.

I'm crying inside too, you know, but what can I do but stick my hand down the pan, into the pissy water, that's right, oh dark, dark, dark, and fish around until my fingers sink into the turd, get a muddy grip and yank it from the water. For a moment it seems to come alive, wriggling like a fish.

My instinct is to calm it down, and I look around the bathroom for a place to bash it, but not if it's going to splatter everywhere, I wouldn't want them imagining I'm on some sort of dirty protest.

By now they must have started eating. And what am I doing but standing here with a giant turd in my fist? Not only that, my fingers seem to adhere to the turd; bits of my flesh are pulled away and my hand is turning brown. I must have eaten something unusual, because my nails and the palms are turning the colour of gravy.

My love's radiant eyes, her loving softness. But in all ways she is a demanding girl. She insists on trying other drugs, and in the afternoons we play like children, dressing up and inventing characters, until my compass no longer points to reality. I am her assistant as she tests the limits of the world. How far out can she go and still be home in time for tea? I have to try and keep up, for she is my comfort. With her I am living my life again, but too quickly and all at once.

And in the end, to get clear, to live her life, she will leave me; or, to give her a chance, I must leave her. I dream, though, of marriage and of putting the children to bed. But I am told it is already too late for all that. How soon things become too late, and before one has acclimatised!

I glance at the turd and notice little teeth in its velvet head, and a little mouth opening. It's smiling at me, oh no, it's smiling and what's that, it's winking, yes, the piece of shit is winking up at me, and what's that at the other end, a sort of tail, it's moving, yes, it's moving, and oh Jesus, it's trying to say something, to speak, no, no, I think it wants to sing. Even though it is somewhere stated that truth may be found anywhere, and the universe of dirt may send strange messengers to speak to us, the last thing I want, right now in my life, is a singing turd.

I want to smash the turd back down into the water and hold it under and run out of there, but the mother – when the mother comes in and I'm scoffing the trout and she's taking down her drawers I'm gonna worry that the turd lurking around the bend's gonna flip up like a piranha and attach itself to her cunt, maybe after singing a sarcastic ditty, and she's going to have an impression of me that I don't want.

But I won't dwell on that, I'm going to think constructively where possible even though its bright little eyes are glinting and the mouth is moving and it has developed scales under which ooze – don't think about it. And what's that, little wings . . .

I grab the toilet roll and rip off about a mile of paper and start wrapping it around the turd, around and around, so those eyes are never gonna look at me again, and smile in that way. But even in its paper shroud it's warm and getting warmer, warm as life, and practically throbbing and giving off odours. I look desperately around the room for somewhere to stuff it, a pipe or behind a book, but it's gonna reek, I know that, and if it's gonna start moving, it could end up anywhere in the house.

There's a knocking on the door. A voice too – my love. I'm about to reply 'Oh love, love' when I hear other, less affectionate raised voices. An argument is taking place. Someone is turning the handle; another person is kicking at the door. Almost on me, they're trying to smash it in!

I will chuck it out of the window! I rest the turd on the sill and drag up the casement with both hands. But suddenly I am halted by the sky. As a boy I'd lie on my back watching clouds; as a teenager I swore that in a less hectic future I would contemplate the sky until its beauty passed into my soul, like the soothing pictures I've wanted to study, bathing in the colours and textures of paint, the cities I've wanted to walk, loafing, the aimless conversations I've wanted to have – one day, a constructive aimlessness.

Now the wind is in my face, lifting me, and I am about to fall. But I hang on and instead throw the turd, like a warm pigeon, out out into the air, turd-bird awayaway.

I wash my hands in the sink, flush the toilet once more, and turn back to life. On, on, one goes, despite everything, not knowing why or how.

Nightlight

'There must always be two to a kiss.'
R. L. Stevenson, 'An Apology for Idlers'

She comes to him late on Wednesdays, only for sex, the cab waiting outside. Four months ago someone recommended her to him for a job but he has no work she can do. He doesn't even pay himself now. They talk of nothing much, and there are silences in which they can only look at one another. But neither wants to withdraw and something must be moving between them, for they stand up together and lie down beside the table, without speaking.

Same time next week she is at the door. They undress immediately. She leaves, not having slept, but he has felt her dozing before she determinedly shakes herself awake. She collects herself quickly without apology, and goes without looking back. He has no idea where she lives or where she is from.

Now she doesn't come into the house, but goes straight down into the basement he can't afford to furnish, where he has thrown blankets and duvets on the carpet. They neither drink nor play music and can barely see one another. It's a mime show in this room where everything but clarity, it seems, is permitted.

At work his debts increase. What he has left could be taken away, and no one but him knows it. He is losing his hold and does it matter? Why should it, except that it is probably terminal; if one day he feels differently, there'll be no way back.

For most of his life, particularly at school, he's been successful, or en route to somewhere called Success. Like most people he has been afraid of being found out, but unlike most he probably has been. He has a small flat, an old car and a shabby feeling. These are minor losses. He misses steady quotidian progress, the sense that his well-being, if not happiness, is increasing, and that each day leads to a recognisable future. He has never anticipated this extent of random desolation.

Three days a week he picks up his kids from school, feeds them, and returns them to the house into which he put most of his money, and which his wife now forbids him to enter. Fridays he has dinner with his only male friend. After, they go to a black bar where he likes the music. The men, mostly in their thirties, and whose lives are a mystery to him, seem to sit night after night without visible discontent, looking at women and at one another. He envies this, and wonders if their lives are without anxiety, whether they have attained a stoic resignation, or if it is a profound uselessness they are stewing in.

On this woman's day he bathes for an hour. He can't recall her name, and she never says his. She calls him, when necessary, 'man'. Soon she will arrive. He lies there thinking how lucky he is to have one arrangement which costs nothing.

Five years ago he left the wife he didn't know why he married for another woman, who then left him without explanation. There have been others since. But when they come close he can only move backwards, without comprehending why.

His wife won't speak. If she picks up the phone and hears his voice, she calls for the kids, those intermediaries growing up between immovable hatreds. A successful woman, last year she found she could not leave her bed at all. She will have no help and the children have to minister to her. They are inclined to believe that he has caused this. He begins to think he can make women insane, even as he understands that this flatters him.

Now he has this inexplicable liaison. At first they run tearing at one another with middle-aged recklessness and then lie silently in the dark, until desire, all they have, rekindles. He tells himself to make the most of the opportunity.

When she's gone he masturbates, contemplating what they did, imprinting it on his mind for ready reference: she on her stomach, him on the boat of her back, his face in her black hair forever. He thinks of the fluffy black hairs, flattened with sweat, like a toff's parting, around her arsehole.

Walking about later he is both satisfied and unfulfilled, disliking himself for not knowing why he is doing this – balked by the puzzle of his own mind and the impossibility of grasping why one behaves so oddly, and why one ends up resenting people for not providing what one hasn't been able to ask for. Surely this new thing is a web of illusion, and he is a fool? But he wants more foolishness, and not only on Wednesdays.

The following weeks she seems to sense something. In the space where they lie beneath the level of the street, almost underground – a mouse's view of the world – she invites him to lie in different positions; she bids him touch different parts of her body. She shows him they can pore over one another.

Something intriguing is happening in this room, week after week. He can't know what it might be. He isn't certain she will turn up; he doesn't trust her, or any woman, not to let him down. Each week she surprises him, until he wonders what might make her stop.

One Wednesday the cab doesn't draw up. He stands at the window in his dressing gown and slippers for three hours, feeling in the first hour like Casanova, in the second like a child awaiting its mother, and during the third like an old man. Is she sick, or with her husband? He lies on the floor where she usually lies, in a fever of desire and longing, until, later, he feels a presence in the room, a hanging column of air, and sits up and cries out at this ghost.

He assumes he is toxic. For him, lacking disadvantages has been a crime in itself. He grasps the historical reasons for this, since his wife pointed them out. Not that this prevented her living off him. For a while he did try to be the sort of man she might countenance. He wept at every opportunity, and communicated with animals wherever he found them. He tried not to raise his voice, though for her it was 'liberating' to get wild. Soon he didn't know who he was supposed to be. They both got lost. He dreaded going home. He kept his mouth shut, for fear of what would come out; this made her search angrily for a way in.

Now he worries that something has happened to this new woman and he has no way of knowing. What wound or hopelessness has made her want only this?

Next week she does come, standing in the doorway, coat-wrapped, smiling, in her early thirties, about fifteen years younger than him. She might have a lover or husband; might be unemployed; might be disillusioned with love, or getting married next week. But she is tender. How he has missed what they do together.

The following morning he goes downstairs and smells her on the sheets. The day is suffused with her, whoever she is. He finds himself thinking constantly of her, pondering the peculiar mixture of ignorance and intimacy they have. If sex is how you meet and get to know people, what does he know of her? On her body he can paint only imaginary figures, as in the early days of love, when any dreams and desires can be flung onto the subject, until reality upsets and rearranges them. Not knowing, surely, is beautiful, as if everything one learns detracts from the pleasures of pure imagination. Fancy could provide them with more satisfaction than reality.

But she is beginning to make him wonder, and when one night he touches her and feels he has never loved anything so much – if love is loss of the self in the other then, yes, he loves her – he begins to want confirmation of the notions which pile up day after day without making any helpful shape. And, after so many years of living, the expensive education, the languages he imagined would be useful, the books and newspapers studied, can he be capable of love only with a silent stranger in a darkened room? But he dismisses the idea of speaking, because he can't take any more disappointment. Nothing must disturb their perfect evenings.

You want sex and a good time, and you get it; but it usually comes with a free gift – someone like you, a person. Their arrangement seems an advance, what many people want, the best without the worst, and no demands – particularly when he thinks, as he does constantly, of the spirit he and his wife wasted in dislike and sniping, and the years of taking legal and financial revenge. He thinks often of the night he left.

He comes in late, having just left the bed of the woman he is seeing, who has said she is his. The solid bulk of his wife, her back turned, is unmoving. His last night. In the morning he'll talk to the kids and go, as so many men he knows have done, people who'd thought that leaving home was something you did only once. Most of his friends, most of the people he knows, are on the move from wife to wife, husband to husband, lover to lover. A city of love vampires, turning from person to person, hunting the one who will make the difference.

He puts on the light in the hall, undresses and is about to lie down when he notices that she is now lying on her back and her eyes are open. Strangely she looks less pale. He realises she is wearing eyeshadow and lipstick. Now she reaches out to him, smiling. He moves away; something is wrong. She throws back the covers and she is wearing black and red underwear. She has never, he is certain, dressed like this before.

'It's too late,' he wants to cry.

He picks up his clothes, rushes to the door and closes it behind him. He doesn't know what he is doing, only that he has to get out. The hardest part is going into the children's room, finding their faces in the mess of blankets and toys, and kissing them goodbye.

This must have turned his mind, for, convinced that people have to take something with them, he hurries into his study and attempts to pick up his computer. There are wires; he cannot disconnect it. He gathers up the television from the shelf. He's carrying this downstairs when he turns and sees his wife, still in her tart garb, with a dressing gown on top, screaming, 'Where are you going? Where? Where?'

He shouts, 'You've had ten years of me, ten years and no more, no more!'

He slips on the step and falls forward, doubling up over the TV and tripping down the remaining stairs. Without stopping to consider his injuries, he flees the house without affection or dislike and doesn't look back, thinking only, strange, one never knows every corner of the houses one lives in as an adult, not as one knew one's childhood house. He leaves the TV in the front garden.

The woman he sees now helps kill the terrible fear he constantly bears that his romantic self has been crushed. He feels dangerous but wants to wake up in love. Soft, soft; he dreams of opening a door and the person he will love is standing behind it.

This longing can seize him at parties, in restaurants, at friends' and in the street. He sits opposite a woman in the train. With her the past will be redeemed. He follows her. She crosses the street. So does he. She is going to panic. He grabs her arm and shouts, 'No, no, I'm not like that!' and runs away.

He doesn't know how to reach others, but disliking them is exhausting. Now he doesn't want to go out, since who is there to hold onto? But in the house his mind devours itself; he is a cannibal of his own consciousness. He is starving for want of love. The shame of loneliness, a dingy affliction! There are few creatures more despised than middle-aged men with strong desires, and desire renews itself each day, returning like a recurring illness, crying out, more life, more!

At night he sits in the attic looking through a box of old letters from women. There is an abundance of pastoral description. The women sit in cafés drinking good coffee; they eat peaches on the patio; they look at snow. Everyday sensations are raised to the sublime. He wants to be scornful. It is easy to imagine 'buzzes' and 'charges' as the sole satisfactions. But what gratifies him? It is as if the gears of his life have become disengaged from the mechanisms that drove him forward. When he looks at what other people yearn for, he can't grasp why they don't know it isn't worth wanting. He asks to be returned to the ordinary with new eyes. He wants to play a child's game: make a list of what you noticed today, adding desires, regrets and content-ments, if any, to the list, so that your life doesn't pass without your having noticed it. And he requires the extraordinary, on Wednesdays.

He lies on his side in her, their mouths are open, her legs holding him. When necessary they move to maintain the level of warm luxury. He can only gauge her mood by the manner of her love-making. Sometimes she merely grabs him; or she lies down, offering her neck and throat to be kissed.

He opens his eyes to see her watching him. It has been a long time since anyone has looked at him with such attention. His hope is boosted by a new feeling: curiosity. He thinks of taking their sexuality into the world. He wants to watch others looking at her, to have others see them together, as confirmation. There is so much love he almost attempts conversation.

For several weeks he determines to speak during their

love-making, each time telling himself that on this occasion the words will come out. 'We should talk,' is the sentence he prepares, which becomes abbreviated to 'Want to talk?' and even 'Talk?'

However his not speaking has clearly gladdened this woman. Who else could he cheer up in this way? Won't clarity wreck their understanding, and don't they have an alternative vocabulary of caresses? Words come out bent, but who can bend a kiss? If only he didn't have to imagine continually that he has to take some action, think that something should happen, as if friendships, like trains, have to go somewhere.

He has begun to think that what goes on in this room is his only hope. Having forgotten what he likes about the world, and thinking of existence as drudgery, she reminds him, finger by finger, of the worthwhile. All his life, it seems, he's been seeking sex. He isn't certain why, but he must have gathered that it was an important thing to want. And now he has it, it doesn't seem sufficient. But what does that matter? As long as there is desire there is a pulse; you are alive; to want is to reach beyond yourself, into the world, finger by finger.

Lately

After Chekhov's story 'The Duel'

1

At eight, those who'd stayed up all night, and those who'd just risen, would gather on the beach for a swim. It had been a warm spring and was now a blazing, humid summer, the hottest of recent times, it was said. The sea was deliciously tepid.

When Rocco, a thin dark-haired man of about thirty, strolled down to the sea in his carpet slippers and cut-off Levi's, he met several people he knew, including Bodger, a local GP who struck most people, at first, as being unpleasant.

Stout, with a large close-cropped head, big nose, no neck and a loud voice, Bodger didn't appear to be an advertisement for medicine. But after they had met him, people began to think of his face as kind and amiable, even charming. He would greet everyone and discuss their medical and even psychological complaints in the pub or on the street. It was said that people took him their symptoms to give him the pleasure of attempting to cure them. The barbecues he held, at unusual and splendid locations, were famous. But he was ashamed of his own kindness, since it led him into difficulties. He liked to be curt.

'I've got a question for you,' said Rocco, as they made their way across the mud flats. 'Suppose you fell in love. You lived with the woman for a couple of years and then – as happens – stopped loving her, and felt your curiosity was exhausted. What would you do?'

'Get out, I'd say, and move on.'

'Suppose she was on her own and had nowhere to go, and had no job or money?'

'I'd give her the money.'

'You've got it, have you?'

'Sorry?'

'Remember, this is an intelligent woman we're talking about.'

'Which intelligent woman?' Bodger enquired, although he had already guessed.

Bodger swam vigorously according to his routine; Rocco stood in the waves and then floated on his back.

They dressed at the base of the cliffs, Bodger shaking sand from his shoes. Rocco picked up the papers he'd brought with him, an old copy of the *New York Review of Books* and the *Racing Post*.

'It's a nightmare living with someone you don't love, but I wouldn't worry about it,' advised the doctor, in his 'minor ailments' voice. 'Suppose you move on to another woman and find she's the same? Then you'll feel worse.'

They went to a vegetarian café nearby, where they were regulars. The owner always brought Bodger his own mug and a glass of iced water. Bodger enjoyed his toast, honey and coffee. The swimming gave him an appetite.

Unfortunately, Rocco craved almond croissants, which he'd once had in a café in London; every morning he'd raise his hand and ask the manager to bring him some. Of course, in their town they'd never seen such things, and each request annoyed the manager more. Bodger could see that one day Rocco would get a kick up his arse. He wished he had the nerve to make such enjoyable trouble.

'I love this view.' Bodger craned to look past Rocco at the sea. Rocco was rubbing his eyes. 'Didn't you sleep?'

'I must tell someone. Things with Lisa are bad.' Rocco ignored the fact that Bodger was drumming his fingers on his unopened newspaper. 'I've lived with her two years. I loved her more than my life. And now I don't. Maybe I never loved her. Maybe I was deluded. Perhaps I am deluded about everything. How can people lead sensible lives while others are a mess? You know what Kierkegaard said? Our lives can only be lived forward and only understood backwards. Living a life and understanding it occupy different dimensions. Experience overwhelms before it can be processed.'

'Kierkegaard! I've been intending to read him. Is he great?'

'Perhaps I enjoyed stealing her from her husband. What?'

'Which book of his should I start with?'

Rocco said, 'She was always up for sex, and I was always hard. We fucked so often we practically made electricity.'

Bodger leaned forward. 'What was that like?'

'We wanted to leave London. The people. The pollution. The expense. We came here . . . to get a bit of land, grow stuff, you know.'

'The dope?'

'Don't be fatuous. Vegetables. Except we haven't got them in yet.'

'It's a little late.'

'Maybe you or your friend Vance would have started a business and a family and all that. But this town is getting me down. And Lisa is always . . . always . . . about the place. That's what I'm saying.'

'I wouldn't leave a beautiful woman like that.'

'Even if you didn't love her?'

'Not her. Romance doesn't last. But respect and co-operation do. I'm a doctor. I recommend endurance.'

'If I wanted to test my endurance I'd go to the gym like that idiot Vance. I think I've got Alzheimer's disease.'

The doctor laid his hand on Rocco's forehead. It was damp. Rocco seemed to be sweating alcohol. Bodger was about to inform him that his T-shirt was inside out and back to front, but he remembered that when his friend's shirts became too offensive he reversed them.

'I don't think so. Does she love you?'

Rocco sighed. 'She thinks she's one of those magazine independent women, but without me she'd be all over the place. She's useless really. What can she do? She has irritating ways.'

'Like what?' said Bodger with interest.

Rocco tried to think of a specific illustration that wasn't petty. He couldn't tell Bodger he hated the way she poked him in the stomach while trying to talk to him; or the way she blew in his nostrils and ears when they were having sex; or the way she applied for jobs she'd never get, and then claimed he didn't encourage her; how she always had a cold and insisted, when taking her temperature, that insertion of the thermometer up the backside was the only way to obtain a legitimate reading; or how she was always losing money, keys, letters, even her shoes, and falling off her bicycle. Or how she'd take up French or singing, but give up after a few weeks, and then say she was useless.

Rocco said, 'What can you do when you're with a person you dislike, but move on to another person you dislike? Isn't that called hope? I'm off.'

'Where?'

'Back to London. New people, new everything. Except we've got no money, nothing.'

Bodger said, 'You're intelligent, that's the problem.'

Rocco was biting his nails. 'I miss the smell of the tube, the crowds in Soho at night, men mending the road outside your window at eight in the morning, people pissing into your basement, repulsive homunculi in ill-fitting trousers shouting at strangers. In the city anything can turn up. There's less time to think there. My mind won't shut up, Bodger.'

The doctor collected his things. 'Nor will my patients.'

'Don't mention this, because I'm not telling her yet.' Rocco pulled out a letter. 'Yesterday this arrived. It fell open – accidentally. Her husband's not well.'

Bodger leant over to look at it, but stopped himself.
'What's wrong with him?'

'He's dead.'

'Aren't you going to show it to her?'

'She'll get upset and I won't be able to leave her for ages.'

'But you took her away from her husband, for God's sake.
Marry her now, Rocco, please!'

'That's a good idea, when I can't bear the girl and couldn't
fuck her with my eyes closed.'

Bodger paid, as he always did, and the two friends
walked along the top of the cliff. When they parted Bodger
told Rocco how he wished he had a woman like Lisa, and
that he didn't understand why she would live with Rocco
and not with him.

'Those shoulders, those shoulders,' he murmured. 'I'd be
able to love her.'

'But we'll never know that for sure, will we?' said Rocco.
'Thanks for the advice. By the way, have you ever lived with
a woman?'

'What? Not exactly.'

Rocco sauntered off.

Bodger hoped he wouldn't be thinking of Rocco and Lisa
all morning. Occasions like this made him want to
appreciate what he had. He would do this by thinking of
something worse, like being stuck in a tunnel on the District
Line in London on the hottest day of the year. Yes, he liked
this seaside town and the sea breeze, particularly early in the
morning, when the shops and restaurants were opening and
the beach was being cleaned.

'Karen, Karen!' he called to Vance's wife who was jogging
on the beach. She waved back.

2

When Rocco got home Lisa had managed to dress and had
even combed her hair. She wore a long black sleeveless dress

and knee-high leather boots. The night before she'd been at a party on the beach. Most people had been stoned. She couldn't see the point of that any more, everyone out of it, dancing in their own space. She had got away and rested in the dunes. Now she sat at the window drinking coffee and reading a magazine she'd read before.

'Would it be okay if I went swimming this morning?' she asked.

She was supposed to sign on but had obviously forgotten. Rocco was about to remind her but preferred the option of blaming her later.

'I don't care what you do.'

'I only asked because Bodger told me to take it easy.'

'Why, what's wrong with you now?'

She shrugged. He looked at her bare white neck and the little curls on the nape he had kissed a hundred times.

He went into the bedroom. His head felt damp, as if sweat was constantly seeping from his follicles. He was too exhausted to even gesture at the ants on the pillow. They were all over the house. If you sat down they crawled up your legs; if you opened a paper they ran across the pages. But neither of them did anything about it.

He lay down. Almost immediately, though, he groaned. He could hear, through a megaphone, a voice intoning Hail Marys. The daily procession of pilgrims to the local shrine, one of Europe's oldest, had begun. They came by coach from all over the country. People in wheelchairs, others on crutches, the simple, the unhappy and the dying limped up the lane past the cottage. A wooden black madonna was hoisted on the shoulders of the relatively hearty; others embraced rosaries and crucifixes. The sound echoed across the fields of grazing cattle. Cults, shamen, mystics; the hopeless searched everywhere. To everyone their own religion, these days. Who was not deranged, from a certain point of view? Who didn't long for help?

In their first weeks in the cottage, he and Lisa had played

a game as the pilgrims passed. Rocco would put on a Madonna record, run up the steps of their raised garden, and piss over the hedge onto the shriners, crying, 'Holy water, holy water!' Lisa would rush to restrain him and they would fuck, laughing, in the garden.

The day was ahead of him and what did he want to do? He thought that having intentions, something in the future to move towards, might make the present a tolerable bridge. But he couldn't think of any projects to want.

Rereading the letter he looked up and saw Lisa observing him. He was about to stuff it back in his pocket, but how would she know what it contained?

Three years ago he had fallen in love. Lisa wasn't only pretty; plenty of women were pretty. She was graceful, and everything about her had beauty in it. She was self-aware without any vanity; and, most of the time, she knew her worth, without conceit. With her, he would make an attempt at monogamy, much vaunted as a virtue, apparently, by some. She would curb his desire. Running away with her would also represent an escape from futility. Now, however, he felt that all he had to do was abandon her, flee and somehow achieve the same thing.

He said, 'I'll ask Bodger if you can swim. I need some advice myself.'

'About what?'

'Everything.'

Rocco knew he was talented: he could play and compose music; he could direct in the theatre and on film; he could write. To release his powers he had to get away. Action was possible. That, at least, he'd decided. This cheered him, but not as much as it should, because he didn't even have the money to travel to the next railway station. And, of course, before he got out he'd have to settle things with Lisa. He needed a longer discussion with Bodger.

At twelve they had lunch because there was nothing else to do. He and Lisa always had the same thing, tinned tomato soup with cheese on toast, followed by jelly with condensed milk. It was cheap and they couldn't argue about what to have.

'I love this soup,' he said, and she smiled at him. 'It's delicious.' It was too much, being nice. He didn't think he could keep it up. Not even the thought of her dead husband brought on compassion. 'How do you feel today? Or have I asked you that already?'

She shook her head. 'Stomach pains again, but okay.'

'Take it easy then.'

'I think so.'

The sound of her slurping her jelly, which he hoped that just this once she would spare him, made him see how husbands murdered their wives. He pushed away his bowl and ran out of the cottage. She watched him go, the spoon at her lips.

3

'Scum. Rocco is scum,' said Vance. 'He really is. And I can tell you why.'

'You had better,' said Bodger.

Bodger was studying Feather, the local therapist who lived nearby, because he was drawing her.

Vance was glancing at himself in Bodger's mirror, not so much to admire his crawling sideburns, floral shirt, ever-developing shoulders, and thick neck, but to reassure himself that his last, satisfying impression had been the correct one.

He ran the town's hamburger restaurant, a big place with wooden floors, loud seventies music and, on the walls, rock posters and a T-Rex gold disc. In the basement he had recently opened the Advance, a club. Nearby he owned a clothes shop.

Vance was the most ambitious man in the town. It was no secret that his appetite extended further than anything or anyone in front of him. Looking over their heads, he was going places. But it was here, to his perpetual pique, that he was starting from.

Like numerous others, he often dropped by Bodger's place in the afternoon or late at night, to gossip. Most surfaces in Bodger's house were covered with bits of wood that he'd picked up on walks, or with his drawings or notebooks. There were towers of annotated paperbacks on astronomy, animals, plants, psychology; collapsing rows of records; and pieces of twisted metal he'd discovered in skips. The chairs were broken, but had a shape he liked; his washing, which he did by hand as 'therapy', hung in rows across the kitchen. To Vance it was detritus, but every object was chosen and cherished.

Vance said, 'Did you know what he said about this shirt? He asked if I were wearing the Nigerian or the Ghanaian flag.'

Feather started to laugh.

'Yes, it's hilarious,' said Vance. 'He provokes me and then wants my respect.'

Bodger said, 'I saw him this morning and felt sorry for him.'

'He's rubbish.'

'Why say that of someone?'

Vance said, 'Did you know – he's probably told you several times – that he's got two degrees in philosophy? He's had one of the best educations in the world. And who paid for it? Working people like me, or my father. And what does he do now? He drinks, hangs around, borrows money, and sells dope that gives people nightmares. Surely we should benefit from his brilliant education? Or was it just for him?'

'Is it the education that's useless, or just Rocco?' Feather asked.

'Exactly,' said Bodger.

'Both, probably. Thank God this government's cutting

down on it.' Vance turned to Feather. 'Can't you therapise him into normality?'

'Suppose he turned out worse?'

Vance went on, 'You know what he said to me? He called me greedy and exploitative. And no one has fucked more of my waitresses. Did I tell you, he was in bed with one and she asked him if he'd liked it. I teach them to be polite, you see. He said . . what was it? "The whole meaning of my life has coalesced at this timeless moment."' Neither Feather nor Bodger laughed. 'How idiotic can you get? Last time he came into the restaurant, he raised his arse and farted. The customers couldn't breathe.'

'Stop it,' said Bodger to Feather, who was laughing now.

'The worst thing is, girls fall for him. And he's got nothing! Can you explain it?'

'He knows how to look at them,' said Feather.

She herself had a steady gaze, as if she were deciphering what people really meant.

'What d'you mean?' asked Vance.

'Women look into his eyes and see his interest in them. But he also lets them see his unhappiness.'

Vance couldn't see why anyone would find Rocco's unhappiness amatory, but something about the idea puzzled him, and he considered it.

When they'd first come to the town, Vance had welcomed Lisa and Rocco. He didn't let them pay for their coffee, ensured they had the best table, and introduced them to the local poets and musicians, and to Bodger. She was attractive; he was charming. This was the sort of café society he'd envisaged in his restaurant, not people in shorts with sandy feet and peeling noses.

Bodger was drawing. 'Calling the man scum – well, that's just unspeakable and I don't agree with it.'

'His problem is,' said Feather, 'he loves too many people.'

Vance started up again. 'Why defend someone who sleeps with people's girlfriends – and gives them diseases –

borrows money, never works, is stoned all the time and tells lies? These days people don't want to make moral judgements. They blame their parents, or society, or a pain in the head. He came to my place every day. I liked him and wanted to give him a chance. People like him are rubbish.'

Bodger threw down his pencil. 'Shut up!'

Feather said, 'The desire for pleasure plays a large part in people's lives.'

'So?' Vance stared at her. 'Suppose we all did what we wanted the whole time. Nothing would get done. I'll tell you what riles me. People like him think they're superior. He thinks that doing nothing and discussing stupid stuff is better than working, selling, running a business. How does he think the country runs? Lazy people like him should be forced to work.'

'Forced?' said Bodger.

This was one of Vance's favourite subjects. 'Half the week, say. To earn his dole. Sweeping the streets, or helping pensioners get to the shops.'

'Forcibly?' said Bodger. 'The police carrying him to the dustcart?'

'And to the pensioners,' said Vance. 'I'd drag him to them myself.'

'Not everyone can be useful,' said Feather.

'But why shouldn't everyone contribute?'

'I've lost my concentration,' said Bodger.

They went out into his garden where everything grew as it wanted. It was hot but not sunny. Cobwebs hung in the bushes like hammocks. The foliage was dry and dusty, the trees were wilting, the pond dry.

The liquefying heat debilitated them; they drank water and beer. Bodger fell asleep in a wicker chair with a handkerchief over his face.

Feather and Vance went out of the back gate arm in arm. He asked her to have a drink with him at the restaurant.

'I would, but I've got a client,' she said.

'More dreams?'

'I hope so.'

'Don't you get sick of all those whingeing people and their petty problems? Send them to me for a kick, it'll be cheaper.'

'People's minds are interesting. More interesting than their opinions. And certainly, as Rocco might have said, as interesting as hamburgers.'

She was smiling. They had always amused one another. She didn't mind if he mocked what she did. In fact it seemed to stimulate her. She liked him in spite of his personality.

'Come to me for a couple of sessions,' she said. 'See what sort of conversations we might have.'

'I'll come by for a massage but I'll never let you tinker with my brain. Words, words. How can talking be the answer to everything? There's nothing wrong with me. If I'm sick, God help everyone else.' After a while he added, 'Rocco's dangerous because he uses other people and gives them nothing in return.'

'Some people like being used.'

'I'm giving you notice, Feather, I'm going to kill that bastard.'

'As long as there's good reason for it,' she said, walking away.

4

Too weak to move, ravers from the previous night sat on the beach in shorts. Some slept, others swigged wine, one had set up a stall selling melons. A woman, a regular who came every morning with her cat in a box, walked it on a lead while the kids barked at her.

Lisa snoozed on the sand until she thought she'd boil, and then raced into the sea.

She loved her black dress. It was almost the only thing that fitted her. She put on her large straw hat with its broad brim pressed down so tightly over her ears that her face seemed to be looking out of a box. As she passed them the boys called after her. She was tall, with a long neck and a straight back. She walked elegantly, with her head up. In another age a man would be holding a parasol for her.

Nearby sat a middle-aged woman, a TV executive, who kept a cottage nearby, commuted to Los Angeles, and read scripts on the beach. She had most of what anyone could want, but was always alone. She dressed expensively but she was plump and her looks had faded. The boys, barking at the cat, also barked at her. Lisa shuddered. Men wanted young women – what a liberated age it was!

Maybe Lisa would ask her for a job. But working like that would bore her after a few weeks. How would she have time to learn the drums? At least . . . at least she had Rocco.

What conversations they had had, hour after hour, as they walked, loved, ate, sat. If she imagined the perfect partner, who would see her life as it was meant to be seen, absorbing the most secret confessions and most trivial incidents in a wise captivated mind, then he had been the one. What serenity and unstrained ease, without shame or fear, there had been, for a time.

Lately he had been hateful. She would have threatened to leave him, except his mood was her fault; she had to cure him. It was she who'd insisted they leave London, imagining a place near the sea, with the countryside nearby. They would grow their own food and read and write; there would be languorous stoned evenings.

There had been. Now they were going down. She'd spent too much on jewellery, bags, and clothes in Vance's. The manager, Moon, had 'loaned' her Ecstasy too, which she and Rocco had taken or given away. She owed Moon too much. Beside, she was wasting her life here, where very little happened. But what were lives for? Who could say? She didn't want to start thinking about that.

She and Rocco rarely fucked now. If they did, he would smack her face before he came. She was always left in a rage.

But he was curious about her body. He watched her as she did up her shoes; he would lift her skirt as she stood at the sink; he would look her over as she lay naked on the bed, and would touch her underwear when she was out. But she ached for sex. Her nipples wanted attention; she would pinch them between her fingers as she drank her tea. She felt desire but didn't know how to deliver herself of it.

She walked through the town. Vance's shop was beside two shops selling religious paraphernalia; there was nothing of use to buy in the high street. The pubs were priest-ridden; the most common cause of argument was Cardinal New-man.

Several of the local boys who worshipped Rocco, including the most fervent, a lad called Teapot, liked to hang around the shop. They copied Rocco's mannerisms and peculiar dress sense, wearing, for instance, a jean jacket over a long raincoat or fingerless gloves; they carried poetry, and told girls that the meaning of life had coalesced over their breasts.

Fortunately Teapot's group were still on the beach and only Moon was sitting in Vance's tenebrous shop, fiddling with his decks. He spent more time deciding which music to play than organising the stock. Sometimes Vance let him DJ at the Advance.

The blinds were down. A fan stirred and rippled the light fabrics. Moon had a mod haircut and wore little blue round shades. Lisa wanted to wave, so uncertain was she that he could see her, or anything.

She moved around the shop, keeping away from him as she asked if he had any E. She was going somewhere that she couldn't face straight and needed the stuff today.

'How will you pay me?' he asked outright, as she dreaded he would.

'Moon – '

'Leave aside the money you owe me, what about the money you owe the shop? The leather jacket.'

'It was lifted from the pub.'

'That's not my fault. Vance is going to find out.'

'Rocco's sold an article to the *New Statesman*. He'll come by to pay you.'

Moon snorted. 'Look.' He scattered some capsules on the counter, along with a bag of his own brand of grass, with a bright 'Moon' logo printed on it. 'Is it right to play games with someone's head?'

If she found a man attractive she liked to kiss him. This 'entertained' her. She would explain that there was no more to it than that, but the men didn't realise she meant it. She had had to stop it.

'You made me like you. You opened your legs.'

He came towards her and put his hand inside the front of her dress. She let him do it. He started kissing her breasts.

He was keen to hang his 'back in five minutes' sign on the door for an hour. But, unusually, some kids came in. She snatched up the caps from the counter and got out.

From the door he yelled, 'See you later!'

'Maybe.'

'At the Rim.'

She stopped. 'You coming, then?'

'Why not? By the way, don't mess with me. You don't want me spreading stuff about you, do you?'

5

They would drive five miles out of town along the southbound road, stop at a pub at the main junction, and then head up to the Rim.

Rocco, Bodger and Moon led the way in Bodger's Panda, followed by Karen, Vance, Feather – holding her cat – and Lisa in Vance's air-conditioned Saab. The boot was full of food and drink.

'Two years from now,' Vance was telling Feather, 'when I've raised the money, I'll – I mean we – ' he added, nodding at his wife Karen. 'We'll be off to Birmingham. Open a place there.'

'If we can ever afford it,' said Karen. 'I can't see the bank allowing it.'

'Shut your face,' said Vance. 'I've explained. I'm not making the mistake of going straight to London. I need experience. Coming with us?'

Feather stroked her cat. 'Whatever for?'

'Because however comfortable you are now, rubbing your pussy and listening to people moaning about mum and dad, in five years you'll be bored. And older. There's a lot of people there need serious head help.'

Karen cried out, 'Look!'

They were speeding along a road carved out of a sheer cliff. Everyone felt they were racing along a shelf attached to a high wall and that at any moment they would go hurtling over into the abyss. On the right stretched the sea, while on the left was a rugged brown wall covered in creeping roots.

They had several drinks in the pub garden, before moving on.

'I don't know what I'm doing here,' said Rocco. 'I should be on the train to London.'

'What about the view?' said Bodger.

Rocco shrugged. 'I have a busy internal life.'

As they walked back to the car, Vance said, 'Why does Rocco have to come with us? He spoils everything with his moaning.'

'You've got to come to terms with Rocco,' said Feather. 'He's obviously doing something to you. What is it?'

'It's making me mad.'

They drove through quiet villages and past farms. Tractors blocked their way. Dogs barked at them. They left the road for a dirt track. Then they had to unpack the cars and walk up the chalky hill to the Rim. Moon carried his music box and bag of tapes, Bodger a pile of blankets and his ice box, and the others brought the provisions. Soon, to one side, the town and the sea were below them, and on the other the hills looked brown, pink, lilac, suffused with light.

Karen threw up her arms and danced. 'What a brilliant idea! It's so quiet.'

'Yes, it is beautiful,' said Rocco. Sometimes he talked to Karen in the restaurant. He felt sorry for her, married to Vance. 'But I like it when you dance.'

'Always the flattterer,' said Vance.

Rocco knew Vance didn't like him, and he was afraid of him too. When Vance was around he felt awkward. Ignoring this last remark he walked away and regretted having come.

Bodger called after him, 'Everyone – get some wood for the fire!'

They wandered off at random, leaving Karen and Moon behind. Moon, with a sleepy look, like he'd been woken against his will, spread out the blankets and set out the spliff, wine and beer. When Vance had gone Karen smoked grass as if she were holding a long cigarette at a cocktail party, and then lay down with her head nearly inside the music.

Lisa wanted to skip, laugh, shout, flirt and tease. In her cotton dress with blue dots and the straw hat, she felt light and ethereal. She had stopped bleeding at last. A few days ago Bodger had told her she was having a miscarriage. She hadn't understood how it had happened. It had been Moon. Her body had bled for him, her heart for Rocco.

She climbed a hill through prickly bushes, and sat down. They'd been late getting away. Dusk was approaching. Down below a bonfire was already burning. Feather's shadow moved in a radius around the fire as she piled on wood and stirred the pot with a spoon tied to a long stick.

Bodger fussed around the fire as though at home in his own kitchen.

'Where's the salt?' he called. 'Don't say we've forgotten it! Don't laze about, everyone. Have I got to do everything?'

Vance and Karen were having a casually bitter argument,

looking away from one another, as if just chatting.

Feather began unpacking the basket, but stopped and walked off, looking at the sea. After a while some strangers came into view. It was impossible to make them all out in the flickering light and bonfire smoke, but she saw a woollen cap and grey beard, then a dark blue shirt, and a swarthy young face. About five of these people were squatting in a circle: travellers. Shortly after, the people struck up a slow-moving song, like those sung in church during Lent.

Moon clambered up the path. Lisa was aware of him behind her. Had there actually been a time when this boy had attracted her?

'It was a mistake,' she said immediately. How could she explain that she wanted him for some things and not others.

'I'll wait until you want me,' he said.

'Do that.'

It became an amusing game again. She still owed him, of course. They had made a baby. For a short while, in the weeks of her pregnancy, she had been a woman and had imagined that people were beginning to take her seriously. She had stood in front of the mirror, sticking out her stomach and stroking it, imagining herself big.

'I must go now.'

She walked quickly, so that Moon knew not to follow her; when she turned she saw him taking another route. But after a few minutes walking she heard a sound and was frightened. She took a few more steps.

'How are you feeling?' said Bodger.

She was startled. He seemed to have concealed himself behind a tree and jumped out on her, surely an unusual practice for a doctor.

'Not physically bad,' she said, grateful for the inquiry. 'Strong again, in that way. But I'm lost.' He was looking at her strangely. 'I liked the last medicine you gave me, but what prescription can anyone give for lostness?'

'A kiss.'

'Sorry?'

'Let me kiss you.'

He closed his eyes, awaiting her reply, as if it were the most important question he'd ever asked.

She left him standing in that position. Down below the soup was ready. They poured it into the bowls and drank it with that air of ritual solemnity exclusive to picnics, and declared they never tasted anything so appetising at home.

They lay in a jumble of napkins, water bottles and paper plates. It got dark; the bonfire was dying. Everyone felt too sluggish to get up and put on more wood. Lisa drank beer after beer and let Moon watch her.

Rocco felt awkward sitting there. His back was hot from the fire, while Vance's loathing was directed at his chest and face. The hatred made him feel weak and humiliated.

'A great picnic and enchanting evening,' said Rocco.

'Glad you liked it.'

In a cringing voice he said, 'You know, Vance, occasionally I envy your certainty about everything.'

Lisa interrupted. 'I don't. I'll never know how anyone can have so much when so many people have almost nothing.'

Vance shook his head at both of them and Lisa got up and ran away. Rocco stared into the distance.

6

It was past one when they got into the cars. Everyone was ready for bed, apart from Moon and Lisa, who were chasing one another in the woods.

'Hurry up!' shouted Bodger, who had become irritable.

'Too stoned,' said Vance, jangling his keys. 'I'm off.'

Exhausted by the picnic, by Vance's hatred of him, and by his own thoughts, Rocco went to find Lisa. She was in high spirits; when she seized him by both hands and laid her head on his chest, breathlessly laughing out loud, he said, 'Don't be vulgar.'

She lost heart. She climbed into the car feeling stupid.

'Typical of the sentimental unemployed,' Vance said, closing his eyes, the better to concentrate on his opinions. Karen was driving. 'They think people are suffering because I've taken their money. They think I don't care. That I see an unemployed man and woman who can't feed their kids or pay the mortgage, and I fall about laughing. Meanwhile he swaggers around at exhibitions, museums and theatres, passing judgement, puffing himself up.'

'Music and books,' said Bodger. 'The best things in life. Reason for living. What men and women make. The best. And what will remain of us, if anything.'

Vance went on, 'You'll never find one of these people – whose dole I provide – sticking out their hand and saying, thank you for wanting to be rich, thank you for making this country run and for taking risks! There's more and more of them about. People don't contribute. What we'll do with them is the problem of our time.'

Bodger said, 'Lisa. She said something simplistic. And you're jumping on her because you hate Rocco. But she's a lovely woman!'

'Bodger, if you met a man who giggled all day and never worked, you'd say, a job will do you good. But you let her off because she's a beautiful woman.'

'What would you do with her, then? Hit her?'

Vance said, 'I might let her peel my potatoes.'

7

It would be too hot to sleep. Even with the windows open the air was not disturbed. Lisa sat down and looked at Rocco.

'Why did you speak to me like that? Rocco, please.' He was pulling something from his pocket. 'What's that?'

'It came for you.'

'When?'

'The other day.'

'Which day?'

'Read it.'

He went into the bedroom and lay down in the dark. She was weeping. 'Rocco.' Thinking he was standing behind her chair, she sobbed, 'Why didn't you tell me this? I wouldn't have gone on the rotten picnic and laughed like that. Moon said such dirty things to me. I think I'm losing my mind.'

He was suffocating. He put his fingers in his ears. Then he climbed through the window, over the fence, and went down the street. Above his head a brightly lit train shot across a bridge.

Rocco peeped through Bodger's windows.

'Are you asleep? Hey. What's happening?'

He heard some coughing. Then, 'What d'you think I'm doing at this time?'

Bodger stood there in his underpants scratching.

'I'm going to kill myself, Bodger.'

'Thanks for the information.'

'Put the light on! I can't stay at home. You're my only friend and my only hope. Bodger, I've got to get away from here.'

Bodger let him in and put three bottles of wine and a bowl of cherries on the table.

'I want to talk.'

It was a monologue, of course, but Bodger – unfortunately for him – considered Rocco to be the only person in town worth talking to.

'How much frustration can a person bear?' Rocco asked. 'How much should one bear? Is stoicism a great or a foolish thing? Without it life would be unliveable. But if there's too much of it, nothing happens, and you can only ask, why are you stopping new shapes forming?' Without waiting for Bodger to express an opinion, he said, 'Please lend me the money to get away. I only need enough to last a few weeks, until I get a room or a flat. If you can lend me a grand, I'd be grateful.'

'One thousand pounds!'

'London's expensive. Seven hundred and fifty would do it.'

'You already owe me more than that.'

'You think I don't know that?'

Bodger said, 'I'll have to borrow it myself. I haven't got any loose cash. I went on that holiday. I've got the mortgage, my mother, and I bought the car. I – '

Rocco could tell that his friend didn't want to let him down. To cheer him up, Rocco offered Bodger one of the cherries and poured him some of his own wine.

'What about Lisa?' said Bodger. 'She's not staying here, is she?'

'I'm going to set things up in London for her. She'll join me after. If there's two of us there at first, it'll cost twice as much.'

'I'll miss you both,' said Bodger.

He raised his glass. 'You're a good man. I love you. Come with us.'

'Oh God, why do you have to be so weak? Can't you make up with Vance before you go?'

'I'm going to try. But I'm too lazy and useless for him. The only thing is, you don't know how he treats his staff. He's the sort of person who thinks that the more ruthless, cruel and domineering they are, the better boss they'll be. You wouldn't work five minutes for him. Poor Vance, why doesn't someone tell him the eighties are over?'

Rocco drank and ate the cherries cheerfully. 'People exist for him not as interesting human beings, but as entities to work. I'm surprised he hasn't suggested the weak be exterminated. And all this to make our society more affluent, more rationalised, more efficient. Will that bring happiness to people?'

'Aren't you trying to exterminate Lisa?'

Rocco sat back. 'I don't understand your problem,

Bodger. One only sees these things as tragic if one has a certain view of relationships. That they mustn't end. That their ending is tragic rather than painful. That the duration of a relationship is the only measure of its success. Why see it like that?'

'People aren't disposable items, are they? It's chilling, Rocco. You sound rational and ruthless at the same time, not always a propitious combination, as you surely know.'

'Certain people are good for certain things and not for others. One wants something from some people, and they want something from you. You go on until there's nothing more.'

'Vance would agree with you.'

'Yes. I see that. I'm not saying it's not painful. Only tonight I believe in another possible future. Will it kill you to give me that chance?'

'Not immediately.' He started to put the drinks away. 'I must go to bed.'

Rocco was lying across the sofa with a bottle in his hand. 'Can I stay?'

He would sit up all night and listen to Bodger's classical records. Even though Rocco would weep at certain musical passages, Bodger liked having someone there.

8

Three days after the picnic Lisa opened the door to find Karen standing there with her son. When she saw Lisa was in, she sent the boy to play football in the garden and stepped inside. It was the first time Karen had been inside the cottage, and even as she looked around disapprovingly she was saying, 'Is it true, your husband died?'

Lisa wondered why she had come. They had never been friends. In fact Karen had often been condescending towards her. Perhaps there was something she had to tell her. But what?

Lisa said, 'It is true.'

'Is that terrible?'

Lisa shrugged.

'Oh God, Lisa.' For a moment Karen hugged her. 'It makes me think of Vance dying.' Looking over Lisa's shoulder she said, 'Books everywhere. Didn't you go to college?'

'University.'

'Is there a difference? I'm a pea brain. I expect you've noticed. What did you do there?'

'Had a lovely time at parties. And read – stuff I'd never read again.'

'Poetry?'

'Psychology. My husband – the, er, dead man – was a lecturer.'

'I'd like to read books. Except I don't know where to start. People who read too much are snobby, though.'

Lisa said, 'I know I didn't make enough of it. All that free education, and no one told me not to waste it. No one had my best interests at heart – least of all me. Isn't that funny?'

Karen said, 'You can get married to Rocco now.'

'But I haven't lived yet.'

'I'll tell you, from experience – marriage will make you secure. I know I'm all right with Vance and he'll take care of me. If I ask for something he writes a cheque.'

Lisa just laughed.

Karen look startled. 'You think he'll run off with someone else?'

'Do you?'

'Soon we're going to get out of here. In the next few years.'

'So are we.'

'But when though, when? Vance keeps saying we will but I know it won't happen!' Karen stood watching her son in the garden. She began to tug at her hair. 'The worst marriages – they aren't the most violent or stifling. Or the cruellest even. You could take action then. It would be obvious. The worst are the ones that are just wrong. People stay because it takes ten years to realise it, and those years are thrown away and you don't know where.'

Lisa murmured, 'I woke up startled the other night. He was kissing me.'

'Who?'

'He didn't know he was doing it. All over my face. Rocco's at his sweetest when he's unconscious.'

'You know, he did this thing with me once,' Karen said. Lisa looked up at her. 'He was carrying a book of poems. I said, "What's that junk about?" "Listen," he said, and read me this one song. It made me feel strange. He made me see what it was about. Vance never liked Rocco. Or you.'

'Have we ever harmed anyone? Vance can be very hard.'

'D'you think so?'

'How d'you stand all that rushing about?' asked Lisa. 'More like thrashing about, actually.'

'We went to the Caribbean. But Vance was always busy. He says I'm out of focus. Men only think about work . . . they never think about love, only sex. I always get up before Vance, to clean my teeth and shower so he won't see me looking ugly. He doesn't like my accent.'

'What d'you mean?'

'He hears me in front of other people, in a restaurant in London, or in front of you – '

'Me?'

'And he looks at me as if he's never seen me before. He says we've got to change if we're going to get anywhere.' Suddenly she cried out, 'What's that?'

'Where?'

'There – on the table.'

'An ant.'

'Kill it!'

Lisa smiled.

Karen stood up. 'They're swarming everywhere! It's unsanitary!' She sat down again and tried not to look around, but said, in her confusion, 'Don't you ever want to . . . to go to bed with another person, someone else?'

'Sorry?'

'Just to try another body. Another thingy. You know.'

Lisa was about to say something but only cleared her throat.

Karen said, 'Is that your only dress? Haven't you got anything else? Moon says you're always in the shop.'

'I like this dress. It's cool.'

'Vance might have to close that place. You're the only person who goes in there.'

'And the club?'

'Vance doesn't tell me much.' She said, 'A lot of the men round here go for you. Like Moon.'

'Oh Moon,' sighed Lisa. 'As Rocco said, Moon's on another planet. Men think that if they put their hands on you or say filthy things you'll want them.'

'Only if you ask for it,' Karen replied sharply. 'What will you live on in London?'

'I'll . . . I'll do journalism. I've been thinking about some ideas.'

Karen nodded. 'A single woman in London. That's a popular scenario. Thing is,' she said, 'however much a woman wants a career, for most of us it's a load of day-dreams. We aren't going to make enough to have a top-class life. The only way to get that is to marry the right guy. You might be brainy, but without money you can't do nothing.'

'Money! Why do people have to have so much of it?'

'People are so envious, it's dirty envy, it makes me mad. They want what we have but won't do anything to get it.'

Waves of heat rolled through Lisa's body; if only the top of her head were hinged and she could let them out.

She said, 'People say of the young people in this town . . . that we don't want to do anything. It's not true. Just give us a chance, we say.' Before Karen could speak again, Lisa went on, 'Did you come for any reason?'

Karen looked surprised. 'Only to talk.'

Lisa was thinking of other things. Her demeanour changed. 'I want to do so much. To learn to sing and dance. To paint. To row on the river. To play guitar and drums. I can't wait to begin my life!'

When she left Karen insisted on kissing Lisa again.

Lisa felt dizzy and feverish. She stepped out of her dress and rolled herself into a ball, under a sheet. She was thirsty, but there was no one to bring her a drink.

She awoke to find Rocco apologising for his rudeness at the picnic.

She cried out, 'Oh God, that woman Karen has done me in!'

'What was she here for? What did she say?'

Rocco noticed the blood on the sheet and went immediately to fetch Bodger.

'Did they teach you at medical school to hold onto your patients' hands that long, while whispering in their ears?' enquired Rocco when Bodger came out of the room.

'So you're jealous?' said Bodger. 'You don't want me to go out with her?'

'If you sorted out the money and I got out, you'd be welcome to have a go.'

'I'm trying to get the money,' said Bodger, glancing back at the door in embarrassment. 'But I'm a doctor, not a financier.'

'I've never known a doctor to be short of money.'

Bodger's voice squeaked. 'You're arrogant! I haven't had time to go to the bank. Are you still sure you want to get out?'

'If I can't get away by Saturday I'm going to go insane!'

'All right, all right!'

'What about by Friday morning?' Rocco put his mouth close to Bodger's ear and whispered. 'When I'm gone, she's all yours. If you knew how I've been praising you!'

'Have you?'

'Oh yes. She likes men. A lot of women do.'

'Yes?'

'But they keep it to themselves – for fear of encouraging the wrong sort.'

Bodger couldn't help believing him.

9

'You don't look well,' said Vance as Bodger came into the restaurant. 'Shall I call a doctor?'

'I thought I'd see the enterprise culture at work,' shouted Bodger over the music, removing his bicycle clips and putting his hands over his ears. 'Without conversation, clearly. What, er, are you up to?'

'Creating work, satisfying demand, succeeding.'

'Lend me £300, will you, Vance? No, £400.'

Vance put his arm around him.

'The place next door is for sale. Come and look. I'm thinking of buying it and knocking through. Put the kitchen in there. More tables here.' While Bodger looked around the almost empty restaurant Vance spoke to a waitress. 'Better food, too.' The waitress returned; Vance put the money on the table with his hand on top of it. 'If it's for Rocco you can forget it.'

'What if it is? That would be none of your business!'

'I won't let you lend money to any sad sack.'

Bodger waved his arms. 'It is for him! But no one tells me what to do!'

'Shhh . . . People are eating.'

Feather, who was writing her journal at the next table, started laughing.

Bodger said, 'Don't be inhumane. You think you're letting people be independent, but really you're just letting them down. How can it be wrong to help others?'

'But I'm all for charity. Is Rocco going away?' Bodger nodded. 'Without her?'

'At first.'

'The bastard's doing a runner. With my money! He's going to leave her behind. You'll get stuck with her.'

'Will I?'

Vance regarded him beadily. 'You want her?' Bodger gulped. 'Do you?'

'I would love her.'

'I can't guarantee to lay on love, but she'll sleep with you.'

'Are you certain? Did she mention it?'

'She'd do it with anyone. Haven't you asked her yet?'

'Asked?' Bodger was shivering. 'Once I'd said it . . . if she said yes, I'd be too excited, you know, to do anything. I sort of imagine that there are, out there, people who know how to ask for everything they want. They're not afraid of being rejected or laughed at, or of being so nervous that they can't even speak. But I'm not one of them.'

'You'll soon get sick of Lisa. She'll be so expensive to run. Can't imagine her working. High ideals and no prospects. Your great friend Rocco is making you an idiot.'

'I'll make him promise to take her with him.'

'Promise! In a year you'll run into him in London doing your Christmas shopping, and he'll be with another woman saying this time it's true love.'

Bodger put his head in his hands.

Vance said at last, 'You're a good man and people respect you. But this is weakness.' He passed the money over. 'There's one condition. Lisa goes with him. If she doesn't, I'll kick his backside into the sea.'

10

Next day, a Thursday, Karen closed a part of the restaurant and held a small party for her son's birthday. When Rocco and Lisa arrived Vance was giving the boy his present.

'He's going to be a businessman,' Vance told Bodger. 'But not in this country.'

'What's wrong with this country?'

Vance was looking across at Rocco and Lisa.

'That woman doesn't know she is about to be betrayed, does she? Or have you spoken to him?'

'Not yet.'

Vance told the waitress to give them drinks and then said, 'Sometimes I look around and think I'm the only person working in England – keeping everyone else alive, paying ridiculous taxes. Maybe I'll just give up too, chuck it all in, and sit in the pub.'

'Someone's got to run the pub, Vance.'

'You're exactly right.'

Rocco was greeting people; he smiled unctuously at Vance. They shook hands. Then Rocco guided Bodger into a quiet corner.

'Tomorrow is Friday.' He was biting his nails. 'Did you get me the loan?'

'Some of it. I'll get the rest later.'

'Thank God!'

'No, thank me.'

'Yes, yes. You've saved me.'

Bodger said, 'Look at Lisa! How could you go anywhere without those shoulders?'

'We owe so much money here, we can't leave. And where will we both stay in London? I've got friends, but I can't impose her on people. How come you've suddenly got a problem with our agreement? Have you been talking to someone? It's Vance, isn't it? I thought you had a mind of your own.'

Bodger blurted out, 'Take her with you, or I'll give you no more money.'

'Don't you know how to love a friend?'

'Don't you know how to love Lisa?'

Karen came over with her son. 'Am I interrupting? Rocco, look at this.'

She made the boy show Rocco his essays and drawings. 'Excellents' and 'very goods' danced before Rocco's eyes.

Karen remarked in the posh voice she adopted on these occasions. 'They push them hard at private schools.'

'I know,' said Rocco. 'I am hoping, in the next few years, to make a partial recovery.'

He wanted his freedom; he didn't want Lisa. If he stayed the bills would mount up. He would get more frustrated. Other people wanted you to live lives as miserable as theirs. This they considered moral behaviour.

He thought of the moment the train would pull away and how he would open a bottle of beer to celebrate. Of course, when Lisa did get to London he would have to squirm and lie to get rid of her: as if everyone didn't lie at times, as if the lie were not protecting something, the integrity of a life. Lying was an underrated and necessary competence.

From across the room Lisa felt Moon's eyes on her. She wanted to go with him to the beach. And then she felt she had no control over herself. Her desire made her want to leave Rocco. He would protest, of course. He needed her more than he acknowledged. But she would make plans secretly, and then announce them. It was time to get away.

Moon and Rocco nodded at one another and went outside to try some weed Moon had been growing using a new method involving human shit. Moon was intending to set up as a dealer, and move to London. He was awaiting Rocco's opinion.

Rocco's bloodshot eyes had closed. Then he started chuckling. Moon nodded confidentially. 'Cool, cool.' But after a time Rocco was clucking, and his head started to thrash as he reacted to some welling disturbance or internal storm. He started looking at people with a wild, frightened disposition, as if he feared they would attack him, his guffaws became shriller until he sounded like a small dog. He tried to get up from the table but his legs would not obey him and his right arm started jumping about on the table. Bodger was so alarmed that he and a frightened Moon led Rocco downstairs, supporting his head from behind while

Feather held a glass against his teeth, and water spilled onto his chest.

Lisa was clutching the back of the chair, afraid she would fall, terrified that Moon had told Rocco about them.

She went to Bodger. 'What's wrong with him?'

'He's smoked too much.'

'Not more than normal,' said Moon hastily.

'What is it, the stuff you gave him?'

'Mellow Wednesday. Because it's mellow.'

'I'm still alive,' Rocco moaned, and said quietly to Bodger, 'If I can get out of here I'll be okay.'

Later, they all walked along the front under a violet sky.

Fearing that Moon might try and talk to her, Lisa tried to stay close to Karen and her son. Fear and dejection weakened her; she could hardly move her legs. But she didn't go home, thinking Moon would try and accompany her. They went down to the beach.

11

'I'm going,' said Rocco at last.

Lisa took his arm. 'Me too.'

Rocco said, 'Thanks for the smoke, Moon. I'll do the same for you some day.'

Moon said he was going in her direction. What a fool she'd been to provoke Moon, but she had been stupefied by desire. Now she had to take the consequences.

Rocco turned away. 'I've got stuff to do. See you later.'

'I must talk to you,' said Moon, when he'd gone. 'You're playing games with me.'

Lisa said, 'But I'm depressed.'

'That's not going to stop me fucking you this evening. Otherwise what you've been doing will get around. People round here will certainly be interested, you know what they're like. In fact I think I'm going to fuck you today and tomorrow. After, you can do what you want.'

Lisa stopped at her front door. It was getting dark. She listened to the steady sea roar, glanced up at the star-strewn sky and felt she wanted to finish with everything.

'You're right, I've messed you around.'

She walked rapidly away and then turned up a side street leading away from the town. Pale patches of light from illuminated windows lay here and there on the road and she felt like a fly, perpetually falling into an inkpot and then crawling out again into the light. Moon was following her. At one point he stumbled, fell, and started laughing.

She turned. 'Not in my house.'

12

Rocco had decided to spare Lisa all the lies at once. He would spread them out. He had also had another brilliant idea: to tell Bodger that she was going to accompany him, and, at the last moment, announce that she wasn't well enough. If Bodger wouldn't give him the money he'd leave anyway, hitch-hiking to London and sleeping on the street. After yesterday's embarrassing paranoid fit, staying in the town was impossible.

Having decided this he felt better. He would visit Bodger for lunch, and charm him, and put him at ease. As soon as he walked in he saw Vance and Feather.

Before Rocco could get out, Vance said, 'How d'you feel after your little fit? I thought only women had hysterics.'

'Hysteria is ridiculous, yes. But most people recognise that paranoia is a kind of language, speaking to us but in a disguised way.'

Vance was looking at him with contempt. 'You're hopeless. Always scrounging money and talking rubbish.'

'What? What did you say?'

'You heard.'

Rocco went into the kitchen where Bodger was preparing lunch.

He began to yell, 'If you haven't got the money, just say that. But don't go round town telling everyone about my problems! Don't you know how to keep a confidence? I suppose, as a doctor, you tell everyone about your patients' illnesses!'

Bodger threw a wooden spoon at him. 'Come back later!'

Rocco rushed out of the kitchen.

'Everyone's spying on me now!' he cried. 'There's nothing better for people to talk about! I borrow money! I ask someone to help me! And for that I am crucified! Then people say I get paranoid . . . End this surveillance now – that's all I'm asking!'

Bodger followed him out of the kitchen, red-faced with rage. 'No one accuses me of such shit!'

Feather began to laugh.

Rocco shouted at Bodger, 'Just leave me alone!' He looked at Vance. 'Particularly you – you fascist Burger Queen.'

'Sorry? Did I hear you right? I think I might have to kick your head in.'

'Try it.'

This was the moment Vance had been waiting for. He took it slowly.

'Not your head. Maybe I'll break a few fingers, or an arm. It'll be educational for you.'

Vance moved towards Rocco with his fists up. Rocco stood there. Bodger extended his arms between them.

'But you can't even fight,' Vance told Rocco across Bodger. 'I don't think there's anything you can do.'

'No? Burger Queen – bring me some French fries too. Two French fries and a knickerbocker glory! Ha, ha ha!'

Vance said, 'I'm tempted, but I'm not going to fight you now – because I might kill you. I'll fight you tomorrow.'

'I used to be a skinhead.'

'Ha! See you tomorrow morning. On the Rim. No rules, skinhead.'

'Bastard, I'm going to stick your head in a bun and eat it

with onions and relish! Ha, ha, ha!'

Vance smacked his fist into his palm. 'I'm afraid you're going to get damaged. Badly. Oh, oh, oh, you're going to cry!'

'Can't wait,' said Rocco. 'And by the way, can I have a green salad on the side?'

A few drinks made Rocco feel even better. And when his mood declined he had only to recall Vance's sneering face, manicured hands and Nigerian shirt to lift himself. How could a fool from a nothing place upset him? He would get the first punch in, and stamp on the bastard.

Teapot was in the pub and when Rocco told him about the fight they went into a field and practised karate kicks. It had been some time since Rocco had kicked anything but Lisa out of bed, and he kept tripping over even as he imagined his boot meeting Vance's balls.

Struggling for breath, he got up and declared, 'It's desperation not technique that's required. I'm going to rely on insanity.'

'That's right,' said Teapot. 'Go mental.'

'Now fuck off.'

He was glad to be alone. But when it got dark he became uneasy. He wanted to be in bed, but knew the night would be sleepless. He would have to think about Vance and prepare the lies he had to tell to Lisa. It was better to go from pub to pub.

He had been doing this for some time when Teapot tracked him down.

'I've been looking everywhere for you,' said the teenager. 'Come here!'

Rocco tried to swat him away. 'I'm saving my energy for tomorrow.'

Teapot almost picked him up and dragged him out of the pub. Rocco had no idea why Teapot should be in such a hurry. Teapot pushed him through the town's narrow streets to the beach and along the wall. There, Teapot took his hand and told him to be quiet.

Bewildered, Rocco followed him, and was helped onto the top of the wall. They lay down; at a sign from the ever-helpful Teapot they peered over the top. In the gloom Rocco could see Moon lying with his head between a woman's legs. Looking at the sky, she was humming to herself, as she liked to. He had imagined she only did that for him.

13

Bodger was ashamed of his outburst. He wanted to apologise to his friend and explain that fighting was childish.

Searching the pubs he stopped and sat down several times, recognising that it had been Rocco who'd insulted him and that he'd always done everything he could to help him.

When he opened the door of his house, Bodger heard Vance and Feather.

'Tomorrow there's going to be a fight,' Vance declared. 'We're civilised people, but we want to beat each other's brains to porridge. The strongest will triumph. Love and peace – out of the window! The thought of a fight – it's frightening . . . but don't we love it?'

Feather said, 'Strength and wisdom aren't the same.'

Bodger hurried in. 'The weather will spoil everything anyway.' He sat down. 'We have to care for one another. Yes! Otherwise we lose our humanity.'

Vance went on, 'We have the weak – people like Rocco – dominating the strong with their whingeing. They want others to do everything for them. But they will deplete our strength and drag us down. Selfishness, wanting something for oneself, is the law of reality. But if I benefit, others will benefit.'

Feather took all this equably. 'Who says who is weak and who is strong, and in what sense?'

'Him, presumably,' said Bodger. 'The new God enterprise.'

'Get real,' said Vance. 'Half the people who drag themselves to your surgery are skivers. They watch soap operas day and night. Why should we spend valuable resources keeping them alive?' He turned to Feather. 'I hope you're coming tomorrow.'

'I'm a pacifist.'

He smacked his fist into his palm.

'That's just voluntary ignorance. You should come and see what life is like.'

14

Rocco lay on the sofa and became aware of an unusual clattering sound. Wondering if children had got in upstairs, he ran to the stairs. No, it couldn't be that – the entire atmosphere had altered, as if there'd been a collision in space and the world would be extinguished. He moved to the window. The earth had turned grey. It was raining on the hard ground. Tonight, surely, was the end of summer. The evenings would draw in; no one would lie on the beach or gather at the War Memorial; the coach parties and foreign tourists would leave. Only they would remain.

For most of his life, at this time of year, he would be returning to school, and a new term.

He remembered as a kid running into the garden with two girls and getting soaked. They had snuggled up to one another in fear. No longer was he afraid of thunderstorms and now he ruined girls. Never had he planted one tree and never had he denied himself the opportunity to say something cutting or cruel, but he'd only wrecked everything.

Already aching from the exercises he had attempted with Teapot, he would feel worse tomorrow. What did it matter? He would encourage Vance to do him in, not only to break his arms – which wouldn't affect his brain – but to destroy his spirit and remaining hopes. It would be a relief.

It seemed not long after that Teapot turned up with his

motorbike and spare helmet. He and Rocco smoked some of Moon's Mellow Wednesday, practised some kicks, and went off.

Lisa had returned as it was getting light and had fallen asleep on the sofa with a coat over her. Rocco kissed her face and smoothed her hair.

There had been a moment – Moon was lapping between her legs and her mind was running free – when she'd projected herself into the future and looked back. She saw that these people, like the teachers and children at her first school – all pinches, curses, threats and boisterous power – were in retrospect just pathetic or ordinary, and nothing to be afraid of. She knew, at that moment, that she had already left.

When she thought of what she'd been through she didn't know how she hadn't gone mad. Her own strength surprised her. How much more of it might she have?

15

Feather rose early, meditated restlessly, and started out with a rucksack and stick. Why was she going? It was ridiculous for a pacifist to be present at such an event. But she was curious. She thought of Rocco. He had suffered; he understood something about life; he liked people. There was no cruelty in him; yet he fucked everyone up. And the person he made suffer the most was himself.

She stopped on the way to eat and drink; she washed in a rain-filled stream. For a change the air was moist. She wondered why this journey wasn't more enjoyable and when she sat and thought about it she realised she was tired of being alone; it was time to find a lover, particularly with winter on its way.

The others drove as far as they could and then walked up the chalk downs, until they could see the town in the distance, and the sea beyond.

She was walking up the Rim when a car approached. It was Karen, who was distressed. But Feather didn't want a lift.

She walked to the very top, a flat area with a pagan pedestal. The first thing she saw was Vance unpacking new running shoes. He wore sweatbands around his head and wrists, a singlet and a pair of shorts. Rocco hadn't given a thought to what he would wear, and had turned up in his ordinary clothes. He noticed that Bodger had arrived, but refused to acknowledge him.

Teapot rushed over to Vance. 'Please, Mr Vance, Rocco's terrified. He's shaking all over. Don't hurt him. He's had some Mellow Wednesday. You can't beat up a man in that condition.'

'I'll teach him a lesson,' said Vance, hawking and spitting. 'After the beating he'll be an improved person.'

'Look at him.'

Vance glanced over at Rocco and guffawed. 'He's disgusting, it's true. But that doesn't change anything.'

Teapot said, 'And he's upset.'

'So?'

Bodger was standing nearby with his doctor's bag. 'What about?'

'He saw his girlfriend being fucked – last night.'

'Who by?'

Teapot leaned towards them. 'Moon.'

Bodger went pale.

Across the way, practising his kicks and trying to make himself usefully mad, Rocco twisted his ankle. Teapot helped him up, but Rocco could barely walk and, when everyone was ready, Teapot had to cart him to the fighting place. Rocco stood there on one foot, breathing laboriously.

Karen stood a few feet away, tugging at her hair. She was watching her husband but seemed, also, to be thinking about something else.

Vance was dancing around and when he turned away to

give Karen the thumbs up, Rocco, windmilling an arm as he'd seen guitarists do, took a tremendous swing at him, which missed. Then he hobbled towards Vance and attempted a flying kick.

Rocco collapsed and lay there shouting, 'Beat me, Burger Queen. Kick my head in. Kick, kick, kick!'

'Get up. I'm not ready yet. Get up, I said!'

Vance reached out a hand to him, and Rocco got up. Then he tried, once more, to attack Vance who danced around him until, taking aim, he landed a nice punch in the centre of Rocco's face. Rocco fell down and Vance bestrode him, picking up his arm and bending it back over his knee. Rocco refused even to whimper but his face was screaming.

Bodger, with his hand over his mouth, murmured, 'Don't, don't . . . '

'A fight's a fight, ain't it?' said Vance.

'Please, Vance, you're just making more work for me.'

'Kill me, kill me, Queen,' begged Rocco.

'Don't worry,' said Vance. 'I'm on my way.'

Suddenly there was a sound from the bushes. Feather, naked but covered in dirt and mud, rushed screeching into the space and began to dance. Vance stared at her, as they all did, but decided to take no notice – until Feather took up a position in front of him and held up her hands.

'I'm breaking my fingers,' she said.

Vance continued his bending work.

Feather snapped her little finger and waved it at everyone.

'Now the next,' she said. 'And the next.'

'No, no, no!' said Bodger.

'What the hell is going on?' cried Vance. 'Get her out of here!'

Bodger rushed into the centre of the fight and threw himself on Vance.

Rocco had thought, somehow, that he would never get home again and had no idea that he'd be so glad to be back.

The books, records and pictures in his house and the light outside seemed new to him. He thought he might read, listen to music and then go and look at the sea. Vance had been right, the fight had done him good.

Lisa, pale and thin, didn't understand why he was being so gentle. Somehow she had thought he would never come back. She was prepared for that. But he had returned.

He stroked her face and hair, looked into her eyes and said, 'I've only got you.'

After, they sat in the garden.

16

It had been raining. A strong sea was running. It was early evening when Bodger, Feather and Vance came up the lane past Lisa and Rocco's house. Bodger carried a couple of bottles of wine and Feather some other provisions. They were on their way to her place. She had arranged to massage both Bodger and Vance, but now her right hand was bandaged. All day Vance had been fussing around her, both contrite and annoyed, and kept touching her reassuringly, as if to massage her.

'I'm not apologising to them,' said Vance.

'I wonder what they're doing,' said Feather. 'Stop for a minute.'

'Just for a second,' said Bodger.

They all looked over the hedge.

'Well, well,' Vance said, 'Who would have believed it?'

Rocco had dragged a couple of suitcases outside and was attempting to throw the contents – papers and notebooks – onto a shambolic bonfire. As the papers caught fire, the wind blew them across the garden. In the doorway Lisa, with a cardigan thrown over her shoulders, was folding her clothes and placing them in a pile. As they worked, she and Rocco chatted to one another and laughed.

'It's true,' said Feather.

Bodger turned to Vance. 'You're a bloody fucking fool.'

Vance said, 'What's wrong with you?'

'This didn't have to happen!'

Feather said, 'Go and tell them.'

'It's too late,' Vance said.

'Tell me if this pleases you!' Bodger cried. 'Be glad then – and dance!'

'Bodger, they've been wanting to get out for weeks. And I'm paying for it.' Vance added, 'It's amazing, he's actually doing something. And we're left behind.'

He turned and saw Moon scurrying up the lane, calling out, 'I'm not too late, am I?'

'You're always late, you little shite. Who's minding the shop?'

'Vance, please,' said Moon. 'I've shut it for a few minutes.'

'Get back there and open up – before I open you up!'

Moon looked over the hedge. Vance was about to grab him when Feather gave him a look; Vance noticed that Moon was crying under his shades.

Rocco had seen them by now, but he didn't look up. He stood by the fire flinging balls of paper into the flames.

Wearing her black dress and straw hat Lisa stood in the doorway smiling. In a strange, abstract motion, she raised her flat hand and waved to all of them. Vance turned and walked away up the lane, lowering his head and shoulders into the wind. Lisa went back into the house. Without moving, the others stood in a line watching Rocco until it began to drizzle and the fire went out. At last they went away, wondering what they would do now. It was raining hard.

The Flies

'We hadn't the pleasure now of feeling we were starting a new life,
only a sense of dragging on into a future full of new troubles.'
Italo Calvino, 'The Argentine Ant'

One morning after a disturbed night, a year after they
moved into the flat, and with their son only a few months
old, Baxter goes into the box-room where he and his wife
have put their wardrobes, opens the door to his, and picks
up a pile of sweaters. Unfolding them one by one, he
discovers that they all appear to have been crocheted. Not
only that, the remaining threads are smeared with a viscous
yellow deposit, like egg yolk, which has stiffened the
remains of the ruined garments.

He shakes out the moths or flies that have gorged on his
clothes, and stamps on the tiny crisp corpses. Other flies,
only stupefied, dart out past him and position themselves on
the curtains, where they appear threateningly settled, just
out of reach.

Baxter hurriedly rolls up the clothes in plastic bags, and,
retching, thrusts them into the bottom of a dustbin on the
street. He goes to the shops and packs his wardrobe with
fly killer; he sprays the curtains; he disinfects the rugs. He
stands in the shower a long time. With water streaming
down him nothing can adhere to his skin.

He doesn't tell his wife about the incident, thinking, at
first, that he won't bother her with such an unimportant
matter. He has, though, spotted flies all over the flat, which
his wife, it seems, has not noticed. If he puts mothballs in his
pockets, and has to mask this odour with scents, and goes
about imagining that people are sniffing as he passes them,
he doesn't care, since the attack has troubled him.

He wants to keep it from himself as much as from her. But at different times of the day he needs to check the wardrobe, and suddenly rips open the door as if to surprise an intruder. At night he begins to dream of ragged bullet-shaped holes chewed in fetid fabric, and of creamy white eggs hatching in darkness. In his mind he hears the amplified rustle of gnawing, chewing, devouring. When this wakes him he rushes into the box-room to shake his clothes or stab at them with an umbrella. On his knees he scours the dusty corners of the flat for the nest or bed where the contamination must be incubating. He is convinced, though, that while he is doing this, flies are striking at the bedsheets and pillows.

When one night his wife catches him with his nose against the skirting board, and he explains to her what has happened, she isn't much concerned, particularly as he has thrown away the evidence. Telling her about it makes him realise what a slight matter it is.

He and his wife acquired the small flat in a hurry and consider themselves fortunate to have it. For what they can afford, the three rooms, with kitchen and bathroom, are acceptable for a youngish couple starting out. Yet when Baxter rings the landlord to enquire whether there have been any 'outbreaks' before, he is not sympathetic but maintains they carried the flies with them. If it continues he will review their contract. Baxter, vexed by the accusation, counters that he will suspend his rent payments if the contagion doesn't clear up. Indeed, that morning he noticed one of his child's cardigans smeared and half-devoured, and only just managed to conceal it from his wife.

Still, he does need to discuss it with her. He asks an acquaintance to babysit. They will go out to dinner. There was a time when they would have long discussions about anything – they particularly enjoyed talking over their first impressions of one another – so happy were they just to be together. As he shaves, Baxter reflects that since the birth of their child they have rarely been to the theatre or cinema, or even to coffee shops. It has been months since they ate out. He is unemployed and most of their money has been spent on rent, bills, debts, and the child. If he were to put it plainly, he'd say that they can hardly taste their food; they can't even watch TV for long. They rarely see their friends or think of making new ones. They never make love; or, if one of them wants to, the other doesn't. Never does their desire coincide – except once, when, at the climax, the screams of their child interrupted. Anyhow, they feel ugly and their bodies ache. They sleep with their eyes open; occasionally, while awake, they are actually asleep. While asleep they dream of sleep.

Before the birth, they'd been together for a few months, and then serious lovers for a year. Since the child their arguments have increased, which Baxter imagines is natural as so much has happened to them. But their disagreements have taken on a new tone. There was a moment recently when they looked at one another and said, simultaneously, that they wished they had never met.

He had wanted a baby because it was something to want; other people had them. She agreed because she was thirty-five. Perhaps they no longer believed they'd find the one person who would change everything.

Wanting to feel tidy, Baxter extracts a suit from his wardrobe. He holds it up to the light on its hanger. It seems complete, as it did the last time he looked, a couple of hours before. In the bathroom his wife is taking longer than ever to apply her make-up and curl her hair.

While removing his shoes, Baxter turns his back. When he looks again, only the hanger remains. Surely a thief has rushed into the room and filched his jacket and trousers? No; the suit is on the floor, a small pyramid of charred ash. His other suits disintegrate at one touch. Flies hurl themselves at his face before chasing into the air.

He collects the ash in his hands and piles it on the desk he's arranged in the box-room, where he has intended to study something to broaden his understanding of life now that he goes out less. He has placed on the desk several sharpened but unused pencils. Now he sniffs the dirt and sifts it with the pencils. He even puts a little on his tongue. In it are several creamy ridged eggs. Within them something is alive, hoping for light. He crushes them. Soot and cocoon soup sticks to his fingers and gets under his nails.

Over dinner they drink wine, eat good food and look around, surprised to see so many people out and about, some of whom are smiling. He tells her about the flies. However, like him, she has become sarcastic and says she's long thought it time he acquired a new wardrobe. She hopes the involuntary clear-out will lead to sartorial improvement. Her own clothes are invariably protected by various guaranteed ladies' potions, like lavender, which he should try.

That night, tired by pettiness and their inability to amuse one another, she sits in the box-room and he walks the child up and down in the kitchen. He hears a cry and runs to her. She has unlocked her wardrobe to discover that her coats, dresses and knitwear have been replaced by a row of yellowish tatters. On the floor are piles of dead flies.

She starts to weep, saying she has nothing of her own left. She implies that it is his fault. He feels this too, and is ready to be blamed.

He helps her to bed, where the child sleeps between them. Just as they barely kiss now when they attempt love, he rarely looks into her eyes; but as he takes her arm, he notices a black fly emerge from her cornea and hop onto her eyelash.

Next morning he telephones a firm of exterminators. With unusual dispatch, they agree to send an Operative. 'You need the service,' they say before Baxter has described the symptoms. He and his wife obviously have a known condition.

They watch the van arrive; the Operative opens its rear doors and strides into their hall. He is a big and unkempt man, in green overalls, with thick glasses. Clearly not given to speaking, he listens keenly, examines the remains of their clothes, and is eager to see the pyramidal piles of ash which Baxter has arranged on newspaper. Baxter is grateful for the interest.

At last the Operative says, 'You need the total service.'

'I see,' says Baxter. 'Will that do it?'

In reply the man grunts.

Baxter's wife and the baby are ordered out. Baxter runs to fetch a box in order to watch through the window.

The Operative dons a grey mask. A transparent bottle of greenish liquid is strapped to his side. From the bottle extends a rubber tube with a metal sieve on the end. Also feeding into the sieve is a flat-pack of greyish putty attached to a piece of string around the man's neck. On one thigh is a small engine which he starts with a bootlace. While it runs, he strikes various practised poses and holds them like a strangely attired dancer. The rattling noise and force is terrific; not a living cretin could proceed through the curtains of sprayed venom.

The Operative leaves behind, in a corner, an illuminated electrified blue pole in a flower pot, for 'protection'.

'How long will we need that?' Baxter enquires.

'I'll look at it the next couple of times. It'll have to be recharged.'

'We'll need the full Operative service again?'

The Operative is offended. 'We're not called Operatives now. We're Microbe Consultants. And we are normally invited back, when we are available. Better make an appointment.' He adds, 'We're hoping to employ more qualified people. By the way, you'll be needing a pack too.'

'What is that?'

From the van he fetches a packet comprised of several sections, each containing different potions. Baxter glances over the interminable instructions.

'I'll put it on the bill,' says the Operative. 'Along with the curtain atomiser, and this one for the carpet. Better take three packs, eh, just in case.'

'Two will be fine, thanks.'

'Sure?' He puts on a confidential voice. 'I've noticed, your wife looks nice. Surely you want to protect her?'

'I do.'

'You won't want to run out at night.'

'No. Three then.'

'Good.'

The total is formidable. Baxter writes the cheque. His wife leans against the door jamb. He looks with vacillating confidence into her tense but hopeful eyes, wanting to impress on her that it will be worth it.

She puts out the potions. The caustic smell stings their eyes and makes them cough; the baby develops red sores on its belly. But they rub cream into the marks and he sleeps contentedly. Baxter goes to the shops; his wife cooks a meal. They eat together, cuddle, and observe with great pleasure the saucers in which the dying flies are writhing. The blue pole buzzes. In the morning they will clear out the corpses. They are almost looking forward to it, and even laugh when Baxter says, 'Perhaps it would have been cheaper to play Bulgarian music at the flies. We should have thought of that!'

The next morning he clears the mess away and, as there are still flies in the air, puts out more saucers and other potions. Surely, though, they are through the worst. How brought down he has been!

Lately, particularly when the baby cries, he has been dawdling out on the street. A couple of the neighbours have suggested that the new couple stop by for a drink. He has noticed lighted windows and people moving across holding drinks. Leaving his wife and child in safety, he will go out more, that very night in fact, wearing whatever he can assemble, a suit of armour if need be.

His wife won't join him and she gives Baxter the impression that he hasn't brought them to the right sort of neighbourhood. But as he is only going to be five minutes away, she can't object. He kisses her, and after checking that the blue pole is functioning correctly, he begins at the top of the street, wearing an acrylic cardigan purchased from the charity shop, inedible combat trousers and a coat.

The first couple Baxter visits have three young children. Both adults work, designing household objects of some kind. Kettles, Baxter presumes, but it could be chair legs. He can't remember what his wife has said.

He rings the bell. After what seems a considerable amount of hurried movement inside, a bearded man opens the door, breathing heavily. Baxter introduces himself, offering, at the same time, to go away if his visit is inconvenient. The man demurs. In his armchair he is drinking. Baxter, celebrating that night, joins him, taking half a glass of whisky. They discuss sport. But it is a disconcerting conversation, since it is so dark in the room that Baxter can barely make out the other man.

The woman, harassed but eager to join in, comes to the foot of the stairs before the children's yells interrupt. Then she stomps upstairs again, crying out, 'Oh right, right, it must be my turn again!'

'Will they never stop?' shouts the man.

'How can they sleep?' she replies. 'The atmosphere is suffocating them.'

'All of us!' says the man.

'So you've noticed!'

'How could I not?'

He drinks in silence. Baxter, growing accustomed to the gloom, notices a strange gesture he makes. Dipping his fingers into his glass, the bearded man flicks the liquid across his face, and in places rubs it in. He does the same with his arms, even as they talk, as if the alcohol is a lotion rather than an intoxicant.

The man stands up and thrusts his face towards his guest.

'We're getting out.'

'Where?'

He is hustling Baxter by the arm of his black PVC coat towards the door. Immediately the woman flies down the stairs like a bat and begins to dispute with her husband. Baxter doesn't attend to what they are saying, although other couples' arguments now have the ability to fascinate him. He is captivated by something else. A fly detaches itself from the end of the man's protuberant tongue, crawls up the side of his nose, and settles on his eyebrow, where it joins a companion, unnoticed until now, already grazing on the hairy ridge. It is time to move on.

Taking a wrong turn in the hall, Baxter passes through two rooms, following a smell he recognises but can't identify. He opens a door and notices an object standing in the bath. It is a glowing blue pole, like the one in his flat, and it seems to be pulsating. He looks closer and realises that this effect is caused by the movement of flies. He is reaching out to touch the thing when he hears a voice behind him, and turns to see the bearded man and his wife.

'Looking for something?'

'No, sorry.'

He doesn't want to look at them but can't help himself. As he moves past they drop their eyes. At that moment the woman blushes, for shame. They give off a sharp bleachy odour.

He isn't ready to go home but can't stay out on the street. Further down the road he sees figures in a window, before a hand drags the curtain across. He has barely knocked on the door before he is in the room with a glass in his hand.

It is a disparate crowd, comprising, he guesses, shy foreign students, the sorts of girls who would join cults, an oldish man in a tweed suit and rakish hat, people dancing with their shoes off, and others sitting in a row on the sofa. In the corner is a two-bar electric fire and a fish tank. Baxter has forgotten what exactly he is wearing and when he glimpses himself in a mirror and realises that no one minds, he is thankful.

His neighbour is drunk but oddly watchful. She puts her arms around his neck, which discomfits him, as if there is some need in him that she has noticed, though he can't see what it is.

'We didn't think you'd come. Your wife barely speaks to any of us.'

'Doesn't she?'

'Well, she's charming to some people. How is the flat?'

'It's fine . . . Not too bad.'

Becoming aware of an itching on his forehead, he slaughters a fly between finger and thumb.

She says, 'Sure?'

'Why not?'

He feels another fly creeping across his cheek. She is looking at him curiously.

'I'd like it if you would dance with me,' she says.

He dislikes dancing but suspects that movement is preferable to stasis. And tonight – why not? – he will celebrate. She points out her husband, a tall man standing in the doorway, talking to a woman. Warm and fleshy, she shakes her arse, and he does what he can.

Then she takes the index finger of his right hand and leads him into a conservatory at the back. It is cold; there is no music. She shoves down her clothes, bends forward over the arm of a chair and he slides the finger she's taken possession of, and two others, into her. It is a luxurious and well-deserved oblivion. Surely happiness is forgetting who you are! But too soon he notices a familiar caustic smell. He looks about and sees bowls of white powder placed on the floor; another contains a greenish-blue sticky substance. Injured specks move drowsily in the buckets.

He extracts his hand and holds it out. Up at the wrist it is alive with flies.

She looks round. 'Oh dear, the little babies are hungry tonight.' She flaps at them unconcernedly.

'Isn't there a remedy?' he asks.

THE FLIES

'People live with it.'
'They do?'
'That is the best thing. It is also the worst. They work incessantly. Or drink. People all over the world endure different kinds of bacteria.'
'But surely, surely there is a poison, brew or . . . blue light that will deter them for ever?'
'There is,' she says. 'Of a kind.'
'What is it?'
She smiles at his desperation. 'The potions do work, for a period. But you have to replace them with different makes. Imported is best, but expensive. Try the Argentinian. Then the South African, in that order. I'm not sure what they put in that stuff, but . . . Course, the flies get used to it, and it only maddens and incites them. You might need to go on to the Madagascan.' Baxter must be looking disheartened because she says, 'In this street this is how we keep them away – passion!'
'Passion?'
'Where there is passion you don't notice anything.'
He lies over her from behind. He says he can't believe that these things are just inevitable; that there isn't, somewhere, a solution.
'We'll see to it – later,' she grunts.
After, in the living room, she whispers, 'Most of them have got flies round here. Except the newly-weds and adulterers.' She laughs. 'They got other things. Eighteen months, it takes. If you're lucky you get eighteen months and then you get the flies.' She explains that the flies are the only secret that everyone keeps. Other problems can be paraded and boasted of, but this is an unacceptable shame. 'We are poisoned by ourselves.' She looks at him. 'Do you hate her?'
'What?'
'Do you, yet? You can tell me.'
He whispers that it is dawning on him, as love dawns on

197

people, that at times he does hate her; hates the way she cuts up an apple; hates her hands. He hates her tone of voice and the words he knows she'll use; he hates her clothes, her eyelids, and everyone she knows; her perfume makes him nauseous. He hates the things he's loved about her; hates the way he has put himself in thrall to her; hates the kindnesses she shows him, as if she is asking for something. He sees, too, that it doesn't matter that you don't love someone, until you have a child with them. And he understands, too, how important hatred is, what a strong sustaining feeling it is; a screen perhaps, to stop him pitying her, and himself, and falling into a pit of misery.

His neighbour nods as he shivers with shame at what she has provoked him into saying. She says, 'My husband and I are starting a microbe business ourselves.'

'Is there that much call for it?'

'You can't sing to them, can you?'

'I suppose not.'

'We've put a down payment on our first van. You will use only us, won't you?'

'We're broke, I'm afraid. Can't use anyone.'

'You can't let yourself be invaded. You'll have to work. You haven't been using the Microbe Consultants, have you?'

'They have passed by, yes.'

'They didn't sell you a pack?'

'Only two.'

'Useless, useless. Those men are on commission. Never let them in the house.'

She holds him. Dancing in the middle of the night, while he is still conscious, she puts her mouth to his ear and murmurs, 'You might need Gerard Quinn.'

'Who?'

'Quinn has been hanging around. He'll be in touch. Meanwhile, behind that door' – she points at a wooden door with a steel frame, with a padlock hanging from it – 'we are working on a combination potion, a deadly solution.

It's not yet ready, but when we have a sample, I'll bring it.'
He looks at her sceptically. 'Yes, everyone would be doing it.
But the snag is, what prevents a definitive remedy is that
husbands and wives give the stuff to their partners.' Baxter
feels as if he will fall over. 'Have you actually mixed it in
with her cereal yet, or are you still considering it?'

'One time I did do that, but I put it down the drain.'

'People use it to commit suicide too. One can't be too
careful, you see.'

She leaves him. He notices that the bearded man has
arrived, and is laughing and sprinkling himself with alcohol
beside the fish tank. He raises his hand in acknowledgement
of Baxter. Later, before Baxter passes out, he sees the bearded
man and the female neighbour go into the conservatory
together.

Early in the morning his neighbour's husband carries
Baxter home.

Baxter is still asleep beside the bed, where he has
collapsed, when the landlord visits. Fortunately he has
forewarned them, and Baxter's wife has stuffed the blue
pole, potions and any devoured items into a cupboard. The
man is susceptible to her; when necessary she can be both
charming and forceful. Even though a fly lands on his lapel
as they are talking, she convinces him that the problem is 'in
remission'.

After lunch, Baxter empties the full saucers once more,
and sets out new ones. Once more the flies begin to die. But
it is no longer something he can bear to look at. He stands in
the bedroom and tells his wife that he will be out for the
afternoon, and will take the kid with him. No, she says, he
has always been irresponsible. He has to insist, as if it is his
last wish, until she gives in.

It has made her sullen, but it is an important victory. He
has never been alone with his son. In its sling, weighted
against his body, he carries this novelty about the city. He
sits in cafés, puts it on his knee and admires its hands and

ears; he flings it in the air and kisses it. He strolls in the park and on the grass gives it a bottle. People speak to him; women, particularly, seem to assume he is not a bad character. The child makes him more attractive. He likes having this new companion, or friend, with him.

He thinks of what else they might do. His lover's phone number comes into his mind. He calls her. They cross the river on the bus. At her door he wants to turn back but she is there immediately. He holds up the child like a trophy, though Baxter is fearful that she will be unnerved by the softened features of the other woman alive between them.

She invites them in. She is wearing the ear-rings he gave her; she must have put them on for him. They find themselves sighing at the sight of one another. How pleased she is to see them both; more pleased than he has allowed himself to imagine. She can't stop herself slipping her hands inside his coat, as she used to. He wraps her up and kisses her neck. She belongs in this position, she tells him. How dispirited she has been since he left last time, and hasn't been in touch. Sometimes she hasn't wanted to go out. At times she has thought she would go mad. Why did he push her away when he knew that with her everything seemed right? She has had to find another lover.

He doesn't know how to say he couldn't believe she loved him, and that he lacked the courage to follow her.

She holds the baby, yet is unsure about kissing him. But the boy is irresistible. She hasn't changed a nappy before. He shows her. She wipes the boy down, and rubs her cheeks against his skin. His soother stops twitching and hangs from his lips.

They take off their clothes and slip into bed with him. She caresses Baxter from his fingertips to his feet, to make him hers again. She asks him to circle her stomach with kisses. He asks her to sit on her knees, touching herself, showing herself to him, her thumbs touching her pubic bone, making a butterfly of her hands. They are careful not to rock the bed or cry out suddenly, but he has forgotten how fierce their desire can become, and how much they can laugh together, and he has to stuff his fingers in her mouth.

As she sleeps he lies looking at her face, whispering words he has never said to anyone. This makes him more than peaceful. If he is away from his wife for a few hours he feels a curious warmth. He has been frozen, and now his love of things is returning, like a forgotten heat, and he can fall against any nearby wall and slide down it, so soft does he feel. He wants to go home and say to his wife, why can't we cover each other in affection forever?

Something is brushing his face. He sits up to see a fly emerging from his lover's ear. Another hangs in his son's hair. His leg itches; his hand, too, and his back. A fly creeps from the child's nose. Baxter is carrying the contagion with him, giving it to everyone!

He picks up the sleeping child and wakes the dismayed woman. She attempts to reason with him, but he is hurrying down the street as if pursued by lunatics, and with the desire to yell heartless words at strangers.

He passes the child to his wife, fearing he is looking at her a little wildly. It has all rushed back, what he owes her: kindness, succour, and something else, the details elude him; and how one can't let people down merely because one happens, one day, to feel differently.

Not that she notices his agitation, as she checks the baby over.

He take a bath, the only place in the flat they can feel at peace. Drinking wine and listening to the radio, he will swat away all thoughts. But the vows he made her aren't affection, just as a signature isn't a kiss, and no amount of promises can guarantee love. Without thinking, he gave her his life. He valued it less then, and now he wants it back. But he knows that retrieving a life takes a different courage, and is crueller.

At that moment his heart swells. He can hear her singing in the kitchen. She claps too. He calls her name several times.

She comes in irritably. 'What do you want?'

'You.'

'What for? Not now.' She looks down at him. 'What a surprise.'

'Come on.'

'Baxter – '

He reaches out to stroke her.

'Your hands are hot,' she says. 'You're sweating.'

'Please.'

She sighs, removes her skirt and pants, gets in the bath and pulls him onto her.

'What brought that on?' she says after, a little cheered.

'I heard you singing and clapping.'

'Yes, that's how I catch the flies.' She gets out of the bath. 'Look, there are flies floating on the water.'

A few days later, when the blue pole has flickered and died – and been smashed against the wall by Baxter – and the bowls of powder have been devoured, leaving a crust of frothing corpses, the Operative is at the door. He doesn't seem surprised by the failure of his medicaments, nor by Baxter's fierce complaints about the hopeless cures.

'It's a course,' he insists. 'You can't abandon it now, unless you want to throw away the advances and go back to the beginning.'

'What advances?'

'This is a critical case. What world are you living in, thinking it'll be a simple cure?'

'Why didn't you say that last time?'

'Didn't I? I'd say you're the sort who doesn't listen.'

'The blue pole doesn't work.'

He speaks as if to a dolt. 'It draws them. The vibration makes them voracious. Then they eat. And perish forever. But not if you kick it to pieces like a child. I passed your wife on the doorstep. She's changed since the last time. Her eyes – '

'All right!'

'I've seen it before. She is discouraged. Don't think she doesn't know what's going on!'

'What is going on?'

'You know.'

Baxter puts his head in his hands.

The Operative sweeps up the remains of the blue pole and offers Baxter a bag of grey crystals. 'Watch.' He pours them into a bowl – the sound is a whoosh of hope – and rests it on the floor. The flies land on it and, after a taste, hop a few inches, then drop dead.

The Operative kisses his fingers.

'This is incomparable.'

'Argentinian?' asks Baxter. 'Or South African?'

The Operative gives him a mocking look.

'We never disclose formulas. We have heard that there are people who are mixing their own poisons at home. This will make your skin bubble like leprosy, and your bones soften like rubber. It could be fatal. Leave these things to the experts.'

Baxter writes a cheque for five packs. At the end of the afternoon, he sees the Operative has parked his unmarked van outside the bearded man's house and is going in with plastic bags. The man glances at Baxter and give a little shrug. Several of the local inhabitants are making slow journeys past the house; as Baxter moves away he notices faces at nearby windows.

Baxter discovers his wife examining the chequebook.

'Another cheque!' she cries. 'For what?'

'Three packs!'

'It doesn't work.'

'How do you know?'

'Just look!'

'It might be worse without the poison.'

'How could it be worse? You're throwing money away!'

'I'm trying to help us!'

'You don't know where to start!'

She blinks and nods with anger. The baby cries. Baxter refuses to recount what the Operative said. She doesn't deserve an explanation. It does occur to him, though, to smash her in the mouth, and at that instant she flinches and draws back. Oh, how we understand one another, without meaning to!

What suggestions does she have, he enquires, trying to keep down self-disgust. She doesn't have to consider this; she has intentions. Tired of the secrecy, she will discuss the contagion with a friend, when she has the energy. She wants to go out into the world. She has been lonely.

'Yes, yes,' he agrees. 'That would be good. We must try something new.'

A few days later, as soon as his wife has left for the park, there are several urgent taps on the window. Baxter ducks down. However, it is too late. At the door, with a triumphant twirl, his female neighbour presents a paint pot. She wrenches off the lid. It contains a sticky brown substance like treacle. Her head is thrown back by the reek.

Holding the paint pot at arm's length, she takes in the room. By now they have, piece by piece, removed a good deal of the furniture, though a few items, the curtains and cushions, have been replaced by spares, since it is imperative to uphold belief. Baxter and his wife can't encourage visitors, of course. If old friends ring they arrange to see them outside. The only person who visits regularly is his mother-in-law, from whom his wife strives to conceal all signs of decay. This loyalty and protectiveness surprises and moves Baxter. When he asks his wife about it, she says, 'I don't want her to blame you.'

'Why not?'

'Because you're my husband, stupid.'

The neighbour says, 'Put this out.'

Baxter looks dubiously at the substance and grimaces. 'You're not an expert.'

'Not an expert? Me?'

'No.'

'Who told you to say that?'

'No one.'

'Yes they did. Because who is, may I ask? You don't know, do you?'

'I suppose not.'

'Experts steal our power and sell it back to us, at a profit. You're not falling for that, are you?'

'I see what you mean.'

'Look.'

She sticks her finger in the stuff, puts it on her tongue, waggles it at him, tastes it, and spits it into a napkin.

'Your wife's not going to eat that, even if you smother it in honey,' she says, gagging. 'But it'll draw the little devils from all over the room.' She gets on her knees and makes a cooing sound. 'You might notice a dungy smell.'

'Yes.'

'In that case – open the window. This is an early prototype.'

She puts out the treacle in his saucers. There is no doubt that the flies are drawn by it, and they do keel over. But they are not diminishing; the treacle seems to entice more and more of them.

She turns to him. 'Excellent! The ingredients were expensive, you see.'

'I can't pay!' he says forcibly. 'Not anything!'

'Everybody wants something for nothing. This then, for now.' She kisses his mouth. 'Remember,' she says, as she goes.'Passion. Passion!'

He is staring into the overrun saucers when his wife comes in, holding her nose.

'Where did you get that?'

'An acquaintance. A kind neighbour.'

'That harridan who stares at me so? You're swayed by the oddest people. Any fool's flattery can seduce you.'

'Clearly.'

'But it stinks!'

'The houses are old, the century is old . . . what do you expect?'

He sticks his finger in the muck, licks it and bends forward, holding his stomach.

'Baxter, you are suffering from insanity.' She says softly, 'You would prefer her opinion to mine. But why? Is something going on there?'

'No!'

'You don't care about me now, do you?'

'I do.'

'Liar. The truth counts for nothing with you.'

He notices she has kept her coat on. She puts the baby in his cot. She has finally arranged to visit her best friend, a well-off snobbish woman with two children whose exhibitions of affluence and happiness can be exasperating. He notices now the trouble his wife has taken to look her best. A woman's face alters when she has a baby, and a new beauty may emerge. But she still looks shabby in her ragged clothes, and strained, as if from the effort of constantly keeping something bad away.

From the window he watches her go, and is happy that at least her determination hasn't gone. There is, though, nothing left of their innocence.

Baxter digs a hole in the garden and throws in the odoriferous paint pot and saucers. To avoid his neighbour, he will have to be sure to look both ways and hurry when leaving the house.

He gets the boy up and lies on the floor with him. The kid crawls about, banging a wooden spoon on a metal tray, a noise which delights him, and keeps away all flies. He seems unaffected by the strange tensions around him. Every day he is different, full of enthusiasm and curiosity, and Baxter doesn't want to miss a moment.

He looks up to see the Operative waving through the window Baxter has never seen him so genial.

'Look,' he says. 'I've nabbed some of the latest development and rushed it straight to you.' He puts several tins of a sticky treaclish substance on the table. 'It's a free sample.'

Baxter pushes him towards the door. 'Get out.'

'But – '

'Pour the tins over your head!'

'Don't shove! You're giving up, are you?' The Operative is enraged but affects sadness. 'It is a common reaction. You think you can shut your eyes to it. But your wife will never stop despising you, and your child will be made sick!' Baxter lunges at him. The man skips down the steps. 'Or have you got a solution of your own?' he sneers. 'Everyone thinks that at some time. But they're deceived! You'll be back. I await your call but might be too busy to take it.'

When Baxter's wife returns they sit attentively opposite one another and have a keen discussion. The visit to her friend has animated her.

'She and the house and the children were immaculate and practically gold-plated, as usual. I kept thinking, I'm never going to be able to bring the subject up. Fortunately the phone rang. I went to the bathroom. I opened her closet.' Baxter nods, understanding this. 'She loves clothes, but there was virtually nothing in there. There were powders and poisons in the bottom.'

'They've been married six years,' says Baxter.

'He's lazy – '

'She's domineering – '

'He's promiscuous – '

'She's frigid – '

'Just shut up and listen!' She continues, 'The rich aren't immune but they can afford to replace everything. When I brought up the subject she knew what I was talking about. She admitted to a slight outbreak – from next door.' They both laugh. 'She even said she was thinking of making a radio programme about it. And if there's a good response, a television investigation.' Baxter nods. 'I'm afraid there's only one thing for it. There's this man they've found. All the top people are using him.'

'He must be expensive.'

'All the best things are, and not everyone is too mean to pay for it. I'm not ready to go back to work, but Baxter, you must.'

'You know I can't find a job.'

'You must stop thinking you're better than other people, and take anything. It's our only hope. They're living a normal life, Baxter. And look at us.'

Once he loved her tenacity. He thinks of how to close this subject.

'What will I wear?'

'You can go to my mother's in the morning and change there, and do the same in the evening.'

'I see.'

She comes towards him and puts her face close to his; her eyes, though darkly ringed and lined now, shine with optimism.

'Baxter, we are going to try everything, aren't we?'

Feeling she will stand there forever, and ashamed of how her close presence alarms him, he talks of what they might do once the contagion is over. He thinks, too, of how little people need, and how little they ask for! A touch, a hug, a word of reassurance, a moment of warm love, is all she wants. Yet a kiss is too much for him. Why is he so cruel, and what is wrong with him?

For a few weeks he thinks that by keeping away from her, by self-containment and the avoidance of 'controversial' subjects, she will forget this idea. But every few days she brings up the subject again, as if they have both agreed to it.

One night when he leans back, the new cushion disintegrates. It is a charred pile. He jumps up and, standing there, feels he will fall over. He reaches out and grabs the curtains. The entire thing – gauze, he realises – comes apart in his hand. The room has darkened; shadows hang in menacing shapes; the air is thick with flies; the furniture looks as though it has been in a fire. Flies spot his face; his hair turns sticky and yellow even as he stands there. He wants to cry out but can't cry out; he wants to flee but can't flee.

He hears a noise outside. A quarrel is taking place. Crouching below the windowsill, he sees the bearded man on the doorstep of his own house, shouting to be let in. A window opens upstairs and a suitcase is flung out, along with bitter words and sobs. The bearded man eventually picks up the suitcase and walks away. He passes Baxter's house pulling the wheeled case. Certain that Baxter is watching, he waves forlornly at the window.

Baxter feels that if the plague is to be conquered it is unreasonable of him not to try everything. Even if he doesn't succeed he will, at least, have pleased his wife. He blames and resents her, and what has she tried to do but make him happy and create a comfortable home? No doubt she is right about the other thing: in isolation he has developed unreasonably exalted ideas about himself.

But he goes reluctantly to work. The other employees look at him knowingly the day he goes in to apply for the job. It is exhausting work, yet he soon masters the morose patter, and his body becomes accustomed to the physical labour. The spraying is unpleasant; he has no idea what effect the unavoidable inhalation of noxious gases will have. Seeing all the distressed and naive couples is upsetting at first, but he learns from the other men to detach himself, ignore all insults and concentrate on selling as many packs as possible in order to earn a high commission. The Operatives are a cynical and morose group who resemble lawyers. None of the many people who need them will insult these parasites directly – they can't survive without them. But they can never be liked.

Baxter and his wife have more money than before, but to afford the exceptional Exterminator they must save for much longer and do without 'luxuries'. Baxter is hardly at home, which improves the atmosphere during the day. But there is something he has to do every night. When his wife and baby are asleep he turns off the light, sinks to his knees and turns onto his back on the living-room floor. There, as he hums to himself, working up a steady vibration from his stomach, moths graze on his clothes, in his hair, and on his closed eyes. It is a repellent but – he is convinced – necessary ritual of accustomisation. He tells himself that nothing can be repaired or advanced but only accepted. And, after acceptance, there will occur a liberation into pure spirit, without desire, a state he awaits with self-defeating impatience. Often he falls asleep here, imagining that the different parts of himself are being distributed by insects around the neighbourhood, or 'universe' as he puts it; he regards this as the ultimate compliance. His wife believes that his mind has been overrun.

One morning a youngish man in a black suit stands at the door. Baxter is surprised to see he carries no powders, illuminated electrifying poles, squirters, or even a briefcase. His hands are in his pockets. Gerard sits down, barely glancing at the chewed carpet or buckets of powder. He declines an offer to look in the wardrobe. He seems to know about it already.

'Has there been much of this about?' Baxter asks.

'In this street? A few cases.'

Hope rushes in again from its hiding place. Baxter is almost incoherent. 'Did you cure it? Did you? How long did it take?'

Gerard doesn't reply. Baxter goes and tells his wife she should talk to Gerard, saying he has a reassuring composure. She comes into the room and looks Gerard over, but she cannot bring herself to discuss any of their 'private matters'.

Baxter, though, tells Gerard the most forbidden, depressing and, particularly, trivial things. Gerard likes this stuff the most, persuading Baxter to see it as an aperture through which to follow the labyrinth of his mind. After, Baxter is more emotional than he has ever been, and wheels about the flat, feeling he will collapse, and that mad creatures have been released in the cage of his mind.

When Gerard asks if he should come back, Baxter says yes. Gerard turns up twice a week, to listen. Somehow he extends Baxter's view of things and makes unusual connections, until Baxter surprises himself. How gloomy one feels, explains Baxter, as if one has entered a tunnel which leads to the centre of the earth, with not an arrow of light possible. Surely this is one's natural condition, human fate, and one can only instruct oneself to be realistic? The wise will understand this, and the brave, called stoics by some, will endure it. Or is it very stupid? suggests Gerard. He turns things around until revolt seems possible, a terrifying revolt against one's easy assumptions.

Baxter begins to rely on Gerard. His wife, though, resents him. Despite all the ardent talk, the flat remains infested. She claims Gerard is making Baxter self-absorbed, and that he no longer cares about her and the baby.

Baxter wonders about Gerard too. Does this man know everything? Is he above it all? And why is he expending his gifts on Baxter without asking for money? Why should the 'clean man' be immune from the contagion? What can be so special about him?

One time the Operatives bring up the subject in the canteen. Baxter, who normally pays no attention to their conversations, looks up. 'There are people now who think they can talk the contagion away,' they scoff. 'Like people who think they can pray for rain, they won't accept it is a biological fact of nature. There is nothing to be done but await a breakthrough.'

Baxter wants to ask Gerard why he is interested in these conversations, but it soon ceases to matter. Something is different. Gerard has aroused in him a motivating desperation. At night he no longer lies on the floor being devoured. He paces, yes; but at least this is movement, and nothing will stick to him. There is something still alive within him, in both of them, which the flies have been unable to kill off.

Near dawn one night Baxter wakes up and can't go back to sleep. In his cot the boy sucks at his bottle. Baxter places his finger in the boy's fist; he holds his father tight. Baxter waits until he can withdraw without waking him. From the cot he takes a little wooden rattle. He dresses in silence, puts the rattle in his pocket, and walks towards the wardrobe. It is a while since he has poked at anything in there. It seems fruitless now.

He steps out onto the street. As he goes past the bearded man's house and that of his female neighbour he sees a black cloud in the sky ahead of him. There will be a storm, no doubt about it. Soon he is lost, but he keeps his eyes on the cloud, making his way through narrow streets and alleys; he traverses wide roads and, eventually, crosses the river, trying to think of what, yet, might be done. He sees other men who are, perhaps, like him, travelling through the night with mementoes in their pockets, searching for different fears; or popping out of doorways to stand still and stare upwards, thinking of too much to notice anyone, before walking determinedly in one direction, and then in another.

The cloud, as he walks towards it, seems to explode. It separates and breaks up into thousands of tiny fragments. It is a cloud of flies which lifts and breaks, sweeping upwards into the indifferent sky.

CPSIA information can be obtained at www.ICGtesting.com
Printed in the USA
BVOW031031081212

307626BV00001B/35/P